EARLY HOLISTIC SCORING OF WRITING

EARLY HOLISTIC SCORING OF WRITING

A Theory, a History, a Reflection

RICHARD HASWELL
NORBERT ELLIOT

UTAH STATE UNIVERSITY PRESS
Logan

© 2019 by University Press of Colorado

Published by Utah State University Press
An imprint of University Press of Colorado
245 Century Circle, Suite 202
Louisville, Colorado 80027

All rights reserved

 The University Press of Colorado is a proud member of the Association of University Presses.

The University Press of Colorado is a cooperative publishing enterprise supported, in part, by Adams State University, Colorado State University, Fort Lewis College, Metropolitan State University of Denver, Regis University, University of Colorado, University of Northern Colorado, University of Wyoming, Utah State University, and Western Colorado University.

ISBN: 978-1-60732-911-4 (paperback)
ISBN: 978-1-60732-912-1 (ebook)
https://doi.org/10.7330/9781607329121

Library of Congress Cataloging-in-Publication Data

Cataloging-in-Publication data for this title is available online at the Library of Congress.

Cover illustration, "Sea Spiral Mandala Mosaic," © Margaret Almon. www.margarentalmon.com

To Janis Haswell and Frances Ward

Like a mad carpenter making a box. Were he ever so convinced that he was King of Jerusalem, the box he would make would be a sane box.
—Joseph Conrad

Do you think there is anything not attached by its unbreakable cord to everything else? Plant your peas and your corn in the field where the moon is full, or risk failure. This has been understood since planting began. The attention of the seed to the draw of the moon is I suppose, measurable, like the tilt of the planet. Or, maybe not—maybe you have to add some immeasurable ingredient made of the hour, the singular field, the hand of the sower.
—Mary Oliver

CONTENTS

Acknowledgments ix

Introduction 3

1 Nine Maps 7
2 Two Premises 30
3 Holistic Scoring and Great Britain, 1936–1949 49
4 Great Britain and the Rejection of Holistic Scoring, 1949–1988 75
5 Paul B. Diederich and AP Holistic Scoring in the United States, 1954–1980 98
6 Osmond E. Palmer, Fred I. Godshalk, and the ECT, 1960–1972 119
7 California Schools, 1960–1982 152
8 Independent Researchers, 1960–1980, and NAEP, 1969–1984 188
9 What Does a Score Mean? 226
10 Reconsiderations 263

Glossary: Technical Terms Connected with Early Holistic Scoring of Writing 291
References 301
About the Authors 325
Index 327

ACKNOWLEDGMENTS

We would like to thank the following colleagues for their many contributions to the present volume: Laura Aull, Stephen A. Bernhardt, Jeffrey Backstrand, Doug Baldwin, Glenn Blalock, Isaac Bejar, Kate Blickhahn, Rexford Brown, Sydell Carlton, Robbi Chang, Christiane K. Donahue, Peter Elbow, T. J. Elliott, Lester Faigley, Mary Fowles, George Gadda, Joan Graham, Liz Hamp-Lyons, Robert L. Hampel, Carol Holder, Brian Huot, Lisa Johnson-Shull, Catharine Keech Lucas, Diane Kelly-Riley, Kathleen J. Klompien, Susan MacLeod, Karen L. McQuillen, Robert M. Mislevy, Sandra Murphy, Miles Myers, Thomas Newkirk, Paul Newton, Maria Elena Olivetti, Irvin Peckham, Les Perelman, Louise Wetherbee Phelps, Mya Poe, Alastair Pollitt, Hillary Persky, David Slomp, Mary Ann Smith, Patty Stock, Edward M. White, Susan Wyche. We also thank our two reviewers, John C. Brereton and Diane Kelly-Riley.

Thanks also to these library and institutional archivists: Tara Kaiser and Joelle Cheng, Bay Area Writing Project; Barbara Gilbert, Special Collections Research Center, University of Chicago; Jay Satterfield and Elena M. Cordova, Dartmouth College Library; Lisa M. Schmidt, University Archives and Historical Collections, Michigan State University; Halle Mares, The Ohio State University; and especially Nick Telepak at the Educational Testing Service and his colleagues at the library there, Catherine L. McQuillan, Charlotte L. Kirby, and Kelly S. Bergman. With Laura L. Runge, the Publications Council of the University of South Florida provided support for book development. The manuscript was edited by the incomparable Kami Day.

We also thank Rachel Levay, acquisitions editor at Utah State University Press, for her early faith in our book. As always, the staff at the press made everything perfect.

EARLY HOLISTIC SCORING OF WRITING

Introduction

> *In the case of all things which have several parts and in which the whole is not, as it were, a mere heap, but the totality is something besides the parts, there is a cause of unity; for as regards material things contact is the cause in some cases, and in others viscosity or some other such quality.*
> —Aristotle, *Metaphysics*

In a review of *On a Scale: A Social History of Writing Assessment in America* (Elliot 2005), the first author of the present volume notes that the second author has missed the mark. *On a Scale* is not about "writing assessment in America," as its subtitle declares: "It's about one kind of writing assessment, a kind that has held odd sway in the United States for a century but by no means held universal or even majority sway" (Haswell 2006b, 2). *On a Scale*, Rich writes, is an inside history of the way the College Board and the Educational Testing Service (ETS) have constructed writing assessment. Instead of a history of writing assessment beyond the world of standardized testing, readers discover an insider's view of just one big-business world within the many interpenetrating worlds of writing assessment.

Well.

While the second author of the present volume is not necessarily participating in atonement, Norbert certainly does recognize his own book as a periodization of a particular sort—one in which evidence is gathered across multiple sites and inferences are made across settings. Unlike the US assessment programs described in this book, most of them designed to be local, those of national testing firms are born to be distributed and to be profitable. Conversely, the national examinations in Britain were never meant to make money. During the period of this study—the mid-1930s to the mid-1980s—the examinations were under the control of the local boards. Perhaps now is the time for another history with special attention to the early history of assessment, a history informed by international perspectives with more attention to localized practice.

Historians of writing assessment fall along a continuum in which three distinct scholarly traditions can be identified. In the first, writers focus on history in its own right with the primary aim to discover documents and analyze the perspectives of their authors. *On a Scale: A Social History of Writing Assessment in America* (Elliot 2005) is just such a book in all but its final chapter. Following a second tradition, authors call for a serviceable sense of history. Brian Huot, Peggy O'Neill, and Cindy Moore (2010) wanted a usable past for writing assessment. As they correctly propose, by understanding the importance of assessment historically, we can center our evaluative practices more effectively in the present. In the third tradition, authors, also calling for actionable history, join the social justice turn in writing assessment. For scholars J. W. Hammond (2018), Sean Molloy (2018), and Keith L Harms (2018), historiography becomes a way to chart specific paths for action associated with justice and fairness.

The book you are about to read—a history of holistic scoring from around 1936 (the London publication date of *The Marks of Examiners* by Philip Joseph Hartog, Edmond Cecil Rhodes, and Cyril L. Burt) to around 1982 (the date Liz Hamp-Lyons joined the English Language Testing System Validation Project, the subject of her 1987 University of Edinburgh dissertation)—borrows from all three traditions. Our definition of formal holistic scoring is straightforward: *the use of a scale to assign a single value mark to a whole essay and not separately to individual aspects, with scorers trying to apply the scale consistently, and with the final score for each essay derived from two or more independent ratings.* Our book constructs the early history of this definition. In service to that task, we bring forward documents and studies that are often underappreciated. We firmly believe our past is usable, and we focus that practical sense into a call for action in terms of research based on forms of evidence and a stance of justice. If we are indeed approaching an age in writing assessment when the key concern is fairness, our history is worth exploring.

In their study of thirty-four books published on writing assessment within a thirty-eight-year period, William Morris, Curt Greve, Elliot Knowles, and Huot found that the ownership of writing-assessment research by writing-assessment scholars can be seen as "limited, with a constant agenda being set outside the purview of writing teachers and administrators" (2015, 132). Our book—more mosaic than fresco, more sea-spiral mandala than battened-down argument—tells stories that reveal the force of local assessment and therefore demonstrates how agendas were established by those who worked according to their own lights, sometimes outside hegemonic systems, often modifying the agendas of those who designed assessments to be distributed across local settings. As one reviewer of the original manuscript that led to this book said, as well as we ever could, our history shows how "holistic scoring was developed by specific individuals within certain locations working for specific institutions in response to specific conditions." The central metaphor of our book is captured in the Sea Spiral Mandala mosaic art by Margaret Almon, shown in the cover for this book.

As for the focus of this history on one particular genre of writing assessment—holistic scoring of essays—we admit our shortcomings. The truth is that we felt enough mettle to write one book but not twenty books. Addressed from the ground up, local histories of writing assessment would be a massive undertaking. Each school, each school district, each local educational authority (in the United Kingdom), each college, each university system, each state (in the United States) has its own history. Each is myriad and chameleonesque. And even such a massive effort would fail to address the history of international external examinations designed to rate students on their compositional skills—examinations that go back at least to the Sui dynasty (Lederman 1986) with fruition in the eight-legged essay during the Ming Dynasty (Elman 2009)—and that extend to the present. Our choice of just two countries is more a matter of expediency than historical importance. Yet, as we show, attention to global developments is just as revealing as genre specification if we are to understand how a profession came to establish a body of knowledge about writing assessment and, in turn, writing itself.

Our choice of just one of those assessment methods, holistic scoring, therefore needs no apology. From the mid-1930s to the mid-1980s, holistic scoring of student essays stood front and center in the arena of writing assessment. It was the newcomer, but rapidly it became the mark against which all other testing tested itself. For a history that wants to narrate writing assessment within the theoretical, the political, the social, the cultural, and the human—as this book does—holistic scoring of essays is a given. As for the sequel to this book, the history of holistic scoring from the mid-1980s on—some would say the history of its heyday, decline, and fall—we gift that massive undertaking to other historians of the profession and wish them as rewarding a journey as ours has been.

Published with our book is WPA-CompPile Research Bibliography, No. 27 (Haswell and Elliot 2019). Containing over 1,000 annotated entries, our bibliography provides detailed and searchable information on the full scholarship of holistic scoring covered during the period of this book.

The long list of colleagues in our acknowledgments is fitting. We owe much to many. With their counsel, we offer a history that is theoretical, historical, and reflective—of use to historians and others interested in the history of ideas and the genesis of professions. Ours is a history by, of, and for teachers, researchers, and administrators who work in the field of writing studies. Here is a story of genre in context.

1
NINE MAPS

True maps are made of experiences.
—Paulette Jiles, *North Spirit*

In the United States, holistic scoring of student essays spread like a diet fad. During the mid-1960s some testing experts were still gingerly handling the upstart term *holistic* with scare quotes (e.g., Godshalk 1966, 2). Twenty years later, nearly every English teacher knew what the method entailed. Or thought they knew. One incontestable historical truth about holistic scoring is that from its beginnings, it was not monotypic. Despite persistent efforts to sway it toward that condition, the activity perversely remained polymorphous and indeed grew more and more so. Holistic scoring seemed to have been owned by the imp of the perverse.[1]

Practitioners, for instance, kept hunting and never finding a method of scoring essays that achieved high levels of interrater agreement leading to high interrater reliability coefficients. No matter how rudimentary the rubric, how long the training, or how strict the monitoring, the experience of doing holistic scoring varied according to writing task, individual scorers, and those scorers' singular responses to the scoring environment. One of our informants, who supervises online rating of a commercial essay test, told us that the morning after the US presidential election in November of 2016, the agreement of raters "went to hell," and that was using a simple four-point scale. As we show in chapter 8, when research began exploring the "ecology" of holistic scoring, a panoply of affects was shown to influence silently the agreement rates of individual scorers (Lucas 1988).

In fact, at every point in the art and act of holistic scoring, complexity reigned. This fact should not surprise. Whatever its stripe, holistic scoring is not one activity but a nexus of many. It is much more than just a technique for rating texts, a procedure in which people can be trained. As this book illustrates, holistic scoring acts as a ritual for crossing social and educational boundaries, an expression of symbolic power, a service for hire and a commodity for sale, a chance for in-group camaraderie and solidarity, a tactic to meet political demands for accountability, a shibboleth of insider taste and knowledge, a temptation to join a bandwagon or follow a craze, a tactic within a plan of research, an academic classroom practice, an act of psychological perception and interpretation. This list is random and truncated. The course of holistic scoring is entangled without recourse in its human enactments.

THE CONCEPT OF ORGANICISM

The history of holistic essay scoring, however, has one clear-cut moment, in 1926 when Jan Smuts published *Holism and Evolution*, thereby coining the terms "holism" and "holistic." The book by Smuts covered all of nature, physical and biological, and his concept of holism rested on a broad intellectual movement that extended back at least to European Romanticism. For simplicity's sake, let's call that movement *organicism* (although other terms would work as well—*holism, structuralism, field theory, systems theory*). The core energy of organicism opposed a Cartesian, part-focused explanation of things. Organicism responded with its own explanation that focused on wholes and their properties and functions. As Smut put it in his beguiling style, "The creative intensified Field of Nature, consisting of all physical organic and personal wholes in their close interactions and mutual influences, is itself of an organic or holistic character—that Field is the source of the grand Ecology of the Universe. It is the environment, the Society—vital, friendly, educative, creature of all wholes and all souls" (1926, 354–55).

In the decades when holistic essay scoring was starting up, the decades covered by this book, organicism flourished in all professional fields: anthropology, architecture, art studies, biology, education, environmental studies, learning theory, neurology, nursing, philosophy, psychology, psychiatry, religious studies, social work, sociology, the list goes on. Most appropriated the term *holistic* as soon as Smuts offered it to the public. Holistic essay scoring was a small plant growing in an intellectual field teeming with holism.

Watch organicism prosper, for instance, in intellectual domains close to holistic essay scoring. Psychology: in 1932 a review of "early holistic psychologists" notes that they had "much in common with the modern proponents of the configurationist viewpoint . . . a more organismic, phenomenalistic, and 'holistic' approach to the study of psychology" (Commins 1932, 217). Psychoanalysis: in 1943, Abraham Maslow is promoting his concept of the psychic "syndrome" as a whole that "can be seen in any of its parts if these parts are understood not reductively, but holistically" (528). Learning theory: in 1954, Louis Thorpe and Allen Schmuller include in their textbook of learning theories a chapter called "Gestalt Psychology: A Holistic Outlook," which offers the fundamental principle "that the organism reacts to total situations and proceeds from whole to part and from general to specific on the basis that the whole is always greater than the sum of its parts" (247). Linguistics: by 1963, in a collection called *Parts and Wholes*, linguist Roman Jakobson is warning about the danger of the *pars pro toto* fallacy in analysis of language, "the illicit conversation of a mere part into a seemingly self-sufficient whole," resulting in "the artificial treatment of messages without reference to the superposed context" (159). Education: by 1967, educationist Paul Hanna is defending his theory of spelling on the grounds that it includes phonemic, graphemic, morphological, and syntactic cues, in short, assumes a "holistic language structure" (216). Literature: by 1974, literary critic James Bennett is editing a special issue of *Style* called "Holistic Criticism," "a conceptual framework for the full description of the dynamic design of a literary text (syntagmatic and paradigmatic) as it connects with author, audience, and world. And, I should add, with the critic" (288). Composition and rhetoric: by 1975, Joseph Comprone is arguing that first-year college students should study "holistic" communication systems and that the study of rhetoric should "adopt the language of quantum physics, gestalt psychology, dialectics, cybernetics, general system theory, or half a dozen other disciplines. One could describe a shift of emphasis from stasis to process, entity to relationship, atom to gestalt, scaler to tensor, component to system, analytics to dialectics, causality to constraint, bioenergetics to communication, or at least a dozen other parallel shifts" (2).

These fields have varied degrees of closeness to writing assessment, but that proximity is another book for others to write. Except for the next chapter with its history of gestalt perception theory, we provide no systematic chart of the vast country of organicism. Even in our restricted terrain of holistic essay scoring, however, history makers and history readers can get lost. It seems a map is needed, but one map won't do. We need a portfolio of maps. Here are nine.

MAP 1: CONSTANCIES IN THE HISTORY OF HOLISTIC ESSAY SCORING

Over the decades this book covers, some constancies do emerge. One is the fact that today in both the United Kingdom and the United States, the universal popularity of holistic scoring has markedly diminished, presenting a pattern of rise and decline historians and their readers find familiar.

Running opposed to this decline and fall, however, is a second constancy, the uninterrupted ascent in national attention to literacy proficiency.[2] Educational accountability almost always includes measurement of writing proficiency. After WWII there was a striking growth in the practice, study, and discussion of formal assessment of writing. In 1949 no professional journal devoted itself solely to educational evaluation or assessment; by 1999, eight did.[3] Over the same span of time, the volume of published scholarship on evaluation of writing increased thirtyfold. The newcomer on the block, holistic scoring, received especially intense scrutiny on both sides of the Atlantic. Did the scrutiny eventually work against the establishment of the method?

The question, answered in chapter 9, leads to a third historical constancy, which was the preoccupation of scholars and practitioners with one particular aspect of the rating of proficiency or performance in writing: the formal methods by which that rating can be accomplished. So those methods also grew, at least in number. And as they grew, they competed. What works better—counting misspellings, scoring multiple-choice questions on grammar and vocabulary, appraising the revision of a poorly written text, turning the student essay into a cloze test, applying a content scheme, or summing up the scaled ratings of eight different writing traits? In formal holistic essay scoring, two or more independent raters label the worth of a whole essay with a single score and do so without first assigning numerical value to separate accomplishments of the writing (recall the definition provided in the introduction). The mystery is why, over many decades, holistic scoring connected so centrally to every other method of writing evaluation—connected in theory, practice, ethics, cost, doability, and faculty esteem. How did that centrality come about? And what happened to it? And is it gone forever?

MAP 2: HISTORICAL EMPLOTMENTS

Simply put, this book studies the early histories of holistic scoring of writing in the United Kingdom and the United States from the mid-1930s to the mid-1980s. Histories, in the plural.

This book disavows a single unified history of holistic scoring, however complex that one history might be depicted. Holistic scoring has many histories because history itself is constructed. The human past was made by humans, true, but history is made by historians. In a phrase current around the same time our own account of US holistic scoring starts, history is an "imaginative reconstruction" (Dray 1963, 108–10).[4] The English philosopher R. G. Collingwood captured the gist of this concept in one sentence: "Historical thinking is that activity of the imagination by which we endeavor to provide an innate idea with detailed content" (1946, 247). The nub of this definition is the word *innate*.

One innate or a priori idea historians bring to their history making is a sense of time passing. This fact is not entirely self-evident. Historians may suggest that temporality inheres in the past, but actually it inheres in the telling of the past. In his summary of constructivist historiography after WWII, Donald E. Polkinghorne puts this point deftly: "Historians have to set forth their presentations as sequences of events, which gives the impression that their conclusions are inferences from the evidence, when really they are only indicators of the way the evidence has been ordered" (1988, 52). Note Polkinghorne's shift from "sequence" to "order." History is not one thing after another nor even one thing over and over. It is one thing seemingly connected to another.

History is a sequence, cohering through narrativity, plot, or in Hayden White's eye-catching word, "emplotment." And, as White famously argued, emplotment comes in different configurations. The historian can narrate the French Revolution as a triumph over repressive rule (romance), a flowering of a union between youthful natural energy and aged social order (comedy), a failed effort to achieve a better society (tragedy), or a hopeless struggle against inevitable forces (satire) (1973, 45–80).[5] Nested within White's "archetypes" or "governing metaphors," and more directly shaping the accounts of most historians, can be read scores of more specific narratives, storylines usually widespread in the historian's own day and culture, plots such as rags to riches or pure intentions corrupted by material realities. The personal anecdote, seemingly unique ("Once I . . ."), usually takes shape in the form one or more of these cultural storylines.

The point is worth dwelling on since it is crucial to this book's particular method of seeking and displaying its history. We glimpse five loose and intermeshing narrative structurings.

- **History as annals.** To begin, we have tried to gather new data connected with holistic scoring in its early days. We have scoured archives, interviewed survivors, tried to sort the accurate from the inaccurate, recorded names, places, and dates—all to construct a new annals—a day-by-day record of an important period in UK and US education.
- **History as story.** But of course, we could never escape from narrative. If, as Collingwood and Pilkinghorne say, historicizing begins

with innate orderings, the search itself for new data will be constructed. Fingering through a dusty filing cabinet is usually searching *for*. We found that with holistic scoring, stories abound, both anecdotes and cultural plotlines. But our finding was part of emplotments we ourselves were writing. Who can resist a good story?

- **History as trajectory.** We mean by historical trajectory a segment or unresolved span of an emplotment. Naturally, the shorter the historical narrative stretch, the greater the chance it will be unfinished. Indeed, it can be argued that historical storytelling differs in one essential way from fictional storytelling in that history is never resolved. Unsettling as it might be, history is nonteleological. In her 1999 end-of-the-century account of US writing assessment, Kathleen Blake Yancey plots a hopeful trajectory of three progressive waves, from objective testing to holistic scoring to portfolio scoring, but who can say that difficulties with innovative assessments won't bring back multiple-choice testing?[6]

- **History as social exploration.** As was the case with work preceding this volume (Elliot 2005), the present volume assembles circumstances surrounding key assessment episodes in order to place them in their social context (316). Because the early practice of holistic scoring had important stakeholder consequences, its social history and social justice are deeply related. We realize that how we write our histories matters, and we encourage new interpretations of our social explorations that focus on impact. Especially promising here is the social justice historiography proposed by J. W. Hammond (2018), with special attention to stakeholder representation, measurement consequences, critical reflection, and practice implications. While this volume attends to each of these analytic frames, extended social justice historiography allows extended interpretation of the history we recount and the creation of assessment histories yet unwritten.

- **History as global journey.** In her study of contemporary trends in historiography, Eileen Ka-May Cheng (2012) finds that the most important recent methodological development is the shift to a global perspective. Along with an emphasis on narrative and cultural context, recent scrutiny of world connections has allowed historians to focus on specific events, such as those scoring genres described in our book, while locating them in a transnational context. We return to the need for a global perspective based on demographic trends in chapter 10. Meanwhile, we hope readers will welcome the transnational stories we tell and the revisionist potential they hold for histories of the profession and, by extension, for fair opportunities for all within the profession.

The danger with historiographic emplotments is that they may exclude some historical evidence and, worse, may curb the search for more evidence. "Every story that is told obscures the stories that go untold," writes Verlyn Klinkenborg (1992, 5). We add that every story told tends to obscure other stories that, often contradictory, lie hidden within it, waiting to be told.

MAP 3: FOUR VIGNETTES

These points beg for illustration. Four vignettes of holistic scoring follow, picked and condensed from the many we reconstruct in this book. Think of them as movie trailers.

Vignette 1: 1940, spring, England. With little warning, the school population of County Devon in the west of England suddenly doubled within a few months. The new students were largely evacuee children from London, sent to the country for safekeeping from the predicted German blitz. At the time, R. K. Robertson was Chief Examiner for Devon, in charge of the 11-plus examinations, mandated assessment that largely determined whether children eleven or twelve years old would complete their formal schooling (Wiseman 1929, 205n2). For an examiner faced with a huge increase in exam-taker population, Robertson headed in a most unexpected direction. In the language-proficiency part of the exam, all students took an objective short-answer examination. Then the roughly 2,500 of them who had scored in the middle third were given a second examination. It required them to write an impromptu essay that was then rated on a thirteen-point scale by four independent teachers. The raters read very quickly, and their rates were averaged. Robertson's method of scoring essays had been investigated for decades in England but had never been used in large-scale governmental examinations. Called general-impression marking at the time, it was the scoring method we term pooled-rater, and we see no reason it doesn't deserve the term holistic.

What is the narrative here for a history of essay-scoring methods? The local story finds home easily enough, a necessity-is-the-mother-of-invention tale or perhaps a good-comes-of-war story. An ironic version might be found in the story that in 1941, Pearl Harbor ended the essay the College Board had used for their admission test since 1900 (Elliot 2005, 99–101). The narrative, however, also fits into a longer trajectory. Robertson's method of scoring was borrowed by US testing experts in the 1950s and 1960s. So the plot is of emigration and taking root in a foreign land. This narrative looks quite different from the plot currently favored by US composition scholarship, that holistic scoring was homegrown, developed by the US testing industry by Educational Testing Service (ETS) employees Fred I. Godshalk, Frances Swineford, and William E. Coffman and published by the College Entrance

Examination Board in 1966.[7] In fact, for that experiment Godshalk, Swineford, and Coffman used a pooled-rater scoring method very similar to Robertson's. We return to this story in chapter 3.

Vignette 2: 1966, Princeton, New Jersey, and the University of Connecticut. The same year the College Board published Godshalk, Swineford, and Coffman's ETS study, ETS was sponsoring an Invitational Conference on Testing Problems. One of the presenters was Ellis Batten Page, who gave an interim report on his and Dieter Paulus's experiment at the University of Connecticut in scoring student essays by computer—a venture first funded by the College Board. To secure a trustworthy predictor variable, Page and Paulus had human raters score each of the essays to be analyzed by their FORTRAN program. They used an analytical approach, scoring five criteria separately on five-point scales and summing the scores (Page and Paulis 1968). This particular five-criteria scale, one that became enormously influential in the following decades, had been developed by an ETS researcher, Paul B. Diederich, and was first published in the *English Journal*, also in 1966. So the same year marks the public announcement of three distinct scoring methods: Diederich's analytic scale, ETS pooled-rater holistic scoring, and computer analysis of written communication.

The evidence undermines the common cultural story that within organizations—such as ETS and big science university programs of research—innovations arise through coordinated teamwork: a win-the-prize-by-rowing-in-unison story. Just as disorienting is the trajectory the story pieces out. It doesn't look like a one-thing-after-another history. It doesn't much fit progressive emplotments Hayden White called "romance," histories that narrate one force being replacing by a better force, a storyline signaled by words such as *post* (posthuman) or *beyond* (beyond outcomes), or by metaphors such as "generation" (Guba and Lincoln 1990), "turn" (Trimbur 1994), "phase" (White 2005), or "wave" (Behm and Miller 2012). Instead, the historical evidence suggests multiple and simultaneous plots, parallel and competing and unresolved, as in the first act of a play that cannot yet be taken as tragic, comic, or satiric.

Vignette 3: 1979, fall, University of Southern California. Louise Wetherbee Phelps joined the University of Southern California's department of rhetoric, linguistics, and literature and heard that faculty and graduate students were reading Subject A examinations, essays written by entering students for placement within or exemption from USC's first-year writing program. She asked to participate in their holistic scoring of the essays. But she lasted only one session. She just "couldn't obey their rubrics." She felt she "didn't belong" (pers. comm., January 7, 2015).

This personal narrative vibrates, antithetical, within the orthodox professional narrative that holistic scoring sessions, when run by faculty, give rise to a greater sense of camaraderie and solidarity. For instance, Carol Holder was coordinator for composition programs in the California State University system and involved with the scoring of its English Placement Test, and she remembers that "because of the fun faculty from different campuses had at the 3–4 day holistic scoring sessions, it wasn't hard to recruit scorers. We enjoyed wonderful dinners wherever we met—usually the San Francisco Bay Area—and developed friendships with faculty on sister campuses" (email to authors, March 4, 2015). But Phelps's experience is not really an anomaly, and this book records a number of similar personal anecdotes, some from scholars in the profession as eminent as Phelps became. Charlotte Linde, scholar of institutional storytelling, calls these stories "unspeakables": "Institutions have occasions that permit the telling of certain narratives. Other potential narratives, the unspeakables, are often difficult to speak because there is no sanctioned public occasion for them" (1997, 287). The underground resistance to holistic scoring forms a history of its own, as we recount in chapter 7.

Vignette 4: 1981, July, New Orleans. At a conference sponsored by the National Institute of Education called "Feasibility of Assessing Writing Using Multiple Techniques," discussions among school and college administrators revealed much confusion over terminology and scoring methods. One administrator heard descriptions of ETS holistic scoring and said that "what he used and called holistic scoring was nothing like the procedure developed by ETS." Other administrators agreed and described their own "unique" systems with pride. To them, other methods apparently had little appeal (McCready and Melton 1981, 80–81).

Is this evidence from a narrative of holistic scoring as fad? When narrating movements as popular as holistic scoring, it is easy to homogenize. Sociological research into popular trends, however, always finds a certain amount of internal conflict to explain their rise and decline. The peak of a fad may contain features that will lead to its decline: oversaturation, self-consciousness, misinformation, exaggeration, and departure from the original (Meyerson and Katz 1957; Miller 2013, 206–8). To this list, as noted above, we add resistance. Are these stages in the natural history of popular trends duplicated in some of the trajectories of holistic scoring 1949–1983?

We hope our reliance on narrative does not imply that this book will take lightly the profession's past agency connected with holistic scoring or will assume blithely that the current profession can only fictionalize those connections. With every sentence, this book tries to get as near to the actual territory as it can. Maybe history can draw only maps of the past, but maps can be more or less accurate, can lead people to where they want to go more or less well. Novelist and poet Paulette Jiles, who spent some years living in the "trackless" northern provinces of Canada, warns, "You must understand how useless a map is. You must also study them with great care" (1995, 192). In our analysis of splitters, rubrics, and profiles, we return to this theme in chapter 9.

MAP 4: EVIDENCE

Should historytelling be descriptive, explanatory, or predictive? Should it be qualitative or quantitative? Should it use a mixed or multiple methodology? Our answer to all these questions is "yes." To that methodological eclecticism, we added the ballast of old-fashioned documentary evidence. We have gone to newspapers, federal and state regulations, funded research reports, individual research articles, institutional and commercial testing archives, and current testimonials of those who were there.

- **Archives.** We located important and unanalyzed materials in archives, for instance, at the University of Chicago, Michigan State University, and ETS. The photo of James Britton in chapter 4 at the Dartmouth Conference, found for us in the Rauner Special Collections Library, may well be the only image that exists of that esteemed UK researcher at that event. Left unknown and untapped by us lies a vast body of evidence in archives around the world.
- **Structured interviews.** As we note in the acknowledgments, we interviewed people who were there—some face to face, some on Skype, some by email, some by telephone. We asked questions tailored to their individual experience. Taken from chapter 6, here is a question from our interview with Sydell T. Carlton on July 2, 2014:

    One of the milestone events in the history of writing assessment is your famous study with John W. French and Paul B. Diederich on factor analysis in 1961. Can you provide the context for that study? Were its findings understood at ETS to be justification of a type of scoring that would focus on total reader impression— that is, a justification of holistic scoring?

    As might be imagined, the answers to such pointed questions helped paint the holistic enterprise in new, complicating, and contradictory detail.
- **The authors' experience.** There is no objectivity in history because history does not make itself. Humans make history by writing it. But historians can be closer to or further from the events, with advantages either way. The authors of this book were tangentially involved with holistic assessment only in the last years this account covers,

but they have not exactly maintained a hands-clean or heads-clear distance since. Although Richard Haswell was using holistic scoring for personal research as early as 1981, it was ten years later that he started considering and then modifying the method as part of a first-year and third-year campus-wide assessment of writing at Washington State University. Norbert Elliot worked for ETS during the summer of 1984, but it was a year later that he started applying and evaluating holistic scoring as part of a campus writing assessment at East Texas State University (now Texas A&M Commerce), 1985–1988. Throughout their careers, both taught, applied, and researched writing assessment. For good or bad, that experience is part of the baggage they brought with them to write this book.

- **Published empirical research**. Formal assessment of writing walks hand and hand with empirical evidence. By its nature, assessment collects and produces data. It shapes, records, validates, defends, critiques, and revamps itself through data. We took extra care to read the data-infused record, at first to explore how it, too, practiced, legitimized, and self-policed its culture. Slowly we became aware of an argument embedded in the data, an evidence-based perspective we present in the final chapter. Over the decades, in investigating and reporting holistic scoring, researchers enlarged their sources of evidence. The new evidence helped unpin holistic scoring yet perhaps at the same time pointed a way to revise and better holistic scoring. The empirical record, we argue, can help turn the history of a scoring method—however incomplete, in fact because it is incomplete—into a history that is actionable. History cannot be recounted just by re-counting it. We report numbers we were lucky enough to find, but we also sought out the underlying habitus and motivations of the people who produced the numbers. It is easy to see holistic scoring as shaped by numerical data—so many essays rated in so many hours with such and such a rater reliability. But holistic scoring was also shaped by philosophy, politics, economics, psychology, pedagogy, and personalities. In a phrase, this history pursues the praxis of the holistic, a praxis reproducing and validating the society and economy that privileged and sustained it. As students, teachers, researchers, and entrepreneurs were practicing the holistic, they were, chiefly unaware, practicing and legitimizing their culture (Bourdieu and Passeron 1990; Douglas 1986).

MAP 5: TERMINOLOGY

While examination and use of an evidence-based approach is the last step of this book, the first step was to take care of the terminology. From its start, discussion surrounding holistic scoring was plagued with synonymy and polysemy. A single concept or method attracted different names, and a name sometimes referred to quite different concepts or methods. This semiotic slide has been a problem since the early days of educational measurement when Truman Lee Kelley referred to definitional challenges as the "jangle fallacy" (1927, 64). Dwell a moment on any term provided in our glossary, and the next stop is a rabbit hole.

Everyone agreed, for instance, that *holistic evaluation* or *holistic assessment* dealt with the value of an essay taken as a whole rather than broken down by parts. But what does one call that wholeness? Around the end of the nineteenth century, *general merit* was popular, but later so was *total merit*, *general impression*, and *overall quality*. Philosophers, psychologists, linguistics, and educationists were adding *holism, wholism, interconnectedness, syndrome, template, agglutination,* and *glosso-dynamic* (Titone 1973). The adjective *holistic* could appear as *organic, organismic, nonanalytic, global, integrated, total, relational, configurational, unstructured, systemic, unitive,* and *molar* (Tolman 1932, from the Latin *moles*, a "whole"). The most common opposite terms were *analysis* and *analytical*, but synonyms spread like nonnative weeds: *atomistic, decompositional, featural, structured, synthetic, dimensional, trait-based, registered* (Braungart-Bloom 1984), and *meristic* (Bhatia 1977, from the Greek *merismos*, a "division").

Synonyms pose problems, but they are lesser problems. Far worse is when contemporary accounts use the same name to refer to different events, such as when *holistic* refers to scoring methods that, in fact, are analytical at root.[8] For our meanings of the host of technical terms writers are obliged to use when seriously discussing evaluation of writing, in application or research, we provide a glossary (and readers provide the rabbit hole). During the period of our study, we found some terms are often used and so are crucial to this book's map of the territory. The citations provided are typical uses in the United Kingdom and the United States. Let's begin with *analytic scoring* and move, by contrast, to *holistic*.

In the practice of analytic scoring, readers assign separate scores to different aspects or accomplishments of the writing. The scorers often use a checklist identifying the parts to be scored with scales for each part (Wiseman 1949). In using scaled criteria, readers fill out a scoring grid—in the United Kingdom, a *marking scheme* or *schedule*—that provides values for individual writing traits such as ideas, organization, or support, each on a scale from low to high (e.g., 1 to 4, or 1 to 20) (Diedereich 1966). Primary-trait scoring is also a scaled-criteria method in which the criteria are limited to a few relevant rhetorical requirements established by the writing task (Mullis 1976). For scoring short essays in academic-subject examinations, a content scheme—in Britain *mark scheme* or *marking scheme*—stipulates the points awarded for each relevant claim of the writer (Mather, France, and Sare 1965).

In the practice of holistic scoring, a scale is used to assign a single value mark to a whole essay—not separately to individual aspects. Holistic scoring is informal if there is only one rater per essay and if there are no preset schemes establishing parameters, such as anchor essays or a given distribution of rates (Gray and Ruth 1982). Typical informal methods are the time-honored grading of teachers; open ranking, in which essays in a set are simply rank ordered from worst to best; and sample matching, in which an essay is assigned a score or rank by fitting it within a given set of essays arranged from best to worst.

In distinction, formal holistic scoring—the subject of this book—compares the scores of two or more raters using a scale on each essay to provide a single value mark (Britton, Marten, and Rosen 1966). Formal holistic scoring ranges from open to controlled, depending on how well the scale levels are predefined by definition, description, or sample essays—"anchors," "range-finders," "exemplars,"—or, as Miles Myers (1980) put it, "prototypes." Two common but crucially distinct ways of controlling essay ratings are rubrics and scoring guides. The first arranges the selected criteria and numbered scale in a table format so each criterion is described and scaled in the same way (see fig. 9.2). The second describes the selected criteria in a way that connects to the holistic scale, but the connections are not uniform across the criteria (see fig. 5.2). Formal holistic scoring schemes can be imagined as closer or nearer to analytic schemes (see table 1.1).

Finally, in formal holistic scoring there have been three distinct ways the final score of an essay is calculated from the scores, often unalike, of independent raters. In pooled-rater scoring—also called "consensus scoring," "collective judgment" (Boyd 1924), or "multiple marking" (Head 1966)—scores based on a shared scale are simply summed or averaged, however many independent raters there are for each essay. Each score represents the perspective of one rater and is taken as no better or worse than another rater's score. In adjusted scoring each essay has two independent raters, but if their scores differ by more than a specified degree, a third rater is used to adjudicate and determine the final score of the essay, often during the reading itself (Breland and Gaynor 1979). In consulted scoring the two original raters discuss and resolve discrepancies (Pilkington 1967). Finally, in office-adjusted scoring a post hoc adjustment is made to reduce rater error (Hartog, Rhodes, and Burt 1936).

Returning to the jangle fallacy, we must emphasize the confusion that ensues when the major elements, defined above, are misnamed or confounded. At base, primary-trait scoring is analytic, and when it is designated "holistic" (e.g., Lloyd-Jones 1977, 37), it skews a narrative of holistic scoring that respects its perceptual underpinnings described in chapter 2. Again, by our definition, formal holistic scoring does not apply when student essays are read by only one rater with a supervisor occasionally spot-checking the scores, as has been standard with governmental school examinations in the United Kingdom (Office of Qualifications and Examinations Regulation 2014) and is growing more common in the United States as automated scores are used to provide a second score (Bridgeman 2013). We acknowledge the contested nature of our definition yet want our definitions to be clear lest our own interpretations become part of the jangle. With adjusted scoring, it is common practice to treat scores one point apart (e.g., 3 and 4 on a six-point scale) as a match and to treat as discrepant scores two or more points apart (e.g., 3 and 5). But when the scores of 3 and 4 are averaged within a group or scores of 3 and 5 are decided by a wiser third party, it is unwise to classify this mixture of pooled scoring with adjusted scoring under a single category of rater precision. Such classifications confound two different underlying philosophies of evaluation. Similarly, it is unwise to treat interrater reliability as a preferred, or (worse yet) only, measure of reliability.

As our book illustrates, many in the United Kingdom and the United States implicitly assumed they had provided evidence of validity by measuring degree of interrater agreement and interrater reliability. Evidence of validity, however, cannot be established by reliability measures alone, and those reliability measures themselves differ widely. Today, we think of reliability as characteristics of Differential Reader Functioning over Time (DRIFT): differential severity, differential accuracy, and differential scale category use (Wolfe et al. 2007). In early holistic reading reliability research, when a sample is only one twenty-minute impromptu essay from each student, early researchers radically simplify the notion of reliability, tacitly excluding basic questions such as the following: Would those same raters score the writing sample consistently a few weeks later (intrarater reliability)? If two tasks are given, are the forms parallel (test reliability)? Does the writer perform consistently on different tasks—and, if so, how many tasks are needed to make a claim about writing proficiency (writer reliability)? Each of these questions has implications for both validity and fairness.

We leave the glossary to provide definitions of other elements related to formal holistic scoring as they were used during the period of our study. As these terms are encountered, it is important to remember that the specialized vocabulary used in this book follows standard usage of the period from the mid-1930s to the mid-1980s in the United Kingdom and the United States. This historical resection means definitions do not include significant change in terms beginning in the late 1980s, as is the case with evidence related to validity (Messick 1989). Only in chapter 10 do we shift to contemporary definitions in order to propose an actionable future for writing assessment. Let chapters 2 through 9 therefore serve as evidence of the history-boggling permutations and combinations of these technical terms as they were applied by actual first-generation researchers working with methods of holistic scoring.

MAP 6: A DEFINITION

These terms provide context for our definition of formal holistic scoring of essays, whose early history this book will construct.[9] We define formal holistic scoring as *the use of a scale to assign a single value mark to a whole essay and not separately to individual aspects, with scorers trying to apply the scale consistently, and with the final score for each essay derived from two or more independent ratings.* Ancillary to this definition is the number of scale levels, identification of a scale as interval, degree of openness or control of rater training, use of rubrics or scoring guides or anchor essays, number of independent scores per essay beyond two, and scoring calculation involving pooling, adjusting, and consultation methods.

MAP 7: A CONTINUUM OF POPULAR ESSAY-SCORING PROCEDURES

Over the decades, several holistic scoring procedures stand out. Table 1.1 arranges nine of the most popular along a continuum from holistic to analytic.

Four observations are important in terms of table 1.1. First, often these methods are distinguished by number of raters per essay, a matter of historical importance. For instance, the United Kingdom did not adopt a two-rater method during the history we present in our book—and does not universally support one today. Following Cyril Weir's own analysis of the British history of interrater reliability, Weir, Ivana Vidakovic, and Evelina D. Galaczi note that, despite "a growing consensus in the profession on the need for and value of double marking . . . practicality is still proffered as an excuse for not utilizing this means of improving scoring validity even in the 21st century" (2013, 201). As a result of a program of research beginning in 2008, researchers and policymakers in the Office of Qualifications and Examinations

Table 1.1. Popular essay-rating methods arranged along a continuum of holistic to analytic

Holistic, open pooled-rater	Raters score each essay relying solely on a shared scale, with all scores summed or averaged (e.g., Britton 1963).
Holistic, controlled pooled-rater	Raters score each essay using a common scale and guidelines such as anchor essays, scoring guides, rubrics, or a given distribution of scores (e.g., Godshalk, Swineford, and Coffman 1966).
Holistic, office adjusted	Raters score each essay with scores later adjusted by standardization techniques, such as applying the overall standard deviation to each score (e.g., Hartog, Rhodes, and Burt 1936).
Holistic, controlled adjusted-rater, with anchor essays	Raters score each essay independently with a third reader resolving discrepant scores and a sample essay to illustrate each scale level (e.g., Myers 1980).
Holistic, controlled adjusted-rater, with scoring guide	Raters score each essay independently with a third reader resolving discrepant scores, using a guide that roughly describes each scale level (e.g., White 1973).
Holistic, controlled adjusted-rater, with unscored rubric	Raters score each essay independently with a third reader resolving discrepant scores, using a tabled checklist of specific writing traits but without points assigned for each trait at each scale level (e.g., Bossone 1969).
Analytic, primary trait	Raters score an essay on a restricted number of traits that are appropriate to one rhetorical requirement of the essay topic, with each trait given points on its own scale (e.g., Mullis 1976).
Analytic, scaled criteria	Raters score an essay using a tabled checklist of specific writing traits that have points assigned for each trait at each scale level, and the final score is the sum of all those points (e.g., Diederich 1966).
Analytic, profile	Raters score an essay using a tabled checklist of specific writing traits that have points assigned for each trait at each scale level, and the final score is the sum of those points (e.g., Hamp-Lyons 1987).

Regulation (Ofqual), a nongovernment regulatory department in the United Kingdom, concluded in 2014 that there is "a strong body of evidence from the 1940s to 1980s that double marking is a more reliable method of marking than single marking." Nevertheless, Ofqual (2014) notes the "significant logistical and financial challenges associated with the implementation of double marking" (10). As a result, "none of the exam boards offering general qualifications in England currently use double marking in its true sense. Instead, all choose to quality assure marking through a sampling approach" (6). In this approach a student essay is scored only once, by a junior marker, whose scores are occasionally checked ("sampled") by a senior marker. In the United States, however, multiple marking in formal assessment was legitimated early and largely remains. Examination of cultural values and subsequent historical interpretation are thus related to the number of raters in a given writing-assessment episode.

Second—and here is an important similarity between the two nations—the essay-rating schemes are directly related to evidence of validity. As Hartog, Rhodes, and Burt argued, "No test can be a 'valid test' unless it yields consistent results in the hands of different examiners, i.e., unless its 'reliability' (to use the word generally employed by educational psychologists), or, as we should prefer to say, its 'consistency,' is 'high'" (1936, 68). It is not simply that reliability is a prerequisite to validity in our studies; rather, it is that evidence of reliability stands as evidence of validity. The forms of validity that were used from the mid-1930s to the mid-1980s on both sides of the Atlantic—which we inferred from construct, content, concurrent, predictive, and conceptually related evidence—often emerge as a concern, albeit too often tacit and too often related to reliability, of the researchers we examine. In similar fashion, fairness is based largely on evidence of scorer reliability. Research into factors of gender and ethnicity, for instance, began quite late in the 1970s (e.g., Breland 1977; with the exception of Martin 1972). Again, we return to Hartog, Rhodes, and Burt in their belief, present for most of our history, that a "fair decision" involves the elimination of random variation related to scoring reliability (1936, 235). Therefore, while our understanding of marking schemes is directly related to the number of raters used in a given assessment episode, these rating schemes are not merely methodological; rather, they are tacitly related to evidence gathering used to draw conclusions about validity and fairness.

Third, the marking schemes shown in table 1.1 reveal research highly restricted in terms of investigating the writing construct. To say writing was undertheorized until the early 1970s (a good milestone date is the 1971 publication of Janet A. Emig's *The Composing Processes of Twelfth Graders*) is an understatement. The sociocognitive models that currently shape the design of writing assessment episodes in the United Kingdom (Weir, Vidakovic, and Galaczi 2013, 212–14) and the United States (Poe, Inoue, and Elliot 2018, 3–38) were not present during the first half-century of our history. As a result of restricted construct representation, table 1.1. may be understood as a taxonomy related to historically embodied forms of evidence. We turn to the use of taxonomies in chapter 10 as the basis of actionable future based on historical patterns.

Fourth, table 1.1 brings forward the importance of genre as constitutive in studying the history of writing assessment (Wood 2018). Popular in the testing of students, these essay-rating methods functioned also as tools of formal research. It worked both ways. Test manufacturers researched scoring methods before making them operational, and those testing methods were borrowed and adapted for independent research, sometimes to investigate the methods themselves. The same method, then, often belongs to two different discourse genres, and the information genre analysis provides, historically, should be interpreted and narrated differently. While ours is not a genre study, the force of genre runs throughout the early history of holistic scoring. In presenting genres of holistic scoring, we see the formation of writing research itself.

MAP 8: FOUR TRADITIONS OF HOLISTIC SCORING

Popular and traditional are not necessarily the same. Tradition implies a transmission and evolution of a practice over generations and, in some cases, across international boundaries. This book discerns and hopes to disambiguate four different traditions of formal holistic essay scoring. They perhaps mark the main departure of our account from previous histories. Map 8 therefore serves as an extension of the continuum of popular essay-scoring procedures shown in table 1.1.

1. **Connoisseurship scoring.** Raters, usually teachers, work from an internalized scale, often a traditional set of academic grades, and assign scores based on their knowledge and experience of students and the educational consequences of the examination. The method may differ little from ordinary teacher grading and thus has deep historical roots. But both in the United Kingdom and the United States, it was used in formal, external examinations for which multiple rating was utilized. Connoisseurship scoring is sometimes described as the inferior form of evaluation that holistic scoring replaced. But it lived on post–WWII in local placement testing, general-college examination boards, teacher-scored exit examinations, and elsewhere. (We take our term *connoisseurship* from the history of the Cambridge English Examinations [Weir, Vidakovic, and Galaczi 2013, 208]).

2. **Trait-informed scoring.** Scorers are trained to focus their reading on a limited set of writing traits (organization, vocabulary, ideas, and so forth) and are sometimes asked to ignore other writing accomplishments. The traits to be used are sometimes defined in a scoring guide or rubric. Like connoisseurship scoring, trait-based scoring has a long tradition, deep rooted in informal classroom practice. It borders on formal analytical scoring methods such as the Diederich scale (1966) or ELL profile scoring (Hamp-Lyons 1987), in which writing traits are scored separately. In the United States the method escalated in popularity during the 1980s and 1990s and is now installed, for instance, in online essay-response schemes, designed for teachers and censured by teachers (e.g., Wilson 2006).

3. **Pooled-rater scoring.** Scorers read papers rapidly—names for the method were "rapid-impression marking" (Britton 1963) or "rapid-impression reading" (Godshalk, Swineford, and Coffman 1966).

Typically, there are three to five independent raters for each essay, and their scores are all accepted, then summed or averaged for a final score. In some forms used in the United Kingdom during the period of our study, post hoc adjustment was undertaken to adjust for consistent variation among raters, and the difference in leniency between the two methods of marking could be standardized afterward. In pooled scoring rater training is usually light, although scorers, usually experienced teachers, may have sample papers to suggest some scale levels or a distribution of scores to shoot for. An experimental testing of the method was reported by British researchers Hartog, Rhodes, and Burt in 1936, and the method was made operational with 11-plus examination essays in Devon by Chief Examiner R. K. Robertson in 1939 (Wiseman 1949). Although it was sporadically used and heavily researched in the United Kingdom into the 1980s, it never caught on. But in the United States, ETS borrowed, tested, and applied it and, eventually, advocated by Fred I. Godshalk and Gertrude Conlan and others, made it the standard scoring procedure for its English Composition Test discussed in chapter 6. Along with the next tradition, pooled-rater scoring stands at the center of the holistic essay-scoring enterprise.

4. **Adjusted-rater scoring.** Typically, each paper has two independent readings, and if the two scores are discrepant, usually more than one point apart, the paper is read a third time, "adjusted," often by the chief readers. Sometimes the method is called "controlled" (e.g., White 1973). Raters are trained with sample papers illustrating the scale and given some sort of scoring guide or rubric to use as they score. The concordance of their scoring with other scorers may be periodically checked by chief readers. As we propose in chapter 5, possibly the first use of this method was in large-scale scoring with undergraduate end-of-course essays graded by the Board of Examiners of the University of Chicago beginning in 1943. The designer was Diederich, who started working for ETS in 1949. Around 1956, adjusted-rater holistic scoring became the standard rating system with Advanced Placement English essays and from there spread around the nation through teachers who had served as AP readers (Advanced Placement Program 1980, 10). In the first half of the 1970s, important high-profile college-essay-assessment programs used adjusted-rater scoring, including the Georgia Regents Testing Program instituted by the Board of Regents of the University of Georgia and the English Equivalency Examination instituted by the California State University system. In the United States, adjusted-rater scoring was probably the most widely used method of holistic scoring.

These four traditions have different provenances, different cadres and followers in practice and research, and different trajectories over the decades. They also ground themselves in different theory and philosophy, as this book hopes to show.

MAP 9: CHAPTERS

We have organized the book into ten chapters. The main narrative chapters, 3 to 9, roughly chronological, focus on particular tests, studies, people, and locales.

- Chapter 2 presents two premises underlying the early historical course of holistic scoring. Social-contagion modeling helps explain the swift and enormous growth of the method in the last half of the twentieth century. Gestalt psychology emphasizes the importance of perception theory in deriving principles behind the dynamic human ordering of the act of holistic scoring. Practitioners of the scoring may have been unaware of these premises, but the principles remain.

- Chapter 3 narrates the attempts at holistic scoring in the United Kingdom up to 1949. It celebrates UK researchers Philip Joseph Hartog and Edmond Cecil Rhodes and educational measurement specialist Cyril L. Burt, who, in their 1936 publication *The Marks of Examiners*, were the first to report and study formal holistic scoring, at least by our definition. The chapter ends with the remarkable use of pooled-rater holistic essay scoring in Devon with government sponsored school examinations, 1939–1948. The history repositions formal holistic scoring within an international context and challenges the received view that the method was invented in the United States.

- Chapter 4 brings the UK history up to the mid-1980s, when it became obvious that in the huge school-leaving and college-matriculation examinations, multiple-marker holistic scoring had lost out to single-marker content-scheme and profile scoring. Despite steady increases in examinees, both first- and second-language students, British researchers and teachers remained faithful to the academic-subject essay and to feedback from examination results to teachers and students. We pay special attention to *Multiple Marking of English Compositions: An Account of an Experiment*, a rigorous study conducted by James N. Britton, Nancy C. Martin, and Harold Rosen into holistic and analytic scoring. The UK assessment experience contrasts with US history, where large-scale distributed assessments largely scored writing competence, not academic-subject knowledge, and where multiple-choice tests of writing gained ground. The chapter concludes with a summary of five major studies, each published in the *annus mirabilis* of 1966.

- Chapter 5 crosses the Atlantic to the United States and explores the role assessment icon Diederich played in devising and installing controlled adjusted-rater holistic scoring, beginning in 1942, through the undergraduate Examining Board at the University of Chicago. In 1949 Diederich moved to ETS, and we pay close attention to changes in early essay assessment of the Advanced Placement Program (1954–1980), changes that solidified the program's widely influential nine-point scale and its method of addressing interrater reliability.

- Chapter 6 features one of the unsung heroes of holistic scoring, Osmond E. Palmer, who directed the Basic College examinations board at Michigan State College for twenty-five years. Palmer was familiar with holistic scoring since he had worked with Diederich at the University of Chicago from 1942 to 1946. Years later, in 1960, as chair of the English Composition Test Committee of Examiners, he may have definitively shaped the series of ETS studies that ended with the famous vindication of holistic scoring in Godshalk, Swineford, and Coffman's *The Measurement of Writing Ability* (1966). Palmer is an exemplary early case of the influence of the educational-writing community on the educational-measurement community. Individuals, as we show, can shape industries.

- Chapter 7 turns away from postsecondary education to a history of holistic scoring in the California schools from 1960 to 1982. The main story recounts a resistance of school teachers to mandated state accountability testing. We feature unexamined work of Albert "Cap" Lavin at Sir Frances Drake High School and of Catherine Keech with the Bay Area Writing Project. In exploring tensions arising around the first assessment of teacher-led curricular initiatives by Michael Scriven, we come to see the value of resistance to restrictive forms of accountability. As we claim, the integrative processes of teaching and assessing writing established in California remain in schools and colleges across the United States.

- Chapter 8 reviews the contributions of independent academic-assessment researchers to the early support and critique of holistic scoring. It continues with a narration of another independent study of writing assessment, the first assessments conducted by the National Assessment of Educational Progress (NAEP) between 1974 and 1984, featuring the friction between holistic essay scoring and primary-trait scoring and between early Education Commission of the States approaches to assessment and those of ETS, who administered the 1984 assessment. The chapter explores the fluid research relationships that arose between independent researchers and large-scale testing organizations in the creation of a body of knowledge for writing studies that relied on holistic scoring. The chapter closes with a recollection of the work of Rexford Brown and his role in the early years of NAEP.

- Chapter 9 ends our histories of holistic scoring by focusing on the inferences, interpretations, and uses of three artifacts of holistic scoring: splitters (writing samples associated with failure in inter-rater reliability), rubrics (scoring methods utilizing a checklist of selected writing traits), and profiles (outcomes reported to students in the form of separate trait scores). In doing so the chapter identifies the limits of holistic scoring associated with score interpretation and use and pays special attention to Liz Hamp-Lyons's 1987 dissertation, which argued, in effect, for abandonment of holistic scoring.

- In chapter 10, we explore the possibility of actionable history. Continuing our attention to validity, reliability, and fairness, we reanalyze the major studies conducted from the mid-1930s to the mid-1980s using a category-of-evidence (CoE) framework. As we argue, rapid demographic shifts over the next forty years necessitate new genres of assessment in which lessons learned from the early history of holistic scoring return to play an important role in our common future.

These chapter maps are intended as interpretative guides to our historical recovery project. Our intention in providing them is to prevent closure and encourage further historical study of writing assessment. The history we now present is, as we say, more mosaic than fresco, dwelling in depth on a few places, stories, and documents (such as those identified in tables 10.1 and 10.2). Tesserae can be found in the over 1,000 annotations in our accompanying WPA-CompPile Research Bibliography, No. 27 (Haswell and Elliot 2019). While we trust our history provides insight on the origin, development, and significance of the assessment genre of holistic scoring, much work remains that can be informed by the maps provided here.

NOTES

1. T. J. Elliott, Chief Learning Officer at the Educational Testing Service, wrote to us that above all, readers of this book should understand the "hybrid and even variegated nature of holistic scoring," that "there is no 'sure' or standard version" (pers. comm., May 2018).
2. Today US students spend up to six weeks of the academic year preparing and sitting for mandated tests (Nelson 2013, 3). A study sponsored by the Center for American Progress found that "students take as many as 20 standardized assessments per year and an average of 10 tests in grades 3–8," with "urban high school students spend[ing] 266 percent more time taking district-level examinations than their suburban counterparts" (Lazarín 2014, 3–4). Those of us who were at our school desks in the 1950s and 1960s remember nothing like that fixation.
3. In order of start-up: *Studies in Educational Evaluation* (1974), *Assessment and Evaluation in Higher Education* (1975), *Evaluation Review* (1977), *Notes from the National Testing Network in Writing* (1982, ceased in 1990), *Language Testing* (1984), *PARE: Practical Assessment, Research & Evaluation* (1988), *Assessing Writing* (1994), *Educational Assessment* (1995). Today we can add three more to the list: *The Journal of Writing Assessment* (2003), *Research and Practice in Assessment* (2006), and *The Journal of Writing Analytics* (2017).
4. In essence, history is not what happened in the past because, as Sartre's protagonist Roquentin famously puts it, "Le passé n'existe pas" (the past no longer exists). As we argue in chapter 10, the past is interpretatively fluid.
5. White borrowed his four overarching emplotments from the literary theory of Northrop Frye—a reasonable source given White's insistence that history is an imaginative construct.
6. It may seem that the term *trajectory*, with its common meaning as the path of an energized physical object, is inappropriate for our application to historicizing. But

the trajectory of a fired missile is only part of its story. Why was it fired and aimed in the first place, and what will be the outcome? Note that Hayden White (1980) defined "chronicle" as a genre of historytelling that "lacks closure," does not provide the "summing up of the 'meaning' of the chain of events" that one expects in a "well-made story" (20). White's "chronicle" and our *trajectory* are roughly synonymous.

7. Claims such as these are common: ETS "laid the foundations for holistic scoring" (Burstein, Leacock, and Schwartz 2001); ETS was "the originator of holistic scoring" (White 1993, 82).

8. Over time, one of the most counterproductive instances of polysemy has been interrater reliability. The term can refer to statistical methods that, in fact, calculate reliability estimates quite differently and point toward opposing premises in theory (for critique, see Cherry and Meyer 1993).

9. The genre of the essay is used throughout this history because it is that form that is most identified from the mid-1930s to the mid-1980s. We recognize that the essay is not merely a form of writing but, rather, is part of traditions of artifact production, use, and interpretation—ideologies that shape the very contexts in which they emerge (Elliot 2016; Gee 2012; Miller 1984; Spinuzzi 2003, 2015; Wood 2018). Readers may well wonder how diverse genres and stakeholders have shaped the history we present—and how the future of teaching and assessing writing will be shaped by broader representation.

2
TWO PREMISES

How does a tale end that was only a promise of no ending? In the same way as a difference comes to inhabit a world that is otherwise the same in all respects; in the same way that a picture which shows a complex urn alters, as you stare at it, to two faces contemplating each other.
—John Crowley, *Little, Big*

First and foremost, holistic scoring worked. But why and how?

Deducing the why is easy. Its affordances were wide reaching. To testing experts it appealed because, as a method for assigning value to whole pieces of writing, it was relatively quick and therefore relatively cheap. It also appeared relatively reliable and valid. With a modest scale and little training, two or more raters working independently could produce scores that correlated highly with one another and moderately with most other measures of writing proficiency, such as writing-course grades, at statistically significant levels. It appealed to teachers because it was direct, appraising whole essays, not indirect, inferring writing competence from filled-in bubbles on multiple-choice tests. Holistic scoring just made good sense. It is therefore of little surprise that, as we have said, in the United States the innovation of holistic scoring became entrenched with rare dispatch.

But is the popularity sufficiently explained by these pragmatic reasons, or were subsurface principles also operating of which test maker, teacher, administrator, or even scorer might be unaware? What was really being witnessed when, in 1952, readers of the *Journal of Educational Measurement* saw the phrase "wholistic method" applied to the rating of essays (Coward 1952, 83)? What, exactly, were researchers learning when, thirty years later, a sampling of college composition administrators "overwhelmingly favored" "holistic scoring" over other measures of writing (Purnell 1982, 408)? What really occurs when a holistic scorer reads an essay on a six-point scale and sees a 4? How did holistic scoring become so popular, and how did it work? This chapter offers two premises: contagion and gestalt.

GROWTH IN THE SYSTEM: 1969 TO 1987

Social contagion involves cases in which individuals join collective gatherings and "typically observe and copy the behavior" of others (Rohlinger and Snow 2006, 508). It provides a handshake model that helps explain the proliferation of holistic scoring in the United States.

The method's rise in popularity is demonstrated by a mathematical model of social contagion developed for us by our colleague Jeffrey Backstrand, a specialist in quantitative analytic techniques applied to social and public health issues. His model is essentially a version of the ancient chessboard fable in which the wise man accepts as payment for services one grain of rice on the first square of the board, two on the second, four on the third, and so on to the last, sixty-fourth square. The wise man would have more than eighteen quintillion grains of rice. In Backstrand's model for our study, in one year, half again as many people learn about holistic scoring as those who have already learned about it.[1]

The exponential rise in holistic scoring's popularity among elementary- and secondary-school instructors—those who experienced the method in the United States first and in the greatest numbers—is illustrated in figure 2.1 below. The index case—that is, the case in which K–12 instructors first changed their status from inexperienced to experienced holistic scorers—occurred in Iowa City in 1969 as eighty-five English teachers read 9,634 essays at the first National Assessment of Educational Progress (1978).[2] To observe the model in action, we note that the National Center for Education Statistics (Snyder, DeBrey, and Dillow 2019) recorded that there were 171,000 high-school English teachers in 1987–1988 (table 209.10). As figure 2.1 demonstrates, the model shows complete saturation of the high-school teachers by 1987 (n = 188, 431). Consequently, it is entirely feasible that, by the end of that year, one could have walked into any high school in the nation, used the term *holistic scoring* in conversation with an English teacher, and been pretty sure the listener would know the meaning of that term, if not a great deal more. Twenty years earlier, as we noted in chapter 1, the term was used gingerly even by specialists.

In the case of college proliferation, the rise in holistic scoring's popularity among postsecondary instructors is illustrated in figure 2.2. The index case, in which college instructors changed their status from inexperienced to experienced holistic scorers, has two points of origin. The first is on the West Coast, in Pomona, where seventy-five English language and literature instructors scored 8,143 student essays in the spring of 1973 using the holistic-scoring method of the California State

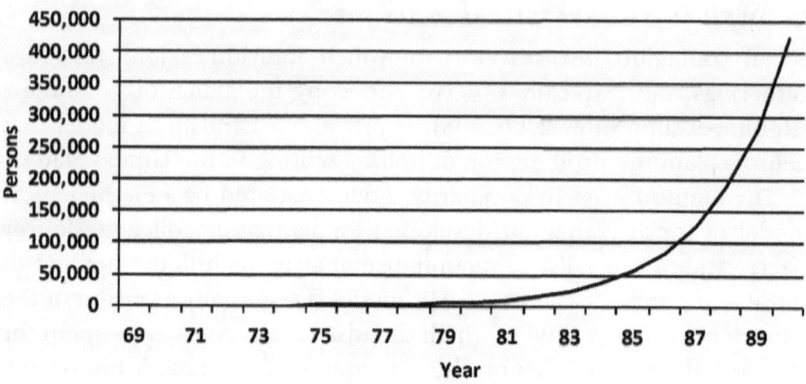

Figure 2.1. Social-contagion model for high-school instructor exposure to holistic scoring

University College Freshman English Equivalency Examination.³ On the East Coast, in Princeton, 200 readers provided holistic scores for 42,984 student essays in the fall of 1978 as part of the New Jersey Basic Skills Placement Test.⁴ Figure 2.2 employs the same model used with the K–12 instructors. Historical information on postsecondary English teachers is harder to find, so we turn to an NCES study undertaken with support from the National Endowment for the Humanities and the National Science Foundation (Conley and Zimbler 1997). In this study we find that, in the fall of 1992, there were 23,063 English language and literature instructional faculty in four-year institutions (fig. 2.2). As figure 2.2 reveals, the model shows complete saturation by 1987 (n = 32, 842). It is entirely possible that by that date, recognition of a term known to secondary-school instructors was equally known to their postsecondary colleagues.

Backstrand's equation does no more than mathematically chart exposure, or mere contact, between two humans. It is designed to model contagion. There are, of course, good reasons that exposure would have actually been contagious in holistic-scoring sessions. Usually holistic scoring was a social affair, intensely open and close, at least in the United States (Dressel 1958). In the United Kingdom, pooled-rater schemes (Wiseman 1949) often had markers work in private because of logistical and financial issues (Office of Qualifications 2014). But in the United States, the adjusted-rater method, the most contagious kind, was almost always conducted in group settings.⁵ For rater training the full corps met together, openly debated, and calibrated their scores on a blackboard. Actual scoring was done at tables of six or more in one large room. Frances Swineford and Fred I. Godshalk of ETS compared

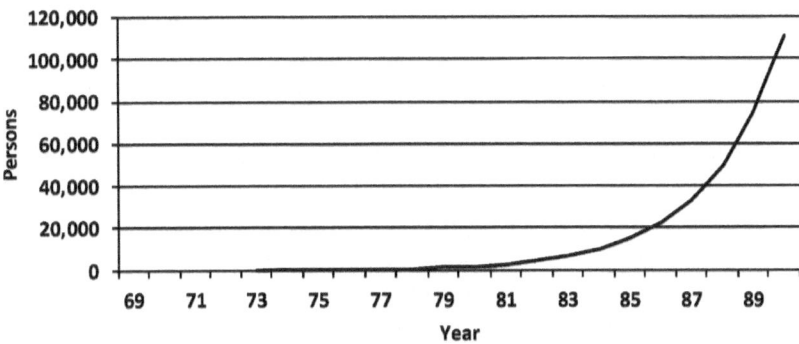

Figure 2.2. Social-contagion model for postsecondary instructor exposure to holistic scoring

holistic scoring to the panel judging of public contests, "whether it be diving, piano-playing, or walking out on the runway in a bathing suit" (1961, 5). During the period of first-generation scoring, reading aloud of papers, often decried, was as often encouraged. At a reading at ETS's western office building in Berkeley of Foreign Service Examination in English Composition given as part of officer qualification testing, with twenty-four readers at three tables, Godshalk encouraged group listening to papers high in "quality," "stupidity," or "sheer wrong-headedness," or papers that were just "refreshing oddities" (1966, 5). He compared the scoring venue to a theatre or sports arena. The readings provide "comic relief," and "the important concept throughout is that readers will do best, like athletes, if they stay loose" (7n7).

We will return to the dynamic contagion of holistic scoring. For the moment we stress that figures 2.1 and 2.2 illustrate both contagion and social action, people coming together and sharing ideas. In the United States holistic scoring also required that each act of actual scoring be independent—one rater deciding on one score, an act personal and introspective, perceptual and cognitive. To address that internal agency, equally a driving force of holistic-scoring methods, we now turn to the theory of it. It is a theory whose history itself must be told.

BORDERLINES: PETER ELBOW AND THE PETER/PAUL OPTICAL ILLUSION

Figure 2.3 is a curious insertion at the end of a book published in 1973 with an ironic argument: people do not need teachers to learn to write. The author is a college teacher with an impeccable education—undergraduate and graduate degrees from Oxford University and a PhD from Brandeis University. Ever an academic, regardless of the chatty and commonsense tone of the book, Peter Elbow could not resist an appendix essay that is "heavily theoretical" (147). Seemingly unrelated to the self-help manual it appends, the essay is about epistemology.

A reader, he argues, can choose either to believe or doubt the text. Believing and doubting are not strictly logical processes; they are filled with romantic turns of thought in which readers make metaphorical extensions, analogies, and associations. These processes help the reader "find potential perceptions and experiences in the assertion" (Elbow 1973, 149). To explain such processes of reading, Elbow turns to perception psychology, a field of research in which meaning making can be characterized as gestalt making. Readers find a gestalt, Elbow explains, as they identify that which is coherent instead of that which is disconnected. At this rhetorical juncture, there is only one move for Elbow to make as words fail—to insert that image, shown in figure 2.3. "A gestalt," Elbow writes, "is the form, shape, or organization that we find in something, say, a picture or a view—that permits us to see it as coherent instead of just disconnected, buzzing, blooming marks" (166–67).

The figure-ground optical illusion, first published by Danish psychologist Edgar Rubin in 1915 (shown in fig. 2.3), initially provides a visualization of wavy images that, as we gaze, coalesce either into a vase or nose-to-nose Peter/Paul silhouettes (Ash 1998, 179–80). Elbow provides an analysis:

> The making or seeing of a gestalt is central to vision. It was the contribution of gestalt psychologists to show that we tend to see coherence not only in its normal views or pictures, but even when we are looking at something broken or disconnected. Visual mistakes *add* coherence as often as they take it away. The act of seeing seems inherently an act of construction that makes wholes out of fragments. The same thing goes on in sound: we hear as melody and shape what are disconnected sounds. (1973, 167)

And the same things goes on in language processing. "Reading or listening is like seeing," Elbow concludes, because "you have to build the gestalt that makes the most coherence out of an ambiguous semantic field" (168).

In interaction, borderlines emerge.

Would this gestalt explanation of reading apply to a holistic reading of a student essay? Elbow himself provides an answer. Around 1995 at the State University of New York at Stony Brook, when he and Pat Belanoff were training teachers to grade end-of-semester student portfolios as "pass" or "fail," he would distribute a "middling example." The writing-teacher trainees sometimes fell into "rancorous disagreement." At that

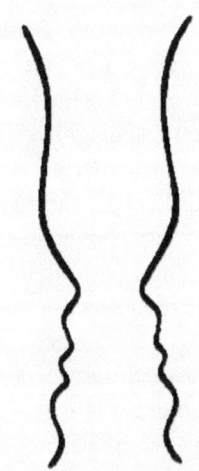

Figure 2.3. Figure-and-ground illustration from Writing without Teachers (1973) (by permission of Oxford University Press)

point he asked them to play the believing game. All would envision the portfolio as passing and then give reasons to support that grade. "This process is magic. Not only is there MUCH more agreement—the rancor goes out of the disagreements" (email to authors, February 5, 2015). As the gestalt psychologists would have noted, a held belief ("passing") changes the perception.

In interaction, borderlines are set.

NEISSER AND ZUCKERKANDL: TURNS LINGUISTIC AND AESTHETIC

To shore up dense epistemological views delivered at breakneck speed, Elbow references two volumes: Ulrich Neisser's *Cognitive Psychology* (1967) and Viktor Zuckerkandl's *Sound and Symbol* (1956). From our point of view, he could not have chosen better studies to explain how humans perceive degrees of quality in unique pieces of language. Neisser extends gestalt theory to linguistics, and Zuckerkandl to aesthetics.

Fetlock deep in the twenty-first century and its belief in a science of the mind, readers of our book will find it difficult to imagine a time when cognitive psychology was new to the research landscape. Yet, when Elbow was writing his first book, the centrality of cognition was still taking shape. Written as a textbook, Neisser's *Cognitive Psychology* (1967) stands as the seminal work that established neurological function as the most important element of perception. The book's importance for us, as it was maybe for Elbow, is its extension of gestalt theory to the process of reading.

The author, German born, was deeply influenced by gestalt theory. After graduating from Harvard University, Neisser matriculated to Swarthmore College to study with Wolfgang Köhler—a founder of gestalt theory who had fled Nazi Germany in 1935 to begin his long career in the United States at this private liberal arts college. When Neisser argued for similarities between language and gestalt phenomena, he stressed their shared origins in cognition. "Whether beautiful or ugly or just conveniently at hand, the world of experiences is produced by the man who experiences it" (1967, 3). By his definition, cognition therefore refers to "all the processes by which input is transformed, reduced, elaborated, stored, recovered, and used" (4). That input includes written words.

In chapter 10 of *Cognitive Psychology*, "Sentences," Neisser demonstrates that linguistic theory has much in common with gestalt theory. The commonality is structure. Neisser gives special attention to Noam Chomsky's *Syntactic Structures* (1957) and *Aspects of the Theory of Syntax* (1965). Ever dissenting, especially so in his early career, Chomsky refuted associationist and behaviorist accounts of reading by pointing to their inability to explain how readers can comprehend novel and unique sentences. (In fact, most sentences readers meet are novel and unique.) To generate meaning, readers must fit the sentences into preexisting, internalized structures. Syntactic "rules" are not enough. Neisser demonstrates this fact with a linguistic parallel to the ambiguous Peter/Paul figure (1967, 247–48). Just as you can see either one goblet or two faces, you can read *they are eating apples* two incommensurate ways. Is the meaning *people are consuming apples* or *these apples are not cooking apples*? The words alone cannot determine the meaning—some internal gestalt must be applied. The second meaning, perhaps intended by the writer, will not be seen by a reader who does not already possess the structure cooking-fruit-is-different-from-eating-fruit. Ambiguity—two interpretations derived from identical input—turns out to be definitive in explaining the act of gestalt meaning making. As Neisser says about the figure-ground image, "In the face of such an example it would be difficult to maintain that structural organization is irrelevant to the process of seeing" (245). An obvious parallel is the student essay seen by one holistic reader as meaning a 3 on a six-point scale and by another reader as meaning a 5, a phenomenon we define as splitters and examine in chapter 9. "Not even psycholinguists can ignore meaning indefinitely, however difficult it may be to treat," Neisser quips (275).

If Neisser's *Cognitive Psychology* suggests a linguistic turn in psychology in which observed phenomena are inextricably linked to language structures, Zuckerkandl's *Sound and Symbol* signals an aesthetic turn. Born in Vienna in 1896, Zuckerkandl was a child of Jewish intellectuals. With a 1927 doctorate from Vienna University and experience as a music critic in Berlin, he emigrated to the United States in 1939. He taught in music departments at Wellesley College, the New School for Social Research, and St. John's College in Maryland, and published *Sound and Symbol* in 1956. The subtitle, *Music and the External World*, establishes its cognitive approach. Following Immanuel Kant's question "How is natural science possible?" in *Prolegomena to Any Future Metaphysics* (1783/2004), Zuckerkandl asks, "How is music possible?" Kant did not seek to know *if* natural science is possible; instead, "he sought to know what the world must be like, what I must be like, if between me and the world such a thing as natural science can occur." "What must the world be like," Zuckerkandl wonders in the foreword to his book, "what must I be like, if between me and the world the phenomenon of music can occur?" (1956, 6–7).

To understand how that can happen, Zuckerkandl argues, as did Chomsky, that we need to depart from mechanistic or stimulus-response views and consider the psychology of motion. "In music, parts of a melody are given in temporal succession or sequence, but these parts are perceived as a whole, or a gestalt." If ten listeners hear one tone simultaneously, "the totality of their sensations is an and-sum," mere arithmetic addition. However, "if one listener hears ten tones in succession, the totality of his sensations is a gestalt—a melody" (1956, 229). Melody is both a thing of beauty and a perceptual construction. For Zuckerkandl, the insight—that epistemology, experimentally confirmed, is a basis for aesthetics—endured. As he wrote in the foreword to the second volume of *Sound and Symbol*, subtitled *Man the Musician* and published posthumously in 1973, "Music still is, just as it has always been, the *other* power which, along with language, fully defines man as a spiritual being" (2–3).

Elbow, a life-long violin player, must have felt the thrill. The new cognitive science, the old aesthetic philosophy, the game of doubting and believing, and the activity of writing were four strings tuned in perfect fifths.

THE BEGINNINGS OF GESTALT THEORY, 1912: THE ILLUSION OF MOTION

As Zuckerkandl's work makes clear, his insight that melody—"notes in succession"—constitute a gestalt was not new. In 1890, Christian von Ehrenfels, professor of philosophy at the University of Prague, used the folk tune *Muss i denn, muss i denn zum Städtele hinaus und du mein schatz bleibst hie* ("Do I Have to, Have to Leave the Village, and You, My Dear, Stay Here?") to offer "proof of the existence of gestalt qualities" (1988, 90). When played in C major, von Ehrenfels observes, the song does not contain a single one of the notes it contains when played in F sharp major. As von Ehrenfels concludes, "From this it necessarily follows that the melody or tonal gestalt is something other than the sum of the individual tones" (90). The fact that listeners recognize melodies across key changes remains prima facie evidence for gestalt perception.

Twenty years later, however, a student of von Ehrenfels's, Max Wertheimer, invented an experiment that produced the definitive physical evidence of a gestalt phenomenon. Wertheimer published "Experimental Studies on Seeing Motion" in 1912 (2012). His experiments established the Φ (phi) phenomenon: an illusion of motion produced when a person sees two still images in rapid succession. Wertheimer had a kymograph drum project two identical vertical lines in succession, the first (*a*) to the left of the screen, the second (*b*) to the right. Neither the viewer's head nor eyes move, but if the time lapse between *a* and *b* is around sixty milliseconds, the viewer sees *a* move from the first position to the second. (This is the illusion that makes flip books and motion pictures work.) Despite prolonged observations and acknowledgment that the appearance of motion was not real, participants in the experiment time and again confirmed their "seeing" motion.

Wertheimer states the epistemological implications with precision.

> Here it cannot be a question of illusion over something physically real, but rather an illusion over something given physically. It is not a matter of: "I am deceived over something physically present," but: "I am deceived in the judgment of something seen. I have actually seen only the stationary *a* and *b*; the deception lies in my believing that I have also seen motion." (1912, 1077)

The illusion of a pencil half submerged in water as broken is "physically real" since the eye picks up two different refractions of light. In contrast, the phi phenomenon illusion of motion is created by the viewer. A purely perceptual construction had been experimentally demonstrated, with evidence drawn from the foremost categories of scientific evidence: reliability and validity.

Participants in the experiment included Kurt Koffka and Wolfgang Köhler, the other two founders of gestalt psychology. In 1922, Koffka explained the theory with von Ehrenfels's example: "When one hears a melody, one hears the notes *plus* something in addition to them which binds them together into a tune—the *Gestalt-qualität.*" A decade later, in

1931, Koffka remembered that moment when he had his first inkling of the momentous nature of the phi phenomenon, in Wertheimer's room in Frankfurt, when he explained the outcomes of his experiments. "I can still feel the thrill of the experience when it dawned on me what all this really meant" (quoted in Ash 1998, 131).

WOLFGANG KÖHLER: FOUR PRINCIPLES OF GESTALT THEORY

By any stretch of the imagination, can (1) a controlled empirical experiment in cognitive perception ever move to (2) a popular method of scoring student essays? It is possible if we keep three similarities in mind. During the Weimar Republic, the early gestalt psychologists were trained in rigorous experimental science. Chemistry, physiology, and physics developed through experimental methods. To achieve the intersection of "scientific and sociocultural discourse," as Mitchel G. Ash describes the processes of the professionalization of the pioneer psychologists (1998, 20), they had to do likewise. By the time Wertheimer published "Experimental Studies on the Seeing of Motion" in 1912, he was the benefactor of a long effort to bring the rigor of physics into the humanities. Similarly, early holistic scoring, from the mid-1930s to the mid-1980s, was largely conducted in the spirit of scientific rigor. The assessment of writing ability was heavily researched, and that quantitative research was informed by a desire for precision. When used in large-scale testing, the outcomes were always validated using statistical methods of the social sciences that were at one with those used by the gestalt psychologists.

Second, the early experimenters and developers of holistic scoring were as committed to the search for theoretical principles as were the gestalt scientists. Both believed theory was nonstatic and proactive. They would have agreed with Andrew Morton, who, in *Frames of Mind: Constraints on the Common-Sense Conception of the Mental*, proposed that theory "is a body of assertions whose terms refer to individuals and properties, and which is transmitted and evolves in accordance with the intention that it asserts truth about them" (1980, 5). Just as gestalt science evolved a body of knowledge by testing hypotheses, early holistic scoring treated its own testing as a series of hypotheses that needed confirmation.[6] As the method became more familiar, explicit references to hypotheses became less common, but the research was theory driven. One need only spend a delightful day reading *Multiple Marking of English Compositions: An Account of an Experiment* (1966) by James Britton, Nancy C. Martin, and Harold Rosen and *Properties of Writing Tasks: A Study of Alternative Procedures for Holistic Writing Assessment* (1982) by James Gray and colleagues to realize how deeply these researchers were committed to theory on both sides of the Atlantic.

Third, gestalt inquiry did not remain confined to the laboratory and has, in fact, been criticized for basing its observations on quotidian human behavior in the real world, free of artificial experimental controls. Just as holistic scoring was felt in the heads and seats of thousands of school and college students as their teachers used sample papers to help students become better readers and judges, so too were the rules of gestalt perception constantly in play—such as when a parent "sees" the posture of a child on hearing its voice from another room and isolates that voice by "unhearing" a hundred other simultaneous sounds. Elbow's "act of construction that makes wholes out of fragments" is something our conscious and unconscious self performs seamlessly every moment of our waking day.

These three points are best illustrated by a book Elbow and other early post–WWII compositionists quite likely read, Wolfgang Köhler's *Gestalt Psychology: An Introduction to New Concepts in Modern Psychology*. The edition we reference, indeed, might be the very one they held in their hands—a slim little paperback reprint published by New American Library in 1947. In *American Pulp: How Paperbacks Brought Modernism to Main Street* (2014), Paula Rabinowitz claims mass-market paperbacks such as Köhler's were agents of cultural enlightenment that carried readers from provincialism to the cultural enlightenment needed to support the United States' new leadership role after World War II. These pocketbooks were popular, and their influence was significant for a wide readership. Here is how those readers were introduced to the gestalt theory and its functioning.

Köhler begins his exposition of gestalt psychology with examples of sensory organization culled from his real-time experience writing notes for the book while sitting on a rock by Lake Michigan. He worries about delivering his manuscript on time; thinks of tax paying instead of book writing; remembers wanting his own face to be like that of Douglas Fairbanks (in fact, it was more similar to that of Ronald Colman); drinks a glass of cold beer after a hot walk and the pleasure momentarily wipes out other sensations; visually organizes his desk—a piece of paper, a pencil, an eraser, a cigarette. Through such personal and cultured examples, his principles of gestalt theory unfold. (Had he been occupied in scoring student papers holistically instead of sitting on a rock, the same principles would have emerged.)

Principle one: *Order is dynamic.* The gestalt, the impression of wholeness, does not derive mathematically from objective experience. The phi vision of motion cannot be statically deduced from two projected lines, just as a holistic scorer's impression of totality (this essay is a 4) cannot be totaled from separate parts of the essay. Indeed, Wertheimer, Koffka, and Köhler never claimed that the whole is the sum of its parts. Phrasing gestalt theory in this way relies on machine metaphors and behaviorist orientations, explaining a gestalt by mere addition, by Zuckerkandl's "and-sum." Koffka insisted that what he had always said was "the whole is *other* than the sum of its parts" (Heider 1977).

Principle two: *Dynamic distributions are functional wholes.* When Ehrenfels used the term "Gestaltqualitäten" in 1890, he designated both shapes and their qualities—a specific form (a dancer) and a related characteristic movement (jumping). The study of gestalt is more than the study of form: it is the study of how organisms organize. As Köhler speculates, the study of dynamic distributions and how they form into wholes may have to include "the processes of learning, of recall, of striving, of emotional attitudes, of thinking, acting, and so forth" (1947, 105). So, a holistic scorer's minutes reading and scoring a student essay are no less dynamically distributed than the student's minutes spent writing the essay.

Principle three: *Dynamic order is isomorphic.* Defined by Köhler, "the principle of isomorphism demands that in a given case the organization of experience and the underlying physiological facts have the same structure" (1947, 177). In other words, experiences and the processes that underlie these experiences are as one. In terms of figure 2.3, for example, seeing the goblet and the face are not products of habit but, rather, two actual modes of the optic sector. This sameness of form exists between experiences and the processes, the theorists held, because neurological processes underlie both. Since isomorphism was understood in psychophysical terms, Köhler was therefore able to align his program of research with that used by theoretical physics, thus creating an experimental model akin to that used by Einstein and Planck. When commentators such as Ash refer to the physicalism of the isomorphic process, they recognize both the unifying functionality and the reality of the processes under observation. While isomorphism could not be examined until the think-aloud protocols of Linda Flower and John R. Hayes in the early 1980s revealed that thought processes and writing behaviors were related, recent studies using eye-tracking software (Hacker, Keener, and Kircher 2017) and keystroke logs (Guo et al. 2018) reveal relationships between processing time and cognitive effort measures. As such studies suggest, underlying physiological facts and the organization of experience have related, if not the same, structure.

Principle four: *Language reveals perception.* Language—uttered, scribed, or printed—offers itself no less as an objective experience than does a chair. While Wertheimer, Koffka, and Köhler did not experiment directly with language, these early experimental researchers nevertheless realized the role language plays in perception. In ending the chapter, for example, Köhler returns to the example of a chair to note that "a sentence which I am formulating is not a part of objective experience in the way in which a chair before me is an experience. And yet my statement about the sentence is no less simple and obvious than were the others, which referred to order in experienced time and space" (1947, 40). The holistic score on a student essay reveals organized perception, reveals an "order in experienced time and space." Köhler concludes, "Why then should language, which is one of the most instructive forms of behavior, be ignored by the experimenter?" (41). Why indeed!

PROTOTYPE, GESTALT, AND SOCIAL CONTAGION: THE HOLISTIC-SCORING SYSTEM OF MILES MYERS

To demonstrate the application of the theory to large-scale practice, no better guide can be found than *A Procedure for Writing Assessment and Holistic Scoring*, published by the National Council of Teachers of English in 1980. The handbook was written by Miles Myers, an Oakland high-school teacher, University of California Berkeley doctoral candidate, administrative director for the Bay Area Writing Project, and future executive director of NCTE. We interviewed Myers before his death on December 15, 2015. He made it clear that in the late 1970s, many Bay-area people who advocated holistic scoring were influenced by gestalt theory.

One case of such influence is that of the eminent cognitive psychologist Eleanor Rosch, whose office was just down the hall from the Bay Area Writing Project at the University of California, Berkeley. In *A Procedure*, Myers uses Rosch's work on human categorization to establish the relationship between holistic-scoring procedures and prototype theory, a cognitive descendant of gestalt theory. "The prototype approach," Myers writes, "says that words have a meaning structure not captured in hierarchies, that, in fact, the structure is built around a range of what is typical" (1980, 2). This may need explaining. Take robins, a concept studied by Rosch. When people imagine the classification birds, they do more than just put robins in it. They have an unconscious mental map of the classification, and that gestalt is structured by typicality. Usually they locate robins somewhere near the center of the map. Robins are *typical* birds, a prototype for birds, just as emus may be included in the category of birds as nontypical, residing somewhere near the periphery. Classical or Aristotelian grouping classifies robins and ostriches equally because it abstractly considers only a few physical traits (feathered biped), but prototype categorizing recognizes human gestalt ways of organizing experience, among them *typicality effects*. You can't logically deduce the impression of the typicality of robins from the sense impressions of robins, just as you can't deduce the impression of motion from two lines seen in sequence.

Just as you can't deduce a 4 essay from just its objective language traits. Rosch wrote that "for object categories, prototypes are the objects which most strongly reflect the attribute structure of the category of a whole; thus, by means of prototypes, categories can be made to appear simpler, more clear cut, and more different from each other than they are in reality" (1977, 3). In *A Procedure*, Myers brings the point home: "The same situation exists in holistic scoring. Even though one can list all of the characteristic of a good piece of writing (clarity, coherence, complete sentences, smooth transitions, good spelling and punctuation), the best way to identify a good piece of writing is to ask people to select typical samples which they rate highly" (1980, 2). Dynamic distributions are indeed functional wholes. Holistic scoring may have become so quickly popular because it had scorers treat essays much like they unconsciously treat, gestalt-wise, every other classifiable object in their lives.[7]

In the slim sixty-nine-page monograph, Myers devotes seventeen pages to the scoring process (1980, 30–46). There are six basic steps: (1) from the set of papers due to be rated, table leaders pick possible anchor papers to illustrate each of the scale levels; (2) all the table leaders independently score the papers and then discuss all their scores openly; (3) in training of teacher raters, the chosen anchor papers are scored independently by all readers, shown publicly, and then discussed openly; (4) actual rating proceeds with final anchor papers spread out in front of each rater for ready review; (5) table leaders give a paper a third scoring if the two independent scores are more than a point apart; and (6) teacher readers whose scores are consistently discrepant are retrained and sometimes removed from the scoring. This was a system that by 1980 had already spread widely across the United States.[8] All the steps seem unconsciously designed to tap gestalt dynamics and encourage social contagion.

For instance, the anchor papers, the "prototypes" according to Myers, possess gestalt qualities. Their overall configuration fits one or another level or score of the scale, and ideally the fit is self-evident. "Those papers on which there is quick agreement for a particular score become the anchor papers" (Myers 1980, 34). Each scale level is a distinct gestalt, and the idea is for readers in training to internalize the prototypes so that in actual scoring they can "read fast," "not think about a paper too much," score on "first impression" (42). Not surprisingly, Myers cautions about using a "rubric" that isolates writing traits to identify scale levels. He allows that one might be constructed after, and only after, the anchors are picked for inexperienced readers to consult.[9] The gestalt-like dynamics of prototype categories fit holistic scoring of essays in that the value structure is built in. It is not totally by coincidence that categories with prototypical structure are sometimes called *graded*, and category members are sometimes ranked according to goodness of fit.

As for social contagion, the ingredients are easy to see. As we have said, most holistic readings are highly public. The main intent, at every moment, is to achieve "consensus" openly. In training, the session leaders asks for scores on a six-point scale by a raising of hands: "How many gave paper A a 6? How many gave it a 5? How many gave it a 1, a 2?" (Myers 1980, 42). All scores are posted for all to see. If there is too much dissent, areas of consensus are identified and then more sample papers are introduced "until the trouble spots disappear in the voting" (43). Even though in actual rating the score of a reader is shielded from other readers, the table leader knows who gave what, and public humiliation can follow. "If the table leaders find that an individual reader continues to give odd scores, the table leaders should assign that reader to the head reader [session leader] for special duties, such as collecting papers and counting them" (43–44). "Odd scores" lead to odd man out—demotion to gofer, for all to see. The purpose of public scapegoating, of course, is to increase social bonding and reinforce cohesive structure. Most of the scorers successfully complete a rite of passage, achieve and partake of consensus, and leave to tell the tale eagerly to others.

The volatile combination of gestalt dynamics and social contagion is mapped by the floor layout provided by Myers, shown in figure 2.4. Prototype essays are displayed publicly, once on a bulletin board and again in front of each scorer. The scorers themselves are displayed publicly, arranged around open tables. Consensus in gestalt recognition is also on display in the open box gradually filling up with scoring completed. All is accompanied with the classic gestalt of social bonding: coffee and cookies on a side board. The entire scoring session looks like a political convention: banners of candidates held aloft, loudspeaker announcement of delegates' votes, revoting, some delegates leaving the action, consensus finally achieved, then the start of that mad social contagion known as the campaign.

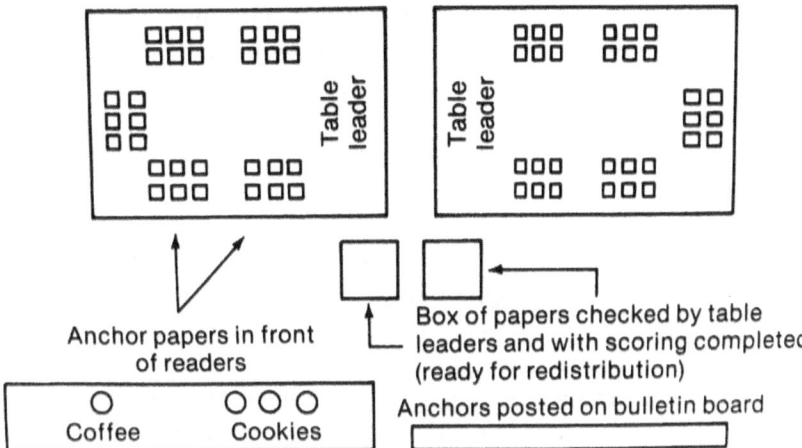

Figure 2.4. Room arrangement from A Procedure for Writing Assessment and Holistic Scoring *(Myers 1980, 45)* (© 1980 by the National Council of Teachers of English; used with permission)

In terms of evaluation methods and procedures, *A Procedure for Writing Assessment and Holistic Scoring*, we should remember, was nascent, emergent, very much a book of its time. Use of the term *prompt*, for example, signals the stimulus-response prevalence of behaviorism—and a disconnect between the spirit of gestalt theory and the terms used to deploy its principles. Discussion of topic selection is rushed and does not distinguish among aim, mode, and genre. Painstaking efforts to pretest topics, now common, are absent. Categories of evidence such as validity and fairness are inferred, not fully discussed. Conceptually, there is no mention of construct validity or the relationship between score use and potential student disenfranchisement. Technically, there is no mention of sample size needed for generalization inferences or of interrater reliability coefficients needed for consistency evidence.

What is clear, however, is that a system was in place that could be replicated across time and circumstance. It worked because the procedure was dynamic and, as such, writing samples expressing a range of ability on a written task could be organized through a scale of values so others familiarized with the scale could reach the same value gestalts. The individual notes differed, but the melody would be recognized. It worked because such a distribution was dynamic, and the readers therefore grouped the papers into functional wholes. The reading act and the resulting score were not mechanical cause and effect; process and product, form and shape, were as one. And it worked because in that reading room, the language used to describe the levels of writing expressed realities that were there in the world. Language constituted meaning.

And because the system made sense—that is, worked—it spread like wildfire.

LEGACY

"Once it is formulated," Köhler concluded, "the present theory is so simple that it may almost appear to be banal" (1947, 203). This banality disappears, he continues, as soon as the reader realizes how the ideas expressed, such as the dynamic perceptual nature of order, would be interpreted were a machine interpretation of perception applied. No one believed anymore in the mechanistic system of Hermann von Helmholtz, expressed in "On the Conservation of Force," first read before the Physical Society of Berlin in 1847, but behaviorism with its stimulus-response orientation toward complex phenomena remained. Not named by Köhler, B. F. Skinner was surely one of those who led "the Homeric assault of Behaviorism against direct experience" (1971, 31). In the simplest concepts, major tensions are forever present. Similarly, Myers's *A Procedure* contained not just a process: it contained a philosophy of language. From the beginning, holistic scoring procedures, among them the process described by Myer, were adopted as bulwark against the assault on English teachers led by those advocating the elementalism—the assault—of multiple-choice testing.

References to gestalt principles in connection with rating of essays were few, and in the last decades have nearly disappeared.[10] In cognitive circles, the names of Wertheimer, Koffka, and Köhler may have survived. In many ways, however, the 1947 publication of Köhler's *Gestalt Psychology* signaled an end to the program of research begun in Germany. Perhaps it was already over by the time Hitler ordered that all classes begin with the Nazi salute in 1933. Ash (1998) makes the case that important students of gestaltism remained in Germany during the Nazi period; and in the postwar period, research continued in East Berlin. But the founders abandoned Germany before the war. Koffka, whose wife was of Jewish descent, left in 1924 to teach at Cornell and never returned. Wertheimer saw the danger of his own Jewish roots and moved to the United States in 1933. Köhler could not tolerate the dismissal of his Jewish colleagues and left in 1935. While all three obtained positions in US colleges, none of those colleges had doctoral programs in psychology. Without doctoral students, their research could not survive. Failure to produce sustainable research was compounded by the early deaths of Koffka in 1941 and

Wertheimer in 1943. Köhler lived the longest, dying on June 11, 1967, in Enfield, New Hampshire.

The legacy of gestalt theory today in holistic scoring nevertheless remains. The direct connections have largely been lost, but the principles endure: the significance that the theory was based on a foundation of aesthetics in which language constitutes meaning through cognitive structure; the reality that perception, and the language that describes it, are dynamic; and the creation of an alternative way of thinking that recognizes human fluidity and celebrates experience. Each facet of this legacy played a central part, although often tacit, in the history of holistic scoring we present in this book. If we are as respectful of human perceptual creativity as were Wertheimer, Koffka, and Köhler, each facet will continue to play an important part in writing-assessment practice and research.

NOTES

1. Each number of the series equals the previous number plus one-half the previous number. If the initial seeds of grain were 8, then 8, 12, 18, 27, 40, 60, 90, 135, and so forth.
2. The report was kindly lent by Hillary Persky. For a history of NAEP writing assessment, see Persky (2012).
3. Estimates drawn from Edward M. White (1973).
4. Estimates drawn from Donald Edge (1979).
5. An exemption was Diederich, as chapters 5 and 6 detail. When Diederich was running holistic scoring of first-year English papers at the University of Chicago, he wrote a fervent memorandum to his boss, Ralph Tyler, arguing that his scorers should be allowed to read and score papers at home (1946c).
6. As psychometrician Robert J. Mislevy has noted in his 2009 treatment of validity from the perspective of model-based reasoning, researchers operate *as if* the reasoning at hand will lead to new knowledge that, over time, results in a body of knowledge. One of the characteristics of early large-scale testing that used holistic scoring was its restless modifications test after test, a process we examine in chapter 5 as we examine the history of Advanced Placement essay-scoring methods.
7. Organizing by prototype shares much with organizing by gestalt. Just as Wertheimer's participants could not stop seeing motion even when they knew the projected lines were stationary, participants in a categorization study could not stop seeing the number *4* or the number *8* as prototypical members of the category "even numbers," where logically *6* or *10* are equally bona fide members of the category (Armstrong, Gleitman, and Gleitman 1983). In the enormous enterprise of cognitive research into prototypical categorization that followed Rosch and her generation, every category studied was found to have prototypical effects (Barsalou 1981, 111).
8. See chapters 5 and 7. In our terms, Myers describes a *controlled, adjusted-rater* system. It was, for instance, used to score the College Board's Advanced Placement essay, in Bay Area Writing Project research, and in essays written for the California State University English Equivalency Examination. For years all three used substantial numbers of teacher readers, a seedbed for social contagion. The The California State University English Equivalency Examination scoring supplied a detailed and influential description of the entire scoring process (Green and Goodrich 1977, 68–75).

9. Myers, nevertheless, understands possible "slippage within a given category" (1980, 31). As prototype theory argues, categories have fuzzy boundaries. In a short article, "Prototype Theory and Holistic Scoring," published three years later, Myers states that "defining score categories by a list of features can mislead readers to expect scoring to be a matter of yes or no, not more or less." That is, actual essays—they all do—lie closer or further from the central gestalt (1983, 20).
10. References, for example, appear in Cyril Burt (1917), Stephen Wiseman (1949), Earle G. Eley (1953), James Burry and Edys Quellmalz (1983), and Brian Huot (1993). For a handbook emphasizing the importance of gestalt psychology in holistic scoring, see Norbert Elliot, Maximino Plata, and Paul Zelhart (1990).

3
HOLISTIC SCORING AND GREAT BRITAIN, 1936–1949

> *The course in all learning, says a French psychologist, is from the conscious to the unconscious. Whatever the truth of the formula in other realms, it is the ideal in this matter of marking.*
> —William Boyd, *Measuring Devices in Composition, Spelling, and Arithmetic*

Gestalt psychology did not flourish in Great Britain.[1] German experimentation that had occurred before 1933 under Wertheimer, Koffka, and Köhler did not survive in the postwar years as it did in the United States. Two reasons may be given. First, as Geoff Bunn, A. D. Lovie, and G. D. Richards have established in *Psychology in Britain: Historical Essays and Personal Reflections* (2001), there was no psychological laboratory in the United Kingdom in the 1930s. While Herbert Spencer and Francis Galton had carried out research as individuals, programs of research were unknown in the universities. Second, the emphasis in England and Scotland was on shaping education toward meritocratic ends. The 1944 Education Act, as Adrian Wooldridge demonstrates in *Measuring the Mind: Education and Psychology in England, 1860–1990* (1994), was embraced by the Labor Party as a way to leverage the examination system for societal good. In this environment the relationship between perception and education was unlikely to be readily acknowledged.

Nevertheless, this misalignment does not mean educators in Great Britain were averse to formal holistic scoring. On the contrary, we argue that the method found its origin there. Upon reflection, one reason is apparent. The principles of gestalt psychology—order is dynamic, dynamic distributions are functional wholes, dynamic order is isomorphic, and language reveals perception—are a constant lived experience in every individual's life. Using the principles does not require the approval of a graduate school. They are experienced every time an essay is composed or evaluated. During the formal evaluation of an essay, they are perhaps experienced least fettered during what we call open pooled-rater holistic scoring.

BALANCED EVALUATIVE ENERGIES: OPEN POOLED-RATER HOLISTIC SCORING

This earliest form of holistic scoring, *sensu stricto*, was deceptively simple. During open pooled-rater holistic scoring, readers assign only one mark to an essay. Usually the mark is a number from a determined scale, typically twenty points or less. Scorers read rapidly, spending one or two minutes per essay, rarely rereading. They do not dwell on small matters but focus on the whole impression. They face scant or no rater training, no scoring guide or rubric or benchmark essays, and no system by which discrepant scores will be detected and adjusted. Each essay has a number of independent readers, three or more, but the scores given to an essay are not deemed "discrepant" or too distant from a "right" score. The essay's final score—the best approximation of the value of an essay—is the sum or mean of the independent scores.

The simplicity of open pooled-rater holistic scoring hides a clever balance of evaluative energies. The reduced scale imposes a tightness to the scoring yet can free markers from individual inclinations, attached from habit, to traditional classroom-based scales such as 100 to 0 or A to F.[2] The focus on general impression or overall merit directs attention to deeper accomplishments such as logical progression and serious thought and draws attention away from surface errors. The brisk reading pace demands a sustained and heightened perusal yet forbids fixation on oddities of little force such as a wrong date or off-topic aside. The summing or averaging of scores of multiple readers respects the singular bents and insights of individual scorers yet pools them into a kind of democratic consensus. Above all, the absence of a scoring guide frees the reader to value a wide range of writerly moves yet helps develop a whole picture. The method abides more closely with the tenets of gestalt perception than do other forms of holistic scoring.

The history of open pooled-rater scoring deserves to be retold from its UK point of origin. In the United States it may have been first formally applied in 1950 by Educational Testing Service researcher Ann F. Coward, but that was an isolated study. In 1963 ETS applied the method for the first time in an actual external writing examination, in ETS's English Composition Test, and it was used there quite sporadically, as we show in chapter 6, until that test's demise in 1992. Otherwise, few writing evaluators in the United States defended or applied open pooled-rater holistic scoring. The truth is that this particular kind of holistic scoring was invented and first applied in Great Britain.

The first formal investigation we have found into this method was published by British researchers Philip Joseph Hartog and Edmond Cecil Rhodes in 1936, with a memorandum by Cyril L. Burt, nearly fourteen years before Coward's ETS trial. The holistic scoring system of Hartog and Rhodes—which they called "marking by impression"—was quickly challenged and retested by British researchers. The earliest extended use in actual external examinations took place 1939–1949, developed and overseen by two Chief Examiners of the Local Education Authority of Devon, England. The method was prominently published in 1949 so was no doubt known by Coward and her US colleagues. By 1956, the method, now called general-impression or rapid-impression marking, had become so well known in Great Britain that it sparked a research symposium, published in the *British Journal of Educational Psychology*. Much of the commentary was rather critical or skeptical. The method never really caught on. The British had begun to reject this form of holistic scoring before the Americans had started applying it.

The time line leads to some puzzles. Why was a kind of holistic scoring first researched, applied, and debated in Great Britain and not in the United States? And—a matter for the next chapter—why, despite its earlier start in Britain, did it not take hold there? And—a matter for the rest of this book—why did relatively open, pooled-rater scoring never really catch hold in the United States?

DISTURBING UNRELIABILITY: SCORING OF ESSAYS IN GREAT BRITAIN BEFORE 1936

By the eve of World War II, on both sides of the Atlantic, researchers in education had convinced themselves that one-person grading of a student essay was an evaluation procedure not suitable for external examination of writing skill.[3] The hitch was interrater agreement and interrater reliability, early forms of Differential Reader Function over Time discussed in chapter 1. It didn't matter whether the examiner was a seasoned high-school teacher employed by the College Entrance Examination Board or an Oxford don marking for the Joint School Examinations Board. It didn't matter that the most common grading system—the 100-point scale—borrowed a protocol familiar for more than a century in school and university classrooms and examination auditoriums. And it didn't matter that the examiners were connoisseurs of language and language standards and readers of exemplary care. You just couldn't depend on their scores. Another teacher or another don, equally qualified, reading the same essay, would come up with a different score, often shockingly different. Connoisseurship, however revered and workable in classroom teaching, was invalid for external testing. Since these scores were not dependable, they were not fair.

In Great Britain before the Second World War, exposing the unreliability of essay markers became rather a fashion.[4] In 1930, forty-eight literature essays written by Durham secondary students for a school-leaving examination were read independently by seven examiners following an analytic scheme and a 100-point scale; one candidate received scores ranging from 19 to 58, another from 37 to 71, a third from 38 to 70 (Hartog, Rhodes, and Burt 1936, 67). Around the same time, educationist Charles W. Valentine gave thirteen teachers seventeen essays by eleven-year-old students to grade on a twenty-point scale, and eleven of the essays received both first-class and failing marks (Valentine and Emmett 1932). Perhaps the fashion of deconstructing marker reliability was begun in the previous century by Francis Edgeworth, who, in 1888 and 1890, reported studies of marking for a wide range of examinations and found disturbing unreliability in all of them. With British civil-service qualification essays marked by separate examiners, one third received scores so varied that with every fifty clerks appointed, on reexamination seven would be displaced. With English composition essays, the second most unreliable examination analyzed, Edgeworth calculated that the chances of a candidate earning honours a second time with an equally competent group of examiners was as "unlikely as getting a run of six or seven heads or tails at pitch-farthing" (1890, 654). Even more devastating, he concluded the following: "I find the element of chance in these public examinations to be such that only a fraction—from a third to two-thirds—of successful candidates can be regarded as safe, above the danger of coming out unsuccessfully if a different set of equally competent judges had happened to be appointed" (653).

Informal grading needed to be replaced in formal testing, but what method of scoring should replace it? In the first decades of the twentieth century, three stock alternatives were sample matching, item testing, and analytic scoring. Sample matching along the lines of the Milo Burdette Hillegas (1912) scale proved impracticable in large-scale tests either for subject-mastery essays or for composition-skill essays. Because of diminished construct representation, item testing stood only as a proxy for essay writing, at least according to its US detractors. In the United Kingdom, multiple-choice testing was used but never caught on to the extent it did in the United States. The third method of marking essays, analytic scoring, however, had deep roots in teaching and examining and many advocates. One, for instance, was Bertie Cotterell Wallis, teacher of geography, Fellow of the Royal Statistical Society, and Chief Examiner for local scholarship examinations. In 1927 he observed that the "old examiner marked largely by impression of the essay as a whole" whereas "the method in use by the modern examiner is to mark by points." He recommended a "schedule of marking" that awarded from one to seven points each on seven "qualities": vocabulary, accuracy, craftsmanship, consistency, completeness, quantity of ideas, and quality of ideas (1927, 76–77). Wallis's particular schedule is only one of hundreds devised by teachers and examiners over the years. But in large-scale examinations, it was generally disliked by markers, consumed scoring time, and suffered from rater reliability problems of its own (e.g., Lamb 1953; Stalnaker and Stalnaker 1934).

Different from stock alternatives, the fourth alternative, formal holistic scoring, was standing in the wings along with the Second World War. As it turned out, holistic scoring arrived first.

THE FOUNDATION: OPEN POOLED-RATER HOLISTIC SCORING IN GREAT BRITAIN

It's scarcely hyperbole to say that for over a century, British-school students had been examination ridden. They had studied, stood, and sat for external examinations to win prizes, earn scholarships, switch schools, leave secondary school with a certificate proving they had completed their education in good standing, and qualify for entrance into any number of professions including accounting, architecture, dentistry, engineering, law, medicine, teaching, the military, and the civil service. And they had studied, sometimes to the detriment of their mental and physical well-being, for the colossal, life-changing tests, the selection examinations at around age eleven or twelve that would determine how they would continue their schooling, the secondary examinations that would or would not put them on a track toward postsecondary education, and the university matriculation examinations that would decide the higher-education fate for the relatively few sixth-formers left. By 1917 there were as many as 100 different kinds of external examinations for pupils (Bruce 1969, 2). By 1936 there were over 160 different examining bodies, and that does not count the myriad Local Education Authority boards who oversaw their own brand of selection examinations and the university boards who administered their own matriculation examinations (Hartog, Rhodes, and Burt 1936, vii, n. 1).

Critique of the pervasive examination system, of course, persisted in Great Britain along with the system itself. For instance, in 1949 the inaugural issue of *The Use of English*, the flagstaff journal of Britain's largest teacher organization, featured an essay by R. R. Pedley, Headmaster of Chislehurst and Sidcup Grammar School in London, rejecting the proposed new General Certificate Examination that was to become mandatory for secondary students wishing to leave grammar school with graduation credentials. Pedley's essay was just the first of a steady litany of complaints in *The Use of English* from the schools about mandatory examinations. *Washback* (or *backwash*), in the educational sense, originally was a British term, appearing in early issues of *The Use of English* (e.g., Britton 1955). In 1965 a special issue was called "English Versus Examinations." In its position of adversary, the journal did not stand alone. Fulmination against educational examining was common long before *The Use of English* started up. In 1889, Auberon Herbert edited a book called *The Sacrifice of Education to Examinations* containing heartfelt philippic by individuals from all social levels.

Between the wars, it was the selection examination standing between elementary and secondary schooling that affected the largest number of students and attracted the most criticism. This examination could be called free place, special place, promotion, and qualifying (in Scotland), transfer, entrance, control, junior scholarship, and 11-plus, although after WWII it was the last name that stuck in England and Wales. Students taking the 11-plus examination—the Common Entrance Examination instituted in the 1940s—were being tested in order to gauge aptitude and ability at age eleven (Mackenzie 2006). Philip Boswood Ballard, educational psychologist and one of the toughest pre–World War II critics of Great Britain's examination system, provided figures in 1923 that every school teacher knew well from experience.[5]

> The Special Place Examination has become a national institution. It winnows elementary school children into three distinct classes: the best of all (rarely more than 5 per cent) go to secondary schools [that is, grammar schools]; the second best (roughly about 15 per cent) go to some such institution as a central school [later called *comprehensive school*], or a technical school, the remaining 80 per cent stay on at the senior elementary school [that is, secondary modern school].

"It is difficult," he continues, "to over-estimate the importance of the Special Place Examination. Every year, the fate of about a half a million children stands upon its results. In sheer magnitude it dwarfs every other public examination in the Kingdom" (111). Usually the 11-plus examination did test for essay-writing skill, with essays. What if the fate of a half-million students, as many researchers insisted, often depended not so much on their ability but upon the single examiner who chanced to read their essays?

Between 1936 and 1966, external examining became more legitimized, regularized, and entrenched. The 1944 Education Act (the Butler Act, coordinated by Richard A. Butler, commonly viewed as the architect of the postwar educational system) made Ballard's "national institution" of the 11-plus examination mandatory in England and Wales.[6] In 1951 the General Certificate of Education (GCE) examinations were introduced for secondary grammar-school students. Sanctioned were the ordinary-level and advanced-level examinations, the first for students who wanted a school-leaving certificate and the second for students who wanted to continue for two more years and test their way into a postsecondary institution. In 1965 the Certificate of Secondary Education (CSE) replaced a hodgepodge of local school-leaving examinations for the majority of secondary modern-school students, who were stuck in school until age fifteen, as required by an act in 1947. Complaints about the overbearing presence of examinations continued, and not from teachers only. During the House of Commons debate over the Butler Act in January 1944, George Muff, representing Kingston-upon-Hull East, said students ready for university had been "jammed by various examination hurdles. Often they come to the university mentally jaded and cannot do themselves justice for some considerable while" (Hansard 1944). By "jammed," Muff meant hurdles placed too close together, leaving a runner with little room to adjust and little time to breathe. The complaining, however, had little effect on the relentless march of the examining.

It should not be forgotten, though, that in Great Britain between the wars, public examination was as revered as it was disliked. The system expressed some of the nation's most deep-seated beliefs. The nineteenth century and its prolific blend of materialism, liberalism, authority, bureaucracy, fact collecting, and moral urging had brought about the proliferation of external examinations. The same blend was expressed in their administration, which added a trust in local authority and local freedom to experiment. Above all, in England and Scotland there was a prevailing belief that public examination served meritocracy and selection, which were uneasy companions. Required for entry into the military, the professions, and the university, external examining was the level playing field that helped eliminate advantage stemming from privilege, patronage, class, inherited wealth, and other forms of favoritism. Examinations would reward merit and merit alone.[7] Yet there remained only so many places for those who passed them. In 1962 only about 14 percent of secondary British students passed A levels and thereby qualified for college (Bolton 2012). Examinations would reward merit, but only so often.[8]

In sum, by the 1930s external examining was part of the educational landscape, and if there were problems with the marking reliability in some of it, the solution was to change the marking, not change the examinations. Testing experts in the United States who were addicted to objective items might caution their British counterparts about the danger of foundering "on the reef of low reader reliability" (Palmer 1962, 224), but the British had little thought that their examination system would ever sink in any storm.

Nor was there much worry about the written examination-essay, which for decades had ruled the British educational seas. In 1936, essays, brief or extended, had long been the standard mode for examination papers on every subject, from history and English to chemistry and arithmetic. To be sure, in the local special-place examinations, short-answer questions were playing more and more of a part in "general English," but the extended essay tended to hold the lead role. As usual, Ballard put it most bluntly: "The modern examination is dominated by the essay. It is based on the essay; it is built of the essay; it stands or falls by the measurability of the essay" (1923, 52).

These words in Ballard's *The New Examiner* (1923) are often quoted, but they can misrepresent his position. He felt, in fact, that the examination essay should fall since it could not be reliably measured. The central chapter of *The New Examiner* is called "The Rejection of the Essay," and much of the book occupies the reader with illustrations of short-answer questions Ballard felt would better serve the external testing of composition. In essence, he viewed the essay as tragic. He loved the genre for instruction but despaired of it for examination. Ballard, along with Burt, greatly influenced the turn toward item testing in school examinations before WWII in Great Britain. By the end of the war, only 36 percent of Local Education Authorities were using an essay in selection examinations (National Union of Teachers 1949), and experiments in holistic scoring often were carried on in the name of "re-instating the essay" (Edwards Penfold 1956, 128).

In subject examinations, the essay, however, was never in trouble. Under debate was the ability of the essay as a vehicle to account for writing skills in the selection examinations given around age eleven and, occasionally, in the school-leaving examinations given at age fourteen. Beginning in the 1920s, mass-intelligence item tests started becoming popular in 11-plus selection examination, supplementing the two standard subjects of arithmetic and English, and by 1954 around three-fourths of the Local Education Authorities were using the Moray House Tests of Intelligence (Vernon 1957, 25). Other similar tests were available. IQ testing in Great Britain, however, gradually lost favor in school examinations (Wooldridge 1994). Then the huge selection examinations required of everybody in 1944 were largely (though not entirely) legislated out in 1976 in England and Wales.

The history of that ban belongs to the next chapter. Between 1936 and 1966, however, the viability of the external examination essays to judge writing skill was under much scrutiny and experimentation. A vital part turned on the issue of holistic essay scoring.

Politically, selection and school-leaving examining were thoroughly decentralized.[9] Local development and administration of examinations had been entrenched long before the beginning of the century. Decentralization was made official in 1902 with the establishment of the Local Education Authority, whose jurisdiction was reaffirmed by the 1944 Education Act. Each of the roughly 170 county or borough councils in England and Wales had its own Local Education Authority, whose bureaucrats determined funding, establishment of new schools, money for scholarships and, among other responsibilities, approval of their own external testing. But often that approval was perfunctory. Many examinations were created and marked by the headmaster or headmistress of the school or by a band of the school's teachers marking the essays of each other's students. More commonly, the Chief Examiner of the Authority created examinations and organized and paid markers, usually local teachers wishing to put by a bit of holiday money. Sometimes the Authority might further examine and decide on borderline cases.

In 1936 the method of marking essays for writing skill was local, under the control of an unruly group of teachers, headteachers, and Chief Examiners. If they wanted to experiment, there was little to keep them from it. All were under pressure to make the marking process not only fairer but also quicker. Connoisseurship, use of a lone independent but knowledgeable teacher-marker, prevailed. And to replace it, some sort of nonanalytical method with an equally nimble reading pace would have been desirable.

Pooling the marks of three or more raters for each essay had a philosophical as well as political provenance. That ground was British empiricism. Pooled marking was explicitly based on the nineteenth-century scientific rule that since measurement of a variable is always prone to error, the single best measurement is the mean of as many independent measurements as can be applied. The rule is still valid, today sometimes called the law of large numbers (LLN). An economist and statistician, Edgeworth may have first applied the rule to the marking of essays in two articles we have already noted as drawing early attention to low rater reliability. "The true or standard mark of any piece of work," wrote Edgeworth, "is the average of the marks given by a large number of competent examiners equally proficient in the subject and instructed as to the character and purpose of the examination" (1888, 599). Edgeworth's statistical point was that averaging of a number of independent marks reduces random error in the marking, and that the more markers used, the greater the reduction.[10]

In 1911, in an address to the Royal Society of the Arts on the need to study examination marking scientifically, Hartog quoted Edgeworth's definition of "true mark" and noted that Edgeworth considered it a postulate, not an axiom. Still, decided Hartog, "it is a convenient postulate, and is probably generally acceptable" (1918, 103). It may have been a statistical postulate of fields more interested in quantity than quality, but that did not seem to have bothered the early proponents of pooled holistic scoring. Edgeworth, as we have seen, did not hesitate to compare the student's chances of getting a particular examination mark to the tossing of a coin. In classical test theory, probabilistic reasoning was everywhere apparent.

In Great Britain, Edgeworth's probabilistic reasoning was never forgotten. In the 1936 groundbreaking study of relatively open, pooled-rater marking, Hartog and Rhodes note that their system is "used by the physicist when he is estimating the relative importance of several measurements of the same quantity" (1936, 188). James Britton, Nancy C. Martin, and Harold Rosen's *Multiple Marking of English Compositions*, the last and the most passionate defense of pooled-rater evaluation, repeats the rule with precision: "Random error in measurement may be reduced by taking several readings and using the mean" (1966, 9). They offer a number of analogies. One is gunnery, where soldiers know to average all the available estimates to set a range. More telling is their reference to pre–WWII experiments of psychologist Hans Jürgen Eysenck (1939), who found that the rank ordering of aesthetic judgments—for instance, of paintings or poems—was the same for two groups of people when the individual rank orderings within each group were averaged. Most telling, Britton, Martin, and Rosen compared a 1926 experiment in which 200 students were asked to order ten weights so little different in weight that hardly any one student got the order right, yet the average of all 200 hit the correct order on the nose (1966, 9).

How can a quantification undetectable to individuals in a group be correctly detected by the group as a whole? Locating "true value" smacks of the ouija board—or, as Gillian Sutherland (1977) termed it in his study of mental testing and English Education until 1940, "The Magic of Measurement." Yet, scientifically, the concept of true value is related to the concept of the true score from classical test theory. Under this framework, the true score is the average of the scores that would be earned by an individual on an unlimited number of tests. Once put in place, classical test theory allows researchers to view an individual's observed score on a test as the sum of a true score and an independent random error. Under these assumptions, most of our knowledge about student writing during the first half of the twentieth century could thus be stated as $\theta = T - E$. In this system, θ stands for a form of the writing construct, a theory-based concept of behavior that varies according to context. T stands for the score, the value we give that construct as we assess it in a performance. E stands for the unbiased error of that measurement as we observe the construct. Hence, performance regarding the construct of interest is equal to the true score minus error (Elliot 2015).[11]

Within the formula is a familiar mystery. In a democracy, universal suffrage turns the whims of each voter into the election of the best candidate (and, in case of ties in US and British elections, the decision is made by drawing straws, cutting cards, or, shades of Edgeworth, flipping a coin) under conditions in which error is (hopefully) modified or removed. The spirit of averaging marks on an essay had plenty of contemporary support in both the popular and scientific cultures.

If averaging is the last step of pooled-rater marking, the first is individual-marker perspective. In perspectivism resides a second powerful contemporary support for the scoring method. Stephen Wiseman, the most influential proponent of multiple marking in Great Britain after WWII, starts with a very concise definition of the average or "true mark" drawn directly from classical test theory: "that given by the pooled judgment of an infinite number of markers" (1949, 203). His analogy, footnoted but much quoted, is enlightening: "Each composition is illuminated by beams from different angles, and the total mark gives a truer 'all-round' picture . . . lack of high inter-correlation is desirable, since it points to a diversity of view-point in the judgment of complex material" (206n3). Britton, Martin, and Rosen provide an equivalent image, noting "the superiority of a number of photographs from selected angles of view over a single photograph of a piece of sculpture" (1966, 11).

Perspectivism, it hardly bears observing, was an active ingredient in the Western Zeitgeist of the first third of the twentieth century. It empowered advances in a diversity of fields, both quantitative and qualitative, among them aesthetics, anthropology, astronomy, hermeneutics, linguistics, perception studies, philosophy, photography, physics, religion, and sociology. In literature, Ford Maddox Ford and others published novels with multiple points of view. Even as absolutist a literary critic as I. A. Richards admitted a kind of perspectivism. His *Practical Criticism*, published in 1929, begins with the axiom (or is it a postulate?) that "ambiguity in fact is systematic." He explains, in language that could easily apply to multiple marking, that ambiguity is "something comparable to a 'perspective' which will include and enable us to control and 'place' the rival meanings that bewilder us in discussion and hide our minds from one another can be worked out" (18–19). It's hardly coincidental that in 1936, literary reading and examination reading shared parallel terms: *multiple perspective* and *multiple marking*, and *impressionism* and *general impression.*

With the perspectivism that underlies the multiple-marking system, we have circled back to the impulse for meritocracy. The connection may be seen in the word *consensus* that early proponents of multiple marking often used in reference to the mathematical averaging of marker scores. Britton, Martin, and Rosen, for instance, call the average or standard score "a composite mark, a consensus to which judges contribute their particular sensibilities." If the judges are competent and self-consistent—always a given—then their individual insights unique to the group must be given equal weight in the final equation. Indeed, differences of opinion are to be encouraged. Otherwise the student is not given fair representation. "Multiple marking represents the pooling of viewpoints each of which contributes towards the full assessment of what the candidate has written on the page" (1966, 11). To adopt the language of Richards, in judging the quality of a piece of discourse, rival meanings of the readers, often hidden from each other, can be worked out systematically, controlled and placed. In the language of meritocratic democracy, candidates—from the classroom, for the workplace, or on the hustings—can be placed fairly through the controlled system of open election in which no eligible voter is more privileged than another and all votes are mathematically equivalent in the final count.

This is the point at which open, pooled-rater holistic scoring breaks most radically with other kinds of holistic scoring—especially with the kind of essay scoring that features anchor essays, rubrics, scoring guides, or content schemes that eventually became established in both Great Britain and the United States. Yet in the 1930s and 1940s, educationists in England and Scotland were applying and investigating this radical approach. There are a number of suppositions as to why Great Britain first sallied in this direction—its ever increasing number of students due to rise in population and rise in the school-leaving age, its hard-earned trust in the essay as central mode of examination, its ideological attraction to pooled-rater evaluation, and its traditional localization of shaping, setting, and scoring.

This is not, we hasten to add, a history of two contrasting national bents, between objective and subjective, or analytical and integrative, or rational and intuitive. As this book argues over and over, these distinctions are misleading when applied to holistic essay scoring. And certainly, they are false as applied to the early developers and advocates of holistic scoring. Consider Burt, probably the most influential educational psychologist in the United Kingdom during the first half of the twentieth century, a psychometrician and a developer and promoter of analytic scoring methods and short-answer mass-intelligence tests. In 1932 he had succeeded Charles Spearman as professor of psychology at the University of London and was the preeminent educational researcher in the United Kingdom. Yet in a 1918 report on scholarship examinations given by the London City Council, Burt wrote,

> The intuitive or impressionistic method corrects many faults to which a crude, mechanical, quantitative dissection might inevitably lead. . . . It allows us to judge the candidates' work by its general form or *Gestalt*, i.e., as a whole rather than as a mosaic of disconnected items; and thus permits us to grant full value to elusive and organic qualities that could scarcely be catalogued, or decomposed into separate portions (quoted in Cast 1940, 60).

The effort to dissect and catalogue an organic form might not be an unfair description of the early British studies and applications of open pooled-rater holistic scoring, to which we now turn.

HOLISTIC SCORING IN GREAT BRITAIN 1924–1949: THE INNOVATORS

With background established, we now turn to a detailed analysis of the major studies undertaken during this period. While the history we present in this chapter begins with the research study of Hartog, Rhodes, and Burt, we extend our history backwards to capture the first measurement handbook, published in 1924. Following our detailed analysis of the major studies, we conclude this chapter with Wiseman's demonstration that open pooled-rater holistic scoring works in the writing-assessment contact zone where construct representation and efficiency intersect.

Boyd 1924: Pooling of Raters

In England and Scotland in the 1920s, all the main components for pooled-rater holistic scoring were in the air: essay as gestalt, fast intuitive response, multiple marking, pooling of marks, contrast with analytic scoring. Teachers, examiners, and educational researchers had just not found a way to combine the components into a valid or viable marking method. There was no better illustration of this than William Boyd's 1924 handbook *Measuring Devices in Composition, Spelling and Arithmetic*. Boyd began a tradition of writing-assessment handbooks united by their singular emphasis on helping classroom teachers.

The author was a lecturer in education at the University of Glasgow, and when the Educational Institute of Scotland was formed in 1917, he was made director of it. The institute was a response to a perceived crisis in the Scotland qualifying examination, which, similar to the English 11-plus exams, selected elementary-school students at age eleven or twelve to move on to secondary education. The current Scottish system of selection was as localized as the English. Teachers devised and scored examinations, overseen by the headmaster or headmistress. By custom, an inspector of schools only checked and approved the teacher's list, at most questioning a few students or the whole class. But teachers at both ends of the process had problems with the system. "Most primary teachers were never very sure of what the pass requirement was; and some secondary teachers were quite sure that many of the pupils sent to them were not up to it" (Boyd 1924, 6). Boyd feared the selection examination would be taken out of the hands of local educators by a state afraid to "entrust teachers with powers so great" or unwilling to countenance such "inefficiency," that is, such unreliability in marking. His book was an attempt to reestablish the trust by providing teachers with "objective methods of measuring school results" (7).

Quite remarkably, Boyd asks readers to take on his book as a do-it-yourself project—an innovation in the handbook genre. He compares the process to chess players following a game on their own chessboards. Readers should first mark twenty-six actual selection essays, written by twelve-year-olds on the topic "Day at Seaside" and scored on a seven-level scale of excellent, very satisfactory, satisfactory plus, satisfactory, satisfactory minus, moderately satisfactory (or bare pass), and unsatisfactory. Then readers should compare their marks with those given independently by 271 teachers. But the table of these marks shows a staggering variability (1924, 24). How can a reader's own mark be judged when nineteen of the twenty-seven essays received either six or all seven of the marks? Boyd's answer is a kind of pawn sacrifice, asking readers to give up their own mark, if divergent enough, in favor of the mean mark of all 271 previous markers. The theory behind this move is Edgeworth's postulate of averaging to determine true value. The democratic will, this "collective vote," has a "remarkable steadiness" (29), Boyd asserts, and he points out that the order of merit of the twenty-seven essays determined by the mean score of all markers is almost identical to the order determined by the mean score of markers who fell 30 percent above and below the median. The chessboard merges with the ouija board.

How is that standard to be built among current teachers? Boyd uses the mass estimate to build a reduced set of "Day at Seaside" essays, a "standard scale" of seven essays exemplary of the seven levels of merit, a set that can be used for sample matching, similar to the scales of Hillegas or Van Wagenen. Individual teachers compare their marked essays with the essays on the scale until the standards decided by "general vote" become automatized ("the course of learning," says Boyd, "is from the conscious to the unconscious"). It thereby also becomes quick. Practice in comparative marking develops "an immediate sense of values" with which essays can be evaluated with "promptitude" (1924, 86). The teacher then can transfer this "Day at Seaside" standard to sets of scripts written on different topics, as future qualifying examinations would require. Boyd wants teachers to better their connoisseurship, to train themselves to grade exam essays in a manner more "objective" or more consistent with the grades of other marking teachers. He never considers double or multiple marking during actual examination situations, that is, never envisions formal holistic scoring in our terms.

Nonetheless, the elements of holistic scoring, as we say, were in the air, and Boyd had breathed it in. He admits the value in looking at various criteria of compositional skill, such as essay length or sentence structure, but he rejects formal analytic scoring, in which raters are required "to break up the essay into its unit characters and to assign marks to each on some definite principle." Not only does analytic scoring "prove impossible in practice," it works against the final act of marking, which is an "immediate non-conscious estimate" (1924, 58). At one point, Boyd's description of that act stands as an early and memorable vote for holism in the evaluation of essays and deserves quoting in full.

> Lest the discussion of the relative value of elements in composition mislead, it must be added that an essay, like every other product of spiritual activity, is always more than the sum of its parts. We cannot ignore certain of the parts—spelling, for example—but if we are to mark justly as well as steadily we must always keep the whole in mind in our judgements. Our first question should not be: How long? or How many mistakes? or What kind of

words? We should cultivate a temporary blindness to such details, so that we may be able to feel whether the essay in any measure succeeds in conveying effectively the information or idea or feeling it seeks to convey. (63)

True to the UK tradition, no one expressed their devotion to teachers more clearly than Boyd, who recalled that the "main inspiration" of his work was "the thought of helping teachers in the daily work of the classroom by the improvement of teaching methods and by providing means for the more accurate estimation of the results of their work" (7).

Hartog, Rhodes, and Burt 1936: Holistic versus Analytic

At the May 1931 International Conference on Examinations, held in Eastbourne, England, and sponsored by the Carnegie Foundation, the Carnegie Corporation, and the Teachers College of Columbia University, attending national committees were given three-year grants to study the situation of educational testing in their countries. The committee from England completed its work with remarkable dispatch and thoroughness, publishing a bibliography on examinations in 1934, an anthology of essays on examinations in 1936, a directory of examinations in the United Kingdom in 1937, a summary of findings in 1935, and a 344-page presentation of their studies in 1936. The last, *The Marks of Examiners*, still stands as one of the finest explorations of formal assessment, and it includes, as far as we know, historically the first study of holistic scoring as we define that concept.

The authors were Philip Joseph Hartog and Edmond Cecil Rhodes. Hartog was academic registrar at the University of London, with, as we have seen, a high respect for Edgeworth and an ardent interest in examinations going back at least to 1911. He called himself "no statistician," an overly modest epithet, but the book covered its bets by including Rhodes, who was a Reader at the London School of Economics and a leading statistician of his day. The book also added a sixty-nine-page "memorandum" by Burt, serving as professor of psychology in the University of London, on the statistics of aggregated marks. *The Marks of Examiners* studied in detail a variety of external examinations on different subjects at different educational levels—special-place (11-plus) examinations in arithmetic and English; school-certificate exams in history, Latin, French, chemistry, and English; college-entrance examinations in English; and university honor essays in mathematics and history. We discuss only the 11-plus essays in English because that is the only examination Hartog and Rhodes had markers read holistically. This fact, as we will see, is of some significance.

Hartog and Rhodes had two sets of seventy-five special-place essays read by ten experienced markers, one set "by impression" and the other set by "a detailed marking scheme," so they were directly comparing holistic and analytic scoring of essays. The two sets had been prejudged as of equal quality and range. Full marks for both the impression and the analytic scale was 100. Markers, accomplished in special-place scoring, were instructed to score the first set of seventy-five by "impression" before they attempted the second set by "detail," and with the first to make no attempt to conform to the analytic scheme "or to any scheme of the kind" (Hartog, Rhodes, and Burt 1936, 118), instructions with clear intention to remove markers from traditional selection-examination grading routines. This intention was strengthened with further instructions for impression markers to sort essays first into five groups according to quality and control of ideas and then check to see whether there were any radical departures from a normal curve (frequencies provided). The analytic marking scheme—designed by Philip Ballard—was weighted: ideas 50, vocabulary 15, grammar and punctuation 15, sentence structure 10, spelling 5, handwriting 5. For both scoring procedures there was no training and markers worked alone under no time pressure.

The objective of the study was narrow, to see which of the two markings was more reliable or, in their word, "precise." Hartog and Rhodes's close analysis shows that the impression scores had a greater range and the analytic scores were more lenient. But, they point out, this discrepancy would not necessarily affect the candidates' order of merit, a crucial outcome since the number of places available in grammar schools changed year by year. Applying Edgeworth's postulate that the ideal or standard mark is the pool of all the raters' marks, they found that impression markers showed greater numerical distance from the average but their standard deviation, that is, the random error in their marking, was almost identical to that of the analytic markers. Hartog and Rhodes conclude that "on the whole no greater precision of marking is obtained by details rather than by impression" (Hartog, Rhodes, and Burt 1936, 240). Hartog and Rhodes, then, applied a genuine formal holistic scoring, by our definition. They found a way—pooling of the scores of two or more independent raters—to determine an essay's score that was more reliable than the score of a single rater.

Although Hartog and Rhodes offer no recommendation as to how these findings might be applied, application is on their minds. They note that "manipulations in the office of the examination authority" was a well-known method to adjust for consistent variation among raters, and the difference in leniency between the two methods of marking could be standardized afterward (Hartog, Rhodes, and Burt 1936, 122, 240). Post hoc adjustment is a procedure later proponents of pooled-rater evaluation applied. Hartog and Rhodes make no particular recommendation concerning the possible value of double or multiple marking for real examinations, although a recommendation could be derived from their figures. Burt's long memorandum attached to this report, however, argues that estimates of the "true value" of a mark can be better acquired through statistically correlating the scores of pairs of markers. Statistically, he prefers comparing the scores of two raters for each essay rather than the variance of all scores given. He adds that correlating pairs of raters would be "hardly worth while with groups so small" (246n1).[12] Technically, the memorandum by Burt lent statistical support to general-impression marking. His memorandum had the force of law. As he recognized, the total impression is the result of distinguishable elements (identified in the detailed marking scheme) readers may value differently. Consequently, marshaling of evidence is not to be taken as a solution but as an approach.

In the end the authors have pitted holistic scoring against analytic scoring and found that, in theory at least, "nothing apparently is gained" by using the second (Hartog, Rhodes, and Burt 1936, 240). They assume, however, that analytic scoring takes more time than open holistic scoring, and they therefore set an agenda for future researchers to determine the exact number of holistic markers per essay needed to achieve time-efficient, valid, reliable, interpretable, and cost-effective scores. Viewed as more tentative than conclusive in its treatment of validity and reliability pursued in search of fairness, *The Marks of Examiners* is far from a statement of triumphalism. As the preface notes, "We must guard ourselves here against the suggestion that the chances due to divergences of marking are the only ones in the examination system. There is also the element of chance due to the variability of conditions in individual candidates, arising from illness or accident, which it is difficult to estimate statistically. It may be reduced, in a rough and ready way, when examining bodies take into account school-records in borderline cases" (Hartog, Rhodes, and Burt xiii). Even in the earliest studies, British researchers seemed especially concerned with writer reliability and its relationship to forms of evidence related to validity and fairness.

Cast 1939–1940: Relationships among Domains

B. M. D. Cast begins her 1939 masters thesis, directed by Burt at University College London, with a quotation from Philip Boswood Ballard's

The New Examiner. "The modern examination is dominated by the essay. It is based on the essay; it is built of the essay; it stands or falls by the measurability of the essay" (Ballard 1923, 257). As Hartog, Rhodes, and Burt well knew, the genre remained without question a valid means of examination; yet, as a test item that consistently had proven difficult to mark reliably, it was so dreadful it should perhaps have been "cast on the dust heap," just as Ballard recommended (258). Cast saw an opportunity for systematic inquiry.

The most venturesome part of her study, published in 1939 and 1940, was the extension of correlation analysis from the essays to characteristics of the students themselves. To create this conceptually related analysis between writing ability and personality, Cast first established standardization of scores related to the elements of style, vocabulary, subject-matter mastery, logical arrangement, and mechanical accuracy. Then, positive and negative correlations—termed *saturations*—were established between the elements. Based on a table titled "Marks for Different Aspects of English Composition," Cast then drew this inference: "Thus those with positive saturations include the more unstable or extraverted children; those with negative saturations are either highly stable or (more commonly) repressed extraverts. The former are imaginative, well informed, fluent writers, usually (though by no means always) fairly logical in arranging their ideas, but decidedly hurried in their writing and careless in their spelling and grammar. The latter are slow and careful writers, with little interest in eternal subjects as such and comparatively devoid of verbal fluency and elasticity of phrase. We might perhaps call them the fluent and the precise type respectively" (57). In connecting performance to personality in terms of conceptually related constructs, Cast was among the first to propose relationships between what are presently known as cognitive and noncognitive assessments—relationships that were newly arisen in the United States (Zwick 2017).

Robertson and Wiseman 1939–1949: Taking Action

Three years later, in 1939, without waiting for experimenters to provide the ideal number of raters, in a county of England far from the London of Hartog, and Rhodes and Burt, apparently with little fanfare and no publication of method or results, the Chief Examiner for the Devon Selection Examination, R. K. Robertson, began having 11-plus English essays marked by a quite open, pooled-rater holistic method. A better illustration can hardly be found of the decentralization of examinations or of local experimentation in Great Britain. When Butler pleaded for his 1944 bill before the House of Commons, he said that "the variety of the education policy of the country must depend upon local initiative" (Hansard 1944). He could have cited Robertson's venture as a case in point.

According to Wiseman, who had worked with Robertson from the beginning and took over his position as Chief Examiner in 1947, Devon's 11-plus population was about 7,500 students in 1943 and about 4,500 in 1948. The drop can be blamed on World War II. Suddenly, in 1939 and 1940, Devon schools were overflowing with evacuee children, chiefly from London. According to S. J. Hess (2006), the first two waves of evacuees, in September of 1939 and spring of 1940, more than doubled the elementary-school population in Devon. A photo of the evacuees is shown in figure 3.1. That pressure on the educational system was not quickly reduced, as drift back was less in Devon than in other parts of England. Robertson's initial marking gambit may have been a response to a crisis of numbers.[13]

Robertson first separated the top and bottom thirds through "objective" testing—probably short-answer questions involving pluralization, vocabulary, opposites, sentence word order, and so forth. That left in the middle about 2,500 students in 1943 and 1,500 in 1948—students whose proficiency still lay in honest doubt, students occupying the "penumbra of uncertainty" (Mather, France, and Sare 1965, 138). Robertson's innovation, however, did not lie in this maneuver since in his day the majority of British local authorities were following a tradition of giving further scrutiny to students who fell within the "border-zone," the margin of error separating pass and fail decisions. That scrutiny could take the form of an oral interview, a review of course records, or an essay (Dempster 1954).

The breakthrough was having that essay read rapidly by four markers with the four independent impressionistic scores summed for a final mark. For the first time, Robertson put into practice the theoretical and experimental insight of Boyd that experienced marking of a whole essay should be intuitive and fast, and of Edgeworth and Rhodes that pooling of multiple marks achieves the best approximation of an essay's true value. Robertson did not leave an account of his thinking. But it was not slipshod. He first tried marking on a five-letter scale, A to E with plus and minus, like the Oxford system. But that method locked markers into a *grading* pattern, he found, with "favoritism" for particular grades (Wiseman 1949, 206). So he soon switched to a 0–20 scale with 10 as average. He also insisted on markers who were "self-consistent," and he validated them as markers by having them rescore essays they had scored

Holistic Scoring and Great Britain, 1936–1949   69

Figure 3.1. Devon evacuees, 1940 (photo courtesy of the Imperial War Museum)

before. It is unknown how he settled on four as the number of markers, but it simply may have been the most he could afford with the examination funds at his disposal.

What Chief Examiner Robertson lacked in fact-gathering disposition was more than made up by his successor. Wiseman combined his own passion for holistic marking with a shrewd grasp of statistics. Using data from the 1943 and 1948 Devon selection examinations, he analyzed issues few researchers had considered before in "The Marking of English Composition on Grammar School Selection" (1949). He prevalidated topics. He recorded the time spent marking essays (a touch over a minute per essay) and confirmed his claim that four "general-impression" ratings took much less time than one rating by "analytic schedule." He also calculated the *inter*marker reliabilities of impression markers (ranging from 0.44 to 0.92) and the reliability of the sum of four raters (0.93 and 0.97), comparing the coefficients with the marking reliability of the objective test (0.83). And—for Wiseman the most important statistic—the measure of *intra*marker reliability ranged from 0.70 to 0.86, with one outlier of 0.60. As he concluded, "A mark re-mark correlation of less than 0.7 cannot be tolerated . . . and such an examiner would be replaced" (206).

For Wiseman, validity was established in terms of interrater reliability. "The consistency thus being measured," Wiseman wrote in his 1949 study of essays as part of the 11-plus examinations, "is consistency with some supra-individual standard, and it is arguable that this is as much a coefficient of validity as of reliability" (203). General-impression marking, he found, was superior to analytic marking based on an explicit model of the writing construct (spelling, sense, punctuation, vocabulary, power of expression, and grammar). To treat student writing holistically was, by association, evidence of fairness. Also, Wiseman introduced the importance of criterion measures as they are related to scores: "A validity study for 11+ composition must, therefore, be a follow-up into grammar school achievement" (205). As far as he was aware, no validity studies of this kind had been published, and they were needed if the scores were to be examined for their predictive validity.

Wiseman's numbers always are warmly rooted in his first-hand experience as teacher, marker, and Chief Examiner. He cautions markers not to expect certain accomplishments in an essay and then penalize the writer for their absence. "Rather look," he says, "for excellences to reward." He knows eleven-year-old writing and its examiners. He tells markers that "a good deal of crude error can be passed over if there is clear vitality and force" (1949, 209). Most radically, he instructs his markers to look not for attainment but for potential, to use the evidence in the composition "to assess the ability of the candidate to profit by a secondary education. You are judging children, not essays" (208). In these instructions we are seeing why Wiseman proudly calls himself a "general impressionist" and why he distrusts analytical assessment. Ultimately, he argues that "rapid impression multiple marking," as Britton later called it, can be cost effective. The final aim of the numbers, he insists, is to "show the efficiency of these methods in practical use (and, what is very important, with large numbers)" (205).

In his evidence-gathering technique, Wiseman's position is clear. Referring to himself, he writes, "The writer is a confirmed 'general impressionist' having frequently had the experience of marking school essays by analytic methods (which for teaching purposes have obvious advantages) and finding that the obvious 'best' essay is not at the top of the list; the total gestalt is more than the sum of the parts. When we are faced with the task of judging any complex psychological material, it is probable that the method of total impression (provided the observer is suitably orientated) will yield sounder judgments than will analytic methods" (1949, 205). To the best of our knowledge, this passage contains the first use of the term *gestalt* as an explicit classification of impressionistic scoring (although we note that the whole, in gestalt theory, is other than, not more than, the sum of its parts.) The passage is equally remarkable because it contains one of the earliest, if not the first, distinctions between selection of methods and score use. For assessment purposes, impressionistic scoring—compelling the reader to focus, in a principled fashion, on the gestalt of the student work—is ideal. However, for instructional purposes, use of identified traits—inviting readers to provide judgment on an identified model of writing—is superior because the elements of the model provide focus in the classroom. Each method has its use, depending on the assessment aim. In this distinction, Wiseman's study is unique in connecting method to aim.

Wiseman demonstrated that open pooled-rater holistic scoring works with selection essays, works in the gritty terms of place, time, money, and personnel. The findings seemed destined to draw the attention of any Local Examination Authority who wished to rescue the examination essay. But did that happen? When Wiseman first published his scoring system in the *Times Educational Supplement* in April 1949, he said it "evoked a considerable number of enquiries from interested teachers" (206). And when he delivered his findings at the British Association for the Advancement of Science in September 1949, and published them in the *British Journal of Educational Psychology* a month later, educational researchers received the system as formidable enough to warrant more study.

But only a few teacher-researchers, such as Britton, embraced the method with enthusiasm, as the next chapter will show. On the local examination field, pooled holistic scoring seemed to have had limited appeal to Chief Examiners. In 1963, Britton could only say that Devon marking "has been widely used for a number of years at 11+ selection examination" (17). It seems that in the 1950s, 1960s, and early 1970s, when the situation would have seemed most ripe for it, when the majority of local education authorities who were depending solely on objective tests could well have been interested in adding an essay, this earliest system of holistic scoring did not establish very deep roots in Great Britain. Localism and perspectivism seems to have been losing out.

But to what, and why?

NOTES

1. This chapter and the next owe much to neighborly vetting by three British scholars: Liz Hamp-Lyons, Paul Newton, and Alastair Pollitt.

2. In the nineteenth and twentieth century, the 100-point scale was widespread in schools and universities, to grade everything from written science examinations to oral speeches, but it was hardly universal. Yale held to a four-point scheme, Oxford to five Greek letters (Smallwood 1935). Exactly where on the scale fell the point of pass, credit, or honors depended much on local custom.

3. As we define the term, *grading* is a kind of holistic evaluation of essays that does not use a rubric or scoring guide to qualify points or categories on a preexisting scale and relies on just one reader. Attending to cognitive, interpersonal, intrapersonal, and neurologic dimensions, grading is what teachers have long done with their own students' essays. Grading, however, is not restricted to the classroom. As we will see, in twentieth-century Great Britain, a great deal of external marking of examination essays differed little from teacher grading. Often the researcher term for this kind of examination marking was *by impression* or *general impression*. The use of the second term extends at least as far back as Burt's *Mental and Scholastic Tests* (1921, 309). Writing in 2019, we also realize there is often a sharp distinction made between grades awarded by teachers within a classroom setting and scores given to papers under external conditions. In Great Britain the first is usually called a *test* and the second an *examination*. In the United States, while scores are associated with large-scale formal assessments, grades are awarded by teachers to their students.

4. This and the next chapter focus on the external examining of essays in Great Britain, that is, in England, Wales, and Scotland. We have tried to be consistent in referring to reports and legislation that pertain only to England and Wales as "British" or "in Britain." The Scottish education and examination system differed in many ways from the British, although the issues remained similar. Ireland and Northern Ireland usually lie off the map of our history

5. A note for US readers. Free place and junior scholarship are terms used because UK policy makers relied on examinations to advance winners tuition free into a local grammar school. As well, 11-plus is used because students older than eleven sat for it. Most parents still wanted their child in a grammar school since it was the standard no-private-schooling route to university. After WWII, the secondary modern school kept the majority of students until they dropped out or tested out with a certificate (US readers would say diploma) in school-leaving examinations. After 1944, comprehensive schools supposedly combined instruction to prepare students either for a high-school certificate or for higher education, and technical schools (never many in number) prepared students for specific occupations. Minimum school-leaving age was fourteen in 1923, then changed to fifteen in 1947 and to sixteen in 1972. Before 1965, all these schools were state funded. Accounting for around 8 percent of school children in the 1960s, the private or independent schools were so named because they were supported not by the state but by fees and therefore were exempt from external regulations. Some of the most exclusive of independent schools, such as Eton, Rugby, or Winchester, were called public because they drew their students from all around England.

6. The Butler Act (formally known as the Education Act of 1944) enforced the tripartite system of grammar, technical, and secondary modern school as the main choices dependent upon the 11-plus examination. But the number of places available in grammar schools remained small. As Denis Lawton observed, "The Butler Act was essentially a Conservative reform, making the existing system more efficient without disturbing the public school privileges and without encouraging people to think of education in a genuinely democratic way" (45). Grammar schools, with a focus on academic subjects, educated students with the assumption that they would attend college. Yet there were few technical schools in existence. Nor had there been created many comprehensive schools, which supposedly would combine

7. It should not be forgotten that "objective testing" was employed in Great Britain, in part to further meritocratic ideals. Alastair Pollitt recounts some history from the early 1920s: "The county of Northumberland asked Godfrey Thomson to help resolve a problem with the 11+ system for selecting pupils to continue into grammar school education. Data showed that the system was heavily biased towards city children at the expense of those in rural primary schools, probably because all the best teachers applied for, and won, teaching posts in the city of Newcastle. His answer was to develop a group test following Binet's principles for assessing 'intelligence' in a way that would be relatively independent of the quality of a child's teachers" (email to the authors, February 19, 2018). Later, Thomson set up the research unit at the University of Edinburgh that created the Moray House Tests that supplied local education authorities with objective tests for six decades. Pooled-rater holistic scoring and objective testing shared a seat on the meritocratic train. When it derailed after 1949, when many saw the student failure that meritocracy structured, examinations such as the 11-plus were severely criticized (Wooldridge 1994).

8. In 1936 there were about 115 institutions of higher learning in England and Wales (population 40 million), and about 850 in the United States (population 128 million). Roughly, there was about half as much space in higher education available to British students.

9. Not so the matriculation examinations, which were controlled by a small number of universities. Sometimes these examinations were called local, but only because dons travelled to the schools (often in academic robes) to oversee the examination instead of making students travel to the universities.

10. Note that it makes no mathematical difference whether the pooled marks are expressed as a mean or a sum. Averaging, however, is a help in visualizing the whole marking array and is also the first step in a number of calculations that later played a significant role in educational statistics—standard error, margin of error, correlation, regression analysis, and factoring. In Great Britain, critique of marking benefited enormously from having Edgeworth as its forbear. In his application of mathematics to the study of economics, he was not a minor figure, and students of microeconomics still use his insights, such as the Edgeworth series, the Edgeworth conjecture, the Edgeworth box, and the indifference curve. In the study of marking, he was the first to calculate error weights (probable error) and use them to combine independent marker scores into an adjusted score.

11. Neil Dorans summarized the history of psychometrics in educational measurement as follows: "The first generation, which was influenced by concepts such as error of measurement and correlation that were developed in other fields, focused on test scores and saw developments in the areas of reliability, classical test theory, generalizability theory, and validity. This generation began in the early twentieth century and continues today, but most of its major developments were achieved by 1970. The second generation, which focused on models for item level data, began in the 1940s and peaked in the 1970s but continues into the present as well. The third generation started in the 1970s and continues into today. It is characterized by the application of statistical ideas and sophisticated computational methods to item level models, as well as models of sets of items" (2011, 259). The majority of studies in the United Kingdom and the United States during the period of our book were conducted with first-generation theory. However, as Pollitt (email to authors, February 19, 2018) pointed out to us, when he joined the Godfrey Thomson Unit in Edinburgh in 1975, his director, Albert Pilliner, encouraged him to explore

second-generation assessment to see "if there was anything useful in this Rasch business." Pollit soon discovered what he termed as "the ultimate source of IRT theory" in the United Kingdom, Derek N. Lawley's 1943 paper on the application of maximum likelihood method to factor analysis. Pollit thus sheds significant light on this early use of second-generation psychometric modeling in the United Kingdom.

12. Later evaluators, with better technology to calculate correlation coefficients, took Burt's way. Burt's memorandum was written in 1935, an indication that Hartog and Rhodes's studies may have taken place in 1932–1934.

13. If Robertson turned to holistic scoring to meet British war contingencies, an ironic comparison with the United States is hard to avoid. In effect, Pearl Harbor eliminated the College Board's three-hour essay-based examination because it was given in June and students called into the services at their graduation found it expedient to take the SAT objective test because it was given in April (Elliot 2005, 99–101). So in the United States, the war blocked external essay examinations; in Britain, it may have helped foster them. Note, however, that Diederich introduced his more controlled version of holistic scoring at the University of Chicago during the War, in 1944 (see chapter 5).

4
GREAT BRITAIN AND THE REJECTION OF HOLISTIC SCORING, 1949–1988

The word "education" has an evil sound in politics; there is a pretense of education, when the real purpose is coercion without the use of force.
—Hannah Arendt, "The Crisis in Education"

There are multiple reasons for the failure of multiple marking to take root and thrive in the United Kingdom. One can be inferred from the formal studies of the method that followed Philip Hartog, Edmond Rhodes, and Cyril Burt (1936)—and later R. K. Robertson and Stephen Wiseman (1949). But the inferences are not always obvious or direct. The readiest conclusion is that in the last three decades of the twentieth century, external examinations tended to shrug off independent scholarly findings when those findings ran counter to political, economic, logistical, and demographic pressures.

Indeed, the reasons gestalt psychology did not flourish in the United Kingdom were the same ones that prevented holistic scoring from gaining wide acceptance. As noted in chapter 3, the 1944 Education Act (often called the Butler Act after the conservative politician who sponsored it) was embraced by the Labor Party as a way to leverage examinations for social good. Yet this aim did not materialize following World War II. As Adrian Wooldridge writes in a perceptive, common-sense analysis, "In the aftermath of the war, educationalists were more concerned with making ends meet than with ushering in a new meritocratic utopia" (1994, 260). Postwar population growth strained resources and, by 1947, the Ministry would have to provide 1,150,000 seats for children. By 1950 the Ministry was nearly 2,000 seats behind schedule. Existing buildings were old, and there was a shortage of teachers. The alarming absence of reliability that Francis Edgeworth had calculated in 1888 and 1890 remained true. The 11-plus examination, Alfred F. Watts and Douglas A. Pidgeon reported in 1957, misallocated students. Out of every 1,000 students examined, 122 were incorrectly selected and were wrongly placed into selective grammar schools or basic education secondary moderns. "Educationalists," Woodridge concludes, "Simply lacked measuring devices sensitive enough to make fine distinctions between similar children" (283). It is against this background that we must understand UK education after 1945.

RESEARCHED DEFENSE OF HOLISTIC SCORING: 1939–1956

Initially in Great Britain, the open, pooled-rater holistic method of Hartog and Rhodes raised questions mainly about random error in markers. For example, B. M. D. Cast picked forty essays written by fourteen and fifteen-year-old students in a London girls' school, and she and other teachers marked them in four different ways (1939, 1940).[1] Connoisseurship provided one way, which she called "marker's own preferred scheme." A second way was for "sense," as suggested by Clarence Ebblewhite Smith and Hartog (1941). A third followed the method of "general impression"—we would say holistic—from Hartog, Rhodes, and Burt (1936). The fourth used an analytic scale devised by Burt, who happened to be Cast's thesis adviser.[2] The last two methods proved most reliable, yet each had its characteristic faults. General-impression rating tended "to seize on a few salient or superficial points—errors of spelling, grammar or fact, perhaps—and weight those out of all proportion to the rest; on the other hand, the analytic method, by dealing with numerous isolated and possibly inessential points, may overlook certain general qualities that characterize the essays as a whole" (Cast 1939, 264).

Curiously, Cast sides with analytic scoring, which, she says, "though laborious and unpopular, appears almost uniformly the best." She admits that the holistic tends to discriminate candidates more (as Hartog and Rhodes had also found) but says it "tends to judge them by more superficial characteristics." Cast seems to fear the "beams from different angles" Wiseman and other advocates of pooled evaluation welcomed. She stresses the fact that "all subjective impressions are influenced by chance elements and unconscious caprice" (1939, 268).

Other studies replicating and extending Hartog and Rhodes also had trouble exorcising the bugaboo of caprice or, as they put it, random marking error. Philip E. Vernon, then head of the psychology department at the University of Glasgow, also found little difference in interrater reliability between analytic scoring and general impression but concluded with some skepticism regarding Edgeworth's postulate about true value: "Though many of the discrepancies cancel out when the total marks for an essay are summed, there are still considerable divergences between markers" (Morrison and Vernon 1941, 117). Cast and Vernon seem uncomfortable with the scoring method supported by their findings.

After an understandable slack in research during the war, the publication of Wiseman's 1949 study focused researchers on unresolved issues inherent in the Devon scheme. One crux was not *inter*marker reliability but *intra*marker reliability. It makes sense to pool the different views of two or more markers, but not to pool differences with oneself. Robertson and Wiseman thought self-consistency the best indicator of a marker's worth. Any mark-remark correlation below 0.7, and the rater should go. The issue was hardly new. Educators had long known that over time, single-marker connoisseurs shift their judgment on an essay more often than they know or anyone likes. In 1888 Edgeworth found one-seventh of British Civil Service scripts received a different mark when marked again later by the same reader. Surely, common sense said, that sad number could be bettered by formal analytic and holistic marking, with more detailed information from analytic marking.

The first assumption proved true but not the second. Mark-remark reliabilities for holistic and analytic were essentially the same (Morrison and Vernon 1941), or else holistic scorers proved more consistent. Smith and Hartog (1941) had eight raters mark essays written by secondary students ready to take a school-certificate examination; the raters marked the essays separately on the criteria of sense, spelling, punctuation, grammar, vocabulary, and expression, and then by general impression. Five months later, the mark-remark correlations were higher for the holistic than for any of the criteria except spelling. In 1951, using Wiseman's four-marker pooled system but on a thirty-point scale, H. Lamb (1953) found the same, with the mark-remark correlation for pooled raters (0.96) beating the combined analytic (0.91) and the individual holistic (0.86). Trust in the consistency of impressionistic markers did not seem to be a problem, at least not relative to analytical markers.

But what about the consistency of student writers? Robertson and Wiseman had retested their border-zone student writers, but they didn't follow up on an underexamined source of random error in holistic scoring, the uneven performance of student writers over time. It was, however, an issue much studied (in the United States notably by Paul B. Diederich). In 1951, Douglas S. Finlayson had students write two sixty-minute essays one week apart.[3] Explicitly replicating Wiseman, he had six teachers mark them by rapid impression on a 1–20 scale. The average single-marker correlation between the two essays was 0.69.

Finlayson concludes, "The performance of a child in one essay is not representative of his ability to write essays in general" (162). James Britton, Nancy C. Martin, and Harold Rosen (1966) found a correlation of 0.77 between two essays written, back to back, by fifteen-year-old students during a ninety-minute examination period. In one sense the post-Wiseman findings just expressed the old "grave doubt" about the practice of assessing general writing ability "from a single essay marked by a single examiner" (Vernon and Millican 1954, 69). But Wiseman sharpened the question. How many pieces of writing from one student would it take to make that holistic assessment dependable? Twenty years later, no one really knew. Examination conditions, it seems, made the question moot. Finlayson, looking at the possibility of using no more than two essays from each student, said that "it is doubtful whether such elaborations are within the realm of practical politics" (1951, 161).[4]

Examination conditions also affected Robertson and Wiseman's most pressing issue, the number of raters in a pooled-rater scheme. Since more markers meant greater reliability (and, inferentially, enhanced validity) and fewer meant less expense (and, presumably, prudent reform), the natural push was toward as few raters as one could get away with (a law, or postulate, we will see operating with relentless effect in the United States). Using essays by Edinburgh twelve-year-old students and replicating Wiseman's marking method, Finlayson employed six independent raters and then ran intercorrelations. For three markers, the reliability was 0.82, for two it was 0.78, for one it was 0.69 (1951, 133). Finlayson advanced the emerging UK program of research where Wiseman left off and paid particular attention to interrater reliability, intrareader reliability, and predictive validity. Historically, his was the earliest study to use a wide range of evidential forms. In Finlayson's research, we see one of the earliest links of writing ability (assessed through a direct measure) to IQ and EQ (Intelligence Quotient and English Quotient, both measured through limited response, objective items). Working from Moray House at the University of Edinburgh, Finlayson used the tools developed under Godfrey Thompson at the Moray House School of Education. As Woodbridge observed, Thompson was convinced that the educational system of Scotland was prejudiced against children from rural schools and hoped to use intelligence tests to demonstrate injustice and rectify imbalance (1994, 68). As a student pursuing the bachelor of education degree when he performed the study, Finlayson would have used the battery of tests developed at Moray House as criterion variables. In the correlations he found that different constructs were being measured and that writing was, perhaps, a thing unto itself. In his research we can see that both the method used and the inferences drawn anticipate the US research of Diederich, John W. French, and Sydell T. Carlton by a decade.

Analyzing marks given to O-level biology essays in Nuffield, Oxfordshire, a biology teacher, J. J. Head, also found that the most substantial jump in reliability was from one to two markers, from 0.64 to 0.84. Head calculated that examining boards for the General Certificate of Education examination could manage double marking, but multiple marking "would be a practical impossibility" (1966, 71). The use of pairs of raters in government examinations—which would become a staple in US essay assessment—seemed at the British doorstep. But it never really crossed the threshold. Val Brooks, who surveyed double marking in Britain 1940–1989, found that "only a handful of public examinations ever adopted double or multiple marking" (2004, 18).

The main reason, argues Brooks, was feasibility. As Wiseman had cautioned, the practical barrier with multiple marking was not so much cost as time. Today the logistics are hard to quantify but easy to imagine. In many English, Welsh, and Scottish counties, schools were small and far flung, railways far apart, and roads indifferent. Gathering markers at one place often was just unworkable. Even in the city boroughs where distance was not a hindrance, there could be tens of thousands of pupils to be tested. In her contribution to the *British Journal of Educational Psychology* 1956 symposium on 11-plus essay assessment, D. M. Edwards Penfold does the numbers. At Wiseman's marking rate of one essay per minute, to complete 20,000 essays would take a single eight-hour-a-day worker a biblical forty days. Yet the normal turnaround time was two to three weeks. Splitting the job among raters would be a logistical nightmare because duplication of essays, though technically possible, was slow and costly. And Wiseman wanted four markers per essay! "It seems, therefore," Edwards Penfold concludes, "that the case for the essay will probably be decided on the errors of a single rather than a composite mark" (129).

RESEARCHERS CARRY ON, FEW LISTEN: 1956–1966

In fact—and historically this is the point of curiosity—Edwards Penfold's was a hasty conclusion. Most Local Education Authorities had far fewer than 20,000 examinees at a time, even with the 11-plus examinations. In fact, during the 1950s and 1960s, *some* Chief Examiners had made Robertson and Wiseman's open pooled-rater scheme work. Maybe as time passed it was a dwindling remnant, and maybe, in 1963, Britton's note that Devon marking "has been widely used for a number of years at 11+ selection examination" (17) sounds like damning with faint numbers, but it seems under some conditions in Britain, multiple-marking was feasible.

And in fact—and this is curiouser—educational research during the years of 1936 through 1966, the research we have just surveyed, by and large found evidence encouraging the use of pooled-rater holistic marking, not discouraging it. With interrater reliability, pooled-rater holistic fared no worse than analytic; with intrarater reliability, better. On the question of the number of essays needed from one student to achieve a reliable score, both methods left the answer up in the air. On number of raters needed to achieve a reliable score, Wiseman's four proved less costly than one rater using an analytic scheme, and perhaps four was overreaching—three or even two might be acceptable.

Researchers found the pooled-rater rapid-impression method also holding its ground on other issues. With 11-plus examinations, it was as predictive of later grammar-school academic success as was analytic marking (Emmett 1954; Nisbet 1955; Schools Council 1965). Rater training had little or no effect on marker reliability (Black 1962; Edwards Penfold 1956; McMahon 1953). During long rating stints, holistic markers actually enhanced their discrimination, that is, spread their scores more (Farrell and Gilbert 1960). Topic choice did affect holistic markers (Britton 1963; Wiseman and Wrigley 1958), but that was a problem easily solved. Marker leniency affected holistic scoring, though no more so than in analytic scoring, but in either case those effects could be controlled with post hoc statistical adjustment that Hartog, Rhodes, and Burt (1936) termed office adjusted (Edwards Penfold 1956; Mather, France, and Sare 1965). Other predilections of individual markers, Cast's "unconscious caprice," were not on the menu of most researchers and could only be surmised.[5] Finally, teacher-markers preferred rapid-impression scoring over analytic, as researchers—most of whom had taught and marked—seemed unsurprised to discover.

One irony among many of great social significance is that researchers were focused on two losing combatants and were letting the ultimate winners—those conservative forces advocating efficiency—escape largely uninvestigated. While research was busy contrasting open holistic and gridded analytic marking of essays, it was *content schemes* and *rubrics* that eventually prevailed in British government examinations. By content scheme, we mean a guide for markers that lists acceptable points made in response to a subject-based question and sets the amount of credit for each point made by the writer.[6] Such a guide works well for marking content in responses ranging from short answer to short essay. Today, points-based marking (content schemes or mark schemes) is used in General Certificate of Secondary Education (GCSE) and A-level subject examinations. It is difficult to identify the origin, but teachers and local examiners had been using them for many decades before 1966. By the 1950s, something like them was often designated as *new type* testing. The old type restricted response to a word, phrase, or number, but the new type allowed longer and more creative response (Vernon 1957, 127–33). In 1956, Pidgeon and Alfred Yates prophesied that the solution to the stand-off between essay and objective examination formats might be the "new type" objective format with "creative response items" (47).[7] Based on the 11-plus misallocation of students they would write about the following year, eliminating rater response would have seemed a logical strategy in the elimination of systematic error.

A second irony, of more technical significance, concerns rubrics. By rubric, we mean a scoring guide that arranges the selected criteria and numbered scale in a tables format so each criterion is described and scaled in the same way. Such a guide presents markers with a simple table format, with or without cell boundaries drawn, centering on a few criteria such as ideas, organization, and mechanics, arranging each by an identical set of scaled categories or, as the British say, bands. The categories can be numbers (1, 2, 3, and so forth along a scale) or named qualities (superior, medium, inferior). The marker marks the essay according to each of the criteria and then, without adding or averaging, selects one band for the whole essay. With awarding boards in Britain, this process became standard in marking essays for proficiency in written communication. When one band is not chosen as a final score but rather separate marks for the criteria are reported, it is profile scoring, which we will discuss in chapter 9, with attention to the early research of Liz Hamp-Lyons.

It might well be that scoring rubrics, as we define them in this study, were a US invention passed on to the British. The story relates a global journey little told in histories of writing assessment. One route starts with the factoring of reader commentary by Paul B. Diederich, John W. French, and Sydell T. Carlton in 1961, whose criteria influenced a rubric-based scheme created by Holly Jacobs and colleagues at Texas A&M University, College Station and published in 1981, which, in due course, influenced Hamp-Lyons and other British second-language experts revising the English Language Testing System (ELTS) examinations in the early 1980s. Another route proceeds as follows: in 1969, Richard M. Bossone studied remedial writing students at City University of New York community colleges and, with criteria derived from Diederich, French, and Carlton, created a holistic rubric that was parent to the CUNY Freshman Skills Assessment Program Evaluation Scale for Writing Assessment first administered in 1979; that rubric was reproduced by Kyle Perkins in his influential survey of ESL testing published in the *TESOL Quarterly* in 1983, read by all second-language researchers in England. As a reminder of the centrality of English-language learning to writing assessment, an essay-rating procedure first used for basic writing and second-language US students was found fit for British students at A-level and even prerequisite AS-level examinations.

British educator-researchers were finding good reasons to promote open pooled-rater holistic scoring during the years it was struggling and, in the end, failing to take root. Some UK researchers appear conflicted. Finlayson's substantial study of pooled holistic scoring expresses an agreement with Edgeworth's postulate that "the pool approximates the 'true' mark of the essay" (Finlayson 1951, 129) and records a mark-remark consistency for four raters of 0.94. Yet, by the time his study was published in 1951, he was already working for Moray House, the most successful British purveyor of short-answer tests before and after WWII. We have seen Cast and Vernon still concerned over variance in marking even after their figures show pooled-marker strategies controlling that variance. It was as though these researchers were riding a contrary tide of social forces they could not control.

Other researchers, unequivocal in their approval for multiple-marker scoring, had their findings left in the wake. Britton (1963) and Britton, Martin, and Rosen (1966) provided the most rigorous and substantial studies then conducted into holistic and analytic scoring. They used O-level English compositions because they wanted to extend Wiseman's method to sixteen-year-olds, with an eye to the new Certificate of Secondary Education examinations that would soon place large numbers of essays before the examining boards. The researchers compared a large sample of essays marked both by rapid impression (pooling three readers) and the traditional single-marker system (with an analytical marking scheme and sample papers) used by the University of Cambridge Local Examinations Syndicate. The outcomes supported the holistic in every way—interrater reliability, mark-remark consistency, judgment of teachers, and expense (four shillings a paper, equivalent to the syndicate cost). These are findings hard to refute, yet the two studies mark the last hurrah for multiple-marker holistic scoring in Britain as societal forces mounted to allocate resources in less experimental ways. We return to the study by Britton,

Martin, and Rosen at the end of this chapter to establish its importance in larger, transnational research.

By the mid-1960s one can sense among teachers and researchers a kind of helplessness before an impending doom. In 1965, Donald Raymond Mather, Norman France, and G. T. Sare, the first and third secondary-school headmasters, complained about the tendency in UK education "to preserve the status quo for as long as possible and to be chary of change" (25). They note decades of research into marker unreliability and lament that "public examinations are still being conducted as if this research had never been done" (135). Yet when they themselves set about promoting a major change in testing—the Certificate of Secondary Education Mode 3 classroom-based examination in which schools designed their own assessments and had them approved by a regional board—they can only offer a hodgepodge of methods, including multi-marking of scripts, pooling of grades or marks, and the long-discredited method of sample matching (54).[8]

This sense of helplessness and accompanying dissent was recorded by Brian Jackson and Dennis Marsden in their 1962 study of the impact of elite grammar-school education on working-class students who found themselves in unfamiliar territory. Based on eighty-eight men and women from working-class backgrounds that had attended the elite Huddersfield grammar schools in West Yorkshire, their research revealed that the costs of education had outweighed the benefits. While "the few Penguin Classics in the book-case may not mean much," they wrote, "they do seem to point, if slightly, to something" (55–56). Yet that something was not worth the price of alienation these students felt. "'Don't let anybody tell you that tradition doesn't matter,'" one former student recalled. "'It does matter to be able to play cricket and wear the old school tie'" (55). Without these experiences, one graduate reported, there was no use coming to London to work. Jackson and Marsden concluded, "We hope our voice is the voice of the last grammar school generations: for something better can be done" (247).

THE LOCAL AND THE STATE: 1965–1988

Then the state started assuming control and progressed, as Wooldridge (1994) put it, from pamphleteering to policymaking. Beginning in 1965, a series of legislative changes to the British examination system all but doomed holistic multiple scoring of essays because, in an environment of increasing conservatism and efficiency, time spent in such scoring could be better spent elsewhere.

- **1967.** The new Certificate of Secondary Education went into effect, designed for secondary-modern students at age sixteen, a subject-based test that could be scored externally by one of fourteen examining boards but also, in the famous and popular Mode 3, internally by teachers who devised the syllabus, set in-class tests, and graded them. Obviously, teacher-friendly Mode 3 was not friendly to holistic scoring, which, as everyone recognized, provided only a number—good for school-leaving decisions but not for curricular advice.
- **1973.** Mandatory school-leaving age was raised to sixteen, easing unemployment but greatly increasing the number of secondary students taking examinations and making double or multiple marking of essays less likely. Before, the majority of secondary-modern students had left without a certification, flooding a tightening job market. Now they were required to stay for a fifth year.
- **1976.** Labour came into power in 1974 and two years later passed an Education Act that abolished the tripartite system and forbade selection at age eleven.[9] The Education Act of 1944 was supported by Labour on the premise of equality of opportunity for all children in Britain and Wales. Local authorities were required to provide schools offering a variety of instruction and training in three categories: grammar (viewed as essential for university entrance and the professions), modern (a less rigorous curriculum), and technical (focusing on spatial and mechanical aptitude). Children would be streamed into one of these three categories on the basis of an examination at age eleven, and the examination became known as the 11-plus. By 1957, the publication date of Vernon's *Secondary School Selection*, all children who had reached the age of eleven (but not twelve) on September 1 were required to take a three-part examination—categorized according to intelligence, English, and arithmetic—in their own schools on a fixed day. However, the Education Act had not much leveled the playing field, and grammar-school enrollment still remained around 20 percent in Britain. In erasing the 11-plus examinations, the Education Act of 1976 also erased the greatest need for large-scale judgment of essay-writing competence. The remaining secondary examinations, CSE and GCE O-level and A-level, were chiefly based on courses of study, not writing skill, examinations suitable for marking schemes providing feedback on content. Teachers and students needed the feedback because the tests provided not only a way out (with a certificate of school success) but often a way forward. CSE and O-level results could send a student into A-level study, a switch made much more easily in the burgeoning comprehensive schools.
- **1988.** In England, a national curriculum was installed. For accountability, and to accommodate the continued growth of comprehensive schools, the GCSE was implemented. It replaced, combined, and regularized the CSE and O-level examinations, but also, in a legislative stroke with far-reaching and perhaps unforeseen consequences

for government practices, it allowed a school to choose the jurisdiction of any examination authority, not just the local one. That led to a rapid, almost panicky merging of examination authorities and the closing of university examination boards. Today there are only five awarding boards (one of them private, Edexcel, owned by Pearson) responsible for testing epic numbers of students and therefore committed to standardization and economy.

Although at every step there was consultation with educationists to a greater or lesser degree, from start to finish legislators were following interests that had little or nothing to do with essay-marking methods. They were intent on standardizing school curriculum, increasing accurate student placement, lowering unemployment, enhancing working-class opportunity, reducing social class segregation by school, and centralizing educational authority. Related to the advancement of opportunity was the end of Galtonian orthodoxy. In examining the research and conclusions of Vernon, Wooldridge (1994) observes that hereditarian theory was yielding to behavioral psychology, and researchers were becoming increasingly skeptical of the use of IQ tests in the 11-plus examinations as a means of predicting student performance. As is evident in his 1957 handbook on secondary-school selection, Vernon was equally alert to the impact of the entire process of selection on the mental health and personality development of children. The majority of the thirty-two recommendations made in the final chapter of the book may be broadly interpreted as dealing with issues of fairness regarding the limits of the examinations and the need for multiple measures of student ability. In this complex environment, holistic scoring was an easy method to let slip away.

In effect, top-down legislation, far removed from multiple-marker holistic essay scoring, effectively blocked it from teachers (who liked it) and teacher-researchers (who found support for it). The winds of change swept much away. This one-way relationship between political interest and test construction was not confined to Britain, of course. It is so pervasive that we offer a postulate (not an axiom).

1. *Political forces impact external testing methods in many ways, while testing methods impact political forces not one whit.* Political legislation, however, is only one factor in the British demise of relatively open and pooled-rater holistic scoring. Who did kill cock robin? As in the nursery rhyme, those involved make a long list, each with its postulate.

2. *The design of an examination is related to the number of examinees.* There are realistic considerations in terms of delivery, and the greater the demand, the less likely it is that a single-measure use will survive because of the limited information it provides.

3. *Scoring methods rarely enable the technology that allows them.* For logistical, cost, and time problems with multiple marking, solutions came too late.
4. *Real-world holistic-testing conditions rarely allow for multiple measures of reliability.* Rapid turnaround time demanded of school marking discouraged moderat from testing for intrarater reliability, test reliability, and writer reliability. Even examination of interrater reliability is difficult if it results in a reading session being discontinued or discounted.
5. *Scoring methods do not escape tacit social expectations and philosophical premises.* The quarrel between the pooled-score and the adjusted-score methods replicated in many ways the confrontation of the 1950s and 1960s between radical and conservative, underground and established, leveled and hierarchized, populist and elitist.
6. *Distinct from concerns of evidence related to validity, reliability, and fairness, corporatization of essay scoring has its own economic reasons for maintaining single marking.* Because an organization's largest expenditure is work force, centralized concentration of examinations (within fewer and larger boards) encouraged testing methods that used fewer and fewer hires.
7. *As essay-examination systems age, they encounter calls for justice.* The rising corporatization of testing led to a heightened sense of social justice in the United Kingdom and due process in connection with examination procedures, results, and use.[10] When examinations are used to structure opportunity, the basis of that structuring has ethical dimensions. As we note in chapters 1 and 10, resulting calls for justice impact historiography itself.
8. *Testing procedures may look the same on paper, but they actualize differently within local fields for social, political, contextual, and personal reasons.* In the United States, as we show in chapters 5 through 8, holistic scoring took on different dimensions than those observed in the United Kingdom. And, in chapter 9, we offer five additional postulates based on US history.

Today in British secondary schools, compared to 1966, examining is more legislated, regularized, centralized, hierarchical, and corporatized. This does not necessarily mean it is worse. In Britain, more students than ever are proceeding on to higher education. Astronomical numbers of examination scripts are marked each year—24 million was one estimate for 2003—but at all examination levels, the unit is the academic subject and, except for mathematics, the testing is essay based, not multiple choice. Pedagogical feedback from examinations is treated as a given, and one reason that to date the United Kingdom has resisted computerized marking is that "UK culture requires that mark schemes be described in ways that are useful to teachers and candidates" (Meadows and Billington 2005, 71).

For essays, analytic marking prevails, with detailed content schemes. Competence in writing extended prose is expected, though not assumed.

Communication expertise is scored for many subjects through rubric-based holistic schemes, even though the score may count for as little as 5 percent of total marks. Single marking of essays is the norm, but it is much more controlled than the connoisseurship of old—with markers trained, standardized, and checked in progress now and then by senior examiners online. Markers are seasonal hires, usually teachers earning a bit of vacation money, as of old.

And the marking itself is much less a mystery. Up through the 1970s, mark schemes were strictly confidential, and markers were forbidden to confide in anyone about them. This practice may have curtailed teaching to the test, but it made preparing for the test more a game of chance, with unfair advantage for teachers who were also markers. Alastair Pollitt remembers the tutor in his teacher-training college advising him to become a marker as soon as possible (email to authors, February 19, 2018).[11] In Scotland, Pollitt helped convince examination boards to correct this situation. Beginning in 1987 in Scotland and in 1988 in England and Wales, mark schemes had to be published after each examination. About the same time in the United States, Miles Myers was also recommending making rubrics or scoring guides public (1980, 51).

All in all, despite the relentless increase in numbers of examination candidates, it may be argued that British ideals were reasonably maintained. If centralization and standardization have grown, the empirical spirit of universal values still holds sway, the ideal of meritocracy still holds true, and selection still reigns, although with more individual student choice.

As for teachers' part in external examining, after a century and a half they continue to be accused of teaching to the test and they continue to lament Vernon's "harmful backwash effects" (1957, 127). But generally, teacher control has weakened. Traditionally, British teachers often had a direct influence upon examinations. They could contest testing decisions of their Local Education Authority, sometimes appearing before the Chief Examiner with evidence from coursework—attendance and behavior cards, tests and essays, personal opinion—arguing that a failed student really should be passed.[12] That respect for teacher knowledge underwrote the radical CSE Mode 3 option.

But Mode 3, along with pooled-rater scoring, did not last long. After 1967, the teacher input on Mode 3 CSE decisions was trimmed down in stages from 100 percent until it was completely prohibited in 1994. In 1967 the Joint Matriculation Board in northern England began an English O-level system that relied entirely on coursework, a popular choice until it was removed also in 1994. In 2006 the Qualifications and Curriculum Authority, then Great Britain's overarching regulator of external examinations, put severe restrictions on the use of coursework for examination credit due to its concerns over internet plagiarism (Tattersall 2007). The Assessment and Qualifications Alliance (AQA) awarding board allows a portion of the GCSE English/English language test to be teacher-marked coursework, but AQA phased out the option in 2017. Victim to Margaret Thatcher's conservatism as prime minister from 1979 to 1990, Mode 3 may have no lives left.

Sometimes, a comment made in passing achieves aphoristic value as a map through complex terrain. In 2012, Hamp-Lyons wrote this of holistic scoring: "You cannot build a sturdy house with only one brick" (395). Devastated by war and committed to a better future, UK educational leaders sought ways to structure opportunity for the next generation through measurement. In the case of holistic scoring, the benefits did not outweigh the costs: bricks had to be useful, and one that had an odd shape to it was not worth the effort. In that brick we see the whole of writing assessment in the United Kingdom: the shifting political forces tending toward conservatism, the growing number of students, the technological intricacies of measurement, the tacit social expectations and philosophical premises, the force of corporatization, the calls for justice, and the varieties of actualization. There are lots of ways to look at a brick, and in the United Kingdom, usefulness to students was the most important one.

CODA: 1966

The year 1966 may be constructed as a dramatic turning point for our transatlantic glance at relatively open, pooled-rater holistic marking in Great Britain. Five research studies and one conference are especially notable as we leave the United Kingdom and turn to the United States in chapter 5. Taken together, these events shine a bright light on 1966 as an *annus mirabilis*: for the United Kingdom in terms of research leadership in holistic scoring; for the United States in terms of its creative early adaptation of UK innovation; in emerging distinctions between deeply contextual, situated studies and formal, experimental studies; in a new emphasis on measuring growth in writing ability instead of the restricted focus on selection; in emerging sources of evidence related to validity and reliability; and in the first Anglo-American conference aimed at creating a principled UK and US curriculum for teachers across the spectrum from kindergarten through college.

First, that year marked the final major study conducted in Britain sympathetic to pooled-rater holistic essay scoring with the publication of Britton, Martin, and Rosen's *Multiple Marking of English Compositions* in 1966. As noted above, Britton, Martin, and Rosen had hoped to provide empirical support for teacher judgment. In using 500 writing samples from General Certificate of Education (GCE) ordinary-level (O-level) examinations, they aimed to ensure claims could be made about the role of writing in a family of basic academic qualifications used in England, Wales, and other Commonwealth nations. In replicating the marking system used by the GCE, Britton, Martin, and Rosen assured that their experiment would have a criterion measure for the rapid-impression, double-scored measure they used. Evidence of validity was presented in terms of the writing construct.

It is no surprise, then, when Britton, Martin, and Rosen write that the argument for "testing by sampling" the actual work of students was undertaken in opposition to the use of objective tests. If "the practice of continuous writing ought, on the strongest educational recommendation, to be a major part of what a pupil does in his English school work," it follows that "the form of the examination given to him ought to encourage rather than discourage such practice" (1966, 3). If the government is to continue using limited means for assessing complex linguistic abilities, then it must "take responsibility for the 'backwash effect'" of its actions (3). The plot is simply all wrong, so Britton, Martin, and Rosen go further. Among all the data points, it is good to hear their voice and its emphasis on individual difference:

> The ability to use the mother tongue is acquired above all by pursuing, from infancy onwards, our own individual purposes and interests. Rather than a high road to general competence, therefore, there are countless individual routes leading to a competence which will always be related to individual needs as well as general social needs. (3)

The second study published in 1966, *The Measurement of Writing Ability* by Fred I. Godshalk, Frances Swineford, and William E. Coffman (1966), matched the British investigation in many ways and helped continue pooled-rater scoring in the United States for a few more years, in the form of the College Board's English Composition Test (ECT). What is remembered is that the study took the holistic score as the criterion variable—an unprecedented, bold move—and sought relationships between it and eight experiential tests, including both objective items and interlinear exercises. In taking a direct measure of writing as the criterion against which the other measures were validated, Godshalk,

Swineford, and Coffman took that which was lowly and uncertain and riveted it to the center of US writing assessment.

Also in 1966, Albert E. Myers of Yale University and Carolyn B. McConville and William E. Coffman of ETS published the third study, "Simplex Structure in the Grading of Essay Tests" (1966). The question of aim is important as we shift back and forth between the United Kingdom to the United States in the 1960s—as we turn from the Britton, Martin, and Rosen study to the Myers, McConville, and Coffman study. In the former, a study of 500 writing samples was undertaken to support teacher judgment. In the later, a study of 80,000 essays was undertaken to determine interrater reliability. In the former, holistic scoring was viewed as a way to help classroom teachers improve their assessment abilities; in the later, holistic scoring was viewed as a way to manage large-scale assessments. The former is deeply contextual, and the latter is deeply formal.

For Myers, McConville, and Coffman, the occasion for the analysis was significant. In December 1963, some 80,000 students electing to take the ECT in the College Board test administration were required to write a twenty-minute essay. The test was the first ECT to include a twenty-minute essay since April of 1947. The research therefore was a milestone moment of reflection in a sixteen-year period during which the College Board had shifted from an essay examination through various stages of objective and semiobjective format and back to an essay format. Of interest is the team's identification of a new interpretative element related to factor analysis used to infer holism. Subsequent factor analysis of covariances among the twenty-five papers yielded four factors. As had been the case with the 1961 Diederich study, Meyers, McConville, and Coffman demonstrated that the factor loadings were indeed giving global judgments. However, Meyers, McConville, and Coffman also observed that there was a functional relationship between scores and the factors, leading the researchers to conclude that there was a simplex structural relationship at hand. In 1954, Louis Guttman described a simplex as a structural relationship that exists between elements when these elements are ordered on a single dimension of complexity. Using this interpretative framework, Meyers, McConville, and Coffman hypothesized that essays may be classified as complex in the sense that they embody the existence of varied attributes, from good organizational structure to command of conventions. An essay receiving low scores, conversely, is simple in that these attributes may not be present. "Thus," they conclude, "the ordering of papers by their mean could be construed as an ordering by complexity" (1966, 52).

Thus, while the holistic interpretation was maintained, a nuance was provided: when scores were understood in terms of quality, diverse points of view were, perhaps, also part of the assigned score—with high scores based on observations of complexity in the writing sample and poor scores based on observations of simplicity. Construct manifestation was, at least in theory, related to score level.

The fourth study, published in 1966 by Diederich, helped classroom teachers understand how to measure growth in writing ability. Based on a method of sampling across grades, he tells teachers, "You can get a solid and convincing answer to that question [how much growth in writing ability comes about in each year of your program] in a single weekend, starting Friday morning and reporting results at the close of school on Monday" (435). In terms of scoring, teachers simply sort the randomly selected papers across grades into three piles of high, medium, and low. The differences across grades, he reminds readers, will not be "sufficiently reliable for individual measurement" but will nevertheless be "reliable enough to measure the difference between one grade and the next" (437). His was among the earliest studies to bring the concept of program assessment, based on pooled scores from writing samples, into the literature of direct writing assessment.

The fifth study, published by E. Percival in 1966, turned to the Moray House tests for criterion variables—just as Finlayson had in 1951. Percival investigated writing samples of an 11-plus group of students enrolled in Bolter Grammar School in the English county borough of Warrington. Based on low to moderate correlations among measures, he determined that taking a measure of IQ was not taking a measure of writing ability. Similarly, absence of high levels of correlations between EQ and defined elements of writing suggested that objective tests were an inappropriate measure of writing ability. Percival extends the Finlayson study through a reflection on resonances between general-impression scoring (holistic) and the schedule method (trait scoring). Using combined traits, Percival examined the relationship between the general-impression score and the distinct combinations. The relationship among a combination of fluency, effective language, accuracy of composition, and accuracy of spelling was 0.93 for boys and 0.81 for girls. It was not that general-impression scoring was without foundation. Rather, it was that the study had led to a way of systematic identification of the "elements that the marker is most affected by when he makes his assessment by the general impression method" (1966, 211). As was the case with Diederich, French, and Carlton, Percival was more interested in independent-measure reliability concerning traits and general-impression scores than in interrater reliability.

As is the case with most of the UK researchers, Percival was careful to caution readers that the identification of elements did not mean writing instruction was to be made elemental. "Miscellaneous exercises in punctuation, sentence formation, choice of vocabulary, and so on," he wrote, "will not alone produce skill in composition. The final product calls for the integration of these elements, not merely their sticking together. They are ultimately interwoven and they thus form a highly complex product. Part of the skill of teaching composition lies in this action of integration" (1966, 212). Percival had provided one of the first connections between instruction and assessment that emphasized the need for an integration of traits—and that warned readers that limited-response tests worked against instruction so envisioned.

Sixth, and perhaps most notably, 1966 was also the date of the Anglo-American Seminar on the Teaching of English, held at Dartmouth College. According to US composition scholarship, the Dartmouth conference celebrated ideas from Britain on teaching and personal growth, ideas now associated with John Dixon and James Britton. But since the first examinations under the Certificate of Secondary Education had taken place the previous summer, surely there was talk at Dartmouth about Mode 3 under which schools set their own curriculum, examinations, and marking. Since Britton himself was in attendance—there he is in figure 4.1 in the upper left of the photo, smoking his pipe—odds are that US scholars there also heard about the quarter century of British efforts at rapid-impression multiple marking.

Was the emerging transcontinental body of knowledge about writing assessment new to them? If the British preceded the Americans in testing and administering a form of holistic scoring by at least fifteen years, wouldn't Americans have learned about it from the British? That seems an obvious conclusion, but there is an odd silence about the question, on both sides of the Atlantic. This is perhaps so because historical documents settling the issue have yet to come to light. The known evidence is scattered, indirect, and muted. In a study of the Hillegas scale, one of the most popular essay-matching schemes after WWI, US scholars Stephen Witte, Mary Trachsel, and Keith Walters are unusual in stating bluntly that during the first three-quarters of the century generally, Britain took the lead in writing assessment: "Throughout the history of the debates about writing assessment in American educational literature, the published research from England and Scotland has often provided a point of departure for work in this country" (1986, 31–32).[13] We agree, and add that UK leadership applies in particular to pooled-rater holistic scoring of essays.[14]

Figure 4.1. James Britton, published in 1966 (courtesy of Dartmouth College Library)

Without belaboring the point, we note these facts. In what may have been the first US trial of open, pooled holistic scoring, in 1950, Ann F. Coward at ETS replicated Wiseman's study of Devon selection essays that had been published a year earlier: both contrasted holistic and analytic methods, instructed holistic scorers to read rapidly for total merit on a reduced scale with no training or anchor papers, pooled readers' scores, and calculated whether the use of four holistic raters would be equivalent in reliability and cost to analytical scoring. With small variations, this method was repeated for ETS experiments in essay scoring up to and including Godshalk, Swineford, and Coffman's major 1963 study (published in 1966) of the feasibility of holistic essay scoring in large-scale examinations, a research approach that is even more exactly a replication of Wiseman's 1949 study.

In US scholarship the principal names in the British history of rapid-impression multiple marking covered by this chapter are rarely mentioned, but they were known. When Richard Braddock, Richard Lloyd-Jones, and Lowell Schoer were finishing their widely influential survey *Research in Written Communication*, published in 1963, the one British "research specialist" they consulted was Wiseman and, as we have noted, their book took up the Devon method and questioned its claims. Three years later, in *The Measurement of Writing Ability*, Godshalk, Swineford, and Coffman themselves noted that Vernon had "already reached" their conclusion that holistic scoring adds predictability to objective testing (1966, 39), and they cited page numbers from Vernon's *Secondary School Selection* (1957) that summarize Wiseman (1949), Finlayson (1951), John Donald Nisbet (1955), and Edwards Penfold (1956). And even if Vernon's book had not been closely read, in 1957, Vernon himself, supported by a grant from ETS, showed up at Princeton and spent the month of June reading, studying, and discussing "routines of test construction" with ETS's Research and Test Development staff (Vernon 1958, i).[15] More than once it has been asserted that ETS invented holistic scoring, but the evidence is that they did not do so without knowledge of the British precedents. As the years passed, that fact seems to have been lost. The latest clear reference to the British origins we can find dates from 1972, in a footnote buried in an article that discusses ETS's scoring of essays for the first National Assessment of Education Progress in 1969 and 1970. As Henry B. Slotnick writes, "Holistic scoring was used at least ten years before ETS came into existence" on December 19, 1947, and then he cites Cast's 1939 and 1940 studies (1972, 119n11).

He could have cited a US precedent. In 1945, at the University of Chicago, Diederich developed a system of scoring undergraduate essays for course credit, a system that is fully holistic by our definition. But he did not install Robertson and Wiseman's pooled-rater method. Diederich's readers gave an essay a single holistic rate, applied a five-point scale aligned with course grades, referred to model essays rather than a rubric for the scale levels, gave each essay two independent ratings, and required adjustment to resolve an essay that had received anything other than two matching scores. It was a rather laborious method not ever used in Great Britain but, as we will see, easily derived from British precedents, such as the work of Hartog, Rhodes, and Burt. Diederich ran this holistic scoring at the University of Chicago until 1949, when he became employed by ETS. There he may have adapted the system to help shape the College Board's scoring of advanced placement essays, a system—controlled rating with discrepant scores adjusted—that proved one of the most influential types of holistic essay scoring in US history.

The next chapter takes up this story. It was part of an assessment endeavor that never took hold in the United Kingdom: the search for reliable ways to rate essays, using at least two readers, composed by college-bound or college-attending students. These essays, in turn, were scored in the US for writing ability—not for content. To the present day, UK researchers still marvel at the curious intricacies of the US composition industry.

NOTES

1. The work was done for Cast's MA thesis in psychology at University College, London. Her two articles, published in the *British Journal of Educational Psychology*, are often cited, although sometimes as written by a male scholar. Hiding the sex of an author through initials was a beloved protocol in British scholarship before and after WWII. The clearest evidence that Cast was a woman can be found in a footnote of hers: "All the children tested were known to me personally; but I endeavoured to obtain independent character-sketches from the other mistresses in the school" (1940, 57n1). Unguarded lapse or calculated disclosure? Another important student of holistic scoring and contributor to the *British Journal of Educational Psychology*, D. M. Edwards Penfold was also a woman. Even British scholars sometimes cite her as Edward Penfold.
2. Burt's 1921 analytic rubric was sophisticated and influential. The criteria are (1) mechanical, with aspects such as handwriting, spelling, punctuation, grammar, and syntax; (2) literary, with aspects such as appropriateness of information, vocabulary, and rhetorical devices; and (3) logical, with aspects such as organization of ideas, unity, complexity, relevance, and intellectual structure. Maximum points are indicated for each criterion.
3. Amazingly, Finlayson was an undergraduate at the University of Edinburgh when he ran his rigorous and influential study. As it turned out, he was not exactly fond of holistic scoring, by any name, possessing a bent toward the objective. He argues that Wiseman was wrong in saying that pooled holistic testing with a mark-remark reliability of 0.91 was as good as objective testing since objective tests have a mark-remark reliability of "unity," that is, 1.0 (1951, 126–27). In 1955 he published *Clear English*, a school textbook that went through many editions.
4. Ten years later in the United States, in 1966, a team of researchers at the Educational Testing Service—Godshalk, Swineford, and Coffman—will test this issue thoroughly in *The Measurement of Writing Ability*.
5. In a pioneering investigative move, Britton factored marker intercorrelations and located two components that hindered marker agreement. One involved language, some markers favoring "sophisticated and conventional" linguistic forms and others "familiar and honest-sounding (if sometimes slangy) tone of the spoken language of the writers' homes." The other factor involved content, a preference for factual observation over imaginative "flights of fancy into the unreal, the impossible" (1963, 21). Britton was extremely cautious about this factoring, but he need not have been so tentative. Later analysis of holistic scorers in the United States sometimes also found these two factors.
6. Mather, France, and Sare offer a complete content scheme (which they call a "mark schedule") for a CSE reading-comprehension test (1965, 101–3). Test takers are given a paragraph written from the viewpoint of a woman whose husband has been fired. One of many short reading tasks they are set is "Mention three ways in which she proposes to deal with the problems that arise." The marker is supposed to give two points for any three out of the following responses: "Margarine for butter," "Cut down smoking," "Limit children's sweets," "Install slot meter on TV," or "Drink less

milk," for a total of six points. If the test taker provides all five, the candidate still is awarded six points. David Cannadine, Jenny Keating, and Nicola Sheldon (2011) describe a content scheme, much more elaborate, for a contemporary A-level essay question in history.

7. In his exchange with the authors, Paul Newton, research chair at Ofqual, the government department overseeing external examinations in England, underscores Wiseman's comment in 1949 that "local education authorities are extremely reluctant to include 'composition' among the examination papers used for grammar school selection at eleven plus" (200). Newton writes, "My hunch is that the use of composition examinations simply dwindled over time," that "Wiseman and co. were just fighting a losing battle with respect to the inclusion of composition in 11+ tests" (email to authors, January 1, 2018). Maybe at core, educators in Great Britain have never felt an all-compelling reason to test writing skills (as separate from content knowledge) with an essay. The exception, of course, is for students writing English as a second language.

8. All along, objective-item testing retained, even increased, its hold on 11-plus examining. The portion of such examinations that used intelligence and verbal reasoning items rose from 74 percent in 1946 to 95 percent in 1968. Standardized testing in arithmetic and English rose from 43 percent in 1946 to 81 percent in 1960, although it declined back around to the earlier portion by 1968 (Gipps et al. 1983). However, it is important to note that multiple-choice testing of writing ability never caught on in the United Kingdom as it did in the United States. Indeed, as Wooldridge notes, in the 1950s sociologists begin systematically making cases against IQ tests—ever reliant on multiple-choice responses. Among all forms of construed response tests, multiple-choice items remain the object of skepticism throughout the history of UK writing assessment.

9. Some Local Education Authorities, especially in northern England, maintained grammar schools and 11-plus selection. The act forbid selection in new schools but did not rescind it in existing schools.

10. Alastair Pollitt reflects that after Margaret Thatcher was appointed Secretary of State for Education and Science in 1970, "trust in the judgement of professionals was undermined: for us it meant rapid increases in appeals against exam results by disappointed students and their parents. The only defense was careful adherence to 'due process' and an audit trail to back it up" (email to authors, February 19, 2018).

11. The proprietary nature of testing erects barriers for historians of assessment. In 1982, Mike Hayhoe, lecturer in the School of Education at the University of East Anglia and an advocate of unearthing the history of marking methods, lamented that "Boards, Panels, and Mode III schemes have their various documents outlining what is to be valued in assessing 'essays' in English, often suggesting in which mark band particular levels of ability in particular features should appear. Some of these schemes are public: some are not" (103).

12. In 1916, Alfred North Whitehead argued that teacher knowledge was part of an essential element of education that external examinations neglect, "namely the genius of the teacher, the intellectual type of the pupils, their prospects in life, the opportunities offered by the immediate surroundings of the school, and allied factors of this sort. It is for this reason that the uniform external examination is so deadly." This element is "the best part of culture," said Whitehead, and only teachers are able to judge it ([1916] 1948, 113).

13. Before World War II, scholarly exchange between the United States and the United Kingdom was possibly more common than after. The Harvard University Commission on English, for instance, which in 1931 published a study of the validity and reliability of College Entrance Examination Board essay testing, includes a number

of British studies in their bibliography, including Hartog's 1918 study and several reports from the London Board of Education. But that was too early for formal holistic scoring.

14. In their reflective history of the Dartmouth Conference, Cinthia Gannett and John C. Brereton write the following: "The Dartmouth Conference represented a serious effort to connect US and UK teachers across the K–16 levels to create a coherent, unified, and well-sequenced language arts curriculum." Readers are encouraged to consult Gannett and Brereton's account of the conference and its impact on these two historians.

15. In the research report Vernon (1958) wrote for ETS, at the end of his stay at Princeton, he summarizes Wiseman (1956) and Vernon and Millican (1954) and concludes that "there would seem to be ample justification for continued employment of the essay in predictive examinations, even if it is marked only among borderline candidates, or if scaled gradings derived from writing done in schools are substituted for a formal composition examination" (47). He is referring, of course, to Robertson and Wiseman's strategy with border-zone students in Devon and to the use of coursework for external testing as later put into place with the Certificate of Secondary Education's Mode 3 option.

5
PAUL B. DIEDERICH AND AP HOLISTIC SCORING IN THE UNITED STATES, 1954–1980

Paul B. Diederich, the dean of evaluators in the field of English.
—James Gray, *Teachers at the Center*

In the United States there has long been a perceived conflict of interest between the College Board, founded in 1900, and the schools and colleges. Yet from the beginning they were joined at the hip (Elliot 2005, 22–29; Fuess 1950). College Board personnel often began their careers as teachers, and teacher oversight boards reviewed writing tests within the organization. This symbiosis did not change with the advent of holistic scoring. Following the charter of the Educational Testing Service in 1947 by the state of New York, scoring run by ETS always used current teachers as raters, and local testing and independent research often relied on ETS experts, materials, and capabilities (Elliot 2014). The English Equivalency Examination of California State University and Colleges (1973–1981), for instance, was a shared examination from beginning to end (Haswell and Elliot 2017). Yet when Paul B. Diederich left his position at the University of Chicago following his 1949 recruitment by ETS President Henry Chauncey, the classics scholar felt a need to disillusion his fellow university colleagues who thought Diederich was jumping fence and "selling out to the enemy" (Hampel 2014, 110). Yet, as Sydell T. Carlton told us in our July 2, 2014, interview, Diederich never fit in at ETS. He did his own mimeographing and worked alone in the research division housed in Upper Pine, a former university dormitory—away from the administrative offices at 20 Nassau Street in Princeton and test development located in the Princeton Shopping Center.

With a focus on the contributions of two colleagues, this chapter and the next explore the origins of methods the College Board and ETS used to holistically score student essays. As we show, these methods were, at the start, deeply influenced by independent faculty who were already supervising innovative language-testing programs at two universities. Chapter 6 narrates the role Osmond E. Palmer at Michigan State University, a colleague of Diederich's, played in the studies ETS conducted to develop its English Composition Test. While these ETS studies may not have turned out as Palmer wished, his role was important. His were the studies that influenced *The Measurement of Writing Abilities* (Godshalk, Swineford, and Coffman 1966), often cited and popularly believed to be the origin of holistic scoring. Continuing the argument raised in chapter 3 demonstrating the origin of holistic scoring in the UK work of Philip Joseph Hartog, Edmond Cecil Rhodes, and Cyril L. Burt (1936), the present chapter further disputes the 1966 origin date with another history, although an interrelated one, suggesting an earlier US origin. As we show in this chapter, a reasonable date for the first formal application of holistic scoring in the United States is Diederich's program of testing and scoring undergraduate essay writing at the University of Chicago, begun in 1943. That program can also claim direct connections with the College Board's longest adventure in holistic scoring, the Advanced Placement (AP) Program, begun in 1954.

DIEDERICH AT THE UNIVERSITY OF CHICAGO: 1942–1949

More than two decades after the fact, James Gray recollected a story that Michael Scriven had told him about Diederich. Back in 1978, Gray was helping direct the Bay Area Writing Project at Berkeley, Scriven was teaching philosophy of evaluation at Berkeley and had been hired to review the project, and Diederich—Gray calls him "the dean of evaluators in the field of English"—was being considered as an outside reviewer.

> Scriven had immense regard for Paul Diederich. He told us a number of stories about what Paul had accomplished. One such story has Paul solving a major problem when the Educational Testing Service brought a number of university faculty and classroom teachers together to score the first College Board writing samples. The papers were handed out, and the scorers began to read and mark them up the same way they had always done when grading student papers. It didn't take long before everyone knew that this wasn't going to work. If they'd kept at it that way, the scorers would still be there. So, as the story goes, Paul Diederich launched holistic scoring, a one-to-five ranking of papers, based on certain criteria agreed upon among the scorers. (2000, 111–12)

No historian would want to rely on a third-hand story. But in this case, all the historical evidence suggests Gray's tale gets the basic facts right. In 1954, when the College Board took up anew the scoring of student essays

Figure 5.1. Paul B. Diederich, 1969 (courtesy of The Ohio State University)

for advanced standing in composition and literature, through their Advanced Placement Program, they fairly soon settled on a method that does deserve the name *holistic*, and initially Diederich did have a hand in it. The only claim we surely dispute in Gray's story is that Diederich "launched" holistic scoring in 1954. In fact, he had launched it, at least on US soil, ten years earlier at the University of Chicago. That will be our story.

We begin on January 22, 1942, less than two months after the United States entered World War II. Faculty at the University of Chicago voted to allow the College to enter a new and even more radical phase of its New Plan. The College was the undergraduate unit of the University, with an entering enrollment of around 500 students and an attraction to the structure of European universities. The New Plan had been established in 1931 by Robert Maynard Hutchins, president from 1929 to 1945, and Chauncey S. Boucher, dean of the College. Entering students were required to take five three-quarter basic-education courses during their first two years. Attendance was not required and course grade was determined solely by performance on a final examination—a Comprehensive—read and graded not by the teacher but by examiners on a Board of Examinations. One of these five required courses was English composition.

In 1942 the New Plan entered an untraveled and volatile phase. This novel course of study allowed completion of a BA degree by the end of a student's sophomore year, at least on paper. The basic-education curriculum was expanded from five to fourteen three-quarter courses. Each still had its Comprehensive, which a student could take, retake, or challenge at any time. It was a curriculum dependent on testing—with entrance, placement, scholarship, advance credit, the Comprehensive, and other kinds of examinations. In his history of education at the University of Chicago, John W. Boyer (2011) recalls that Ralph Tyler, chair of the Department of the Board of Examiners in 1942, boasted in 1950 that "the results of the Examinations together with the Placement Tests are the sole criteria in the College for awarding the Bachelor's Degree. At the time of entrance, the student's performance on the Placement Tests determines what Comprehensive Examinations he must pass in order to receive his degree" (126).

Universities around the nation were dismayed by Hutchins's New Plan, some refusing to accept its BA. Today the experiment still astonishes. It facilitated advanced credit, individual study, course challenges, and course standards imposed by someone other than the teacher of credit. It radically shortened time to degree. Its curricular plan actually implemented the ideals of competency-based education promoted twenty years later by those same universities, most of whom even then were unable to materialize those ideals.

One of the most astonishing feats of the Chicago New Plan took a couple of years, a change in the English composition Comprehensive. The person responsible was Diederich. Only much later did Diederich attract the sobriquet of "dean of evaluators in the field of English," and when Tyler hired him in 1942, he was best known as an innovator in the teaching of Latin to school students. Tyler, however, already knew firsthand Diederich's potential as an original thinker when it came to testing.

No doubt because of the new expansion of basic courses, Diederich was hired half-time to construct placement tests in reading and writing, to teach the remedial reading and writing course, and to oversee the Comprehensive Examination in English. For the other half of his time, he was employed by the military to construct General Educational Development (GED) tests and admissions examinations for officer training school—a time during which he acquired a deep understanding of item testing for proficiency in writing. Tyler always had brilliant insight into personnel. In fact, Diederich had worked for him earlier. His dissertation in Classics at Columbia University unfinished, Diederich had taught Latin for three years at The Ohio State University's laboratory school, then spent four years on the research staff of the Eight Year Study of students sponsored by the Progressive Education Association from 1933 to 1941. Tyler was part of a team investigating curricular reform in secondary schools, and Diederich's association with Tyler allowed in-depth exposure to innovative educational theory and state-of-the-art evaluation methodologies. Association with Tyler cannot be underestimated. He influenced the greatest minds of a generation, including Bruno Bettelheim, Peter Blos, Oscar Buros, Louis E. Raths, and Hilda Taba (Kridel and Bullough 2007, 78). Diederich finished his dissertation in 1939 and published it the same year with the University of Chicago Press. After a year of postdoctorate study at Harvard, occasionally assisting I. A. Richards in translating Plato's *Republic* into basic English, Diederich found himself working in Tyler's Department of the Board of Examiners at the University of Chicago.

What he saw was not entirely to his liking. Comprehensive examinations were written by a small number of people on the board, who constantly had to run to the instructors of the courses for ideas. Four years later, in a memorandum to Tyler, Diederich (1946c) suggested expanding the board by creating a staff examiner for each Comprehensive Examination in English.

> After all I had heard about the comprehensive examination system at the University of Chicago, it was a great shock to me to find that it was run by three or four young part-time men, most of whom spent the bulk of their time teaching. In such a set-up it was inevitable that they should act as messenger-boys in the production of more examinations than they could possibly handle. If we really mean to produce examinations, we cannot continue with our present skeleton force. If we want to talk big, we have to get big. (3)[1]

Newly arrived in 1942, however, he tended to his own garden: the evaluative methodologies informing the comprehensive examination program.

He found a test lacking in writer reliability. During the last week of the third term of the first-year writing course (English 3), all students gathered in an examination hall to choose a topic and to write an essay. Diederich knew from experience and from previous research that such a grading method was hard to defend (Cast 1940; Lang 1930). Depending upon time, topic, and mood, a student will show quite different proficiencies in writing impromptu essays. What Diederich did then became a habit in his career. He ran a study. Along with Diederich, John W. French, and Sydell T. Carleton (1961) and Godshalk, Swineford, and Coffman (1961, 1966), the study would become one of the three most influential experiments in the history of holistic scoring in the United States.[2]

Under Diederich's direction, for the 1943 end-of-course Comprehensive Examination testing, English 3 students wrote three essays, each a week apart and three hours long. Students had no choice of topic, but each topic was based on a common set of materials made available to students a week before the testing. Topics were within the students' grasp, neither too easy nor too difficult, and they called for familiar discursive forms such as explanation or persuasive argument. (Were topics rotated even among testing episodes, and did each essay have two independent readings? Diederich does not say.) Afterward, the marks on the first essay were correlated with the mean of the first and second essay marks, and then correlated with the mean of all three essay marks. The findings supported Diederich's concern with the instability of student writing. As a result of the second essay, the marks for a quarter of the students shifted at least one letter grade, up or down. The third essay, however, altered their grade less than 5 percent of the time (Diederich 1946b, 586–87). This experiment helped determine the method followed by Diederich's subsequent Comprehensive scoring during his remaining years at the College, from 1944 to 1949.

For the Comprehensive Examination that Diederich redesigned, students wrote two three-hour essays, one from 9:00 to 12:00 in the morning and the other from 2:00 to 5:00 in the afternoon of the same day. Students had no choice in topic, but the test topics were based on materials provided them three weeks in advance. Over the years, outcomes supported Diederich's concern with writer reliability. "In spite of the most careful marking, which will be described later, the mark on the first essay has never attained a correlation higher than 0.55 with the mark on the second" (1946b, 587).[3]

Diederich describes what he means by "most careful marking" (1946b, 587). By way of training, raters, all of them teachers of the English course, were reminded of criteria embedded in the course, and then they marked and openly discussed the same four or five sample papers. The scale was five points, with points referenced to course grade. Then, without recourse to a scoring guide, each paper was scored independently twice—assigning a single mark, not marks on separate traits—and if the scores did not match exactly, the two graders consulted and settled on one. The final mark was the sum of the scores for the student's two essays. Finally, two examiners from the board, the English examiner (Diederich) and the Chief Examiner (Tyler), pondered the distribution of summed marks and determined cutoffs for final course grade. This system was kept up through 1949, as long as Diederich ran it.[4]

Think of the Comprehensive's functioning within Hutchins's New Plan as an additional feature of innovation. A Qualifying Examination consisted of both objective questions and an essay read by a Board of Examinations. The examination placed students within the required first-year English sequence or gave them full credit for the course. A basic reading and writing course was one possible placement, but on teacher recommendation, students could switch to the regular course at any time. Also, at any time, students could challenge the three-quarter composition requirement by taking the Comprehensive Examination in English. If students stayed in the course, they would still have to take the examination, which determined their grade. Teachers of the course followed a common syllabus and had a staff meeting every week, and they gave students a quarterly grade, but the final grade was determined solely by performance on the English Comprehensive. Therefore, teachers operated as coaches and used old Comprehensives for guidance.[5]

Graders of the Comprehensive Examination in English were required to teach at least one section of the course. Criteria for judging Comprehensive essays were accepted by teachers and taught in the course. Students taking the Comprehensive had materials to read well before the examination, wrote two essays, and with each had three hours to plan, write, and revise (three hours!). The comprehensive grade was determined by two independent readings of each essay, and discrepant marks were resolved by mutual consultation between the readers, sometimes with input from the chief English examiner. The teacher of a student could challenge the Comprehensive outcome, although, as Diederich recorded, "The experience of readers at the University of Chicago indicates that not more than one mark in ten will be challenged and that four out of five of these marks will be accepted as fair by the teachers who challenged them, after they have seen the papers" (1946b, 591). Finally, students could retake the Comprehensive any year afterward, and the fee for doing so would be reimbursed should they improve on their original grade.

Another way to compare the quality of this testing of first-year writing might be to look at the old questions for the Comprehensive Examination in English. One is provided by Diederich in a chapter he coauthored with Benjamin Bloom and Jane M. Allison in *The Idea and Practice of General Education: An Account of the College of The University of Chicago* (Bloom, Allison, and Diederich 1950). Three weeks in advance, students knew the theme would be private property and were given a handout of extended passages from the following works: Plato's *Republic*,

Aristotle's *Politics*, Locke's *Second Treatise on Civil Government*, Marx and Engels's *The Communist Manifesto*, William Sumner's *The Challenge of the Facts*, R. H. Tawney's *The Acquisitive Society*, and Pope Pius XI's *Quadragesimo Anno*. On the day of the examination, the question turned out to be a prompt: "Write a unified paper on some restricted aspect of the question of the future of private property in America." A page of "stipulations" followed. Among them were the obligation to write a "pro and con argument," the advice to spend half an hour planning and an equal time revising, and the permission to consult the passages and personal notes on the passages (303–4). A ready conclusion from this example is that during and after WWII, the art of topic writing in the United States does not exactly follow a trajectory of steady progress.

One must consider, of course, the singular genius of Diederich. He seemed always a step ahead of his associates, or at least a step to one side or another. As far as we know, there is no exact historical precedent for his method of scoring English Comprehensive essays at the University of Chicago. Elements of it had been tried, recommended, or imagined, such as drawing more than one writing sample from a student, discussion by raters of sample papers, scoring based on select criteria agreed upon in advance, rating with a single mark on general impression rather than with multiple marks on analytic breakdown, employment of teaching staff as readers, assessment of each essay by two independent readings, adjustment of nonexact scores. But the combination was historically novel. So was the unbroken use of the method in a large-scale examination over several years (not to speak of its regeneration for an even longer run in an even larger examination, in scoring the AP English essays). The only comparison is with R. K. Robertson's method of scoring applied to 11-plus essays in Devon from 1939 to 1949. Yet Diederich would not have known about that system in 1944 since an account of it was not published until 1949 by Stephen Wiseman. In addition, Robertson and Wiseman relied on the radically different system of pooled scoring.

It would be too easy, however, to propose independent births of holistic scoring, one in the United Kingdom and one in the United States. That would disregard the long history of general-impression scoring before World War II, a history at least partially known to scholars such as Wiseman and Diederich. For instance, from Diederich's work in school assessment with Tyler, he surely would have been familiar with the ground-breaking 1936 study of holistic scoring published by Philip Joseph Hartog, Edmond Cecil Rhodes, and Cyril L. Burt. That famous book emerged from the International Conference on Examinations held in May 1931, in which the United States participated, and the holistic procedure described in it follows technics Diederich later preferred: use of accomplished teachers who needed little training, initial sorting of essays into five piles (which reflect academic grades), and assigned marks to approximate a normal curve (discussed in chapter 3 of this text).

It is of some curiosity that Robertson's and Diederich's methods of holistic scoring first materialized during the war. Is there something that occurs during time of war—risk taking—that would have fueled experimental holistic scoring? With Robertson in Devon, the sudden influx of blitz children might have encouraged the development of a novel method fit for processing large numbers of essays. But such was not the case at Chicago. Hutchins's New Plan was fully conceived before Pearl Harbor, although that event might have swayed some faculty when they voted it in on January 22, 1942. According to John W. Boyer, "The crisis occasioned by the coming of the Second World War in late 1941 provided the final impetus for the implementation" of the plan (2011, 123). Perhaps some faculty thought the plan's shortening of time to degree might accelerate the enrollment of qualified officers into the military. Diederich's holistic scoring was launched in May of 1942, with the United States fully at war. April and May had seen the Battle of the Coral Sea, the surrender of General Wainwright to the Japanese in the Philippines, the first tentative successes by the Soviet army over the invading Germans, and the first saturation bombing conducted by the Allies, on Cologne. Yet it is hard to see direct connections. Perhaps there was an undercurrent of feeling that in time of war new measures were called for, or at least novel measures could be risked.

Certainly, the war helped keep Diederich's accomplishment at Chicago from receiving the scholarly notice it was due, at least at the time. But it doesn't explain the inattention to his scoring feat since, a lack of notice even among US scholars preoccupied with the evaluation of writing proficiency. An answer may lie in the shaky interface between assessment scholarship and Diederich's personality. From habit, belief, and personal history, Diederich almost always chose teachers as his primary audience. This choice can be seen in the style of his publications, even those reporting the empirical investigations he loved to conduct: minimal citation of sources, lack of footnotes, and little mention to the elements of experimental design such as parameters, protocols, full data array, and inferential statistics—even when he had utilized all of these. We have called his report of the 1943 experiment with the redesigned Comprehensive Examination in English (Diederich 1946b) one of the most influential documents in the history of holistic scoring, but the influence is tacit, with little or no scholarly notice. Diederich published it with no statistical trappings in the *School Review*, a publication sponsored by the University of Chicago and designed mainly for school teachers.[6]

Diederich's singular genius deserves closer examination. Today he is chiefly known for his analytic approach to evaluating essays—in particular his factor analysis of essay-reader commentary (Diederich, French, and Carlton 1961), his analytic scale for rating school essays (1966), and his writing assessment handbook (1974). Forgotten, or overlooked, is his interest in systematic evidence gathering—no doubt influenced by his work as an early career scholar with Tyler. Seen comparatively, Diederich's Comprehensive Examination in English might be assumed elemental. But, in fact, it surpasses in evidence of construct validity, interrater reliability, and implied fairness many tests of undergraduate "writing proficiency"—holistic or otherwise—given later, even given at the present writing, by many. By our definition, his method is classified as formal holistic scoring, and, by our count, it existed more than seventeen years before the 1966 publication of *The Measurement of Writing Ability*.

As we discuss in chapter 6, Diederich's was the first empirically derived model of the variables, or factors, of writing ability, and his research standards were high. He was brutally honest when his own research did not meet minimal levels of interrater reliability. This commitment to research integrity was exemplified in his extended discussion of bias recollected in *Measuring Growth in English* (1974). With ETS colleague Benjamin Rosner, Diederich had conducted (but not published) an experiment in which teachers were asked to grade papers that had been marked as from either honors or regular students. Rosner had, however, deliberately altered the information so the opposite group had actually written the papers. The result was that, even though the papers were from traditional students, the papers were marked honors and averaged almost one grade point higher that they should have been (based on alternative marking with correct identification). With emphasis on anonymization, we find here an early discussion of bias in writing assessment as "the influence on grades of irrelevant considerations such as liking or disliking the student, disagreement with his views, etc." (99).

Forgotten also is the fact that he was never committed solely to the analytic approach. Of all early writing-evaluation specialists, he was the most eclectic. His one standing commitment was to fit an evaluation scheme to a particular testing environment. As Carlton told us in our July 2, 2014, interview with her, her colleague was devoted more to "making students' lives richer" than to validating tests for their own sake.

So when Diederich needed to construct a valid criterion variable for his study of reader commentary, he had fifty-three readers independently rank 300 essays, and then he pooled their rankings. When he needed a scheme to measure the often-uneven improvement of school essays from year to year, applied by teachers with a weak sense of group criteria or standards, he created an analytic scale of six criteria scored separately. When in Chicago he had a cohesive teaching staff who had internalized a common set of criteria, he created a holistic scoring method on a 5 to 1 scale referenced to an A to F grading tradition, with teachers as readers and two independent readings to account for natural variability in individual perspective found in any corps of teachers no matter how unified. When he taught lay readers, who had little inside experience with the high-school English program for which they were grading student papers, he gave the teachers model essays with ideal commentary representing minimum A, B, C, and D levels (Diederich 1960). "These papers not only served as a guide for grading but suggested also the sort of comment the [lay] reader might make upon a paper" (Palmer 1961, 210). When he imagined a British Subject-A examination in literature, with thousands of candidates needing a rapid turnaround, he placed his bet on a machine-scored test over an essay test: "It will be one of those classic contests: the tailor against the sewing machine, the abacus against the computer, our own tall-tale John Henry against the pneumatic drill" (Diederich 1965b, 150). And in his imagined school profile system, which would over the years accumulate a folder of a student's work, for an example of the student's composing proficiency he would have the teacher copy an essay with comments and grades and attach to it a standard sheet of "values" the school set as its main curricular objectives, with each value scored by the teacher on a Likert scale indicating the degree to which the paper had met that objective (Diederich 1949a). Diederich—polymath, iconoclast, pioneer—could never be pinned down, nor did he wish students, teachers, or evaluators to be pinned to a universal scoring method.[7]

Although he never articulated the idea in print, Diederich's essay-scoring spectrum hints at an inverse relationship between scorer group and criterion specification. A scoring team strong in solidarity and in internalization of writing standards and proficiency levels can handle a method weak in explicit trait guidelines. Community, he inferred, is the key to writing assessment. In the case of Diederich's Chicago teaching staff, all that was needed was a brief reminder of criteria and a discussion of sample papers and the instructors could grade reliably without any printed rubric or scoring sheet. In the case of Diederich's diverse set of school English teachers, a group fixed in their individual teaching ways, they may need an analytical scale with preset traits in order to score student essays for demonstration of curricular improvement. As our history of holistic scoring unfolds, we will see this inverse relationship between group cohesion and trait specificity help explain choices made of essay-scoring method, choices both wise and unwise.

ADVANCED PLACEMENT SCORING OF ENGLISH ESSAYS: 1954–1980

It shouldn't surprise that not long after Diedrich left Chicago for ETS in 1949, he applied his old English Comprehensive scoring method to the College Board's assessment of English essays in the Advanced Placement Program.[8] For once again he had a community of readers who were teachers of the same courses with a common set of writing standards. With Advanced-Placement English essays, Diederich may have played a part in starting up one of the three major strains of early holistic scoring in the United States. The AP method was possibly the kind of holistic essay scoring most often adopted and adapted by schools and colleges. Yet this AP history has never been told.

First, however, a regret. Our narrative of AP scoring of English essays 1954–1980 will take on a scant and ragged mien, for two reasons. The history itself is ragged, with aspects of the College Board's scoring protocol changing nearly every year it seems. We say *seems* because of the second reason. Despite all our efforts, the College Board could not find or would not find for us archival documents relevant to this history of AP scoring, offering only its own widely available 1980 reminiscence, *An Informal History of the AP Readings, 1956–76*. For most years up to 1980, we were not able to see questions, criteria, scoring guides, rater instructions, or calculations of rater reliability. We know ETS statistician Frances Swineford (1956a) wrote a report of the AP scoring every year beginning in 1954, including estimates of rater reliability, but the College Board has now lost, misplaced, or sealed those reports.[9] So our account is based largely on outsider records. This outsider approach is a pity since during the years our history covers,

AP-style holistic scoring of essays played a predominant role in spreading the holistic news.

The College Board's Advanced Placement Program bridged an articulated high-school and college curriculum. High-school teachers taught AP courses that prepared students for AP examinations that could qualify them for advance placement or credit in first-year courses at the college of their choice. The AP curriculum and testing included US history, biology, chemistry, European history, French, German, Latin, literature, mathematics, physics, Spanish—and English, in which literature and composition were not scored separately at first (Elliot 2005, 152–55). The relative novelty of this school-examination-college articulation may help explain why the early history of the bridge in the middle—the AP examination series—was so tentative and changeful, sometimes almost comic, sometimes like a person looking for lost keys under a street lamp because the light is better there.

Chosen to score the English essays were high-school teachers of AP English and college teachers of the courses impacted by the advance standing. So, if Diederich was called to rescue the English-essay scorers, as Scriven claimed, what would he have found? Using the 1980 reminiscence, we can put together a possible scenario.

If Diederich arrived for the reading in 1956, he would have driven a short distance, or walked, to Westminster Choir College in Princeton. Overall, there were eighty readers there to score 2,199 examinations. Essays on English (an examination on written composition) and literature (an examination on textual critique) would have been scored in two rooms. But this was the first AP reading, and something had gone horribly wrong. Each group of readers had decided its own grading scale, with 3 at the low end and 100 at the high end and maximum scores ranging from 24 to 3,000. There was chaos. John R. Valley, the first ETS program director for Advanced Placement, was called in to manage the situation. Did he call on Diederich? We will never know, but the solution certainly has the stamp of his approach. A fifteen-point scale was developed and is recorded in *An Informal History of the AP Readings, 1956–76*:

15-14-13 Demonstrates superiority or mastery

12-11-10 Demonstrates competence

9-8-7 Suggests competence

6-5-4 Suggests incompetence

3-2-1 Demonstrates incompetence (12)

In addition, a zero was added to the scale that could be used if a student gave no answer or was off topic. Reasonably, it appears that Diederich installed the essay-scoring system he had used for years at Chicago, with a similar set of faculty teaching within a well-articulated curriculum. Essentially, a five-point scale was set, papers illustrating the scale were read and discussed, criteria were chosen and reviewed, and then examination essays were rated without a printed scoring sheet. The composition essays were rated twice, independently. Table leaders checked individual raters occasionally for consistency. The method qualifies as holistic, and it remained so over the decades.

When did the nine-point scale used today arise? The 1980 report tells us that, as of 1976, three scoring scales for the essay question were in operation: 1 to 15, 1 to 9, and 1 to 4. So, sometime before 1976, a nine-point scale was installed, with model essays providing prototypes for points 2, 4, 6, and 8. The parent of AP's nine-point scale may have been Diederich, French, and Carlton's study of 1960, published in 1961. Each of their fifty-three readers simply sorted their 300 papers into nine piles, 1 to 9, on an intuition of ascending "general merit." Apparently, Diederich soon recommended the system to rate school papers in an experiment in contrasting pedagogies (Hays 1962, 322). That study used three readers for the College Board's English Composition Test, which was Frederick I. Godshalk's bailiwick, and we soon see Godshalk testing the nine-point scale in another experiment, Ross M. Jewell, John Cowley, and Gordon Rhum's study of the influence of first-year writing on subsequent undergraduate writing proficiency. Godshalk had his readers first imagine their set of sample papers on a normal curve divided into quartiles: "much below average, below average, above average, much above average" (Jewell, Cowley, and Rhum 1966, 19). They then converted this four-point scale (which they were accustomed to in English Composition Test scoring) to scores of 2, 4, 6, and 8. As Godshalk explains in his description of scoring for a Foreign Service Examination in English officer test at Berkeley in December 1965, "The odd numbers are to be used infrequently in cases where the paper just misses a score—little better or little worse" (1966, 4). From these "operational" trials, Godshalk surmised readers preferred the nine-point scale "because they 'feel' that it gives greater scope for discriminating judgment and is more 'comfortable' as well" (1967, 87).

We can't be sure this is how it happened, but this narrative represents our best assembly of chronology based on archived reports and our knowledge of the way Diederich approached large-scale assessment.

CLASSROOM IMPACT AND ENDURING CHALLENGES

The nine-point holistic scale proved unusually contagious, with AP scorers taking it back to their classrooms, schools, or districts. Teacher-raters found it easy to divide a set of papers in half, then each half in half, then move a paper up or down a point depending upon certain features. Figure 5.2 illustrates such an adapted decision guide used by Catharine Keech of the Bay Area Writing Project. The exact origin is unknown—Keech used the illustration without attribution—but perhaps it was taken from a local school assessment.

The image is remarkable in its combination of scale use and decision making. Note that only on the third decision, following deliberation, does the rater assign one of nine points for final assessment of the paper's worth. Note also the criteria, probably established by reading a sample of the papers: voice, ideas, details, freshness, organization, interest. Also note the AP mantra: "Reward what the writer does well."

The nine-point scale, however, did not solve a weakness in previous holistic scales used in AP scoring, and that was interrater reliability. In Diederich, French, and Carlton's study (1961), the average one-reader correlation was 0.31. When Godshalk's ETS readers had applied his nine-point scale in Jewell, Cowley, and Rhum's study (1966), the researchers had required each essay to be read twice, and the interrater reliability coefficients—at least the only two of 0.18 and 0.22 they reported in their final report—were so weak that eventually critics used them to help dismiss the entire study (e.g., McColly 1970, 73). It seems that earlier AP scales had had not much better luck, at least judging from the two Swineford reports on the scales we were able to consult. We know that in 1956 she found that three sections of the English examination and one section of literature were "rather difficult to read reliably" (1956a, 6). This claim is based on correlations ranging from 0.36 to 0.40 on the English sections and .39 on the literature—low correlation coefficients indeed. In the second report, published in 1964, she had 200 essays read twice from the English examination. Two scales were examined: a four-point scale and a fifteen-point scale. For the four-point scale, the correlation between readers was 0.39. On the fifteen-point scale, the correlations ranged from 0.25 to 0.33. The reading reliability featured in the principal findings, 0.74, is not the actual interrater reliability coefficient but, rather, an estimate based on composite score variance. As would be the case in the 1966 study discussed in chapter 6, the actual interrater correlations were remarkably low, yet the featured correlations, always high, were derived from estimation procedures extending beyond the less flattering Pearson correlations.

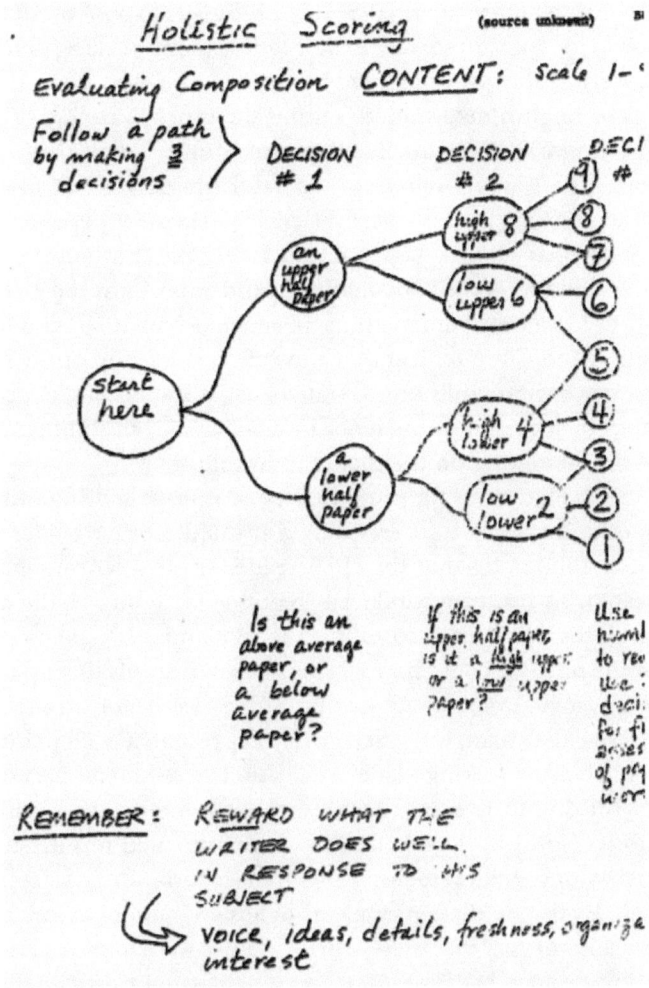

Figure 5.2. Example of an AP-style decision scoring guide (Keech 1979, B8) (courtesy of the National Writing Project)

For years, it seems, AP rater correlations were calculated only on a random sample of the scores. In 1956 the two independent composition scores were still just pooled, but when third-party adjustment of discrepant scores began is hard to say. Other vagaries are also difficult to date. Early on, some examination essays were scored by only one person. When were all essays read by two independent readers? The report *An Informal History of the AP Readings, 1956–76* (Advanced Placement Program 1980) suggests 1972, when intrarater checks were also introduced.[10] Certainly by 1979, because James Vopat (1981), in his caustic exposé of AP English ratings, says he then observed exhausted readers peeking under the sticker covering the previous reader's score. And how were the final cut scores in English determined, setting the crucial ranking of 5–high honors, 4–honors, 3–creditable, 2–passing, and 1–fail that colleges used to assign advanced standing? And did the percent of passing or better change over time? Gerhard Friedrich reports 9 percent in 1957 (1959); and Vopat reports 97 percent in 1980 (1981), when the 2 score was now defined as "possibly qualified." And what were the criteria or standards used to determine writing proficiency? In 1959, at a College Composition and Communication Convention workshop on AP composition scoring, Friedrich listed substance, organization, logic, precision and fluency of style, and proficiency in mechanics, but did that change year by year depending on the model essays chosen?

And, most relevant to the early history of holistic scoring, when did AP composition scorers start receiving a printed scoring guide? An AP report from 1967 notes that the chief reader wrote a scoring guide for each question so his team would be "reading according to the agreed-upon standards, and not according to local standards" (Jamison 2015, 144), but the practice could have started earlier. It seems that up to 1980, the criteria (standards) in AP scoring guides were not arranged in a regular table-like format, with each criterion present at each point in the scale, as in a holistic scoring guide. Again, we can see the impact of these guides by turning to Keech (1979b) and her reference to a classroom-based rubric shown in figure 5.2. The guide was used to rate students, essays for writing achievement. Note that criteria are not consistent across scale levels. So "diction" appears at level 8, but not at lower levels.

Historically, the fact that these scoring guides were used in classrooms acquires importance because it was the schematized rubric that gained sway in US holistic scoring after 1980 that helped undermine holistic scoring's theoretical base in gestalt perception, and that eventually attracted some of the most telling negative critique of "holistic" scoring practices (e.g., Wilson 2006). For years, however, that tendency was counterbalanced by the popularity of AP-style scoring guides, among National Writing Project teachers and assessors for instance, as chapter 8 documents.

The AP examination system was contagious. Enrollment in the English examinations grew exponentially, from less than 200 in 1954, to around 2,000 in 1958, to around 48,000 in 1980. With three essays to rate from each English examinee, by 1960 some eighty readers were needed. At the annual AP readings or at regional conferences on

Following is the set of criteria for judging student papers written this year for our annual (first) writing sample. Please do your best to avoid thinking in past ways when you are reading the paper — read for the stated criteria only.

The reading should be done holistically, and fast. Score the papers from 2(low) to 8(high) with the possibility of adding one (1) bonus point or subtracting one (1) penalty point.

Criteria:

8   The paper represents the top 25% of all papers in this sampling. It has:

   paragraphing
   varied sentence structure
   movement from generalization to concreteness
   transitions
   unity
   organization: beginning, middle, and an end
   freedom from serious mechanical errors
   apt diction

6   The paper is in the upper half of all papers in this collection. It has:

   paragraphs
   complete sentences, but they may not vary much
   a topic that is developed
   pedesttian ideas or mode of presentation
   mechanical errors to some degree

4   This paper is in the bottom half of all papers in this set. It has:

   some plan of organization, but not necessarily involving paragraphs
   the topic stated clearly
   problems with clarity, especially concerning specific language
   ordinary ideas, even for a high school student
   frequent reference problems

2   This paper represents the bottom 25% of papers in this set. It has:

   no apparent plan of organization
   incoherent sentences
   brevity which is not the soul of wit, or uncontrolled ramblings
   limited vocabulary
   gross mechanical errors

Add a bonus point of 1 for complexity of idea
Subtract a penalty point of 1 for distracting mechanical errors
Automatically reject: A. illegible papers
                       B. Papers that do not deal with the topic

Figure 5.3. Example of an AP-style rubric guide, Encina High School, October 4, 1977, Encina, California (Keech 1979, B4) (courtesy of the National Writing Project)

the AP curriculum sponsored by the College Board, new colleagues shook hands, made plans, and returned to their classrooms informed and enthused. By 1980, a number of people later influential in writing assessment, nationwide or at their own institutions, had received their introduction to holistic scoring at AP readings and/or worked as question or table leaders: Robert C. Albrecht, William Carpenter, Peter Elbow, James Frey, Gerhard Friedrich, Reginald Hannaford, Wendell Johnson, Marjorie Kerrie, Albert "Cap" Lavin, Marie Jean Lederman, Christopher C. Modu, Miles Myers, James T. Nardin, Alan C. Purves, Stephen Reid, Robert E. Scholes, Bernard R. Tanner, Ralph E. Voss, Thomas B. Warren, and Edward M. White. Friedrich read AP papers from the start in 1954, led scoring tables, ran CCCC workshops, and became instrumental in installing AP scoring methods (albeit on a six-point scale) for the California State University and Colleges English Equivalency Examination in 1973 (Haswell and Elliot 2017).

Perhaps most influentially, in terms of the early history of holistic scoring in the United States, Myers and Lavin conversed at an airport, both coming back from an AP scoring in the late 1960s. Myers learned that Lavin and other teachers were applying AP holistic scoring in California high schools (email to authors, December 8–14, 2014). Only a few years later, as chapters 7 and 8 detail, Myers and Lavin helped direct the startup of the Bay Area Writing Project, which soon was spreading its AP-style holistic scoring across the United States through National Writing Project sites.

In our terminology, AP-style holistic scoring as conducted during the period before 1980 was formal and controlled, followed a given distribution of scores that were criterion referenced, and used a scoring guide (not a rubric). Typically, scoring leaders took a random sample of essays from the set, determined anchor papers for the points on the rating scale, and derived writing traits (often based on the particular question) for the main points in a nonschematized way; then raters first divided papers into groups that fit the given distribution (usually quartiles on a normal distribution) and then sometimes refined the score by adding or subtracting a point in regards to certain proficiencies (e.g., mechanics). As we have suggested, the method works best with scorers who form a tight community through a common background—they are students in the same class, teach in the same curriculum or the same university system, or, as in the case of AP readers, serve as members of the same curricular articulation. English table leader Mary Rion Hove, from St. Olaf's college in Minnesota, wrote that readers did not return year after year for the money or for the sense of usefulness, but "for the people" (Advanced Placement Program 1980, 32).

Underneath the long-gone playfulness of the yearly AP scoring at Rider College—the traditional volleyball game, the loud fans brought in to cut the stifling heat for readers in the gymnasium, the parodies of passages drawn from the questions, the games during breaks outside where it was cooler, the intermittent romances—lay a solemn professional solidarity, a sense of common ground, that helped make this particular scoring method work.[11]

NOTES

1. Quoted with permission. Special Collections Research Center, University of Chicago Library.
2. It is not easy to find exactly how the Comprehensive Examination in English was being scored when Diederich arrived at Chicago. For instance, was there more than one reader of a student essay? In a piece published in 1934, John M. and Ruth Stalnaker, both faculty members at the University of Chicago, discuss rater unreliability and recommend judging papers analytically, "on the basis of specific, predetermined criteria which trial has shown can be consistently evaluated" (605), and they say that when this system was put into place at the reading of English examinations at the University of Chicago, the reliability improved from 0.42 in October of 1931 to 0.92 in November of 1933. The dates suggest, however, that these essays were for Qualifying examinations, not for the Comprehensive.
3. Diederich may have been influenced by Harold A. Anderson and Arthur E. Traxler (1940), who found that when school students were given material ahead of time, they wrote essays that achieved better interrater reliability. Anderson was in the Education Department at the University of Chicago. As for required topics, educators had long known that grading consistency was highest when graders read essays written on the same topic.
4. See Wilma R. Ebbitt and Diederich (1950), in which Diederich is clear that in 1949, the composition Comprehensive used two three-hour essays from each student and two independent readers for each paper. Later in his career, he stuck to his belief that with two independent scorers, only an exact agreement constituted an agreement, despite the common practice of holistic evaluators accepting adjacent scores as such. In 1951, employed by ETS, he wrote a memorandum criticizing the scoring of the new College Board's General Composition Test because it counted as an agreement two contingent scores (Diederich 1951, 3). Diederich's belief and practice help account for the comparatively low interrater-reliability coefficients he often reported for his studies.
5. Publication of previous examinations was a rule initiated with Boucher's New Plan in 1931. It was a highly radical step. As the previous chapter points out, postexamination publication, even of mark schemes, was finally instituted in 1987 in Scotland and 1988 in England.
6. It seems Diederich did not often file his empirical data. When Earle Eley wanted to use a selection of the 1949 English Comprehensive essays for his dissertation study, he found "no information either as to the reliability of the essay itself, or of the reading of the essay" (1953, 57–58). That is, the essays were saved but not the information of the scores for the two essays each student wrote and the scores independently given by the two raters. The original student script would not have the readers' scores because, under Diederich's system, the first reader tore off the stamped number of the essay and turned the number in with the score, and so did the second reader with the newly stamped number.
7. Edward M. White visited Paul B. Diederich at ETS in the summer of 1962 with questions about how to score CSU's proposed English Equivalency Examination.

White wrote that Diederich went "through the advantages and disadvantages of various scoring scales for the particular test we would be giving. We decided on a six-point holistic scale, for a series of complex reasons, all related to that particular test" (2010).

8. Titles of AP courses and accompanying examinations changed over time. In the first administration in 1954, the two commissioned tests were English (written composition) and Literature (canonical works). In 1958 these two tests were combined into a single test, AP English Literature and Composition, a cost-saving measure. The AP English Language and Composition Examination began in 1980. There are few histories of the AP Program during its early days written by those attending the first readings: one is by Eric Rothschild (1999) and another by the AP Program itself (1980). For a history, see Norbert Elliot (2005, 152–55) and Elizabeth Jamison (2015).

9. ETS archivists have been superbly helpful in allowing us every document in their possession related to the AP Program. However, it does appear that some materials belonging to the College Board may have been lost while being stored by the vendor, ETS. While researching her dissertation on AP English prompts, Jamison was told by ETS that some thirty years ago, two boxes of AP materials were consumed by "an unexplained conflagration" (2015, 147). As confirmation, when Elliot wanted to rescore the papers from the Godshalk, Swineford, and Coffman study (1966), he was told that fire also consumed the student papers scored from *The Measurement of Writing Ability*.

10. In 1972, for examination essays in subjects such as history and English, a consistency index number (CIN) was applied, a measure based on raters scoring ten papers they had scored before: "The best CIN occurs for the Reader whose scores show the least variance. . . . This is a refinement of the process used in English, where Table Leaders spend almost all their time checking the Readers at their tables" (Advanced Placement Program 1980, 28–29).

11. For instance, in 1976, English Table Leader Bernard R. Tanner, from Cubberly High School in Palo Alto, spoofed a quotation from *Beowulf*: "Here they studied the wobbling / flight of frisbees, and if some sample went too wrong, / they sacrificed a Table Reader to make it right" (Advanced Placement Program 1980, 40). The next year Tanner, now a Bay Area Writing Program consultant, would coauthor a holistic scoring of California high-school proficiency essays, faithfully based on the AP method (Bernstein and Tanner 1977).

6
OSMOND E. PALMER, FRED I. GODSHALK, AND THE ECT, 1960–1972

We order our lives with barely held stories.
—Michael Ondaatje, *Warlight*

When US compositionists credit the Educational Testing Service with inventing holistic scoring of essays, they often cite Fred I. Godshalk, Frances Swineford, and William E. Coffman's *The Measurement of Writing Ability* (1966). Yet, as we have said, in that very monograph those ETS researchers note that their method of rating was not new, and they reference a number of antecedent researchers, most notably Phillip Vernon, author of *Secondary School Selection: A British Psychological Society Inquiry* (1957).

They could have cited more.

One person in particular, absent from footnote, bibliography, or main text of the College Board report, deserves to have been mentioned. If the name Osmond E. Palmer does not ring a bell as a scholar in the academy who influenced ETS researchers during an important period in writing assessment, genre bears some of the blame. While the research-report genre is known for brevity, one wonders how much is left out when names of those who lent value and direction to the work are not recorded. As it turns out, Palmer played a consequential part in the US history of holistic scoring, a part that highlights the differences between university and testing-firm attitudes. Reconstructing Palmer's contribution, however, may require a bit of historical excavation. So as archaeologists do, we delve, layer by layer, back down through time.

PALMER: CHAIR OF THE COMMITTEE OF EXAMINERS FOR THE ENGLISH COMPOSITION TEST, 1960

Let's begin in 1967. When *The Measurement of Writing Ability* was reviewed in *Research in the Teaching of English,* one of its critics, Martin

Steinmann Jr., charged that "the competence of the readers used in this study is assumed, not demonstrated" (1967, 83). The critique touches on the old and abiding debate over the calculation of the final holistic score of an essay—whether differences in the perception of independent readers are embraced democratically and their scores just averaged (pooled scoring) or independent scores are compared hierarchically and, if needed, calibrated toward the "correct" score (adjusted or consulted scoring). In the same issue of *Research in the Teaching of English*, Godshalk replied to Steinmann and defended the use of pooled scoring. Little differently than Stephan Wiseman had done in 1949, Godshalk argued that the scorers in the experiment had been highly qualified experts. As if defense enough, he listed the names and institutional affiliations of the scorers. Among them were three college teachers—John H. Middendorf of Columbia University, Marjorie Muirden of Portland State College, and Palmer of Michigan State University. All had been members of the Committee of Examiners for the English Composition Test (ECT), a College Board assessment that had been the subject of research since Edward S. Noyes, William Meritt Sale, and John M. Stalnaker published *The First Six Tests in English Composition* in 1945.

Often forgotten is the fact that it was this advisory committee—formed of English teachers, not ETS personnel—that in 1960 first proposed the idea and a method for Godshalk, Swineford, and Coffman's famous study (1966). The chair of the committee had been Palmer.

Let's now go back to that moment in November 1960, when the Committee of Examiners asked ETS for a new validation of the ECT.[1] At the time, the test consisted of objective items and an interlinear item type. The interlinear gave students a paragraph and asked them to edit it for the better by penning their revisions between the printed lines. To score, the interlinear was time consuming and hence costly. The committee recommended that ETS, the research unit for the board, investigate the contribution of the interlinear by correlating it with a criterion measure of "free writing," paragraphs and essays composed impromptu by the student. As always, the rub was how the freewriting would be produced and scored. As a criterion measure, the writing and the scoring had to be as trustworthy as possible.

The Committee of Examiners recommended "the use of several samples of an individual's writing, produced at different times and covering some variety of communication problems" (Swineford and Godshalk 1961, 2). This recommendation was not surprising since all the committee members had scored essays for the Advanced Placement

Examination in English, where, as we have seen, it had long been practice to take at least two samples of a student's writing—to show proficiency in both literature and composition but also to control for the variability in competence that appears when students compose at different times and on different topics.

What might have been surprising was a particular request of Palmer, the chair of the committee. He wanted five samples of writing from each student, each scored independently by five readers. Swineford and Godshalk's description nine months later of the committee's proposal bears quoting since it details Palmer's unique contribution to the eventual study:

> Also recommended at the instance of the chairman was a reading or rating procedure by which five different readers would rate each sample in order to cancel out as much reader variation in judgmental standards as possible. It was assumed, though it is not a part of the record, that the readings would be holistic rather than analytical, but that they would be based upon a group examination and discussion of selected papers, with consensus reached as to the rating of each paper and the elements that had been considered in arriving at the decision. (Chairman Osmond E. Palmer is Examiner in English at Michigan State University. The procedure is patterned after experimental readings of student essays by which a reading reliability [in] the high 0.80s was attained.) (1961, 2-3)

There is one obscurity in this passage that bears thought. It is not the phrase "at the instance of," which today is simply obsolete. The idiom meant at the suggestion, request, instigation, or insistence of someone. Why was an "Examiner in English" from Michigan State University requesting, and maybe even insisting on, a particular method of scoring essays? Exactly how obscure was such an instance?

One answer is that Palmer was a scholar, kept up on the literature, used it to inform his own program of research, and was someone to be reckoned with in committee. He worked inside the tent.

Earlier in the spring of 1960, *Educational and Psychological Measurement* had published "The New STEP Essay Test as a Measure of Composition Ability," by C. C. Anderson (1960), on the Sequential Tests of Educational Progress (STEP) developed by the Educational Testing Service in 1957, a research study Palmer must have read.[2] While the STEP Writing Test included only multiple-choice questions to be used from grade four through the sophomore year of college to establish continuity of measurement for individual students, there was an accompanying essay test that could also be used. Anderson, a professor of education at the University of Alberta, expressed acute awareness of sources of variance in estimates of student essay-writing competence, especially instability in the quality of essays produced over time by an individual writer and instability of scores given independently by readers. He had fifty-five eighth-grade students write on one STEP topic in the morning and on another topic in the afternoon, then repeat the task three more times at one-week intervals. All five essays were scored independently by three experienced readers on an analytic scale. Anderson found that the two topics, the different testing occasions, and the individual raters all contributed significantly to variance in the scores. The usual suspects were present to cause the usual mischief associated with reliability: "composition fluctuation, the unrepresentativeness of essay samples, and discrepancies among markers" (101). For Anderson, analysis of variance techniques similar to those Douglas Finlayson used in 1951 had explicitly revealed multiple sources of variance related to reliability, with special emphasis on construct representation within tasks. Anderson's experiment, which became well known among writing-evaluation experts,[3] gave Palmer good reason to ask for five essays and five readers in the ECT validity study. But he had other reasons, plentiful as blackberries.

Anderson's research mentions a study conducted only a year earlier, one that turned out even more famous. Published in 1961, the 1959 experiment of Paul B. Diederich, psychometrician John W. French, and their colleague Sydell T. Carlton used fifty-three readers to generate one of the first variable models of the writing construct based on factor analysis.[4] Each reader's solitary job was to rank some 300 essays on a scale of 1 up to 9. The fifty-three readers' rankings of an essay were simply pooled. This method yielded five factors: ideas, form, flavor, mechanics, and wording. A construct model was thus, for the first time in history, empirically derived from the comments of readers responding directly to student written texts. Implicitly, if validity evidence was to be demonstrated, it could be collected as the five-factor model was used. The key finding appears on page 33 of *Factors in Judgments of Writing Ability*: sixteen of the fifty-three readers had loadings on the first factor of 0.25—more than any other factor (appendix A, table A-3, 9). A general factor of writing, associated with ideas, had been identified. We quote the report here: "It is by inspecting this table that we can learn something about the 'general factor' of reader agreement which was discounted by the particular kind of rotation of factors that was chosen. Inspection of the table reveals that we have a table of rank one. That is, if we were to factor analyze this table of intercorrelations, we would find only one 'second order' factor. The over-all agreement of the readers and tests that is not explained by the six factors already discussed appears to be concentrated on one rather than several major aspects of writing" (appendix A, 5–6).

And there it was, empirically verified by state-of-the-art methods: the gestalt qualities that fueled the holistic score.

Notably, Palmer had been one of the readers. He was also aware of a speech Diederich had delivered around 1959 in which Diederich had calculated what a test would need to bring student essays up to the validity and reliability of objective items: six two-hour papers on different topics written at different times, each with four independent readers, with scores pooled (Valentine 1961, 91).

As we will see, Palmer had good reason to pay special attention to the studies and opinions of Diederich—just as Diederich and his colleagues were mindful of Palmer's research at Michigan State. Five years before Diederich, French, and Carlton's experiment in judgment of writing, in February 1954, Diederich wrote an essay called *Notes on Grading Essays*. It offers solutions to combat the notorious unreliability of English teachers in grading essays. "Some staffs have done an admirable job of framing definitions of four or five levels of competence in four or five important qualities on which the papers are to be judged, such as mechanics, style, organization, reasoning, and fullness of content" (4). One such study was being directed by Palmer at Michigan State College of Agriculture and Applied Science (now Michigan State University, as renamed in 1964). In fact, by 1960, Palmer, the chair of the Committee of Examiners for the ECT, had accumulated fourteen years of experience as director of a mandated test in first-year college language accomplishment, including designing tasks for essay assessment. As we will see, the experience could well have led Palmer to be pleased when Swineford and Godshalk (1961) did experiment with his five-essay five-reader stricture and to express reservations for the applicability of the finding to his own institution.

PALMER AT MICHIGAN STATE COLLEGE: 1946–1961

Eleven years earlier, in 1946, Palmer, called Oz by his friends, age thirty-nine, with wife and daughter but without PhD, had been hired at Michigan State College as assistant professor in the Department of Written and Spoken English and director of the Board of Examiners in the Basic College. This medieval job title may need some translation. His department combined instruction in writing, speaking, reading, and listening. Postwar and prelapsarian, it was a midcentury form of the English department, sometimes detached from the literature and linguistics side, a kind of basic-skills, protocommunications department that thrived before speech faculties seceded and formed the hugely successful communications departments we know today.

The Department of Written and Spoken English was lodged within Michigan State's Basic College. The Basic College was an independent administrative unit applying a general-education requirement involving a small set of year-long, three-quarter courses for all first- and second-year students. The other courses were Biological Science, Effective Living, Fine Arts, History of Civilization and Literature, Physical Science, and Social Science. Of these, students had to take four, along with Written and Spoken English. The five-course set comprised a curriculum that occupied half of a student's academic study during the first two undergraduate years. And Michigan State College meant business. To earn credit in each of these courses, the student had to pass an end-of-year comprehensive examination, constructed and administered and graded not by the teacher of record but by a Board of Examiners. As readers of the previous chapter will recognize, the model for Michigan State's Basic College was, unabashedly, the College of the University of Chicago. There were differences, however. For Written and Spoken English, the student at Michigan State had to take an objective test, give a speech, and write an impromptu essay. Devising and managing the scoring of that comprehensive test was part of Oz Palmer's new job.

Palmer became part of the evaluation team coordinated by Paul L. Dressel, director of Education Services at Michigan State. Dressel was trained as a statistician and became passionately devoted to assessment as an opportunity to learn about what students could do under valid, reliable, and fair testing conditions. In 1958 Dressel published *Evaluation in the Basic College at Michigan State University*. The volume covered general-assessment efforts (managed by a Board of Examiners) that had begun in 1944 under a central administrative unit (the Basic College). In 1961 Dressel issued a second volume, *Evaluation in Higher Education*, in which Dressel and his colleagues provided what could be considered the first institutional-research handbook. Viewing evaluation as an "integrative element" in postsecondary education, Dressel stressed that evaluation was both a means and an end to improve quality of instruction (24). Taking Michigan State College as a case study in institutional research, Dressel and his colleagues provided chapters on the nature and role of evaluation; specific evaluation problems in the social sciences, natural sciences, humanities, and communication; the relationship between grades and examinations; and the role of institutional research in planning and policy development. An appendix provided a discussion of technical considerations in measurement.

While limited-response forms of assessment are present throughout the volume, notable is attention to writing in disciplinary settings. In the social sciences, for example, historian Harry D. Berg (1961) well understood tensions between interrater reliability and construct validity and provided advice to "limit the scope" of the task at hand and to "structure the question" so that "its requirements will not be vague and subject to legitimate misinterpretations" (106). In the natural sciences, biologist Clarence H. Nelson (1961) emphasized the "unique structure and distinctive characteristics" of science and the unique forms of its instruction (113). In the humanities, David K. Heenan (1961) called attention to the need to design evaluations that were sensitive to the student's sense of aesthetic values—the "ethereal, nonverbal aspects" that rendered traditional forms of assessment inappropriate. "The humanities, by emphasizing noncognitive experiences, represent, for many students, a wholly new educational experience," he reminded readers (161).

In the discussion of technical considerations in measurement, Joe L. Saupe (1961) presented a primer on reliability that focused on stability (use of the same test at different times) and equivalence (relationships between measures) and internal consistency (relationships among measures). In turning to validity, Saupe followed Lee J. Cronbach (1960) and innovatively focused on evidence. "Under this definition," Saupe noted, "a test may have differing degrees of validity depending upon the various uses to which it might be put" (446). The traditional forms of validity are noted (construct, concurrent, and predictive), and attention is also paid to affective constructs such as inquiry. Again, following Cronbach, Saupe establishes the importance of theory building in establishing relationships between conceptually related constructs. In the measurement of inquiry, for example, "meaningful measurement relevant to this objective requires a theory specifying the meaning of the attitude, other traits or characteristics to which it is or is not related, and situations in which behavior reflecting it might or might not be expected to occur" (448). In establishing the relationship between reliability and validity, he notes that "reliability is a requirement for validity" but that it is nevertheless "more important that a measure be valid than it be reliable" (449). In the twenty-three pages of the appendix, Saupe provides an informed and excellent introduction to measurement.

The conceptual system he describes is the most informed and best presented in the handbooks produced from 1924 to 1985. Indeed, the system supports what may accurately be understood as the first institutional-research handbook featuring writing in the disciplines in the United States.

A local exit examination, to be sure, is different from a national competency measure such as the College Board's ECT, and the validation of the two also differs. In the difference probably lie the reasons for the scoring method Palmer insisted Swineford and Godshalk use in 1960. The reasons turn on the issues of criterion referencing, local pragmatic needs, and, in the end, rater and writer singularity. At base is a profound chasm splitting standardized testing at the national level and testing of curricular standards at the local level. For Palmer, and possibly for the other four members of the ECT advisory committee, the difference led to an unsettling historical irony. Their recommendations for constructing a criterion variable to validate an indirect measure of writing skill (the interlinear) led, unforeseen, to the construction of a predictor variable to serve as a direct measure of writing skill (holistic scoring). The irony is that holistic scoring stood counter to Palmer's methods of assessing student essays for course credit at Michigan State.

A closer look at those methods allows us to revive a scene that risks falling into historical oblivion, programmatic language testing at state-supported universities before the entrance of rhetoric and composition studies (sometimes dated as 1966, with the Dartmouth conference). At Michigan State, Palmer's system of grading written and spoken English comprehensives was rigorous and labor intensive. Student impromptu speeches were scored on a five-trait analytic scale by three independent raters. As for his testing of writing proficiency, half consisted of a battery of objective items. Palmer's how-to guide for test makers, passionate and knowledgeable, advocates short-answer items that measure skill rather than memory (1961, 213–24). As for the impromptu essay, again Palmer used three independent raters. They scored analytically, grading each of five criteria—content, organization, sentence structure, style, and grammar—on a ten-point scale. The top five levels were referenced to the Examination Board's standards for final course grade, equated with A, B, C, D, and F.[5]

It would be sanguine to imagine Palmer's system at Michigan State as fixed in time. Typical of institutional assessment, the Basic College and its examination of Written and Spoken English kept shifting shape in response to internal and external demands and privations. Needed was a manifold approach to assessment, Palmer notes in his 1961 chapter on the evaluation of communication skills in *Evaluation in Higher Education*. Emphasizing what we would today define as a language-arts model of reading, writing, speaking, and listening, Palmer treats each facet of communication individually, with special attention to the evaluation of writing.

Take the scoring criteria. In 1945, the year before Palmer arrived at Michigan State, the criteria had been point, achievement of point, syntax, grammar and mechanics, and paragraphing and organization. Later, after two local studies of the halo effect in board ratings, with results showing that raters were in effect scoring to the tune of only three independent traits, Palmer reduced the criteria to diction, content and organization, and sentence structure and mechanics. Palmer and his colleagues found, also empirically, reasons for other changes. To get a better spread of rates, letter grades were disassociated from the top five scale levels. Before 1950, students had recourse to a booklet of facts about the topic (as at the University of Chicago), but that was discarded because topic difficulty couldn't be controlled. To save students time and maybe reduce enrollment, the Board of Examiners began giving standardized examinations at the end of each quarter of the course. By 1958 the board had acceded to the insistence of the instructional staff that final course grade remain in teacher hands and had limited board scoring to students challenging the course (Palmer and Nelson 1958, 121–23).[6] Then, in 1971, Michigan State's system of general-education examinations ended. It had lasted twenty-seven years, a relatively long life for a university curricular assessment.

In 1992, two decades after Palmer's retirement from Michigan State, one of his old department colleagues, Theodore R. Kennedy, remembered that "Oz was industrious, conscientious, good-humored—totally devoted to the 'objective,' multiple-choice type examination." Kennedy added that with impromptu themes, "Here too Oz made every effort to insure an 'objective' grading, often with less than complete success" (n.p.). Accurate enough, but it would be equally accurate to say Palmer believed no formal rating of a student examination essay will have complete success. Even before he arrived at Michigan State, he was intimately acquainted with different methods of judging essays—including those we call *holistic*. He knew their faults and therefore often tested the tests. He did so in light of four requirements. Were they dependable? Were they referenced to teaching and learning? Were they humanly doable? And did they admit human singularity?

Teacher grading of essays, he knew, was a carnival toss. Palmer had ten papers graded A, B, C, D, or F independently by forty-seven members of his teaching staff. All papers received at least four different grades, and six of them received all five grades (Palmer and Nelson 1958, 127). One paper only, he also knew, was not dependable, at least in verifying a student's writing prowess. "He may not like the topic," Palmer observed, "he may not be well informed upon it, he may not feel like writing on a given occasion, or he may lack inspiration" (1961, 209). How many times had he heard these very reasons given by the students themselves, students whose impromptu essay had not passed the comprehensive test? At Michigan State, Palmer's solution was to have three papers from each student graded anonymously, a procedure that fit the contingencies of the university's basic college—a programmatic infrastructure for evaluation aligned with institutional need.

However, for both classroom grading and formal examination, another method would work better, according to Palmer: ranking. Ranking, of course, is the procedure lying at the core of holistic scoring, and Palmer's comments show remarkable insight for his time (1961, 211–12). They were published in 1961, the same year Diederich, French, and Carlton published their *Factors in Judgments of Writing Ability*. As we have noted, Palmer had served as a reader for that experiment two years earlier, and Palmer and the ETS researchers describe an identical tactic: sort papers into the three piles of high, average, and low, and then sort the papers in each pile into three ranks. Palmer describes the problems.

> It assumes a common assignment. It assumes that one is reading for over-all effective communication (or possibly a single major thing—well-chosen illustration, soundness of reasoning). If one is looking for effective communication and accuracy, the second factor is going to get in the way. When papers are rated or ranked by the composite or averaging of several different factors, the range of scores may be seriously reduced, for the papers good on some factors may be poor on others. (212)

Three years earlier, Palmer had also noted that although ranking erased individual rater differences in leniency, it did not solve the problem of converting a norm-referenced rate (e.g., thirty-sixth best of the set) to a criterion-referenced rate (e.g., B within a local grading system) (Palmer and Nelson 1958, 128).

So a few years before he became chair of the Committee of Examiners for the ECT, overseeing in 1960 Swineford and Godshalk's use of holistic essay scoring, Palmer was identifying some of that procedure's central problems: need for a single topic, intractability of the halo effect, poor range of scores, difficulty in dealing with unevenness of accomplishment. Therefore, at Michigan State he used neither ranking nor any other kind of holistic scoring. He notes that although ranking would prove more valid than an analytic scale, "As yet we have not undertaken this system" (1961, 128). Understandably so, since his Board of Examiners would have had to give students only one topic and then

Figure 6.1. Crowd of students taking exams in auditorium, Michigan State College of Agriculture and Applied Science, December 1946 (courtesy of Michigan State University Archives and Historical Collections)

rank over 1,000 essays—2,100 of them, for instance, in spring of 1952. An earlier examination session, in 1946, is shown in figure 6.1.

Palmer could never escape one contingency: he was in charge of the operation. Pragmatics ruled, and often pragmatics ruled out. For instance, in theory he approved of the use of sample matching, or what he called a "writing scale"—locating the essay at hand, as Milo Burdette Hillegas (1912) had, within a set of model essays that represented points or divisions of the scoring scheme. He notes, shrewdly, that, in essence, Diederich's lay-reader system, STEP testing, and Advanced Placement scoring of essays all were based on sample matching. But that would mean his board would have to devise a new set of model essays for each topic administered, and do so as many as six times a year—a local necessity that differed from the chart-on-a-wall plan of Hillegas.[7] He made the analytic scale his scoring method of choice because it was the most doable. It was also the most teachable. Palmer noted that national large-scale testing would find impracticable scoring schemes that require multiple readings. But, he continued, the schemes "may be useful to the individual teacher, particularly when the device itself serves to indicate to the student areas in which his writing is weak" (1961, 210).

It is not incidental that Palmer expressed this sentiment on the semantic level of singularity: "the individual teacher," "the student." Long before he was an examiner, he was a teacher, and teachers know to the bone that students are all different. Once, when Palmer and his confederate examiners were experimenting with very broad topics for impromptu essays, such as communications, they found a paper he never forgot. It was written by a Korean War veteran about a military radio outpost in the Pacific. The paper only vaguely kept to the topic, was poorly delimited and organized, was just a narrative. Yet it was "well-written and vivid." "It could be graded high and was," Palmer remembered, "but it was not the kind of job we wanted" (Palmer and Nelson 1958, 119). In the final analysis, some writings never fit. No scoring scheme, however justified, could do diagnostic justice to this particular essay or this particular author.

The Korean War veteran's essay is an example of a time, no doubt, when one of Palmer's examination trials had "less than complete success." Yet, after all, he may have been a successful college testing administrator *because* he saw the gap between testing and teaching, saw where standardized measures will never completely succeed in fulfilling their promise to measure the writing proficiency of students. Palmer often changed testing methods during his twenty-seven years at Michigan State.

But his changes always cleaved to the first axiom of his Board of Examiners, that evaluation serve instruction. "Instruction and evaluation are not and should not be separable," he said (1961, 205). To this axiom, Palmer once proposed a corollary, that "statistical reliability had little to do with the extent to which a teacher would rely on the test and value the results" (Palmer and Nelson 1958, 116).[8] He treated all his examinations as trials to be examined themselves.

PALMER AND DIEDERICH AT THE UNIVERSITY OF CHICAGO: 1942-1946

Where did such wisdom come from? Did Palmer learn it all at Michigan State? The likely answer is that he developed much of his knowledge and views earlier, at the College of the University of Chicago, whose general-education system, launched in 1931, served as model for Michigan State's Basic College, as we have noted. The interesting question, as it turns out, is not how he learned about holistic scoring—the answer is obvious—but why he rejected it. To answer that question, we need to return to Diederich and his writing-proficiency examination system at Chicago during and after World War II.

By the fall of 1942, four years before he moved for good to East Lansing, Palmer had returned to the University of Chicago to finish his dissertation. Through a stroke of good fortune, he found himself working under Diederich, who had arrived two years earlier. Palmer was thirty-five, Diederich thirty-six, both raised in Catholic families and schools, both experienced teachers. So paths crossed—although very different paths.

As we have seen in chapter 5, Diederich had been a part of Ralph Tyler's longitudinal study of student development in thirty high schools, had earned his doctorate in classics at Columbia University, had published his dissertation with the University of Chicago Press, and then had been hired by Tyler at the assistant professor level to serve as English Examiner at the College. Palmer had earned an MA in literature at the University of Chicago in 1932, then had spent twelve years as a part-time, itinerant English teacher: St. Bernard's Seminary in Rochester, New York (1930–1932), St. Louis University (1935–1937), Canisius College in Buffalo, New York (1938–1940), DePaul University (1941). During those years, he had published nothing. By 1940 he was pursuing a PhD in literature at the University of Chicago and even had a dissertation proposed: "The Attitude toward Fiction in America to 1870." But he wouldn't finish it for eleven years. No doubt much of his attention was diverted elsewhere during his four years as instructor in the College and as examiner for its Comprehensives in English.

In the four years, Palmer must have learned an enormous amount from Diederich, much of it running research experiments with him. In 1942 Diederich involved Palmer with exploratory and validity studies of the Comprehensives, as well as with other work in testing outside the College. The other half of Diederich's time was spent constructing a series of officer-qualifying tests in English for the United States Armed Forces Institute. On this task, Diederich and Palmer worked together. They created tests that did not look like the standard military fare "in which," they said, "no passage has any connection with any other" (1963, 5).[9] One test from their series consisted of multiple-page quotations on a single issue from two authors (e.g., Aristotle, Plutarch, Bacon, Huxley); around fifty multiple-choice reading questions on these texts; then around twenty items in which students choose the best of four revisions of sentences in an essay written by a student in response to the two quotations. Intense, relentless, head cracking, these armed forces tests today would challenge applicants to graduate school at any university.

Undismayed, Diederich and Palmer, who had been put in charge of the remedial English program in the College, set about transmuting their military testing into classroom pedagogy. Students took one of the multiple-choice reading tests as homework, brought cards to class showing their answers, held up their card for a poll of each question, then discussed questions on which there was disagreement.[10] The third meeting of the week, they read aloud and discussed essays they had written on the issue of the quotations.

Notable is the fact that in Diederich and Palmer's remedial classes, the reading tests tested nothing, just prompted critical thinking and class discussion. For Diederich and Palmer, the real test was the success of their pedagogy in terms of the future English Comprehensives. It was a validation they did not hesitate to document. They found that of seventy students who had been in their experimental sections of remedial English, only thirty-one failed the Comprehensive, whereas of seventy students who took other sections of remedial English, fifty-four failed it (Diederich and Palmer 1963, vii). Palmer may have already held the belief that testing should always serve learning ("Instruction and evaluation are not and should not be separable"). But Diederich helped show him that objective testing, intelligently constructed, had its legitimate place in writing instruction.

More important, Diederich probably helped convince Palmer that the testing should always be tested. Between 1942 and 1946, as discussed in chapter 5, Diederich conducted a series of studies of the Comprehensive Examination in English at the University of Chicago. Palmer probably participated in all of them. Certainly he was involved in Diederich's 1943 experiment in writer reliability, where for their Comprehensives students wrote three essays spaced a week apart (Diederich 1946b).[11] And as instructor and examiner with the 1944, 1945, and 1946 Comprehensives, Palmer experienced from within what the previous chapter has described as the first formal large-scale holistic essay scoring on US soil, in which students wrote two three-hour essays and instructor-readers trained with sample essays agreed on criteria, independently marked papers on a five-point scale, and consulted over papers that had received two different marks.

Palmer probably also participated in another experiment of Diederich's, in which he proved to his teaching staff that students actually were writing better at the end of the course. Papers from the beginning and the end of sections of the course were mixed and scored by letter grade (with pluses and minuses). Only 14 percent of students wrote an acceptable paper at the beginning, but 70 percent did so at the end. This gain was statistically significant (and greater for basic students than regular students), while the slight gain in essay quality written by students not taking the course lacked significance (Diederich 1949b). But Diederich insisted on one proviso. Essays had to be scored only by the "the most reliable and sensitive readers on the staff of the course." In every such evaluation that was conducted at Chicago, he said, "some readers have detected twice as much difference between beginning and end papers as others" (396–98). Diederich also advised that if several readers are used, each reader should get both initial and final papers of the same students in order to level out differences in reader leniency. Such rater personal differences, in perspicacity and leniency, can't be controlled by rater training.

Palmer also learned, however, that although Diederich strove to contain writer and reader unreliability, he never imagined local testing could be rid of it entirely, or even should be. He noted that in English Comprehensive scoring, the correlation between first and second student papers never rose above 0.55 (1946b, 589). So rather than apply scoring methods that masked rater consistency challenges and use correlations that reported such masking, he put in place safeguards. Students could challenge a failing grade by having their essays scored again by different readers, and the fee they paid for doing so would be reimbursed if the grade changed to a pass. Students could also retake the examination without having to retake the course. Apparently they did so frequently. In the 1949 English Comprehensives, more than a third of the 646 students were retaking the examination to raise their grade or challenging it through independent study (Ebbitt and Diederich 1950, 285).

Working with Diederich, Palmer would have learned or seen confirmed an abiding respect for individual differences. To be sure, it was a view common in the 1940s—perhaps because of its origin in differential psychology. The interest is in how Diederich accommodated individual differences with formal, large-scale grading of examination essays. All too easily, individual differences of writers and raters can be erased with stringent scorer norming and simplistic rating scales. Diederich's attitude can be seen in a remarkable memorandum he wrote to Ralph Tyler on June 21, 1946, remarkable even by Diederich standards. He is complaining about the room his English readers had been assigned for the spring Comprehensives, a cramped, below-ground gym in the education building.

> We asked the English 3 staff to read between 1200 and 1800 hand-written pages in a shed with only a few tiny windows high up in the walls—so that every page would have to be read by artificial light. They would have to sit on hard straight chairs around long tables, where other staff members could hardly avoid saying every two minutes, "Listen to this!"—and then reading some prize boner. By the time the other staff members looked

back at their own pages, they would be unable to remember what had been said up to that point. In addition, our girls would be going bang-bang continually with the stamping machine, and reading off numbers to one another, and scurrying back and forth. Every few minutes the door would open, and everyone would look up to see who was coming, and then try to find his place in a paper again. Other staffs at adjoining tables would be conferring loudly about grading standards or disputed papers or grade lines. And every staff member would have to go through about fifty hours of this nerve-racking distraction while performing one of the most difficult intellectual operations in the world—that of judging the quality of writing without even the comfort of a smoke.[12] (Diederich 1946d)

Why, asks Diederich, are we requiring "fourteen distinguished members of the English 3 staff to grade papers under sweatshop conditions?" Why couldn't they just score papers in their own homes?

> How do they usually read papers? Sitting in a comfortable chair at home, preferably from 8 P.M. to about 2 A.M., with smokes and drinks [in their] hands, and with children and other distractions kept firmly out of the way. The difference in comfort alone would justify the English staff in asking to read the examination at home; but there is reason to believe that the grading would be done better amid customary surroundings—in the same chair in which they had graded papers all year rather than in a strange place filled with noise and confusion—and without all the distractions I have noted above.[13]

Diederich recommends instead that one member of the Board of Examinations meet with all the graders, discuss standards, set due dates, hand out packets of essays, and then send everybody home. In part he is lamenting the way heartless bureaucracy has taken over everything in American life, even the administering of academic examinations: "We should do our best to be as courteous as the old-time filling station attendant" (Diederich 1946d).

Under these "sweatshop conditions" of the 1946 administration, Palmer scored English Comprehensives at Chicago for the last time. Probably he heard Diederich's objections directly from Diederich: that holistic rating pushes toward conformism in its raters and that there should be a humane limit to that tendency. Thirty years later, enthusiastic holistic assessors will insist that raters work in the same room and at the same time to improve their interrater reliability. But Diederich, maverick and eccentric, saw the danger—that overinsistence on rater norming risks dulling the discrimination of singular raters to notice and reward singular writing. It wasn't a matter of reading too fast. In the same memorandum, Diederich (1946d) argues that papers may be scored more quickly if readers work at home. It was a matter of reading with the kind of rapt, undivided attention that ferrets out singular language proficiency otherwise hidden in the push of impromptu essay writing and impromptu essay scoring.[14]

In Diederich's day, respect for the singular individual was hallowed at the College of the University of Chicago. It had been favored at the start with Dean Boucher's New Plan in 1931, which allowed a student to take a Comprehensive examination whenever they felt ready, enrolled in the course or not.[15] Palmer and Diederich's closest educational guides believed deeply in shaping assessment to respect individual differences. Tyler's Eight-Year Study created assessments designed specifically to measure the uniqueness of students. As we will see, in his association with the National Assessment of Educational Progress, Tyler came to despise the tendency of ETS—and educational statisticians in general—to shape educational testing in the form of statistical norms. "Most of psychometric theory," he wrote late in his life, "is based on the notion that educational tests are primarily to be used for sorting" (1983, 200), that is, not for singling out but for lumping in, categorizing people in catch-all abstractions. Dressel, who wrote that his conception of evaluation was largely due to his association with Tyler (Dressel 1958, vii), discredited course grades because they erased the singular accomplishments of students.[16] Benjamin Bloom, who was on the Board of Examinations at Chicago during Diederich's stay there, is the best-known theorist of mastery learning, which (like the Comprehensive system at Chicago) allowed individual students to learn at their own pace.

Human singularity, of course, does not necessarily conflict with holistic scoring or with the psychological holism that underpins it. The point is thoroughly explored in Earle G. Eley's University of Chicago dissertation, as the previous chapter notes. Eley's advisor was Bloom, and one of his dissertation directors was Tyler. A large part of the corpus of essays Eley analyzed in his dissertation were written by students for the 1946 Comprehensive Examination in English. The main point Eley makes is that the singular intent of a writer, as it emerges from a unique language context, is what gives the writing its impression of wholeness. Language production then can be viewed "in a way consistent with the gestalt or holistic point of view toward psychology" (1953, 26).[17] At the time he was writing his dissertation, Eley was working for ETS in analyzing the scoring of essays in ETS's short-lived General Composition Test (1950–1954). Eley found shortcomings in the scoring but defended the use of essays eloquently: "The ability to use language creatively is one of the last strongholds of the individual against a growing tendency toward conformity" (1955, 13).

In his May 12, 1946, memorandum to Tyler arguing that each Comprehensive Examination should be scored by one staff examiner and one research assistant, Diederich mentions Palmer twice. Once is to recommend him as his assistant in constructing the English tests. And once is to add a postscript: "I need to talk with you about the status and prospects of Palmer" (1946c). We can only speculate about Diederich's concerns, but probably one issue was Palmer's slow progress in completing his doctorate. The following August, still without it, Palmer moved to Michigan State as assistant professor in the Department of Written and Spoken English and on the Board of Examiners of the Basic College, bringing with him an intimate experience with holistic scoring.

But Palmer did not install Diederich's harbinger scoring method. Why not? He had experienced it as instructor, examiner, and experimenter for four years at Chicago, yet at Michigan State he applied an analytic scale. Probably his choice had to do with the three factors mentioned earlier: rater and writer singularity, criterion referencing, and local pragmatic needs. Of course, he may have felt pressured to maintain a system already in place. But it was a system with its own "surrounding" or "supportive context," as Eley (1953) would say (86). Palmer's office had over 2,000 students to assess every year, more than three times as many as at Chicago, and to assess for both writing and speaking. Students failing would be knocking on his door asking why, and the criterion-referenced analytic scale would give his advisors convincing answers. Palmer's choice also may have come down to personality. Palmer was "conscientious" and "objective," a person with, perhaps, even more of a conviction than Diederich that raters have individual perspectives no training or technique could normalize. As we have seen, Palmer's first study at Michigan State looked at the range of uncontrolled teacher grading of essays (Palmer and Nelson 1958, 127). He also had graduate students at Michigan state who were empirically probing halo effects that beset marking of essays, even trait-based marking (Kincaid 1952; Starring 1952). It is not surprising that he insisted on three independent readers rather than Diederich's two.

Historically, the point is that Palmer had a choice. If we did not know his previous experience with Diederich's holistic scoring at Chicago, it might look as if he was just following a long-standing and entrenched system of scoring essays by analytic trait. But he was not. He was deliberately choosing one system over another. And the system he rejected was holistic scoring, which some say ETS invented twenty years later. And that brings up another historical point worth stressing. After WWII, the formal investigation of essay-scoring methods was not confined to ETS or the College Board. Universities, colleges, and even schools were conducting their own studies, albeit fitful, albeit unevenly supported with inferential statistics, albeit supported by studies run by their own graduate students. Their focus was locality constrained, person centered, and learning based. Findings were designed to serve, and sometimes only to serve, one living curriculum with its anxious students and dubious teachers.

At Chicago, one of Diederich's last studies was suggested by his first-year composition staff to find out whether the Comprehensive English grades matched their own appraisal of their students. Could the evaluation of three essays written impromptu in six hours match the evaluation of a teacher who had seen eight essays and known a student's work through nine weeks of class? So teachers recorded the grade they were sure their students *should* get on the Comprehensive, some 422 students, and that grade was compared with the one the students *did* get. The findings, argued Diederich and his new English staff member, Wilma R. Ebbitt, "show the examination to be a much more accurate measure of writing ability than the English staff itself ever imagined it to be. Ninety-six per cent of the grades were either exactly what the instructors said they ought to be or not more than one grade off" (Ebbitt and Diederich 1950, 286).[18] Palmer, now at Michigan State, did not participate, but he would have approved. The study was informative but so local as to be hardly replicable. This is research shaped for a unique set of students, teachers, and examiners.

GODSHALK AND THE ENGLISH COMPOSITION TEST ESSAY: 1960–1972

It has been a long circuit, but we are brought back to the fall of 1960 and the recommendations of an advisory committee concerning a test of composition skill that supposedly was valid for any student anywhere. Now we can surmise why Oz Palmer insisted on five independent raters for each of five pieces of a student's writing. He knew, from eighteen years of experience at Chicago and East Lansing, that both writers and readers are unreliable, and if essay writing ability was what the ECT purported to test, then many essays from one writer were needed to test the test. He also knew that if raters' scores of the essays were to be pooled, and the raters were not part of a bonded teaching staff, then multiple scores were needed, the more the better. What he didn't know was that his recommendation would trigger a multistage investigation by Godshalk and his ETS colleagues. Where that investigation led is a story that needs telling, events that seem to have been deliberately staged for Hayden White's trope of irony.

As the beginning of this chapter notes, in Swineford and Godshalk's review of their 1960 meeting with the ECT Committee of Examiners, they left one remark obscure. According to Swineford and Godshalk, holistic scoring of the criterion essays was not explicitly mentioned in the notes or minutes of their November 1960 meeting with the committee. Holistic scoring, they say, was "not a part of the record" but rather was "assumed" (1961, 2). But assumed by whom? Did perhaps Swineford and Godshalk assume it and not the committee members? We cannot answer that question. But we do know that around that time Godshalk, as much as any researcher in the United States, was knowledgeable and committed to holistic scoring of a particular sort: fairly open rating with independent scores pooled, not adjusted.

For instance, he drew on ETS researcher Ann F. Coward's isolated and pioneering work comparing "wholistic" scoring with "atomistic" scoring of English composition in the Foreign Service test (Coward 1950, 3). As far as we know, her term "wholistic" is the earliest use of the term to refer to a method of scoring essays. At the time, September 1949, Foreign Service candidates wrote four essays in three hours, and the essays were scored analytically with seven variables on a four-point scale. Coward had 100 papers also scored twice on "total merit," a "subjective, intuitive, over-all judgment" achieved "boldly, decisively, and rapidly" (3). The holistic scale was 1–10, there was no training or anchor papers, scoring time averaged about four minutes, and single-rater reliability ranged from 0.44 to 070. Coward calculated that if each paper was read four times, the wholistic system would equal the atomistic system in rater reliability and reader cost.[19]

Two findings of the Coward study are notable: interrater reliability is related to task; and scoring method, when driven by statistical assumptions, can impact results. Of the four tasks scored in the study, the third (on the basis of a given statistical table, the candidate was asked to write an informative report of 300 words) yielded the lowest correlations (0.44 to 0.63). Because this was not a typical writing task for an essay, it appeared that reliability was related to task. Second, the analysis was subjected to differing statistical treatments that, in turn, led to different conclusions. Third, those who read "wholistically" were advised to place at least one paper in the lowest and one in the highest category; were warned not to place more than ten papers in either extreme category; and were told that all other categories should be used, with a peak near the middle of the ten-point scale. Although there was no evidence that the 100 candidates formed a Gaussian distribution—indeed, the candidates for the Foreign Service examinations were likely to be verbally skilled and would, hence, demonstrate a left-skewed curve with the higher scores on the right of the x axis—the instructions created a normal distribution. Since no such instructions were given to those who scored atomistically, the correlations achieved as a result of holistic scoring may be understood as an artifact of the scoring instructions. In the United States, from the very first, the relationship between scoring and task was understood to be complex, as was the relationship between reader instructions and the inferences that would later be drawn from their scores.

Godshalk called Coward's method "holistic" without hesitation (Godshalk, Swineford, and Coffman 1966, 4), and he repeated her rather unusual phrase for it, "total merit" (Godshalk 1961, 4). Later, after the ECT study was completed, he even continued her holistic reading of Foreign Service essays. His report as chief reader for that test, given in December 1965, contains his most unabashed defense of pooled-rater scoring. "Experienced readers cannot avoid, nor are they expected to, the influence upon a total impression of writing skill that results from a paper's organization, logic, coherence, consistency of point-of-view or attitude, correct grammatical form, acceptable usage, apt phrasing, and the proprieties of mechanics (punctuation, capitals, format). But the readers are expected to disregard them as separate entities combined for a total score," allowing "an integrated and largely unconscious combining of these analyzable outcomes" (1966, 6n5). In the past, he says, essay scoring had been moving "in the wrong direction," toward controlled readings with third-reader adjustment of discrepant scores, and "the solution, it seemed, was in subjecting each paper to the judgment of a number of different readers. This consensus would constitute a valid measure of writing ability, assuming, of course, that the readers were competent" (4). Rapidity of reading is essential, and Godshalk even goes so far as to assert that the most common problem with his scorers was "failure to read holistically, a kind of inability to see the forest for the trees, usually the result of too slow and thoughtful a reading" (4).

Godshalk's notion that a reading may be too thoughtful gives pause for thought.[20] But Godshalk's feelings about holistic scoring, 1960–1966, were almost those of an ideologue. The best example can be found in his work on another College Board trial, the Writing Sample, work that overlapped with his first attempt to validate the ECT interlinear (Godshalk 1961). The Writing Sample was a typical though short-lived

College Board venture. In 1958–1959 the College Board decided that enough colleges would ask applying students for a sample of their writing if there were a trustworthy arrangement for the composing of it. In 1960 the College Board promoted a one-hour impromptu essay with a choice of topics to be first offered early in December as an optional part of ECT testing. However, rather late in the day, the oversight Committee on the Writing Sample (another lay advisory group) decided that the Writing Sample topics should be validated in advance. It was a rush, but Godshalk managed to have entering students at colleges such as Carleton and Reed write on one of ten topics during autumn orientation and shortly thereafter to have the essays scored by seven experienced AP readers. This scoring session must have taken place before Godshalk's meeting in November with the ECT committee and therefore throws light on the statement that "holistic scoring" was "assumed" during that meeting (Swineford and Godshalk 1961, 2).

The earlier scoring of the Writing Sample topic-validation essays used a method devised, overseen, and called "holistic" by Godshalk. As far as we know, it is the first scoring of essays so termed at ETS since Coward's experiment in 1950.[21] The method was radical for College Board scoring. The one-hour student essays were scored as "poor," "average," or "good," very fast, at the rate of three minutes an essay. Godshalk calls it "'skim' or holistic reading" (1961, 12). His idea was that the rating method fit the experimental end. "Since the desired result was a judgment of topics rather than writers, it was theorized that a very rapid reading of many papers might be sufficient for the purpose" (2–3), a "skim" reading "by experienced readers who could arrive quickly at a judgment of total merit" (4). The theory seemed to work, and two of the ten topics were thrown out because they showed an abnormal distribution of scores.

Despite appearances, Godshalk's method was not undisciplined. To begin with, the readers were highly experienced ETS raters.[22] Before scoring, they read twenty samples and had a discussion and planned for a scoring session of no more than three hours that lasted through dinner until ten o'clock. Yet Godshalk insists that this kind of scoring was not appropriate for making judgments about individual writing ability, in part because of its poor rater reliability. Such a session is only a way to score topics relatively similar in difficulty. He also notes that the current analytical way of scoring essays in such sessions takes fifteen minutes and that "skim readings" would cover one essay five times over in that time. "If five independent judgments on this basis were averaged, it seems at least possible that a more reliable judgment of proficiency would result from a like expenditure of time and energy" (1961, 13).

When Godshalk met a month or so later with the ECT committee, not only would he have found quite reasonable Palmer's insistence that five readers per essay were needed to create a valid and reliable criterion variable for validating the interlinear item type, he also might well have assumed the criterion essays would be scored holistically.

But that Palmer would also have assumed it is not so likely. In gist, by the time ETS researchers Godshalk, Swineford, and Coffman had completed their validity of the interlinear—and it took the original study plus two field studies (see Godshalk, Swineford, and Coffman 1966; Myers, McConville, and Coffman 1966)—they had transformed Palmer's predictor variable into their own criterion variable, had made holistic scoring and not the interlinear the testing procedure to validate, and had reduced five raters per essay to two and five samples of writing to one. It was a transformation, they make clear, not planned when they began their validation of the interlinear (Godshalk, Swineford, and Coffman 1966, 26). Palmer could not have anticipated that the procedure he insisted on in November of 1960 would end as an attempt to validate holistic scoring for operational test use. So one irony is that an essay examiner who had participated in holistic scoring and then rejected it unwittingly helped make it a well-publicized method in essay examinations.

A second irony is that the method—fairly open holistic scoring with pooled scores—itself was eventually rejected by the College Board in favor of more controlled methods such as essay-anchored, rubricized, or focused holistic scoring. As we will see, the method of holistic scoring Godshalk, Swineford, and Coffman supposedly invented for ETS proved deeply contentious within ETS.

When Swineford and Godshalk conducted the validation of the ECT's interlinear late in 1961, they obliged Palmer's request. They managed to get 646 juniors and seniors in high school to compose five twenty-minute essays on five rhetorically distinct prompts, and to get readers of the ECT interlinear (including Palmer) to score the essays. Each essay got five independent readings. The scale had only three points, "superior," "average," and "inferior." The readings were fast, averaging less than two minutes per essay. Readers had been given little training. They had scored some sample essays, and the scores were "announced" but not discussed. Other than a warning to avoid the "safe" procedure of putting almost all essays into the middle category, no distribution of scores was set or recommended. The 16,150 essay scorings, as well as the 646 interlinear scorings, were finished in a single five-day session. For the criterion of writing "ability," a student's twenty-five scores—five rates on five essays—were simply summed. It is as if Stephen Wiseman had been directing the study (Swineford and Godshalk 1961).

Wiseman would not have been surprised at one result, the interrater reliabilities recorded by Godshalk, Swineford, and Coffman (1965) in their statistical analysis report that preceded the well-known College Board publication by one year. As expected with open readings, single-rater reliabilities were low, ranging from 0.36 to 0.41. But the five-rater pooled reliabilities ranged from 0.74 to 0.78. And with all twenty-five raters pooled for a student's total "writing ability" score, the scoring reliability was estimated at an astonishing 0.92 (15). Palmer knew what he was asking for in his request for multiple readings.

We are not going to analyze further the studies that led up to *The Measurement of Writing Ability* (Godshalk, Swineford, and Coffman 1966) since that often-cited College Board publication has been thoroughly discussed (Elliot 2005, 158–65). In brief, the first study (conducted in December 1961) validated both the objective items and the interlinear as test worthy, that is, as contributing unique information in predicting a student's writing proficiency. More important, the second study (the field study, conducted in December 1962) validated a holistically scored, twenty-minute essay also as test worthy. As we have noted, this second study switched one of the criterion variables to predictor variable, a clever maneuver devised by statistician Swineford. One by one, each of the five twenty-minute essays was rotated out and correlated with the remaining four twenty-minute essays, combined to serve as the criterion. The predictor essay was read five times on either a three-point or four-point scale. The researchers concluded that one twenty-minute essay, given two or three independent holistic readings on a four-point scale, would add as much predictability as would the interlinear. The cost of scoring the essay and the interlinear would be about the same.

It is important to understand that this experiment did not test the validity and reliability of using an essay or essays, holistically scored, to measure a student's writing proficiency. Instead, the experiment explored how holistically read essays might function within an hour-long, nationwide, high-volume test that also included a battery of objective questions.

Although Edward S. Noyes, a professor of English at Yale University and former director of admissions there, was ecstatic in his introduction to *The Measurement of Writing Ability*—"It is clear from this monograph that colleges can in general accept scores on the ECT in any of its current forms as valid indices of their candidates' ability to write" (1966, vi)—gushing did not make it so. It is, in fact, quite difficult to find information about interrater reliability in the 1966 report. Tables 3 and

4 selectively show average correlations for five readings among the five essay topics. The correlations range from 0.44 to 0.59. The reported reading reliabilities of 0.92 that stick to the mind of the reader and that caused Noyes to gush were, in fact, produced by an estimate: calculation by dividing the mean square for essay scores minus the mean square for error by (that is, using the denominator of) the mean square for scores. Essentially, that 0.92 means that if a second group of twenty-five readers as competent as the first group read the papers again, it might be expected that the two sets of total scores would produce that high correlation. To find what the actual correlations were without the hypothetical adjustment, we must turn from the report monograph to an article published by Coffman in the *Journal of Educational Measurement*. Appearing in 1966 at the same time as the report itself, Coffman's article provided a table (153, table 2) not shown in the College Board report in which the interrater reliabilities are provided in terms of the numbers of topics read. For two readers reading one topic holistically, the correlation was 0.38.[23] The extraordinarily high 0.92 correlation was an artifact; the realistic situation of two readers reading one paper was far lower.

In the final analysis, usefulness, efficiency, and expense trumped reliability and validity. As the authors, appealingly forthright, put it, "Obtaining a reliable essay score in any large-scale reading is difficult if not impossible," but "even relatively unreliable essay scores *in combination with other types of questions* can be useful" (Godshalk, Swineford, and Coffman 1966, 14; our emphasis).

In writing assessment, validity, like reliability, is related to cost. The special contribution of the interlinear to validity, say the authors, again appealingly forthright, "appears to be relatively small when one considers the additional cost of including the interlinear in a test" (Godshalk, Swineford, and Coffman 1966, 21–22).

At the time with the ECT, use and cost were not minor considerations. In 1962 Coffman estimated that with every 50,000 essays, one less reader would save $5,000. In 1963 the test was taken by 142,000 students. The College Board was not a tax-supported state system of education or a governmental-supported enterprise. A nonprofit organization, the College Board could not operate at a loss.

This is not to say that the authors of *The Measurement of Writing Ability* were slaves to efficiency. The authors were indeed quite introspective about the findings of their report. After all, they had read Vernon's *Secondary School Selection* (1957) and referenced the very pages (120–21) in which studies by Hartog, Rhodes, Burt, and Wiseman were discussed in detail. One imagines the ETS researchers were drawn to those pages both because of the Vernon's summary and because of his advocacy of "general impression marking" and the use of "total pooled marks" as strategies by which "the inherent subjectivity of essay-marking can be reduced to reasonable proportions, in examinations where the range of pupil-ability is wide" (121). As Godshalk, Swineford, and Coffman write (1966, 39), their study "supports conclusions" already reached by Vernon. In this light, the US research becomes a replication of previous UK studies.

They saw the replication as a commodity, certainly, but also as a psychometric diagnosis, a learning experience, and a message to educators. They believed in testing writing with writing, despite the cost. They agreed that with the essay, "it is doubtful that the slight increase in validity alone can justify the increased cost," but they still argue for its inclusion in the test because of "the model" it provides for teachers and students (Godshalk, Swineford, and Coffman 1966, 41). And they adamantly believed in fairly open, pooled-rater holistic scoring. Their descriptions match Wiseman's and Britton's in clarity and sincerity. As Gertrude Conlan—Godshalk's devoted collaborator at ETS—claimed in her instructions for essay readers of the 1978 ECT, the scoring method was founded on the assumption that "each of the factors involved in writing skill is related to all the others and that no one factor can be separated from the others," and therefore readers "must read each paper for the impression its totality makes" (1978, 12). In the United States, the Coward-Godshalk-Swineford-Coffman-Conlan line kept pooled-rater, open holistic scoring alive and kept intact its underlying principles of organicism, gestalt perception, and the democratic or probabilistic law of large numbers, and they did so largely through the ECT.

But just as the parallel Hartog-Rhodes-Burt-Robertson-Wiseman-Britton line in the United Kingdom discovered, the resistance was relentless and eventually won out. In May 1962, the Committee of Examiners for the ECT (with Palmer still as chair) recommended that either the interlinear or a twenty-minute essay be included in all five administrations of the ECT per year, but then a paragraph later recanted and, because the two exercises "were more expensive to score," recommended that either be used "in *at least one* English Composition test each year" (Committee of Examiners 1962). The College Board took the committee at its word, and a year and a half later holistic scoring of a twenty-minute essay was finally approved, but just for the December 1963 testing.

A writing sample, scored holistically, never became a staple of the ECT, which remained mainly or totally dependent on limited-response items. The essay was discontinued entirely for the 1967–1968 testing year, and up to the 1971–1972 testing year, it was offered only eleven out of thirty-six times. At that point the College Board's vice president for programs issued a memorandum declaring that "all essay testing in the Admissions Testing Program be and remain suspended until further notice, pending outcomes of studies." The reason—no surprise—was cost. "What is not agreed—indeed, the matter is argued bitterly and incessantly—is whether very large expenses of money and energy should be accepted to preserve some relatively small writing exercise" (Godshalk 1972, 5). "Preserve" and "small" are not friendly words. The memorandum is quoted in a talk Godshalk gave in February of 1972, perhaps at the annual School and College Conference on English held at Princeton. The manuscript angrily breaks off with the words, "This is the end of my report."

It wasn't the end of the battle. Godshalk (1971) studied the results of past ECT testing and found telling differences between scores some students had made on the objective parts and on the essay. It seems for some individuals the essay did contribute unique diagnostic information. Conlan reports "anecdotal reports" that this was especially true of students speaking dialects or writing English as a second language (1976, 6). In 1976 the College Board reinstalled the essay for the ECT, read as before without a scoring guide and again only for December administrations. The ECT continued until it was replaced in 1994 with the SAT® II: Writing Subject Test, scored with a rubric (Bejar 2017, 575; Breland, Kubota, Bonner 1999, 2).

In the history of US holistic scoring, the 1966 publication of *The Measurement of Writing Ability* certainly proved a moment when the "stars had aligned" (Elliot 2005, 164). In the long, back-and-forth history of College Board efforts to demonstrate empirically the value of an essay in a test of writing skill or performance, the publication finally provided convincing tangible proof. In part because of the extensive reviews of it the next year in *Research in the Teaching of English*, the study became a *vade mecum* for assessment researchers, scholars, and practitioners. Furthermore, its significance as a promotional event should not be gainsaid. With its publication, holistic scoring (so named) acquired legitimacy in the United States. If it were to be challenged, the challenge would have to be in accord with the rigorous empirical methods of the report itself.

However, as its final subheading asked, was *The Measurement of Writing Ability* "A Significant Breakthrough?" Did it offer anything new by way of assessment or measurement technique? The ETS researchers themselves, perhaps, provide an answer, though it is not one they expected readers ever to see. A manuscript draft of *The Measurement of Writing Ability* shows one fascinating last-minute alteration.[24] Although the small differences from the published version are nearly all cosmetic, one substantive change occurs in the section called "A Significant Breakthrough?" The draft reads:

> A careful re-examination of the reports of previous studies indicates that our findings are not contradictory; rather, they provide a previously missing key to understanding the totality of the research. And the crucial element in our study is the criterion measure. (Godshalk, Swineford, and Coffman 1965, 47)

In the published report, this passage is replaced with

> A careful reexamination of the reports cited in Chapter 1 and a study of Vernon's review of research conducted in Great Britain indicate that these findings are not contradictory: in fact, they support conclusions already reached by Vernon (1957, 120–124). What the study has contributed is a highly reliable criterion measure which permits the relationships to be viewed in sharp focus. (39)

The penultimate draft has all the scholarly references included in the published report except for this citation of Vernon, and, as we note in chapter 4, the pages indicated from Vernon include the major British studies of open, pooled-rater holistic scoring, such as B.M.D. Cast's (1939, 1940), Wiseman's (1949), John Donald Nisbet's (1955), and Edwards Penfold's (1956).[25]

Breakthrough? Not as far as the scoring method and its outcomes are concerned, as Godshalk, Swineford, and Coffman ultimately say without equivocation. The breakthrough came with the construction of their criterion variable (the five pooled ratings) and the clever way they tested it against other measures. The thanks, one is tempted to say, is due to Swineford for the cleverness and to Palmer for the construction. But for his part, Palmer might have said no thanks.

The year the College Board suspended holistic essay scoring in their admission testing program, 1972, turned out to be both pivotal and ambivalent in the early history of holistic scoring. The ECT essay was withdrawn but managed a tenuous comeback four years later. ETS's budding College Level Examination Program (CLEP) offered an essay test to the California State University and College's Examination Committee, who were still gestating their English Equivalency Examination, but the committee turned CLEP down and the next year administered and scored its own essay, following an AP model (see Haswell and Elliot 2017). The National Assessment of Education Progress was devising a new form of essay evaluation, primary-trait scoring, to replace AP-style holistic scoring, which they had found uninformative in their first round of testing three years earlier—although, as we see in the next chapter, NAEP never fully gave up on the holistic. Finally, in 1972, the Bay Area Writing Project was in the planning stage. Within two years it would start spreading its own preferred style of holistic scoring and, at the same time, would begin empirical studies that questioned holistic scoring and helped undermine it in years to come.

All in all, a year for holistic scoring of essays, 1972, seems to shadow other ambivalent events on the bigger screen, events tailored for histories that follow Hayden White's emplotment of satire, which narrates the ironic struggle of human desires against inevitable underlying forces. In Munich, US swimmer Mark Spitz wins seven Olympic gold medals and Palestinian Black September terrorists kill eight Israeli athletes; in Vietnam, the United States withdraws 24,000 more US troops on the theory that South Vietnam will step up and eventually win their war with North Vietnam; in the Indian Ocean, Ceylon becomes the Democratic Socialist Republic of Sri Lanka and initiates nearly three decades of ethnic civil war; and in Washington DC, members of a committee organized to get President Nixon reelected (although that was a sure thing) are caught wiretapping the Democratic National Committee's headquarters in a residential complex called Watergate.

And in East Lansing, Michigan, after a quarter of a century devoted to local university language assessment, Oz Palmer celebrates his sixty-fifth birthday but postpones retirement for two more years, not knowing that he will enjoy only seven months of it before dying, two weeks before Christmas, during a visit to friends in California.

NOTES

1. The other members of the committee were Philip E. Burnham, English chair at St. Paul's School, Concord, New Hampshire, author of composition textbooks, chair of the National Council of Teachers of English Committee on Language in 1960, and chief reader for Advanced Placement English; Clarence W. Hach, chair of the English Department and coordinator of AP courses, Evanston Township High School in Illinois, author of "Needed: A Sequential Program in Composition" (1960); John H. Middendorf of Columbia University, an eminent scholar of eighteenth-century literature; Marjorie Muirden of Portland State College, a long-time reader of Advanced Placement essays and associate chair of a 1963 National Council of Teachers of English convention panel on "The Testing Programs in English," with Fred I. Godshalk presenting on "Testing Traditions and Trends."
2. According to his obituary, Palmer "contributed examination materials regularly" to STEP designers at ETS (*Town Courier*, December 19, 1974).
3. In December 2014, Miles Myers emailed us that "an Anderson study of another ETS test [1960] showed that this ETS test recommended 'holistic scoring' as the scoring

method." The other ETS test is the STEP. Note that Anderson's scale awarded 50 percent to quality of thought, 30 percent to style, and 20 percent to mechanics—a rating procedure we would call *analytic*, not *holistic*. But Myers is remaining true to his qualification of analytic scales as "holistic" (1980, 2). Anderson's 1960 study does not use the word *holistic*, but it does review the British contribution to pooled scoring, "the average verdict of a team of markers" (96).

4. We must be mindful to recognize that the form of factor analysis Diederich used in his study was not the method created by Charles E. Spearman in 1904. Spearman had operated under a single-factor hypothesis that had led him to identify a general intellective factor—an analysis that began a trend of reductionistic thought associated with the racism of eugenics, the restriction of immigration, and the horrors of genocide. A quick look back a Spearman's sampling plan—twenty-four of the oldest children of a village school in Berkshire, which was particularly favorable for his purpose since the school was located within 100 yards of his home—leads us to two conclusions: with such commonality of the children's experience in that small village, it would have been unlikely that any factor could have been found that did not correlate with another; and that method often creates, rather than identifies, a phenomenon. It is no wonder, then, that Diederich (or, more likely, the psychometrician French, whose 1961 account is a more extended account of factor analysis) chose to follow a procedure derived from, but not related to, that created by Spearman. Based on matrix algebra, the method is described in *Vectors of Mind: Multiple-Factor Analysis for the Isolation of Primary Traits* by L. L. Thurstone (1935) of the University of Chicago. Using matrix theory, Thurstone held that information—in this case, a score—can be expressed as a linear function of a number of factors, not as a single factor. Defined as a theory of multiple factors and presented in chapter 2, the methodology was an expression of Thurstone's desire to create "generalization of the factor problem to n dimension" (1935, vii)—a mathematical solution to what he described as the faith of all science: "that an unlimited number of phenomena can be comprehended in terms of a limited number of concepts or ideal constructs." "Without this faith," he added, "no science could ever have any motivation" (44). In using methods so described, the Diederich team was able to bring the full force of empirical investigation as it had evolved since 1935 to the problem at hand. To perform the analysis, an early IBM computer, unavailable to Thurstone, whose centroid calculations were done by hand, was used at the Littauer Statistical Laboratory, Harvard University, to undertake a principal component solution.

5. In the 1940s a similar system was used at the University of Iowa for testing out of a required communication-skills course (Gerber 1948)—and no doubt at other colleges and universities.

6. Other changes came from other directions. In 1952 the department altered its name to Communication Skills. In 1957, Michigan State College became Michigan State University. In 1960 the Basic College changed its name to University College. In 1961 Palmer's department changed its name once again, to American Thought and Language. Dressel records the facetious remark of one faculty member "that he had developed the habit of stopping by the dean's office each morning to find out who his department head was before going to his office" (1958, 5).

7. As we have noted, on the other hand he knew full well, from research done by his board and by doctoral students at Michigan State, that trait-based scales suffered from halo effects: "In some cases, the rating form was used only as a recording device for a grade previously determined by the rater" (Palmer and Nelson 1958, 123).

8. Palmer's supervisor at Michigan State, Dressel, agreed. In a talk called "Evaluation as Instruction," given at the 1953 ETS Invitational Conference on Testing, Dressel (1954) offered this postulate: "Concern with reliability and validity as statistical

concepts characterizing evaluation instruments or procedures should be replaced by concern with the permanency and relevancy of learning as concepts characterizing the quality of instruction" (26). In words a little closer to earth, if a test isn't useful to a teacher or a student, what matter its relative validity or reliability? Long before Dressel and Palmer, evaluation statisticians were fond of pronouncing that without rater reliability, there is no test validity. Dressel and Palmer, both teachers first, responded that without instructional use, there is no test validity.

9. Their textbook was published by Holt, Rinehart and Winston in 1963, but Diederich and Palmer's preface is dated May 1955. They began writing original test materials in 1942 and by military contract had to validate them with a representative spread of schools and colleges. Teachers responded enthusiastically and wanted more. When the war ended, Diederich and Palmer had enough leftover material for their college textbook. But why did it take nearly twenty more years to be published?

10. In their narrow office, Diederich and Palmer tried out multiple-choice questions by shouting their answers of A, B, C, or D. Later they decided numbers would be better—1, 2, 3, or 4—which would not be confused with letter grades. In class students could just hold up fingers. "Fingers are not so easy to lose or forget to bring to class as cards" (Diederich and Palmer 1963, vi).

11. Palmer participated as reader in the three most impactful early US experiments in whole-essay evaluation: Diederich's 1943 test of writer instability (Diederich 1946b); Diederich, French, and Carlton's 1961 factoring of essay commentary; and Swineford and Godshalk's 1961 validity study of the ECT (Godshalk, Swineford, and Coffman 1966).

12. Quoted with permission. Special Collections Research Center, University of Chicago Library.

13. Quoted with permission. Special Collections Research Center, University of Chicago Library.

14. Diederich loathed reductive language tests, including multiple-choice tests, that looked only for "the lowest common denominator." In a draft titled "The Construction and Criticism of Comprehensive Examinations" and dated May 22, 1946, Diederich formally presents his argument that the construction of Comprehensive Examinations be undertaken solely by members of the Board of Examinations. If the test is written by a teacher, that teacher should also be a member of the board. It "will give him greater freedom to write items above the lowest common denominator of the course if he is in a position to disclaim responsibility for items which one or more of his colleagues dislike" (1946a, 2). Earlier, in a May 12 memorandum, Diederich (1946c) affirms that when tests are created by a group of teachers, "the more penetrating items tended to disappear in favor of items on the lowest common denominator of the course" (2). Conformism of groups can ride roughshod over insights of individuals. The argument became popular among critics who disliked holistic scoring methods. Louie Crew (1977), for instance, defines holistic scores as "a collection of subjective responses, the wise mingled indiscriminately with the foolish, which by way of a number have been reduced to their lowest denominator of possible evaluative significance" (710).

15. All along, of course, the force behind the plan was President Robert Maynard Hutchins. The day after he was inaugurated in 1929, he spoke to the Student Assembly and said, "I favor the best faculty that could be obtained, teaching the best students that could be found, with a curriculum intelligently adjusted to the needs of the individual" (quoted in McNeil 2007, 27).

16. In 1957, Dressel defined an academic grade as "an inadequate report of an inaccurate judgment by a biased and variable judge of the extent to which a student has attained an undefined level of mastery of an unknown proportion of an indefinite

17. material" (1957, 6)—an often-quoted pleasantry with a bitter aftertaste. Doesn't a grade make the singular person ("a student") vanish?

17. The particular writing surround—which later Catharine Keech Lucas would call "ecology" (1988)—Eley called "supportive context." His dissertation argued that writing errors therefore cannot be assessed fairly if they are just counted. "From our discussion of various error categories we have seen that in a large number of cases the error pattern is most easily explained in terms of the strength or weakness of surrounding context. A successful essay would seem to be one flowing from a single and extensive linguistic intention appropriately organized and carried out. The extent to which any piece of writing fulfills these criteria and hence creates a sense of unity for the reader is the extent to which a rich and consistent ground for communication has been constructed" (1953, 86). In the history of writing assessment, Eley's point is well ahead of its time.

18. The University of Chicago club included some odd couples. In 1962, Wilma R. Ebbitt coedited *Dictionaries and THAT Dictionary* on the controversy over *Webster's Third New International Dictionary*. Her coeditor was James Sledd. In 1953, Sledd was one of the members of the English Department at the University of Chicago who attacked the New Plan and its system of Comprehensives and Board of Examinations. He could out-prickle Diederich. In one memorandum he scoffed at the claim by Bloom and other examiners that the New Plan produced sophomores as qualified as seniors elsewhere: "I found graduates of the College pretty much on a level, statistically, with students who had spent two years at Mundelein, Vanderbilt, the Academy of the New Church, or the Central Michigan College of Education" (Boyer 2011, 147–48). Ebbitt went on to write several enormously popular rhetorical handbooks and to end her career with fourteen years as professor in the English Department of Penn State University.

19. Unfortunately, Coward provided no citations, even when the report was published in the *Journal of Educational Research* in 1952. But surely she knew of Wiseman's study of Robertson's pooled-rater, rapid-impression marking of Devon 11-plus essays, published in the *British Journal of Education Psychology* early in 1949. For his open pooled-rater scoring, he had used a twenty-point scale (which she just halved), and his rater-reliability calculations had also recommended pooling the scores of four raters.

20. Two decades later, in a comprehensive and stern caution against holistic essay scoring, Davida Charney used Godshalk's words against him, noting the requirement of rapid reading during scoring and concluding that "testing agencies and researchers must impose a very unnatural reading environment, one which intentionally disallows thoughtful responses to the essays" (1984, 74).

21. Godshalk's account of the session exists as a draft of an article for the *College Board Review*, dated January 30, 1961, sent to Henry Dyer, vice president of the College Board. A report of historical significance, it seems to have remained in the ETS archives, unnoticed by composition scholars. But not unnoticed by ETS personnel. Gertrude Conlan kept a copy in her file cabinet and then, on August 5, 1988, passed it on to colleague Gary Saretzky, with a note saying Godshalk was "the inventor of holistic scoring" and that the "historical interest" of his report is that its "pages record the first glimmerings of the idea for holistic scoring." The document was given to Norbert Elliot by Doug Baldwin of ETS.

22. One reader was Gerhard Friedrich, long-time table leader at Advanced Placement English examinations, who a decade later would prove instrumental in the use of AP-style holistic scoring for the California State University and College's English Equivalency Examination, 1973–1979 (see Haswell and Elliot 2017).

23. How does this correlation—0.38, determined by two readers reading one topic holistically, the most common research design—compare with other studies we have

analyzed from 1936 to 1966? When we turn to Hartog, Rhodes, and Burt, we see that the levels of dispersion (focusing on marking of the English essay) using impression marking were reported in terms of descriptive, not inferential, statistics. In Burt's technical memorandum to *The Marks of Examiners*, he does not take up correlations involved with the essay, but we can get an idea of the range of acceptable correlations in his analysis of the Latin examination. When correlations are established between the marks of each examiner and the hypothetical true mean, the coefficient is high, ranging from 0.72 to 0.96 (Hartog, Rhodes, and Burt 1936, 294, table 141). This result is to be expected because the hypothetical true mean is a determination of calculation in which marks are weighted to achieve standardization; thus, this correlation is not a reported relationship of the compared scores of two readers. In the study by Cast, analysis of variance was used in the first part of the study (1939), but in the second part (1940), the average correlation for twelve examiners using general-impression scoring is 0.49 (52, table 7). For Wiseman, the average correlation for eight markers using general-impression scoring is 0.70 (1949, 203, table 2). For Coward, the correlations for readers using "wholistic" scoring were related to task and ranged from 0.34 to 0.71. For Finlayson (1951), correlations between two readers was established at 0.74. While Anderson (1960) used analysis of variance techniques, he did report (without a correlation table) a correlation of 0.45 in terms of the three examiners. For Diederich, French, and Carlton (1961), the interrater reliability was 0.31. So, in sum, the 0.38 correlation between readers reported by Coffman (1966) was very much a low-to-average correlation, especially considering the highly constrained timed, impromptu nature of the five writing samples that were to be completed in two hours and twenty minutes. The correlation is indeed among the lowest reported at that time. It is worth noting that when the Godshalk, Swineford, and Coffman study published in 1966 was replicated in 1987 (Breland et al.), the reliability for a single essay read twice was 0.53—a somewhat higher coefficient related to the six-point scale used in the replication (60). And so it is that, while the Godshalk, Swineford, and Coffman 1966 publication is remembered for being a landmark study for the rise of holistic scoring in the United States, close inspection of the achieved interrater reliability demonstrates a remarkably low level of correlation between readers. The 0.7 standard had not been met.

24. The penultimate draft of *The Measurement of Writing Ability* can still be found in the ETS archives (Godshalk, Swineford, and Coffman 1965). One of the few changes made to the published version is the decision not to use the original title: *Studies of the Question Types in the CEEB English Composition Test as Predictors of an Essay Criterion*. While awkward, the original title captured the innovative study design.

25. Who added this reference at the last minute? Swineford, Godshalk, and Coffman were all at ETS when Vernon spent a month there in 1957 discussing test construction, and any one of them might well have noted a glaring omission in their survey of previous scholarship. The rewriting of the passage, however, suggests a reevaluation of the "breakthrough" nature of their study. Was there a fourth party? A clue, highly tentative, lies in the strange fact that the published bibliography adds a new item, one not mentioned in either draft or text: Diederich's essay "Reading and Grading," which had been published in 1965 (1965a). Was it Diederich who reminded the authors of Vernon's book and British studies of pooled-rater holistic scoring? Diederich, of course, had no love for pooled-rater scoring in real-life settings: "I have never had much confidence in any scheme for rating papers," he wrote in 1974, "that does not involve comparison with independent ratings of another person and discussion of papers on which there is a substantial difference of opinion" (53).

7
CALIFORNIA SCHOOLS, 1960–1982

> *Moloch the heavy judger of men.*
> —Allen Ginsberg, "Howl"

With its open holistic scoring—few reader constraints except the use of anchor essays—the English Composition Test was sold to students by the College Board as part of their admission testing program. However, it was for accountability in the schools, usually in a form more controlled and rubricized, that holistic essay scoring reached its peak use. That controlled form of scoring—a process in which the readers are guided in various ways with the use of anchor essays, scoring guides, rubrics, and preset distribution of scores, and which is often accompanied by fairly lengthy rater training and recalibration of scorers—largely occurred in the 1980s. Although the history of the end points on a continuum could be documented in nearly every state of the Union, there is no better place to see the borderlands than California, where *la frontera* is starkly drawn.

It is not overdramatic to say that in California, the history of holistic essay scoring began with an act of surveillance and exclusion. California school teachers were watched and excluded, and holistic scoring was one way they resisted. Part of the resistance included the Bay Area Writing Project (BAWP), founded in 1974. The relationship of BAWP with holistic scoring was complex and included forms of resistance in which tests were praised and rejected as they supported or oppressed teachers. In this kind of map, focus on method is sharpened when attention is drawn to learning. Researchers in BAWP learned that resisting state accountability meant accounting for themselves. In the end, they may have found that the interplay between assessment and accountability is not a zero-sum game. Seen through a contemporary lens, the work of BAWP teachers in California helped found the kind of writing assessment environment that Chris Gallagher (2019) describes as informed by "thoughtful critiques *and* workable alternatives rooted in democratic models of engagement" (493). Between 1960 and 1982, the California dream of teacher empowerment—achieved by integrating instruction and assessment at a local level—established communities of research-based practice that remain in place today.

THE CALIFORNIA EDUCATIONAL SYSTEM: 1960

In every way, California is big and manifold. If, heaven forbid, you physically laid California on top of Great Britain, it would extend beyond Land's End at the bottom of Wales and beyond the Duncansby Head lighthouse at the top of Scotland. By necessity, in terms of size and geography, the schools and colleges are also various and far flung. In 1960 the same could be said of the way they formally assessed the writing of their students.

In postsecondary education, language testing depended upon the system to which the institution belonged. State funded California campuses were divided into three segments: the California State University System (CSU), which began as colleges for teachers; the University of California (UC) System, whose campuses are featured as research centers; and the California Community Colleagues, which serve a wide variety of vocational and educational needs. In fact, the three units of California public higher education are, unlike such institutions in many states, not segments of a single system. Each has its own mission, board of governors, and distinct student populations. Even within these three cohorts, there were few uniform rules governing writing proficiency in admission standards, advance credit, or degree requirements. Take the CSUC system. By 1960, there were eighteen campuses, including California's oldest university in San Jose (1857) and one of the youngest in Dominguez Hills (1960). It wasn't until 1973 that CSU installed throughout its system an advance-credit examination in writing (Haswell and Elliot 2017).

It might therefore seem that the seven campuses in the University of California system, from Berkeley (1868) to San Diego (1960), offered an exceptional uniformity since the Subject A examination had been administered system wide since 1898. Originally, in University of California institutions, English was Subject A, Latin Subject B, and mathematics Subject C. Given the nature of the California system, however, the way that the Subject A requirement was administered varied over time. In 1960 that variation had become excessive. Each campus was running that writing-placement test differently. At individual campuses, everything about the examination kept changing like a surrealist film—the students who had to take it, the time they took it, and who paid for it.[1] Up to 1960, and far beyond, the most consistent part of Subject A was the way it was graded, typically by a single faculty member applying connoisseurship. As a result, the scoring itself could hardly be called consistent, and in fact its unreliability had been and would be questioned over and again (Stevens 2000).

This environment produced radically different views of assessment. In developing a placement process for the CSU system, Edward M. White (2001) has characterized his experiences with the Educational Testing Service (ETS)—the vendor for the assessment—as troubled and often antagonistic. In his March 24, 2015, interview with us, George Gadda provided a narrative of collegiality in working with Associate Examiner Mary Fowles of ETS, along with colleagues across campuses in the University of California system. Gadda came to University of California, Los Angeles (UCLA) in 1980 and, beginning in 1985, was invited to chair the development of the university-wide Subject A Examination with colleagues from the UC Council of Writing Programs. With experiences beginning in the 1980s when he was a graduate student at the University of North Carolina at Chapel Hill, Gadda (a medieval scholar by training) came to UCLA to teach in the writing program, worked there with Richard A. Lanham, and has continued to work with a wide variety of vendors to manage what was once the Subject A Examination—and would become, after 2005, the Entry Level Writing Requirement (ELWR), with the test later renamed the Analytical Writing Placement Examination (AWPE) in 1987.

As the histories provided by White and Gadda illustrate, postsecondary admission and placement processes were extraordinarily diverse. Private colleges, such as Stanford, as closed admission as possible, relied on school transcripts, teacher recommendations, and parents' wealth. As for the two-year institutions, in 1960 the fifty or more "junior colleges" were not even united in a state-wide system; the California Community Colleges was formed in 1967. These sites did not test writing or verbal skills for admission. The Donohoe Higher Education Act, signed by Governor Edmund Gerald ("Pat") Brown in 1960, made them officially what most had always been: open admission.

That leaves the public schools. In 1960 the public schools graduated over 40 percent of their students, the highest rate in the nation, yet formal assessment of writing was left up to the districts or schools, who sporadically applied machine-scorable tests at different curricular points, or more commonly imposed none at all.[2] Most school teachers liked it that way, but it gave their opponents an opening. Compared to college teachers, public-school teachers have always been more vulnerable to top-down control—administrative, political, and public. As we will see, distrust of teachers ran powerfully through the post–World War II history of formal writing assessment in California. A major part of the history is the way school teachers fought that distrust, a struggle in which they achieved notable and unique victories. Some of the fight swirled around holistic scoring. The historical evidence for that is compelling. In 1960, formal assessment of writing was rarely direct except for teacher grading and an occasional use of analytic scales. Yet twenty years later it was said of the San Francisco Bay Area alone that it contained "more teachers who are highly trained in holistic scoring than does any other metropolitan area within the United States" (Stansfield 1986, 230). Chapter 2 documents that it happened. Here we show how.

CALIFORNIA SCHOOLS AND MANDATED LANGUAGE TESTING: 1961

As we have noted, the California history of holistic scoring of writing began with an act of surveillance and exclusion. We refer to an actual legislative act, not the 1960 Donahoe Higher Education Act but another that quickly followed: the 1961 minimum-competency legislation that introduced California schools to testing mandated by the state. Starting in 1962, schools had to test students at grades five, eight, and eleven. Subjects covered were, as the legislature oddly put it, "reading, language, mathematics, and intelligence." By "language" they meant "composition skills," and by composition skills they meant whatever it was that "objective type questions" measured (Citizens 1961, 55). A list of objective achievement tests from which schools were compelled to choose was provided by the California State Board of Education. The list included, for instance, the Stanford Reading Tests, the Houghton Mifflin Tests of Academic Progress, and the verbal battery of the Lorge-Thorndike Intelligence Tests.

Support for the testing was solid everywhere except among teachers. It was perhaps thinnest among writing teachers, who as a rule scorned machine-scored bubble-and-booklet tests. "In California," wrote one of them years later, "we have provided other states with an example of how they should not assess student writing" (Peckham 1987, 30). But as early as the mid-1960s, California teachers were also providing other states with an example of how *to* assess student writing. Theirs was a unique dissent.

Not that California was the first state to require language testing in their schools. West Virginia in 1958 and Alabama in 1959 started mandating it for all students at certain grades, and by 1962 many other states, such as New York, Florida, and Washington, were requiring it for students in college-prep programs or for admission to higher education in the state. A larger number of states had installed it on a quasi-voluntary basis—Indiana, Illinois, and New Hampshire, for example, and Iowa, where 95 percent of school districts participated (Resnick 1968). And some other states, such as Arizona, had patchwork testing requirements because they were using money provided by Title V of the National Defense Education Act (NDEA). In 1958 the NDEA was founded by Congress with an eye-opening appropriation of $800,000,000. The purpose was to help the United States compete with the Soviet Union by identifying exceptional students in US schools and colleges. As a measure of talent but also of accountability, the NDEA-funded institutions were required to test students objectively. Probably the most common expenditure of an NDEA grant was the purchase of machine-scorable tests.[3]

In California the 1961 minimum-competency legislation did not appear uniquely vindictive. It is true that in following years the legislature gradually tightened the act as an oversight measure. In 1965 the tests were made uniform across districts. In 1968 the proscription of release of results was rescinded. In 1969, academic grades tested were increased to one, two, three, six, and twelve, and results had to be reported to schools, districts, and the State Board of Education. Still, California minimum-competency test scores were never used for graduation or individual grade promotion, and when a school performed badly, the outcome, supposedly, was increased funding to improve its programs.[4] So how could the 1961 legislation be called an act of surveillance and exclusion?

One clue is the term *national defense* in the name NDEA. Surveillance fit the affective and political climate of the 1950s. Widespread and often voiced was a fear that our educational system had failed to educate our students in ways that could defend the country from Communism, which would if it could subvert or destroy the country. Historically it was no accident that the run-up to federal and state-mandated testing coincided with the Cold War. The symbiosis of the Cold War and accountability may explain much of the motive of the California Legislature in 1958 to authorize a Joint Interim Committee on the Public Education System, an authorization that produced the minimum-competency legislation three years later.

Certainly, the meld of Cold War and testing helped account for the recommendations of the Citizens Advisory Commission, which the Joint Interim Committee had quickly created to gather facts and public opinion. The first words of the commission's preliminary 1959 report struck a note less advisory than admonitory: "With the advent of the Russian 'Sputnik' into the skies of our universe, parents, educators, and legislators were suddenly made aware that perhaps there was something lacking in the system of education as we now know it in the United States." The Soviets had got to space first and our schools were to blame. "What is the matter with the educational system of California, and is the Russian system superior?" (Citizens 1959, 5). Yes to this second question needed only one concrete piece of evidence, the Soviet satellite that passed over the sovereign state of California every two and a half hours, looking down from "the skies of our universe." America must be made great again.

In orbit for only three months during the fall of 1957, Sputnik was not, in fact, looking down on anybody or anything since the USSR had not designed it to do that. It just emitted beeps. Anxiety of US citizens was not allayed. Surveillance from on high was already plugged into their mindset. The first "flying saucers," nine of them, had been sighted near Mt. Rainier in 1947, and by the mid-1950s, hundreds of UFO sitings were being investigated by the US Air Force. In 1956 the Air Force's Project Genetrix sent more than 500 high-altitude balloons equipped with cameras over Eastern Europe, the Soviet Union, and Communist China, most shot down in response to loud diplomatic outrage. In May of 1960, Gary Powers and his U-2 plane were captured on Russian soil.

The "cloud of apprehension," as the Citizens Advisory Commission put it (1959, 5), emerged also from a sense that surveillance was coming from around as well as from on high. Ten years earlier, a little-known US senator named Joseph McCarthy had held up a sheet of paper that, he assured his audience, contained a list of 205 Communists working in the State Department. People took him at his word. Later the same year, California passed the rightly named Levering Act, requiring its state employees to sign a loyalty oath swearing they would defend the United States "against all enemies, foreign and domestic." Thirty-one University of California faculty were fired for refusing to sign the oath.[5]

In this political environment it makes sense that the Citizens Advisory Commission thought of installing a surveillance system to watch some of California's own citizens, namely its school teachers. The commission insisted it was not out to oversee or control teachers. "These tests will set a minimum level of instruction beyond which the teacher should be encouraged to develop the most comprehensive, meaningful, and challenging program of instruction," the commission said, and "will follow the curriculum rather than determine it" (Citizens 1961, 54). But such language would not have fooled many teachers. They knew that if tests locate a "minimum level," the school will expect its instructors to devote their time bringing students up to that level. In the commission's scheme, individual student results were not reported, but school averages were known, and if a school fell below the standard in, say, eighth-grade language, who would be held accountable? If teachers were not threats, why had testing come to their classroom doors?

And why had the commission not come to their doors earlier? As with most fact-finding groups empowered by state legislatures, the selection of members for the Citizens Advisory Commission was highly politicized. One legislator said that over 300 potential candidates came forward, most of them "with axes to grind," and a member of the commission recalled that the requirement for selection was "who had the biggest beef with education" (Inglis 2011, 34–36). Although there was some effort at moderation, in the end, the twenty-seven members of the commission tended to be people whose direct acquaintance with schools was as school students: lawyers, college administrators, university professors emeriti, oil-company executives, bank presidents, textbook consultants, and school-board members. Only two were current school teachers, one of them "recently started" (Citizens 1961, 7–12). The first act of a commission authorized to recommend major changes in the daily work of school teachers was, as might be expected, to exclude school teachers almost entirely from their group.

People in a cloud of apprehension need concrete sources for their fear. Spies and other operatives would work, but as the House Un-American Activities Committee was discovering, they are hard to put a finger on. UFOs, nuclear radiation, racial contamination, and water fluoridation are almost as nebulous as the fear itself. It is no surprise, then, that the most popular scapegoats were school teachers. They were plentiful and closeted with our children behind closed doors five hours a day. Following World War II, the public attack on US teachers was relentless, appearing in hundreds of magazine articles and in popular books such as *Educational Wastelands* (Bestor 1953) or *Quackery in the Public Schools* (Lynd 1953)—none of it likely "to inspire confidence in anyone with high hopes for their children," as education historian William J. Reese dryly puts it (2005, 222).

In some ways, among school faculty it was teachers of English who bore the brunt. In times of national crisis, the state of the English language has always been a target. Suddenly, people note the mother tongue has grown slipshod, vulgarized, error ridden, or has otherwise deteriorated. As for the causes of the decline in "correct" language use, Harvey A. Daniels provides a popular list that includes one-parent families, oral contraceptives, overdoses of television, rock and roll, teenage slang, telephones, *Webster's Third*, and—closer to our point—progressive education, teachers' unions, structural grammar, phonics, picture books, and elective English courses (1983, 25).

To round off the surveillance, the commission recommended and secured "a composition test" given at grades six and eight and during the third or fourth year of high school. Because they were part of the problem, English teachers would have no say in constructing the tests. The commission, of course, did not put it that bluntly, but such was their meaning: "With the state constructing the examinations, the effectiveness of the test will be much more meaningful, because specialists will be constructing them, who have skill and ingenuity far superior to that which many districts could afford with their comparatively small budgets" (Citizens 1961, 54–55). In the absence of sophistication in the teachers, specialists would have to be brought in to construct a test of writing proficiency.[6]

As it turned out, California would get more for its money than the commission had imagined.

ALBERT LAVIN AND SIR FRANCIS DRAKE HIGH SCHOOL: 1966–1972

In the history of the US accountability movement, the absence of composition teachers and specialists from large-scale testing decisions is commonplace. California English school teachers, however, were a feisty lot.[7] In 1961 many had at least one conviction worth fighting for, namely, that multiple-choice tests in themselves were not valid to assess student achievement, proficiency, or potential in writing. Required were direct ways to assess writing proficiency.

Possibly it was through their own advisory commission that they first became acquainted with holistic scoring. The Curriculum Study Commission was established in 1927 by the California State Board of Education for input on issues concerning curriculum, textbooks, and teaching materials. In 1949 the commission sponsored the first of the Asilomar Language Arts Conferences, which continue to this day. From the start, they were popular with teachers, and principals were instructed to let their faculty off early on Friday afternoons so they could make the drive to Asilomar beach on the Monterrey peninsula to swap stories, share insider information, and form communities of practice.

It was at an Asilomar Conference in 1957 or 1958 that Miles Myers, who was teaching English at Washington High School in Fremont,

California, remembers being first introduced to "holistic scoring." He also remembers attending "holistic essay scoring" sessions at California Association of Teachers of English (CATE) conferences about the same time, perhaps when he had moved to Oakland High School, where he taught English from 1959 until 1974. In 1969 he attended essay scoring at Concord High School a few miles east of Berkeley (email to authors, December 8–14, 2014). It seems language-arts teachers in the 1960s were exploring methods of direct assessment, if not in direct response to objective testing of composition skills, at least as a complement to it.

For historians of writing assessment, the problem with these early efforts in the California schools is that the evidence is scant and often secondhand.[8] Even the particular brand of holistic procedure Myers mentions is hard to determine. He had an eclectic definition of holistic, roughly any scaled rating of an essay positioned east of teacher grading and west of numerical analysis of features (such as words per sentence).[9] At Asilomar or CATE in 1957 or 1958, the presentations could have been a report of the California Writing Evaluation Scale since the work on that sample-matching scheme was supported by CATE and began in 1957.[10] Or the talks might have reported on the relatively new method ETS was using to score essays in their Sequential Tests of Educational Progress—a quasi-analytical scoring scheme with 50 percent awarded for quality of thought, 30 percent for style, and 20 percent for sentence structure, all on a seven-point scale with model essays at points 2, 4, and 6. As the two previous chapters describe, teachers serving as scorers for ETS could have brought back holistic methods from the newly formed Advanced Placement (AP) English Literature and Composition examination or from the administrations of the English Composition Test that rated essays. The president of CATE in 1964 and 1965, Gerhard Friedrich, was deeply involved with AP scoring from its start in 1954. Of course, many language-arts teachers would have known Paul B. Diederich's 1966 article in the *English Journal*, "How to Measure Growth in Writing Ability," which set forth both a rapid-impression scoring method with a three-level scale ("high," "middle," and "low") and a weighted analytic scale that scored eight criteria separately.

As our imagined meetings reveal, in the 1960s California schools had a variety of direct-scoring methods available to them, but it is not easy to find out which ones they actually used. Fortunately, there is one application about which we now know a good deal. It was run by the English Department chair at Sir Francis Drake High School in Marin County, Albert "Cap" Lavin. Lavin began his Writing Project as early as 1966 or 1967.[11] Lavin, it should be emphasized, was not a run-of-the-mill English school teacher. According to James Gray (2000), Lavin was the only US school teacher invited to the Dartmouth conference in 1966. When the National Assessment of Educational Progress established a conference in July 1969 to revise their writing objectives, the attendees included eleven experts from outside the National Assessment of Educational Progress (NAEP) or ETS, and one of them was Lavin (Norris 1969).

Actually, Lavin may have experimented with holistic scoring before 1966. Myers (email to authors, December 8–14, 2014) remembers meeting him, perhaps as early as 1964, at an airport after an Advanced Placement reading in Atlantic City, where Lavin told him "some of the Marin County teachers were starting to organize their own holistic scoring of essays." Myers may have been referring to classroom use of holistic scoring, with students rating peer essays. We know for certain, however, that around 1966, Lavin started a six-year study comparing the writing of grade-nine, grade-ten, grade-eleven, and grade-twelve students at Drake. Kate Blickhahn (email to authors, June 10, 2015), who taught with Lavin, describes the purpose:

> Cap convinced our Principal, Harold Allison, to reduce each English teacher's teaching day to four periods, the fifth period assigned to supervise Study Hall, to enable English teachers to reduce the load of papers to be graded and to increase the time for grading and lesson planning. Both Cap and Principal Allison were interested to see whether there might be a way to measure the growth and sophistication of student writing by comparing the work of students at each grade level, partly out of sheer interest, and partly to justify the reduced teaching load given our English teachers.

In effect, Lavin wanted to defend a reduction in his high-school faculty's teaching load by showing that the writing of their students continued to improve despite that reduction.

The purpose and design of Lavin's experiment owed much to Diederich. In 1960 Diederich had published a controversial piece in the *English Journal*, "The Rutgers Plan for Cutting Class Size in Two." In part, the plan proposed that "every high school English teacher may have one day a week completely free of class duties" (158). For rating his Drake essays, Lavin turned to a method in which he himself had been trained, the Advanced Placement scoring of composition essays discussed in chapter 5. In her June 10, 2015, email correspondence with us, Blickhahn pointed out that Lavin taught Advanced Placement courses and "was a member of the ETS scoring team" that read AP essays. Lavin followed AP's scale of 1–9 but not AP's use of sample papers to illustrate scores of 2, 4, 6, and 8.[12] His scoring directions under the term *rubric* only note that an essay not completely addressing the topic can receive a score no higher than 6, and one that evades the question can receive a score no higher than 4. But it repeated nearly verbatim the statement that for years appeared like a mantra on all AP scoring guides: "Students should be rewarded for what they do well in response to the question." And it followed AP's direction to add one point for "exceptionally sophisticated style and grace" and subtract one point "for severe mechanical and stylistic deficiencies that block communication of meaning." Lavin's directions also followed AP's request that in scoring an essay, readers should first settle on an even number from the nine-point scale and then, if suitable, use "odd numbers to reward things which really stand out—language use, freshness, crispness, or to lower the score of a paper which was a struggle to read" (Keech 1979b, appendix B2).[13]

Lavin followed ETS in administering the reading with a chief reader and table leaders. His use of the scores, however, departed radically. Here is Blickhahn's description of Lavin's system (email to the authors, June 10, 2015):

> A committee of teachers designed the writing prompt. Students wrote to the prompt during their English classes, using their initials and a teacher-period code to prevent identification of individual students during scoring. All members of the department gathered during a specified day for the scoring. Papers were randomized. Each paper was read by two readers, the first score covered by a peel-off sticker. Scores were later combined. Papers were recorded by grade [academic grade level] and percentages of each score noted. Scores for individual students were never revealed, nor were scores attained by students in any teacher's particular class. The project was designed specifically to compare the overall writing ability of freshmen, sophomores, juniors and seniors.[14]

The actual scoring guide (Keech 1979b, appendix B2) adds that a paper with two independent scores more than two points apart on the nine-point scale (e.g., 4 and 7) were "given a third reading" by the table leader or chief reader, presumably with all three scores averaged.

During the six years of the English Project, Lavin's eleventh graders were also taking California's minimum-competency examinations. That objective composition test and Lavin's experiment both purport to measure writing achievement, yet they are a study in contrast. One collects data, the other tests an hypothesis. One has students work with fragments of someone else's language, the other has them write their own complete essays. One assumes teachers cannot make or score the test they give, the other that teachers can perfectly well design the test, write the prompts, and score the products. One uses the test results to detect problems in faculty teaching, the other to defend an improvement in faculty job conditions. One testing procedure isolates teachers into their separate classrooms, the other has teachers work together to construct prompts and evaluate essays. To initiate, one needed a legislative committee, a citizen's commission, and an act of the legislature, the other required conversations between a school principal and a head of a department. One was partly motivated by "axes to grind," the other by "sheer interest" in the outcomes.

When we say, in measurement terms, that a construct is either underrepresented or robust in a given assessment, related issues are ever present. You can find out a lot when you focus on genre.

MANDATES: MINIMUM ESSENTIALS AND BUBBLE SHEETS

It is hazardous to typify the mood of school teachers across California in the 1960s in terms of the state's minimum-competency requirements. School teachers were just as heterogenous as the rest of their state. Many of them, including some participating in Lavin's English Project, may have welcomed objective testing of composition skills and the excuse to teach to that kind of testing. But other teachers felt anxiety, anger, and frustration. As Catharine Keech Lucas (email to authors, March 2016) describes it, "They SAW that school children were being taught writing in ways that stultified expression, inhibited fluency and did not necessarily improve even their basic skills. And we all felt that the tests were partly at fault. We certainly knew they took up too much classroom time, without giving us anything we needed to know, and succeeded only in sorting kids into the top dogs and the defeated children who might have been capable of more, if given a chance."

Clouds of apprehension and feelings of opaque resentment are not impossible to document. For many teachers of the language arts in the 1960s and 1970s, resistance to testing mandated by the state interconnected with a number of specific concerns, including minimum essentials, lock-step curriculum, curtailed speech, and bureaucratic machinery. The material manifestation of these concerns included draft cards, punch cards, and bubble sheets.

In reference to the California 1961 mandated testing, authorities speaking for the state always used the term "minimum competency." Teachers, however, sometimes talked of "minimum essentials." It is a revealing choice. *Minimum essentials* was a catchphrase in education dating back at least to the first decade of the century, used in reference to curricular objectives, pedagogical techniques, textbook coverage, teaching aids, and testing goals. The essence of minimum essentials was that at each step of a curriculum or learning plan, teachers should make sure every student understood the fundamentals of that step before proceeding to the next. Only thereby would teaching achieve its greatest efficiency. By 1913, Thomas E. Thompson, superintendent of schools in Leominster, Massachusetts, and self-declared leader of the minimum-essentials movement, averred, "'Minimum essentials' is the topic most discussed in the educational world of today" because "'efficiency' is the slogan in the world of business, of achievement, and of education" (102).

But not all teachers bought into Thompson's movement. Especially educators in the language arts argued that the curricular ideal of minimum essentials assumed a lock-step sequence of learning that did not fit either writing or the acquisition of writing. In 1921 the author of an unsigned editorial in the *English Journal* entitled "Minimum Essentials" argued that unity, coherence, emphasis, illustration, vocabulary, and directness "can never be acquired once and for all but must be matters of slow and simultaneous growth through all the years" and that teachers much give them "*equal* and *simultaneous* attention" (541). "Equal and simultaneous," to be sure, is another way of saying "holistic."

Fifty years later, many California teachers still stood in opposition to the lock-step sequences of minimal essentials. They were reading California-based intellectuals whose best-selling books targeted everything sequential, mechanical, and hierarchical: Herbert Marcuse debunking the "unfreedom" of capitalist technology in *One-Dimensional Man: Studies in the Ideology of Advanced Industrial Society* (1964), Alan Watts bemoaning ontological "isolation" in *The Book: On the Taboo against Knowing Who You Are* (1966), Hubert Dreyfus exposing "context-free rules" in *What Computers Can't Do* (1972). Most English teachers knew Allan Ginsberg's ironic invocation in *Howl* to "Moloch the heavy judger of men . . . Moloch whose mind is pure machinery"—first recited in 1955 at City Lights bookstore in downtown San Francisco. In 1964 some of them had actually heard Mario Savio (1964) on the steps of Berkeley's Sproul Hall shouting, "There's a time when the operation of the machine becomes so odious, makes you so sick at heart, that you can't take part! You can't even passively take part! And you've got to put your bodies upon the gears and upon the wheels, upon the levers, upon all the apparatus, and you've got to make it stop!" Savio was protesting new University of California regulations limiting political activities on campuses, rules limiting free speech, civil rights, and protests against the Vietnam War such as burning draft cards. But he was also protesting the way a faculty member had called the president of the University of California, Clark Kerr, the "manager of a firm," which to Savio made teachers at Berkeley "a bunch of employees" and the students "raw material."

One familiar material object standing for all this was the bubble sheet. Students filled in little circles with #2 lead pencils, and answers were measured as right or wrong either by machines with photoelectric cells or by humans performing like machines with scoring sheets.[15] And bubble sheets were just a version of the old punch card, which had first been used to guide automated weaving looms (machines) in the early eighteenth century. In the 1950s and 1960s, the general public was familiar with punch cards in the form of utility bills, student registration forms, and employment and unemployment checks. They often contained the warning, "Do not fold, spindle or mutilate." For political resisters, the punch card became a symbol of efficient, heartless bureaucracy and what it was doing to people. Lucas (email to authors, March 2016) remembers "chanting, referring to ourselves and people in general, in University of California Berkeley demonstrations: 'do not fold, spindle or staple. . . . The whole California culture was discovering holism, individualism, non-hierarchical decision making." Some of that rebellion is captured in Steven Lubar's 1992 article "'Do Not Fold, Spindle or Mutilate': A Cultural History of the Punch Card," in which the university was depicted as a card-punch machine run by big business, "its product students as identical to one another as IBM cards" (46).

For many California school teachers, objective machine-scored testing attached not only to feelings of surveillance and exclusion but to the entire counterculture of the 1960s and 1970s. Something of the mood can be seen in "The Test Takers," a poem published in 1973 in the *English Journal* and written by Blickhahn, Lavin's old colleague.

The poem describes students confronting a machine-scorable examination, perhaps to satisfy the 1962 California minimum-competency requirement the final year that requirement was in effect. The last line gives the author's feelings away: "The State wants to know something about him." What is the use of this testing? Neither the test requirer nor the test taker really know—just "something." All that remains is the sense of surveillance ("wants to know"). Seated in "parallel" rows like punch cards, the students bow obediently to the task of filling in the bubbles, "little o's," zeros empty of meaning. The students have been coerced into isolating themselves from one another, protecting their answers ("handling his test booklet from inside his rumpled plaid jacket").

But isn't the poem also about the teacher? Mindfully, as the teacher observes the students, a judgment takes place. In place of the

> **The Test Takers**
>
> Seated at desks,
>   their backs bent in supplication, concentration,
>   over parallel pencils poised,
> their faces reflect the white paper.
> One sits,
>   his neck pulled in between hunched shoulders;
> One sits,
>   slouching on the arc of his lower back;
> One sits,
>   stiffly upright,
>   her arms and legs arranged,
>   head carefully tilted,
>   mouth pursed;
> One sits,
>   leaning close,
>   her hair curtaining her desk top.
> One thin, reedy boy works,
>   folded in on himself,
>   handling his test booklet from inside his rumpled plaid jacket,
>   his brown wool pants bunching around his thin legs,
>   his oversized scuffed boots knotted together.
> The long graceful fingers of his right hand pull at his hair,
>   stirring it softly awry around his sharp-featured face,
>   with its wedged nose and sad eyes.
> The slender fingers of his left hand hold the pencil,
>   deftly crossing the page,
>   swiftly swirling little o's.
> The State wants to know something about him.
>
>   Kate Blickhahn
> *San Anselmo, California*

Figure 7.1. "The Test Takers" (Blickhahn 1973) (© 1973 by the National Council of Teachers of English; used with permission)

depersonalized "Ones" lined up like the "little o's" of a bubble sheet, the teacher describes all students in their individuality. The teacher refuses to rubricize students (Maslow 1962). Those seated at their desks are not itemized but singular wholes, meaning-making individuals with unique gestalt perceptions. And yet, the testing situation has excluded the teacher from students and their learning. All that can be done is to watch them work at a task that probably has nothing to do with what needs to be taught and what needs to be learned. The testing situation has appropriated the teacher and made her part of the apparatus of the State—an instrument of surveillance. The teacher's only task is to hand out and collect the tests and, in between, watch for cheaters. In the panopticon, mindfulness does not matter.

In 1969 Diederich defiantly wrote in *Today's Education* that "the Sputnik-inspired demands for superior education did not toll the death knell for progressive education" (1969a, 19). That certainly turned out to be true in California schools, but it took years to become apparent, just as earlier social and political shifts, underground "plate tectonics," produced the tensions, frustrations, and fears that led to the above-ground social disturbances and violent events of the 1970s (Starr 2009, ix).

And so it was that a quiet experiment in direct evaluation of writing in Marin County, California, bodily led to the founding of the Bay Area Writing Project in 1974—historically one of the most progressive of school innovations.

THE BAY AREA WRITING PROJECT: INSERVICE TEACHERS

We mean *bodily* in a literal sense. People who had promoted holistic scoring before 1974 were instrumental in forming BAWP, which quickly started backing holistic scoring in the schools throughout California as a challenge and substitute for state-mandated objective testing of writing for minimum competency. School teacher Lavin became the cofounder of BAWP, along with Berkeley professor of education James Gray. Catharine Keech, who in 1974 as a graduate student at Berkeley shared an office with Lavin, analyzed student papers from six years of his Sir Frances Drake High School experiment for her dissertation and became one of BAWP'S first roving consultants and its shrewdest researcher, defender, and critic of holistic scoring. And at BAWP's first summer institute in 1974, Blickhahn, colleague of Lavin at Drake, gave a presentation on holistic scoring and, as Mary Ann Smith remembers it, teachers leaned forward and started taking notes (email to authors, February 15, 2015).

Something revolutionary was happening at BAWP's summer institute in 1974. School teachers like Blickhahn were teaching university teachers and administrators like Gray. That simple act dismantled one of the oldest hierarchies of the academic establishment. BAWP's mission was in-service teacher development. Traditional methods saw college professionals, most of whom had never taught school, publishing words of wisdom in *English Education* and other professional journals and lecturing teachers during workshops. Years later Gray (2000) remembered well the hostility of teachers at workshops required by school districts and run by university teachers. In 1975, at Lowell High School in San Francisco, an elite institution with high admission standards, a presentation by Gray, Lavin, and Myers started with paper wads thrown at them and ended as a teacher shouted, "Gimme some pencils! If you want to help us, give us some pencils; we can always use pencils." The three presenters agreed thereafter that attendance at BAWP workshops or presentations would never be anything but voluntary (Gray 2000, 63).

In contrast to the old-school way, BAWP held fast to the principle that school teachers know best about school teaching and therefore should be teaching one another, and that college educators should facilitate

Figure 7.2. Albert "Cap" Lavin and James Gray, 1974 (courtesy of the National Writing Project)

that exchange, not co-opt it. This bottoms-up principle ran through all BAWP's staple programs. At summer institutes, both invited and open, professors did not lecture but rather attendees gave presentations of their best practices and shared their own writing in teacher edit groups. School-year inservice workshops lasted no less than five sessions, giving teachers time to report back how a classroom technique, introduced by one of BAWP's experienced school teachers, had worked in their classroom. When schools or districts asked BAWP to solve a problem, they were sent not a university maven from the school of education but a teacher-consultant from the schools who had hands-on experience with the problem. When BAWP research assistants helped school teachers design teacher research, resulting publications cited the teacher as the first author or the only author.

The view of teachers promoted by BAWP was the opposite of exclusion and surveillance. The experience of teachers was accepted as valid, and they were invited to share it openly. No wonder the BAWP franchise expanded rapidly in California and throughout the nation. By 1977, BAWP had approved eight new Writing Project sites in California and five in other states (sponsored by Duke University, Oregon State University at Ashland, Rutgers, The State University of New Jersey, Pace College, and the University of Colorado Boulder). The National Writing Project was established in 1978, with fourteen sites the first year, forty-one the second year, and sixty-nine the third (Gray 2000, 128). In 1980 the California legislature agreed to budget California Writing Projects, and in 2001, when there were 156 national sites, the US Congress agreed to start funding National Writing Projects, citing "a continuing crisis in writing in schools and in the workplace" (*Congressional Record* 2001).

ACCOUNTABLE: THE BAY AREA WRITING PROJECT AND THE CALIFORNIA ASSESSMENT PROGRAM

The grass-roots approach of the Bay Area Writing Project extended to its promotion of holistic scoring of student essays. It is true that from the start the project was formed to improve the teaching of composition in the schools. UC Berkeley was the initial source of funds for the project, and Gray had sold it to administrators as a way to save the university money. He argued that improved teaching in the schools would reduce the number of Berkeley first-year students who had to take the remedial Subject A course. Yet holistic scoring became one of BAWP's most successful programs. Possibly it and subsequent project sites were responsible for more spread of holistic scoring in the 1970s and 1980s than was any other organization, including the College Board. In fact, they often argued that schools and districts could learn to score holistically on their own and not have to pay commercial firms to do it for them.

As it happened, when BAWP started up in the summer of 1974, California schools had a new reason to encourage their teachers to learn direct assessment of student essays. Amazingly, the state had just asked schools to join accountability rather than to resist it. In 1973 the California state legislature replaced the 1961 minimum-competency requirements with the California Assessment Program (CAP). Responding to complaints that the old mandated testing took up too much classroom time and was unrelated to course content, CAP imposed a state-wide testing system rarely seen before or since—a system California itself rejected some twenty years later. It was a bifold system, one that eventually turned into a double-edged sword. The legislature had taken the advice of an advisory committee on testing chaired by the eminent statistician Lee J. Cronbach, and CAP installed a statistical method called *matrix sampling* designed to allow robust construct sampling in group scoring—and first used in large-scale academic assessment by NAEP in 1983–1984 (Applebee, Langer, and Mullis 1986). For school and district accountability, students still had to take objective tests, but each student sat for only parts of the total examination, cutting individual testing time and allowing the construct to be well represented across the student-sampling plan.

On the other hand, for the first time the legislature deemed that not just schools and districts would be held accountable but individual students as well. In fact, graduation would depend on a score of proficient on tests given in the senior year. Legislators were responding to national, local, and sometimes teacher belief that student learning was in decline, especially in language skills. Of course, the belief just retreaded old fears. SAT verbal scores had been in notorious decline since the mid-1960s (Norman Cousins had published "Why Johnny Can't Write" in the *Saturday Review* in 1963). The legislature, uncharacteristically, threw in a sop. They let districts choose the method of testing individual students in math, reading, and writing. So, for the first time in California history, school and district administrators, if they chose, allowed direct evaluation of student essays for state-mandated testing, and they well might have listened to teachers who had learned or heard about holistic scoring.

Caught by surprise in 1973, however, many administrators delayed the development of their local tests and continued to graduate students embarrassing to the state, at least according to the majority opinion of legislators. As a result of manufactured concerns, in 1976 the legislature reinforced CAP with Assembly Bill 3408, known as the California Pupil Proficiency Law. It mandated testing at grades seven, nine, and eleven in order to identify and bring laggers up to snuff. The California State Department of Education called this "enroute assessment" (1979, xi). As one of the drafters of the legislation put it, the bill intended "to restore meaning to the high school diploma by requiring students to meet locally developed standards" (Hart 1978, 592–93). Luckily, California's Pupil Proficiency Law still kept the fate of the individual student at the local level and still encouraged direct testing of writing proficiency.

BAWP did not delay. It sent staff knowledgeable in holistic scoring to interested school districts. Blickhahn remembers, "Soon we were leading holistic scoring sessions in local districts where teachers were still considered people with brains and were trained (by us) to score writing proficiency exams" (email to authors, June 10, 2015).[16] Blickhahn, for instance, took the method to high-school English chair Mary Francis Claggett, who saw that it was used in the entire Alameda School District (in Oakland, a little south of the Bay Bridge). Claggett, who became a BAWP consultant, then took holistic scoring to the Cotati-Rohnert Park

Unified School District (just west of Sonoma State University). Most school districts, of course, preferred indirect, quickly scored tests for measuring writing proficiency, but sometimes teachers took the initiative. Irvin Peckham (email to authors, January 28, 2018) remembers that in Santa Clara County, south of Oakland, English teachers from different schools "bonded together" and formed a writing-assessment committee. Peckham, who taught at Live Oak High School (in Morgan Hill, north of Berkeley), became chair of the committee. Blickhahn came to show the committee how holistic scoring could serve. Peckham also remembers that later, in 1978 or 1979, he was a table leader at a holistic-scoring session directed by Miles Myers that had as many as "a couple hundred teachers," part of a large-scale assessment in Santa Clara County. Myers (email to authors, December 8–14, 2014) also ran an Oakland School District essay scoring for five or six years "in response to the state minimum competency law." In other parts of the state, newly established BAWP sites were spreading the method as well. The California State Department of Education was an ally. In 1977 it published a study of some 4,000 high-school seniors, comparing their scores on an objective test with holistic scoring of an essay (on the now-classic AP scale of 1 to 9) (Law 1977). When it published the *Technical Assistance Guide for Proficiency Assessment* to help schools deal with the Pupil Proficiency Law, the accompanying manuals in 1978 and 1979 included holistic as well as analytic scoring guides for sample topics (California State Department of Education 1979, charts 1, 3, and 5).

Holistic scoring was also spread through the California High School Proficiency Examination (CHSPE), initiated in 1975 and offered three times a year. As in British school-leaving examinations, students who passed CHSPE could drop out without a degree but with a certificate of proficiency. The language-skills portion combined two twenty-minute essays with a multiple-choice section. The examination was run by ETS. According to Ruby S. Bernstein and Bernard R. Tanner, both Bay Area school teachers and BAWP consultants, readers of CHSPE essays were school teachers who had participated in AP or CLEP holistic scoring, or in "composition evaluations held in local school districts or in invitational summer workshops of the BAWP, where they had been introduced to holistic reading as a technique for evaluating student writing." They say, "By now many teachers of English have had direct experience with the holistic reading method, or at least have heard it explained" (1977, 3). Clearly, the spread of holistic scoring in California schools during the second half of the 1970s owed much to state legislation and the response of BAWP sites to it.

THE BAY AREA WRITING PROJECT AND HOLISTIC ESSAY SCORING: HEIGHTENED AWARENESS

As a demonstrable recognition of the force on local adaptation, attitudes toward holistic scoring ranged widely across BAWP sites. Staff tended to mirror the feeling of most English teachers everywhere, that getting students to produce good writing was more important than getting teachers, or anybody else, to assess it. BAWP spent most of its energies on pedagogy: respecting the composing process, creating stimulating assignments, reading drafts aloud, running peer draft-critique groups, compiling anthologies of class writings, writing along with students, and encouraging writing across the curriculum. One of the first applications of holistic evaluation in BAWP sites was to have students use it to respond to drafts of classmates. Peckham remembers that in the Santa Clara district-wide evaluation committee, "there were hackles raised" when people perceived BAWP as having taken "an instructional protocol and used it as a way of assessing student competency and to determine promotion" (email to authors, January 28, 2018). In his book on the early history of BAWP, Gray mentions holistic scoring explicitly only once (2000, 55).

The number of BAWP consultants spreading the use of holistic methods to meet state writing-assessment requirements was moderate—Bernstein, Blickhahn, Claggett, Keech, Lavin, Myers, Mary Ann Smith, Tanner, perhaps one or two others. But even within this cadre there was a division over the way holistic evaluation should be conducted. The issue was whether the scoring guide ought to be generated before or after the anchor essays are selected. Although the issue sounds like a quibble among technicians, it had far implications.

In pragmatic terms, it saves time to bring a preexisting scoring guide to a set of papers. The most difficult task remains finding anchor papers from the set to fit the guide (Godshalk 1966, 4). Teachers did not like that task, but as bad was constructing a new scoring guide for every new topic (Harned 1986/1987, 11). Criteria had to match expected accomplishments of the task imposed by the topic. Top-scoring essays for a narrative topic might generate suspense, whereas top-scoring essays for an argumentative topic might show insight into both sides of a debate.

If a scoring enterprise dealt with large numbers of essays and needed new topics session after session, the use of a preexistent set of criteria was common. Advanced Placement composition tests year after year applied the same basic scoring guide superficially adapted to the current topic—a practice that had been copied by the Drake High School self-monitoring examinations and the California State University

English Equivalency Examination. It was still standard procedure in ETS scoring, however, for scoring criteria to be developed from sample papers, not the other way around. For instance, with CHSPE, table leaders first selected anchor papers for the five points of the scale, then created a scoring guide. "This descriptive guide, or 'rubric,' result[ed] from the team's attempt to describe those anchor papers." The guide was then presented to readers, who during training could suggest change whether they found it "incomplete, unrealistically inflexible, or puzzlingly ambiguous" (Bernstein and Tanner 1977, 4). But during workshops for teachers, leaders usually did not want to spend time having participants generate new scoring guides. Peckham remembers Myers arriving at the Santa Clara scoring session with guide in hand. In his 1980 book on holistic-scoring procedures, Myers was open to either method: "Rubrics can come first or later. The process works well either way" (1980, 31). But Catharine Keech was not so open.[17]

Keech was not somebody to take lightly. She had earned a BA in philosophy at UC Berkeley, married, then spent six years teaching in Europe. She returned to Berkeley in 1974 as a doctoral candidate in education with, as she puts it, "a single burning question, How does a writing teacher reconcile external demands (and systems) for evaluating (i.e., grading, scoring, assessing) student writing with her internal goals to help students write for real purposes, with commitment and authenticity and confidence?" (email to authors, May 2015). She was given an office to share with Lavin and soon was drawn deeply into BAWP work, especially where it connected with evaluation of writing.

She attended holistic-scoring workshops for teachers and worked with teachers in designing, executing, and writing up research. For her dissertation she analyzed a six-year sample of scoring done by Drake High School teachers, with papers provided by Blickhahn and Lavin. Through Lavin, she met Diederich and Roberta Camp, who arranged for her to participate in ETS scoring. Through Allan Seder of ETS, she read for the CHPSE examinations. She knew the history of essay evaluation thoroughly, including the British studies and practices. By the late 1970s, through her hands-on experience, empirical research, and philosophical underpinning, she had made herself one of the top experts in holistic scoring in the United States.[18]

As we will see, her expertise led her to insights into the limitations of holistic scoring. But she held fast to one truth, that there were qualities of essay writing only general-impression scoring could tap: "A primary advantage of holistic scoring is that it allows us to register the total effect of a piece even when that effect cannot be described by naming particular qualities." As a result, she was cautious not only about analytical scoring but also about holistic rubrics or scoring guides. Although she agreed some criteria should be known to teachers and students before a test for proficiency was administered, and she felt a scoring guide of some sort was needed in typical holistic sessions, she maintained that the "scoring guide should not, however, be transformed into an analytic count of certain measures" (Keech 1979c, 4).

It followed in Keech's thinking that as a first step, expert teachers should pick possible anchor essays from the set of essays to be scored, and after that, scorers should extract the criteria of the scoring guide through open debate over the choices. The acceptance of teacher-rater values and opinions in the formation of rating standards distinguished, according to Keech, the "BAWP model" of holistic scoring from the ETS model. She first realized this after participating in ETS scoring at Princeton.

> I realize, belatedly, that this jaunt to Princeton to drink from the source probably did as much as anything else to shape the model of holistic scoring later disseminated by Writing Projects and in wide use today. Where I deviated from the ETS model was in the training of readers to a common rubric. Of necessity, ETS developed a single rubric (with consultation from those select teachers under Roberta Camp) to be used across multiple testings to stabilize scoring standards over several years. Readers for the test were rigorously vetted during training to discover and correct sources of deviation from group standards. I remember a certain level of anxiety as I tried to match my response to a piece of writing to the predetermined "correct" response based on the rubric and samples offered.
>
> That much calibration I sought to keep in what would become the BAWP model. Where I differed was in developing the rubric with on-site teachers, rather than exporting a standard rubric to all participating schools. My primary goal—to use community scoring to raise consciousness among teachers—was best served in those workshops where colleagues had to confront and resolve their differences, letting go of idiosyncrasies (like punitive responses to certain comma errors) and responding holistically to the communicative power of the writing. Working with a sample of essays easily sorted into four levels of accomplishment, teachers could begin to examine why they ordered the samples as they did. At every school I worked with, I used questions to heighten awareness of neglected features and seized opportunities to soften ancient prejudices. (email to authors, May 2015)

Keech assumed, with good reason, that a preimposed rubric could easily slight topic effects and therefore underassess proficiencies of the writers.

Keech's scoring procedure was not inconsequential. It promoted both inclusion and sharing to start with sample papers written to the topic and to then develop the scoring guide with the teacher-scorers. It synced with BAWP's approach to internal teacher development and reservations about external expert consultants.

METHOD: CATHARINE KEECH VERSUS MICHAEL SCRIVEN

Rubric first or sample papers first—the quarrel is well shown in an early confrontation between Keech and, fittingly, an outsider to BAWP. The situation emerged out of circumstances in which BAWP's survival lay in the balance. In 1977, after three years of support from UC Berkeley, the program had to find other funding. To succeed in that, it needed to be evaluated by an expert not affiliated with the project. Enter Michael Scriven, UC Berkeley professor of philosophy and education. Gray remembers him as "a domineering presence, always dressing as if he were about to make a trek across the veldt with his khaki shirt and trousers and holstered knife" (2000, 111).

Nationally known scholar of evaluation in its broadest sense, originator of the distinction between formative and summative evaluation, author of papers and a recent book on evaluation of academic programs, Scriven mapped out an assessment of BAWP that raised hackles among the staff, who saw his approach as contrary to BAWP's central raison d'être. He wanted to see the effect of BAWP on the writing of students. Gray, Myers, Keech, and others wanted to see the effect of BAWP on the teachers. Eventually, that clash of opinion was resolved. For the three-year evaluation, both students and teachers were investigated in a series of studies, many run by Keech. Scriven wrote a positive program evaluation and, along with a second written by Diederich, BAWP survived with substantial funding by National Endowment for the Humanities, the Carnegie Foundation for the Advancement of Teaching, and others. If there were disagreements between Scriven and Keech, the designated research assistant for the program evaluation, they have not survived in print.

Except for one incident. It is well worth recovering since the differences centered over the role of rubrics in holistic scoring. In February 1978, before studies for BAWP's review had been fully designed by Keech and others in the evaluation unit, Scriven sent them a memo called "General Categories for Assessment of Essay Work." He sets forth a "generalizable set of categories for the grading of English composition," shown in figure 7.3.

It is what Keech (1979c) feared: a preset "analytic count of certain measures" (4). It follows the figuration of Diederich's scale, which had

ABBREVIATION	MEANING	WEIGHT	SCORE	SUBTOTALS (WxS)
Spel/Punc.	Spelling, punctuation	1		
Ref/Ack	References, acknowledgements	1		
Cov/Foc	Coverage, focus	2		
Ex/Org	Expression, organization	2		
Reas/Exx	Reasoning, examples	3		
Ins,Orig	Insight, originality	3		
Code: ✓ = commendable, blank or - = acceptable or not applicable, x = deficient			TOTAL/GRADE	

Figure 7.3. General Categories for Assessment of Essay Work (Scriven 1978) (courtesy of the National Writing Project)

been published in 1966 and 1974. In fact, Scriven (1978) mentions he had consulted with Diederich over this particular set of criteria. Although Scriven assures the evaluation unit that his proposed categories lie "quite apart from the specific task of developing a rubric for the particular essay topics that we're using," the timing of the memo left little doubt that Scriven was proposing that his criteria be used by the evaluation team (A1). Specifically, raters should use this "analytic evaluation first in the 'practice runs,'" and then it "should be synthesized in the overall evaluations done on a holistic scale" (A1). As Scriven put it, what is first done "slowly and analytically" should be internalized by raters for the time when they have to score holistically "in a hurry" (A3).

This proposed use of an analytic scale is quintessential Scriven. Fundamentally a top-down thinker, a philosopher of evaluation, Scriven always began with overarching principles. He studied "evaluation" in its largest sense, defining it as "a logical activity which is essentially similar whether we are trying to evaluate coffee machines or teaching machines, plans for a house or plans for a curriculum" (1966, 3). Whatever might need measurement of its potential merit or value, Scriven's preferred method was what he called the checklist. In 1974 he had already published a thorough rationale of checklists. Evaluators agree on a set of criteria (properties, aspects, dimensions, categories, etc.), a set they predict is complete, relevant, and suitably weighted. Ideally, they administer trial runs and use the results to revise the criteria and weighting (Scriven's "formative evaluation"). When satisfied with the checklist, they then rate the "evaluand" on each criterion separately (his "summative evaluation"). In his memo to the evaluation unit, he does not call his generalized essay scale (1966, fig. 3.1) a *checklist*, but he could have. He says he plans on making a stamp of the categories for scorers.

It is important to note that, in 1978, Scriven's program-evaluation model was the norm, and it stayed the norm for decades. Theoretically, the model makes evaluation as objective as possible. The checklist, according to Scriven, reduces the halo effect and the "Rorschach effect, i.e., the tendency to see what one wants to see in a mass of data" (2000/2005, 3–4). His fellow philosophers of evaluation called him an "empiricist," an epithet most program evaluators would happily embrace for themselves in years to come. Even in 1978, however, Scriven's model had been challenged by Harvard University's Carol H. Weiss in her groundbreaking *Evaluation Research: Methods for Assessing Program Effectiveness* (1972). Weiss introduced the current theory-based and action-oriented program-evaluation model. The two models competed throughout the rest of the twentieth century, but Scriven's generally held the day. As chapter 9 relates, the rubricized form of holistic scoring operates not much differently than a Scriven checklist, and in the 1980s and 1990s, it became the dominant form.

In February 1978, Scriven asked for a quick response to his memo, and his research assistant complied. Keech's answering memo, "Michael's Criterion List for Evaluating Written Composition," although not dated, must have been sent within a few days. It is polite and circumspect, as befits a graduate student responding to a full professor, one from whom she had taken an "evaluation training seminar" (Scriven 1974, 10). But Keech does not shy away from expressing her reservations. First, she notes that the set of criteria do not seem appropriate for some kinds of student writing. Several categories, such as references/acknowledgment, apply only to academic writing. Essentially, she is asking the bottoms-up question of whether any set of composition criteria can ever be "generalizable," suitable for any writing task.

Then Keech (1978) takes up Scriven's expression/organization category and makes some comments that, in terms of the history of holistic scoring, can be called prophetic. The passage is well worth quoting in full.

> These two sets of skills will not always (or even usually) coincide— especially in developing writers. Perhaps by college age, students with syntactic maturity and sophisticated diction will have mastered most organizational problems, or those with organizational sense will have developed commensurate levels of syntax and diction, but my own experience is that

these abilities do not always develop in concert. Very talented writers and good readers may have uniform development, but students who depend on classroom education may find their training is somewhat lopsided. The combination of these categories might prevent an evaluator from spotting this uneven development. (appendix A6)

These comments are the seed that ten years later Lucas (through 1984, she signed her publications as Catharine Keech and only later as Catharine Lucas) will bring to consummate bloom in her essay "Toward Ecological Evaluation" (1988). Student writers are complex and their writing is complex, and abstract checklists of criteria Scriven favored may belie such complexity and obviate variables associated with writing performance. Student development in writing, patchy and off-balance, is just one of many contingencies—each present in the learning ecology—affecting evaluation.

At stake is a sequence in the training of raters and the rationale of that sequence. Should raters first internalize a general evaluative scale and then use that abstraction to shape their response to a particular scoring—a sequence Scriven says Diederich recommended. Keech notes that Diederich's scale was "factored-analyzed from actual reader response," a source of evidence that is significant in the design of scoring criteria and generalization inferences made from them, as will be seen in chapter 9. Her main caution, however, is that internalizing a hypothetical set of criteria in raters runs the danger of creating a terministic screen. She ends her memo by making a politic suggestion, that Scriven pilot the scale and then ask what readers "think the categories mean after applying them to several hundred papers of various kinds" (1978, appendix A6). It seems she had her way. In the studies Keech ran for Scriven's evaluation of BAWP, her raters first picked anchor papers and then derived a scoring guide from them (e.g., Caplan and Keech 1980; Woodworth and Keech 1980).

Rhetorical mode was part of the shifting occasion of the testing Keech thought should shape the one-off criteria used by raters in a holistic-scoring session. Naturally, mode—narrative, for instance, or argumentative—was conveyed by the topic or rhetorical task set by the prompt, another major contingency of writing assessment. Different prompts demand different criteria. Particular prompts also affect particular scorers differently, who bring their own Umwelt with them. As for the scorers, Keech was adamant in thinking prompts should be the source of the criteria. Scoring leaders, sometimes strangers, do not hand the criteria to scorers. At the start of rater calibration, it is scorers who suggest the criteria and debate them and agree on them. In Keech we see the power of integrating research-based practice into specific educational sites: the tasks themselves construct responses, and the judgments that result must be based on the specific forms of writing at hand. Generalization must begin at the level of the task, not in response to archetypically developed scoring criteria.

Even in large-scale testing at the time, as in CHPSE or CSU's English Equivalency Examination, standard practice allowed holistic raters some say about criteria, in part to invest them appropriately in the scoring. But that say was minimal. Before training, examination leaders selected the anchor papers and devised a provisional scoring guide, which was given to raters, who could make "slight changes" (Bernstein and Tanner 1977, 4). In the smaller scoring sessions usually run by BAWP, raters generated the guide as they openly debated their scores on the anchor papers with other scorers, citing strong and weak points. "Thus," explains Keech, "their implicit standards for writing this particular kind of paper, their interpretation of the writing task, as well as other constraints surfaced as they evaluated and ranked the anchor set." She stresses that "this discussion is the heart of the training process" (Keech and McNelly 1982, 266). Keech's language, it is worth knowing, refers to a particular training of high-school students to score holistically. Probably she means rater development of the criteria when she mentions "the Educational Testing Service model for holistic scoring, as adapted by the Bay Area Writing Project" (264).

As we have said, the adaptation had far implications. Above all it fit the needs and allowances of local testing, whether that was school district, department, or classroom. It assumed teachers know best and took as primary the neighborhood surround and circumstances of the assessment. It assumed they know circumstances will be different and will determine the purposes of the testing, and that the purposes will determine the scale and the topic, which will guide the selection of anchor essays. From the anchors, the scoring guide will be developed by teachers because they will be the users of it, the scorers. While scoring, the teachers may even find better anchors (resampling). Finally, topics, anchors, and rubrics will be included in the report of the testing, written by teachers. The full sequence is quintessentially BAWP because, throughout, it allows teachers to maintain control of the testing.

THE BAY AREA WRITING PROJECT: ACCOUNTING FOR ITSELF

And also to critique it. During its early years BAWP was a hotbed of empirical research. Early directors such as Lavin, a researcher at heart, encouraged consultants to conduct research studies with school teachers within reasonable driving range. For instance, Keech worked with Patrick Woodworth at Tomales High School northwest of Berkeley to see if audience specification in topics affected holistic evaluation of essays (1980) and with Rebekah Caplan at Foothill High School east of Palo Alto to see if holistic scoring could record improvement in the essay writing of students taught the rhetorical strategy of show and tell (1980). Her study with Woodworth, *The Write Occasion* (Woodworth and Keech 1980), reported what was to become one of the first studies of task design. The study was straightforward: students in three ninth-grade English classes and three mixed junior/senior-level English classes wrote on topics in which no audience was identified, an imagined audience was suggested, and a real audience was identified. While the tasks were varied, they were aligned to classroom assignments in which students wrote about their own experiences and were invited to do so with authority.

While grade-level differences in performance were identified, and women performed at higher levels than men, no statistically significant differences were determined among audience types. As Woodworth and Keech concluded, audience specification for the sample at hand "does not necessarily result in simple and direct improvement of student writing" (1980, 34). Also, audience specification did not appear to result in genre shifts; the informal essay remained the default genre. The implication of this finding was especially interesting: for students well adapted to school tasks, "the general audience of test readers can provide a real rhetorical context for some writers, and for some kinds of writing" (34). At the classroom level, Woodworth interpreted this finding as evidence of the significance of "a sense of occasion" in which students are told they are involved in an unusual writing situation—one in which "a world larger than the immediate class-room—in this case, readers/teachers from other schools—is involved" (38). The sense of occasion, he speculated, may be useful in boosting motivation.

With such well-designed classroom-based research and interpretative prowess, it is not surprising holistic scoring itself quickly came under BAWP scrutiny.

The scrutiny led BAWP to a major investigation into the "potential sources of invalidity in the conduct of holistic assessment" (Gray et al. 1982, 4). Supported by a National Institute of Education grant, the project director was Leo Ruth, and research coordinators were Keech and Sandra Murphy.[19] In order to jump-start their investigation, Ruth asked—who else?—Keech to draft a summary of research into topic effects. It was called "Topic Design: Views from the Profession" and was circulated among experts. The piece was folded into two chapters of the final report: Ruth and Keech's "Designing Prompts for Holistic Writing Assessments: Knowledge from Theory, Research, and Practice" (1982, 31–131) and Keech's "Practices in Designing Writing Test Prompts: Analysis and Recommendations" (1982, 132–213). If BAWP members were among the foremost in spreading holistic scoring, they were also among the first to question its method seriously.

The final report was dated November 1982 and called *Properties of Writing Tasks: A Study of Alternative Procedures for Holistic Scoring* (Gray et al. 1982). Still buried in ERIC Document Reproduction Service files, it stands as the first book-length critique of holistic scoring—a gathering of studies answering questions users of holistic scoring were asking, or should have been. Did scores improve when the prompt specified an audience? What do students remember about writing a test essay a day later? Do students and teachers interpret prompts differently? Do think-aloud protocols show differences in the way prompt constructors, students, and raters imagine the prompt? Do correlations of analytic measures with holistic score change when the rhetorical task changes? Of a range of prompts, which generate the most valid scores? What does test-retest study reveal about writer reliability in holistic scores? What kind of longitudinal irregularities appear in holistic scores?

James Gray and colleagues—the authors and editors of the 1982 542-page study—sought to extend and deepen the research by Woodworth and Keech by differentiating between classroom writing assignments and school writing tests. In classroom contexts, Leo Ruth and Keech noted in their section of the study, interpretation is possible, as well as preparatory help and motivational encouragement. In test conditions, however, no such contextualization is possible. "Each head bent over the page is presumed to be getting the same message to direct his/her writing performance," they noted (34).

Holistic scoring was used to tease out interactive relationships among participants, products, and processes during writing-assessment episodes. Central to the analyses was a model of study of the writing-assessment episode, with identified participants, processes, and products (Gray et al. 1982, 8). Task design, student response, and rating processes were the distinct and interrelated processes that allowed identification of the psycholinguistic and sociolinguistic variables involved in designing the writing-assessment episode. In what was to become among the first systematic study of response processes, Gray and colleagues were indeed able to identify variables associated with writing-task design.

Those variables encompassed the range of task design, from discourse mode (topics that encourage introspection or autobiographical writing by drawing on personal experience) to task structure (using specifications to cue students to topic exploration and tester's expectations). And, because agents were identified in the writing-assessment episode and because response processes were used in the study, the studies did find that students interpreted the writing task in ways that differed from teacher and rater task interpretation. In determining the properties of writing tasks, the episodic model has proven invaluable in allowing granular study of design and impact. While the original report may long have been forgotten, the essence of the work influenced many in its final form: *Designing Writing Tasks for the Assessment of Writing* (Ruth and Murphy 1988).

BAWP researchers discovered that when teachers take on accountability testing, they become accountable themselves. Decades earlier, others had discovered that scary and invigorating fact, such as teacher Stephen Wiseman in Devon (see chapter 3) and teacher Paul B. Diederich at the University of Chicago (see chapter 5). Through the 1980s and 1990s, faculty running independent testing programs in schools and colleges would keep learning it, and their independent research into their testing kept accruing, some of it supportive of holistic scoring, some not. At the same time, teachers also learned another fact, that accountability is inseparable from power. By its nature, *accountable* does not stand alone. It is always *accountable to whom*? If anybody learned this the hard way, it was California teachers.

We will curtail the story, since it extends outside this book's historical focus. It deserves a book of its own. One of the facts about essay scoring in large-scale accountability testing is its tendency to degenerate. BAWP had helped the 1973 CAP minimum-competency writing assessment take the form of scored essays, but Smith, who had attended the first BAWP summer institute in 1974 and became the project's director, sadly observed that by 1987, a single essay had become "standard fare" in many districts, and the essays students produced on the tests were not very palatable. The five-paragraph theme had arrived, or rather emerged. "To read some of these student writing samples is to die a slow death—one formulaic paper after another cut to the pattern offered by well-meaning teachers who have taken refuge in a prescribed form. Minimum means minimum" (1987, 6).

But early that year, 1987, an astonishing solution was already in place. Under the direction of Charles Cooper at University of California, San Diego, and supported by the State Department of Education, a California

Writing Project had completed a new test of writing. Throughout its development, it worked with school teachers. It was cutting edge and technically still stands (along with Diederich's testing program at Chicago in the 1940s) as one of the most valid large-scale assessments of writing proficiency ever made real. Students could choose from three topics. They wrote in one of eight different genres. Each essay was scored three times for specific accomplishments through focused scoring—a rigorous but very expensive evaluation. Matrix sampling meant a district could be evaluated on success in each genre and accomplishment. It also meant the individual student or teacher could not be assessed. The new CAP writing could be called *teacher intensive*. In 1986, half the eighth-grade teachers in the state were involved with inservice work connected with test development. The first test in spring of 1987 took 290 teachers, trained by ETS, eight days to score 282,155 eighth-grade booklets (Cooper and Breneman 1989, 13). For teachers who believed in direct and authentic assessment of writing, it was a dream come true.

Yet the most innovative aspects of the assessment, and its most costly, proved its downfall. In June 1990, Governor George Deukmejian, serving his last term, vetoed funding for the examination in an inconsequential fight with the Democratic legislature over whether the $11,000,000 should come from the state's general fund or from moneys generated by Proposition 98. Twelfth-grade writing tests scheduled for November and December were cancelled. A new assessment, called the California Learning Assessment System (CLAS), was installed in 1991, perhaps too hastily. For language arts, it focused on reading and response to reading and added a radical new element, a portfolio of student writing gathered during the school year. Both the reading topics and the portfolio were designed and scored by school teachers. Crucially, the "new CAP" was supposed to report individual student scores. Right-wing voters wanted individual scores so teachers of poorly performing classes could be identified and parents could keep their children out of them. Then in 1994, the next Governor, Peter Barton Wilson, vetoed a senate bill to extend CLAS through 1999. His stated reason was that the proposed assessment did not score individual students as it was supposed to. There had also been some public outcry over a prompt that had asked students to write about a school rule they disagreed with, under the belief that it was teaching them to defy authority. Critics had also deplored the lack of objective rating and jumped on a few low rater-reliability coefficients in the portfolio scoring. Objections gained momentum, and California ended mandated direct testing of school writing proficiency. Also ended was the long effort of

California school teachers to have a say in the writing examinations the state ordered for their students. In his veto statement, Wilson declared that California teachers would never again be involved in the development or implementation of state school assessment (Dudley 1997, 20). Exactly thirty years had passed since Mario Savio's protest on the steps of Sproul Hall against the view that California teachers were no more than "a bunch of employees."

The trajectory of CAP/CLAS follows a pattern, and the pattern follows a rule. The teachers who take on the responsibility to run state-mandated and state-supported accountability testing are finally accountable to the state, and the state is run by politicians and administrators who ultimately are accountable to no one, not even voters, it seems. When change arrives, as we see with the United Kingdom in chapter 4, hegemonic forces sweep away curriculum and assessment without attention to evidence. No matter how good the test or how much the work, the testing can end on a political or administrative whim. And probably will. California teachers did provide other states with an example of how the testing of writing should be done but also an example of how it usually ends. However, it is equally important to recognize that, as is the case with many democratization processes, work continues at local levels to the benefit of many. While the state may have swept away much, the integrative processes of teaching and assessing writing established for a brief while in California remain today in schools and colleges across the United States. If we look carefully, we can see origins of the body of knowledge we now associate with writing studies.

NOTES

1. Based on his own long association with UC assessment, George Gadda (email to authors, August 13, 2018) challenges this description: "People I know who were in UC in the 1970s claim that there was substantial similarity between campus operations, and as far as I know which students had to take the Subject A exam was always a matter of UC-wide policy."

2. Today it is hard to imagine how few outside tests were imposed on schools and school students in the United States before 1960. Richard Haswell graduated from high school in 1957. During his twelve years in school, he took only two standardized examinations, an aptitude test (whose results indicated he should become either an engineer or an artist) and an IQ test (whose quotient was not divulged to him). On average, students today take 112 mandatory standardized tests over their school years (Hart et al. 2015, 9). A report issued by the Center for American Progress concluded that the testing overload is unbearable (Lazarin 2014). Students in grades three through eight take, on average, about ten large-scale, mandated tests throughout the year; and urban high-school students take three times as many district-level tests, and those students spend up to 266 percent (!) more time taking them compared with suburban high-school students. While students are tested as

frequently as twice per month and, on average, once per month, the report finds, many districts and states may be administering tests that are duplicative or unnecessary. "There is a culture of testing and test preparation in schools," the report concluded, "that does not put students first" (19).

3. By 1978 eighteen states were reporting mandated writing assessment: California, Hawaii, Idaho, Louisiana, Maine, Massachusetts, Missouri, New Hampshire, New Mexico, New York, Ohio, Oregon, Rhode Island, Texas, Vermont, Washington, and Wisconsin (Frederick 1979). By 1991 that number had risen to thirty-six states, not counting the twenty-four that imposed NDEA Title V testing (US Congress 1992, 24).

4. Did that ever happen? Quite the opposite happened four years later when the California legislature passed the Hughes-Hart Education Reform and Finance Act. It set aside special funding for school districts whose seniors *improved* their CAP scores from one year to the next: the more the gain, the bigger the award. Teachers called the act Cash for CAP or Dollars for Scholars. Fifteen million dollars was set aside for it in 1985–86 and 1986–87. Then Governor George Deukmejian, who ran as a fiscally responsible Republican, vetoed it, and the funds were never restored.

5. Originally, in 1958, beneficiaries of NDEA money had to sign an affidavit disclaiming belief in the overthrow of the US government, although that obligation was removed by President Kennedy in 1962.

6. Outright animosity against teachers is hard to find in the commission reports. But it might be noted that one-third of the members voted against a recommendation that "the salaries of teachers be set at a high enough level to attract and hold the best talent in the profession" (Citizens Advisory Commission 1961, 21).

7. And it seems to have always been. The California Teachers Association (CTA) was founded in 1863. Over the years it has fought public opinion and the California Legislature, and has won, on many issues: free public schooling in 1866, special funding for schools that taught nonwhite students in 1867, free textbooks in grades one through eight in 1911, retirement pension for teachers in 1913. During WWII the CTA publicly protested the internment of Japanese Americans. After a decades-long battle, they won the right of teachers to collectively bargain in 1975. Perhaps most amazingly, in 1988 California teachers campaigned with success to pass Proposition 98, which requires the legislature to reserve around 40 percent of the annual general fund for schools and two-year colleges.

8. Nothing is more ephemeral than school documents. In 1978, Keith Caldwell left Morgan Hill High School to work as a consultant and editor for the Bay Area Writing Project. Four and a half years later when he returned to Morgan Hill, he found that all his teaching notes and materials had been thrown away (1983, 6).

9. Myers's definition of *holistic* is close to that of Charles Cooper: "I am using the term 'holistic' to mean any procedure which stops short of enumerating linguistic, rhetorical, or informational features of a piece of writing. Some holistic procedures may specify a number of particular features and even require that each feature be scored separately, but the reader is never required to stop and count or tally incidents of the feature" (1977, 4). Myers and Cooper, then, would call our *analytical* scoring "holistic."

10. The scale consisted of six ranked essays as described in *A Scale for Evaluation of High School Student Essays* (Nail et al. 1960). So essentially it was a sample-matching scheme, but at each of the six levels, users were provided with leading questions about content, organization, style, and mechanics. The lead author of the venture, Pat Nail, taught at Woodside High School near Redwood City, a half an hour's drive south of San Francisco.

11. Myers reproduces two topics used by Lavin's "six-year assessment," taken from a report issued in 1973 by the English Department of Tamaulipas High School, with

Blickhahn as lead author (Myers 1980, 9). That would take Lavin's study back to at least 1967. Blickhahn herself says about Lavin's early holistic scoring at Drake, "I think the dates from 1966 to 1972 for Drake sound correct, as it would have been before I was involved in the Bay Area Writing Project" (email to authors, April 2016). Catharine Keech Lucas wrote her Berkeley dissertation on papers from Lavin's students, arguing that changes in topic over the years confounded evidence for yearly progress in writing proficiency.

12. We are describing the scoring guide provided by Keech (1979b, appendix B12). It is labeled "from the Report of the Writing Assessment, Sir Francis Drake High School," perhaps referring to the same 1973 report "The Writing Project" by Blickhahn and others cited by Myers (1980, 9). We cannot date this particular scoring guide exactly, but Lavin would not have changed his scoring procedure during the six years since he wanted to compare yearly change in student writing. The writing prompt covered by the guide refers to the one provided by Myers from the "six-year assessment of the Tamalpais School District" and labeled "Spring 1970" (1980, 9).

13. As we note in the previous chapter, in December 1965, Godshalk ran a Foreign Service Examination at ETS's western office in Berkeley. Candidates wrote two essays, which were scored on the AP scale of 1–9. Godshalk explains that the system replaces the English Composition Test's scale of 1–4 but is similar in that 1, 2, 3, 4 are replaced with 2, 4, 6, 8 and "the odd numbers are to be used infrequently in cases where the paper just misses a score" (Godshalk, Swineford, and Coffman 1965, 4). Calls for readers were sent to "school and English teachers" in the Bay Area. So here is another possible influence on the Drake Writing Project. Myers remembers that "Cap's district got Evans Alloway (ETS) to come out and help organize essay scoring for the high schools. I sat in for some of that" (email to authors, December 8–14, 2014). But that probably was after Lavin's BAWP research was under way.

14. In an email from February 15, 2015, Mary Ann Smith adds further purposes of Lavin's experiment: "At Drake High School, English teachers used holistic scoring to follow a group of students, from 9th to 12th grade, to score a set of their papers and to reflect on the department/classroom curriculum based on how the students fared. Kate [Blickhahn] emphasized that the students themselves were interested and invested in this annual assessment. Several years later we duplicated the Drake model at our high school in Walnut Creek and experienced the same benefits, including student engagement."

15. Just as males eighteen years or older were burning their draft cards (a kind of personal answer sheet they had to show on demand), younger students had their own resistance to bubble sheets. See Thomas Newkirk's chapter, "The Curse of Graphite." He taught 1970–1973 at an inner-city public school in Boston and remembers students filling in circles just to make pretty designs on the sheet (2009, 6). For a brief history of the technology of limited-response items at ETS, see Elliot (2014, 240–47).

16. In an email from February 15, 2015, Smith adds that many BAWP consultants worked weekends at the ETS office in Berkeley holistically scoring essays from state examinations around the country (e.g., South Carolina) and also from the California Basic Educational Skills Test™ teacher-certification examination.

17. Myers does not much distinguish between *scoring guide* and *rubric*—he may be treating the terms as synonyms. As we argue in chapter 9, the rubric, as we define it, straddled that thin line between holistic and analytic.

18. Keech's contributions to holistic scoring and theory have not received the recognition due them. Despite the enormous amount of work she accomplished for BAWP 1977–1980, she is not mentioned in Gray's memoir of BAWP's early years, *Teachers at the Center (2000)*. She and Blickhahn stopped working on a book on holistic scoring

when they were caught by surprise with the appearance of Myers's *Procedure for Writing Assessment and Holistic Scoring* in 1980. Both Ruth and Scriven, it should be noted, early praised Keech's BAWP expertise. In *Properties of Writing Tasks*, Ruth provides a long and detailed account of Keech's "extensive background" in conducting essay assessment (Gray et al. 1982, 94–95).

19. Ruth was supervisor of teacher education in the Graduate School of Education, UC Berkeley. Murphy was a PhD student in language, literature, and culture and recommended to Ruth by Myers. Although listed as principal investigator, Gray was too busy with BAWP to supervise or work with the study (Murphy, email to authors, December 2017). Much of the final report found its way into Ruth and Murphy's *Designing Writing Tasks for the Assessment of Writing* (1988).

8
INDEPENDENT RESEARCHERS, 1960–1980, AND NAEP, 1969–1984

The elegant interpretation is particularly suspect.
—Donald P. Spence, *Narrative Truth and Historical Truth*

In chapter 6 we identify the year 1972 as pivotal in the early US history of holistic scoring of student essays: the College Board suspended holistic scoring, the National Assessment of Education Progress (NAEP) explored primary-trait scoring, and the Bay Area Writing Project (BAWP) was in the planning stages. It is time to deconstruct this attribution and its implied periodization, at least in reference to research independent of commercial testing firms. Both before and after 1972, academic researchers used holistic measures to describe student writing performance, often in connection with state and national accountability testing and with local university placement, exemption, and certification assessments. Researchers across the United States also applied holistic essay scores as a dependent variable in research studies looking into a wide spectrum of language habits and activities. Furthermore, as we have seen with BAWP investigators, these independent researchers were more likely to question holistic scoring itself as a variable. That meant going beyond purchased test validation concerns with interrater reliability and score predictability. It meant applying psychometric techniques to bring to light the shadowy, underwater, gestalt-like ways holistic scorers arrive at a score in terms of perception, value making, construct representation, rater response, and social context—as well as the ways those scores are used in assessment narratives and interpretation arguments.

The focus of this chapter is US independent research, from 1960 to 1980. As is the case throughout our book, dates are provided to mark general periodization rather than exact demarcation. The chapter first surveys investigations run by academics that used and dissected holistic scoring and then narrates in detail the adventures in essay scoring of the

NAEP during many of the same years. A large-scale census independent of commercial or academic control, NAEP was the first attempt in the United States to collect national data about student proficiency, including writing ability. *Independent*, of course, is another term that must be deconstructed. As will be seen, NAEP relied on academic experts and, in time, contracted with the Educational Testing Service (ETS) to develop and apply scoring of student essays.

INDEPENDENT ACADEMIC RESEARCHERS AND HOLISTIC SCORING: 1960S–1980S

Although academic researchers operate in a free-floating space, even the most independent research was not truly independent. It was swamped with contingencies such as practitioner knowledge, financial support, potential utility, professional obligations, disciplinary pressures, and political mores (Bourdieu and Passeron 1990; Schmidt 2000; Trachsel 1992). The larger the research program becomes, the greater the need for consultants. In the case of NAEP in its early years, researchers sometimes paid ETS-trained scorers and ETS experts such as Fred L. Godshalk or Evans Alloway to collaboratively design their assessments, subsequently administer their scoring of student writing, and perform the required statistical analyses as evidence of the validity, reliability, and fairness of the research. Research methodology itself is deeply situated and never free of its occasion or ecology, a fact the researchers themselves were discovering in these years as sampling plans grew and impact expanded.[1]

On the other hand, during the two decades of the 1960s to the 1980s, academic researchers were handed a certain amount of freedom and independence from an unexpected source: the Cold War. As we describe in chapter 7, in the 1950s many politicians believed US students needed better education if the United States wanted to keep up with Communism; hence, the US educational system needed to be improved; hence, since testing stood at the core of education, educational testing needed to be improved; hence, expert research was needed in the area of evaluation. The outcome of this dubious chain of reasoning took the form of new government granting agencies, regional laboratories, and university research centers.

In 1954, Congress created the Cooperative Research Program to fund study of educational problems. Academic researchers responded with such enthusiasm that Congress expanded the original appropriation of $1,000,000 in 1956 to $3,357,000 in 1961. In the 1960s and

1970s, a number of original research studies applying holistic scoring were Cooperative Research Projects (e.g., Braddock and Statler 1968; McColly and Remstad 1963).[2] Then, in 1965, Congress established ten "regional educational laboratories," spaced around the nation, and the next year appropriated the astonishing sum of $51,000,000 to get them going. In the end, of course, it was up to the laboratories to keep their operations afloat, and they quickly learned that evaluation sold quite well. Soon they were consulting in essay evaluation, running holistic scoring for state assessments, orchestrating conferences on evaluation, and researching and concocting new and easier essay-rating schemes. Their influence on essay-scoring practices was not inconsiderable, in particular the trend toward rubrics in holistic scoring in the 1980s. For instance, in 1980 the Regional Educational Laboratory Southwest published a rubric for scoring sixth-grade stories, with twelve criteria each rated on a three-point scale. Shortly thereafter, the Regional Educational Laboratory Northwest developed its six-plus-one rubric, still popular (Culham 2003).

As we have seen with the BAWP, from 1960 to 1980, universities were establishing their own research laboratories, in which evaluation of writing took on a large and sometimes exclusive focus. In 1966 the Center for the Study of Evaluation sprung up within the UCLA Graduate School of Education. During the 1970s researchers in the center generated rigorous studies of holistic scoring, some of it quite critical of the method (e.g., Spooner et al. 1980). Notable here is the work of Edys Quellmalz. With Eva L. Baker, Quellmalz issued three studies in 1981 investigating areas of research interest on variables related to writing performance: prompt modality, topic familiarity, and score stability. In comparison to the experiential work of James Gray and colleagues (1982) on properties of writing tasks discussed in chapter 7, we see in the UCLA research applications of formal experimental tradition. While Gray and his colleagues rely on teacher knowledge as a basis for evidence, Baker and Quellmalz tended to rely on empirical variable modeling. We note in passing that an early history of writing studies, focusing solely on knowledge creation, could be written from *Properties of Writing Tasks* (Gray et al. 1982) and *Studies in Test Design* (Quellmalz 1981a, 1981b, 1981c).

While the UCLA work remained experimentally focused, aimed at an audience of researchers interested in issues of measurement, at the University of San Francisco, Michael Scriven established an Evaluation Institute, with a more public-facing orientation. By 1981 Scriven and his colleagues had published *The Evaluation of Composition Instruction*, one of the leading early handbooks on assessing academic writing programs, notable for its ecumenical treatment of holistic scoring within the context of other methods (Davis, Scriven, and Thomas 1981) and its clear exposition of complex measurement concepts.[3]

These and other university research centers soon discovered, as had BAWP, that they faced similar challenges. Their institution would support them only up to a certain point. It was not easy to obtain grants from the National Endowment for the Humanities or from private foundations such as Carnegie Foundation for the Advancement of Teaching or the Ford Foundation. For individual academic research projects, however, the Department of Health, Education, and Welfare did grant some work in writing evaluation (e.g., Cohen, Sheldon, and Chadbourne 1971) and then in 1972 founded their National Institute of Education (NIE), whose grants continued to support innovative research into holistic scoring throughout the 1970s. NIE supported Catharine Keech's work on her dissertation with its harbinger argument that to measure student growth with holistic scoring is to look through a very murky and disfiguring glass (Lucas 1984).

It should go without saying that most writing-evaluation researchers ended up relying on their institution, running studies "on shoestring money" (Steinberg 1963, 33). But whatever their home base or their source of funding, researchers steadily increased their use and study of holistic scoring during the years 1960–1980. Historians in writing studies sometimes construct this research activity as a push-me-pull-you contest between the analytic and the holistic, like the oscillation between high and low tide in a river estuary. But a more accurate image is that span of time when river and sea push and pull to a standstill—still on the surface but underneath a restless mingling of salt water and fresh water, tide and current, eddy and flow, sand and mud. The years themselves may mark a turning point, but it was diffuse, ambivalent, and conflicted.

As chapters 5 through 7 demonstrate, US higher education has a long history of using pure and quasi holistic methods to investigate its writing-assessment programs—the California State University and Colleges system, the College of the University of Chicago, Florida State University, the University System of Georgia, Indiana University, Michigan State College, the University of Illinois, the University of Nebraska, to name a few out of many. Around the nation, dissertations were exploring essay composing using both analytic and holistic measures, directed by faculty with interest and expertise in essay-rating systems.[4] And the permanent faculty were doing their own research. Around 1965, at Harvard, John C. Mellon was studying the effect of his sentence-combining practice on school-student essays, relying on AP-style holistic scoring. About a year later at the University of Iowa, Richard Braddock and Charles R. Statler were using both analytic scales and general impression to compare juniors who had taken first-year composition with juniors who had not.

It would take another book to do justice to these first-generation pioneer researchers. They scrambled for funding, bore the scorn of numerophobic colleagues, begged for teachers to try out controlled teaching interventions and to assign essays for research study, talked their students and office mates into scoring essays for free or for measly pay, performed tedious analysis before computers were readily available to ease the tedium, and suffered setbacks in the form of nonsignificant results or dubious rater reliability or post factum discovery of invalid research design. Usually they were attempting investigations that had never been done before. But they persisted. They had to take the plunge into the chancy waters of whole-essay rating because they needed some kind of writing-proficiency score as a dependent or criterion measure for their target variables. Those targets included errors in context, writing improvement during composition courses with greater or less amounts of writing assigned, yearly improvement within a school writing program, sophistication of syntax, improvement from first to third year of college, improvement with practice in sentence combining, junior-level writing with or without the first-year composition course, composing with or without prewriting. All these studies were completed before 1970. Between 1970 and 1980, investigators added more trials in research areas of new interest: effect of typeface on grading, validity of computer grading, and influence on the writing of students of teachers who had attended National Writing Project seminars. Especially popular was the use of holistic scoring to measure the effect on the essay writing of students, using pre- and posttests, from specific pedagogies, such as individual student conferencing in class (the Roger Garrison method), giving only praise to papers, providing teacher commentary between drafts of a paper, and teaching the generative rhetoric of Frances Christensen.

There may be some truth to the charge that these early researchers were naïve to think that a unitary measure such as a holistic score, derived from a scale sometimes as rudimentary as three points, had enough discriminatory power to record differences in research-group performances. A case in point is Joan M. Putz's 1969 dissertation with New York University's School of Education, "The Effectiveness of Non-Directive Teaching as a Method of Improving the Writing Ability of College Freshmen." To rate her pre and post essays, she replicated Godshalk, Swineford, and Coffman's (1966) study, using a three-point scale and pooling five independent scores. She did not find any statistically significant difference between pre and post or regular and experimental student papers (Putz 1970). On the other hand, sometimes holistic scores did distinguish significantly between pre and post essays or between control and experimental groups. In 1962–1963, William McColly and Robert Remstad set up a contrast among three teaching practices in school English courses: (1) "mere writing," (2) functional "non-writing" learning activities such as peer critique, and (3) oral tutoring with immediate feedback. Relying on a pooled-rater holistic scoring system based in Godshalk's new scoring methods for the English Composition Test (ECT), they found that students at grades 10, 11, and 12 achieved higher scores at statistically significant levels. Statistically significant higher scores were also identified in papers from older students and from women.

It is worth noting that McColly and Remstad (1963) also added a measure of error frequency. In reality, from 1960 to 1970 only a few experimenters who chose holistic scoring chose it as their sole measure. In addition, they used misspellings, minutes on task, academic grades, frequency of syntactic forms, and a healthy sprinkling of other analytical variables. Researchers were interested in the concrete breakdown of the situation they were investigating. They had their main eye on a distinctive teaching method, a language-growth pattern, or a problematic curricular route, not on the overall quality of an essay or on the general proficiency or aptitude of a student. They tended to be of a searching, pragmatic, analytical bent. So they chose measures that fished out the particulars. In 1971, three investigators trying to pin down the unruly variance in the writing of California junior-college students put it bluntly: "The holistic approach to grading essays simply will not yield as much useful information as the atomistic approach" (Cohen, Sheldon, and Chadbourne 1971, 13).[5]

And as reflective researchers everywhere, they did not hesitate to question their own measures. By 1960, problems with holistic scoring, loosely defined, had been known for decades. As early as 1923, the lack of diagnostic information with unitary scores was noted by Earl Hudelson, who pointed out that sample matching on an essay scale won't help teachers needing "devices for analyzing composition and diagnosing merits and defects for the purpose of improving instruction" (57). As early as 1940, unevenness in examination essays was noted as an obstacle in making a holistic decision, yes or no, on exemption essays at Indiana University: "A great many papers fall into one or the other of two classes: (1) those with good thought but with errors in mechanics; and (2) those correct in mechanics but with poor thought" (Hendricks 1940, 613). As we saw in chapter 4, in the United Kingdom the influence of topic on holistic raters had been studied by Stephen Wiseman and James Wrigley in 1958 and James Britton in 1963. From 1960 to 1970, on both sides of the Atlantic, other potential problems with holistic readings were being empirically investigated: exclusion of important writing achievements from the chosen criteria set; failure of readers to take syntax into account; lack of attention by raters to rater instructions; asymmetries between stated criteria and score, as when one writing trait unconsciously influences the rating of other traits (the halo effect); poor correlation of one holistic-scoring scheme with other holistic-scoring schemes or with analytic scales; and overconformity among the rating corps, that is, the way the demand for high interrater reliability encouraged raters to see themselves "as though they were all cut like gingerbread men, from a common mold" (Pilkington 1967, 93). In the United States the empirical deconstruction of holistic essay scoring accelerated after 1970, reaching a kind of peak around 1979. Indeed, Keech and other BAWP researchers were catching a wave in the late 1970s since other researchers were also discovering that the quality of essays students wrote and the scores raters produced were affected by topic choice, prompt construction, rater background, norming, and fatigue.

Most surprising was the discovery that holistic scores were affected by essay qualities of which raters were usually not aware, such as handwriting, syntax, stylistic register, and linguistically diverse language. Bringing latent variables to light is not easy, but discovery was aided with fairly new statistical procedures feasible only with high-end computer processing such as the IBM computer at the Littauer Statistical Laboratory, Harvard University, used for a principle-component solution in 1961 by Paul B. Diederich, John W. French, and Sydell T. Carlton. Factor analysis could locate underlying patterns lost in an ocean of data and derive new variables fewer in number than originally identified. Stepwise multiple regression could improve on simple correlations among variables. The process invites the researcher to specify a dependent variable and a series of independent variables—and then to select the most powerful explanatory variables, then the next, and then the next until statistical significance is lost.

One of the earliest uses of this method was undertaken by Ellen Nold and Sarah Freedman of Stanford University and published in *Research in the Teaching of English* in 1977.[6] Stepwise regression was used to tease out which textual elements of two timed writing samples written by twenty-two Stanford first-year students most influenced reader response. The dependent variable was the holistic score on the two essays, reportedly read at a 0.85 correlation between readers. The independent variable was based on four textual elements: the number, development, and logic of ideas; the presence and appropriateness of the organization of those ideas; the complexity, variation, and appropriateness of the syntax; and the richness and appropriateness of vocabulary. Knowledge of conventions associated with mechanical and spelling errors was not part of the analysis because Stanford students, the authors note, make few such errors. Measurement of the variables was established by counts of various kinds—words per T-unit, for instance, and categorization of finite verbs as common or not.

Following stepwise multiple regression using R^2 as coefficient of determination, 20 percent of the variance was explained by essay length, 3 percent by final modifiers (the authors incorrectly report 12 percent in the text for $R^2 = 0.312$), 4 percent by modal verbs, 4 percent by *be* or *have* as auxiliary modifiers, and 4 percent by common verbs. As they conclude, "It is more damning to write a short essay than elevating to write a long one" (Nold and Freedman 1977, 173). As to sophistication in modification, they find that final free modifiers are indicative of good writing in expository and argumentative discourse, just as Francis Christensen claimed in 1967. The young composition teachers used as raters might have sworn that length of an essay did not influence their scores, and they might have had difficulty in finding, much less identifying, final free modifiers since the syntactic structure had gained notice in the profession only a few years earlier. But using their scores as a dependent variable allowed Nold and Freedman to determine which variables most influenced rater judgment.

While Nold and Freedman made clear that they identified some significant predictors of writing quality, they were very alert to the tenuousness of their findings. "Care must be taken" they caution, "that both readers and tasks remain as consistent as possible across studies" so "the research, the test maker, and the composition teacher" may benefit by the discovery of what textual elements most impact reader judgments (1977, 174).

In the late 1970s, multivariate studies added more surprising insights into the "covert, quantifiable written cues," as Nold and Freedman put it, that secretly guide holistic readers (1977, 164). Some of the findings were not only surprising but also unsettling. Over and over, mere length of essay (a proxy for fluency) and poor mechanics (associated with knowledge of conventions) correlated more with high scores than reasoning, organization, or support (all taken as measures of critical thinking.) Over and over, measures reflecting mature or sophisticated sentence construction, such as T-unit length, diminished positive association, and sometimes the association was negative. These interrelationships among essay traits would be impossible for most holistic readers to see and were made visible by multivariate analysis.

In research based on her Stanford University dissertation, Freedman turned to her study of reader response by using the holistically scored essays from the 1977 study as anchors. She systematically manipulated original and revised papers to identify which of four characteristics—content, organization, sentence structure, and mechanics—most influenced reader decisions involved in categorizing student writing. Analysis of variance revealed that the content variable was that which caused readers to score an essay significantly higher. As was the case in her study with Nold, Freedman closed her article with instructional implications. She wrote, "If society values content and organization as much as the raters in this project and many of the earlier studies apparently did, then according to the definitions of content and organization used in this study, a pedagogy for teaching writing should aim first to help students develop their ideas logically, being sensitive to the appropriate amount of explanation necessary for the audience" (1979, 336). While she notes that many college-level curricula begin with a focus on addressing mechanical and syntactic problems, it is important to supplement these curricula with carefully planned curricula for teaching content and organization aspects of discourse.

Significantly, her evidence-based conclusions were to be confirmed by the first metanalytic study by George Hillocks Jr. in 1986 as integral to what he defined as the environmental mode of instruction, yielding an effect size of 0.44, with its attention to clear and specific objectives, problems selected to engage students with each other in defined processes important to particular features of writing, and activities facilitating high levels of peer interaction concerning specific tasks. Freedman's attention to the integrated nature of written communication, experimentally identified, would be associated with knowledge yet to come about effective writing instruction.

Between 1975 and 1980, more than a dozen studies used multivariant analysis (such as multiple regression, stepwise multiple regression, factor analysis) to tease out writing-trait features that lay hidden behind holistic scores. In a few years independent researchers had confirmed the suspicions that testing-firm researchers had long held but little investigated, that halo effects—identified by Edward L. Thorndike in 1920 as a general impulse coloring a specific observation—were operating despite rater training to avoid them.[7] Of course, carefully designed calibration sessions lessened the effect by leveraging gestalt principles.

INDEPENDENT ACADEMIC RESEARCHERS: A BODY OF KNOWLEDGE AND THE QUESTION OF FAIRNESS

Did this body of knowledge developed from 1960 to 1980 influence the future course of holistic scoring? Independent researchers certainly used it as a foundation for even stronger critique in the next two decades, such as Davida Charney's tough interrogation of unproven assumptions about validity (1984), or Catharine Keech Lucas's patient lesson that testing could never escape setting (1988), or Roger Cherry and Paul Meyer's exposé of the deceptive ways rater reliability could be calculated (1993).[8] But the critique did not seem to block or even slow down commercial, state, and local standardized testing. On the contrary, the 1980s mark the heyday of holistic scoring, especially connected with accountability in primary and secondary schooling.

As our analysis reveals, there is evidence that, from the 1960s to the 1980s, US academic researchers were more willing to investigate the contextual impact of holistic essay scoring—an issue of fairness related to evidence of validity and reliability—than were their testing-firm counterparts. (Diederich's 1961 factor-analysis study with French and Carlton is a notable exception of research not directly linked to a product.) No doubt this different path of research is related to occupational context. ETS researchers studied writing traits, but their aim was testing, so traits most amenable to limited-response items were targeted, such as knowledge of conventions and patterns of editing. Academic researchers had different primary goals: to improve reading habits of composition teachers; to validate new teaching practices; to quantify adolescent language growth; to understand the interface between language production and psychological states such as anxiety or audience awareness; to interrogate research measures; and to advance previous research through innovative programmatic approaches that were site specific.

The difference can be seen, for instance, in the study of linguistically diverse language. Only in the late 1970s did researchers developing large-scale assessment start to ask if dialect affected holistic scoring (civil-rights issues came about a decade late to language-evaluation studies). Take 1977. That year, Hunter Breland of ETS published a comparison of performance of students who had taken the College Board's objective Test of Standard Written English (TSWE) with holistic rating of essays the students later wrote in first-year college composition. The Breland study was among the first to report group differences in scores based on a given construct of writing. Breland had an established program of research in fairness. In 1976, with Gail H. Ironson, he had designed a comparative analysis of admission strategies following the *DeFunis v. Odegaard* decision that brought the issue of preferential minority admissions to the Supreme Court. That study demonstrated expert use of psychometric models developed by T. Anne Cleary (1968) and Nancy S. Cole (1973) associated with the determination of fairness. In 1977 he brought that judgment to bear on the TSWE using techniques associated with differences between majority and minority groups on predictors and criteria, correlations between predictors and criteria, and slopes of the within-group regression lines. The results of the regression analyses comparing TSWE scores and writing samples were especially revealing. The difference in the intercept of the regression line between men and women was not statistically significant ($p = 0.057$)—but only barely. Conversely, the differences between majority and minority students were quite statistically significant ($p < 0.001$)—a high statistical significance indeed. But for a rounding decision upward for 0.057 rather than downward of 0.05 (the borderline for statistical significance), differential prediction would have been established for both groups.

Even in the most generous interpretation, it is difficult today to agree with Breland's conclusion that no important group differences were observed. Yet, while we may debate the conclusions drawn, we must also acknowledge that his study paved the way for future research based on the final sentence of his report: "The study was limited to some degree, of course, by the necessity of combining all minorities into one group. Future studies should attempt to focus on single groups. Therefore, sufficient quantities of data should be collected for within-group analysis" (1976, 44).

Beginning in 1977, Edward M. White and Leon L. Thomas would do just that. They had begun a study of the California State University and College's new English Placement Test, which used a holistically scored essay. Published in 1981, their study—"Racial Minorities and Writing Skills Assessment in the California State University and College"—was the first large-scale comparative account on score distributions resulting from limited response and holistic-scoring methods. Information was presented on the performance of 10,719 first-time freshmen admitted to the California State University and Colleges in fall 1977 on both the TSWE and the English Placement Test (EPT). The large sampling plan therefore served as the first large-scale study of a test of prescriptive English using multiple-choice questions (an examination of what White and Thomas termed the "grapholect") and a comparative assessment using both multiple-choice questions and holistic scores (described as a "test of writing ability").

While Breland (1977) had reported statistically significant majority-minority differences in a comparative regression analysis of essay scores on TSWE Scores, White and Thomas provided descriptive statistics in the form of histograms. While Breland had used inferential analysis, White and Thomas presented score distributions that had a straightforward message: direct measurement of writing produced different distributions for minority students than for white students. For the overall group and for white students, White and Thomas reported a Gaussian distribution for the holistically scored essay, accompanied by a left-skewed distribution for the EPT (that is, both the multiple-choice questions and the essay). The TSWE scores were flatter but nevertheless approached a normal distribution. For black students, however, the distribution patterns were described as "dramatic": the TSWE produced a right-skewed distribution, placing approximately 11 percent of the students at the lowest score range, while the ETP and the essay continued to approximate a Gaussian distribution. Similar patterns were reported for Mexican American students and for Asian American students. As White and Thomas concluded, "The TSWE does not distribute minority students the same way trained and accurate evaluators of writing samples do" (1977, 282). A vehicle for construct representation, item type itself was related to the potential for disparate impact.

No doubt White and Thomas were justifiably proud of the EPT. Their findings showed that holistic scoring could be meaningfully associated with an assessment of linguistically diverse students.[9]

Comparison of the two studies demonstrates their historical significance. As we note above, there is no doubt we are witnessing two distinctly different occupational contexts. Breland was, in essence, justifying score use to a society increasingly critical of tests that frustrated equal opportunity. White and Thomas were extending that analysis by comparing one test to another in order to examine differential impact on their own students. Yet lest we repeat ourselves on differences, there is an important similarity between the two studies: they are far too late in appearing. The TSWE was introduced in 1974, but the first study of impact was published in 1977. The Carolina placement test was first given in 1973, but the first study was published in 1981. How could it be, we rightly ask, that tests that had high-stakes consequences for thousands of students had been released before adequate analysis had been undertaken? How can it be that analysis was not conducted before the first student took the first test to determine any unintended racial differences in outcomes resulting from tests that claim to be neutral? Framing differences in terms of joint failures allows a different kind of map to be drawn for the future, as we suggest in chapter 10.

As Mya Poe and John Aloysius Cogan Jr. establish in their study of disparate impact as a vehicle for assessment fairness (2016), the Civil Rights Act of 1964 provided both an ethical and legal framework for the identification of discrimination. From 1960 to 1984, US writing studies researchers—whether employed by testing organizations or the nation's colleges—came to realize that assessment is a moral issue. Because it took us a while to start listening, and because we must listen still, the 1963 Civil Rights Address of John F. Kennedy remains haunting: "This Nation was founded by men of many nations and backgrounds. It was founded on the principle that all men are created equal, and that the rights of every man are diminished when the rights of one man are threatened." In writing studies, everybody knew that the equal right to develop talents and abilities began in language.

And everybody had something to say. In 1977, Louie Crew published his thoughts about an essay he read during a Regents Examination, the rising junior-level test in the University System of Georgia. The essay was composed in African American dialect, and teachers had given it scores of 1, 2, and 3 on a scale in which 4 was the highest score. Crew was selling something: his profound dislike of holistic scoring. His argument turned on the influence of the student's language on raters. Speaking sarcastically, he wrote that "part of the magic of translating a complex linguistic response into a simplistic score is the inaccessibility of the mental processes of the scorer" (708). Crew accused the Regents Examination of racial unfairness, noting that in 1974–1975, the three largest black colleges in Georgia produced a 37 percent passing rate compared to 71 percent for the system as a whole.[10]

To these offhand claims, compare a research study undertaken the same year, 1977, which challenged Breland's finding that differential prediction was absent from the Test of Standard Written English. In *Research in the Teaching of English*, Gene Piché, Donald L. Rubin, Lona J. Turner, and Michael L. Michlin challenged Crew's suggestion that the "mental processes" of scorers were inaccessible. These researchers from Duke University and the University of Minnesota had inservice and preservice teachers apply nineteen seven-interval semantic differential scales to analyze their subjective response to eleventh-grade essays. Nine of the scales together provided a holistic appraisal of an essay.[11] The essays appeared in pairs, one in "standard written English," the other in "black nonstandard written English." The second was deliberately peppered with dialectical markers. The raters also were asked to guess the sex, age, and "racial identity" of the writer. The findings of this mixed-guise experiment were unforeseen. The "nonstandard" papers did not raise beyond chance the luck of the teachers in recognizing the writing as nonstandard, yet a paper (doctored or not) that the teachers judged below average in writing skill tended to be attributed to black authorship. Bias and essay appraisal were intertwined. The researchers concluded that "composition stimuli are salient in eliciting a general impression of *ethnicity-nonstandardness* somehow associated with the presumed writers" (1978, 116). Mental processes of teacher-readers could be accessed, to a degree, and the processes appeared linked to assumptions about race. Holistic scoring of an essay would not necessarily erase this bias. A tradition of such text-based studies continued with NAEP in the work of Geneva Smitherman (1992).

INDEPENDENT ACADEMIC RESEARCHERS: HANDBOOKS AND KNOWLEDGE DISSEMINATION

Acknowledgment of contingency and awareness of intersectionality informed six handbooks that were different than those produced by William Boyd (1924) and Phillip Vernon (1957) in the United Kingdom and Paul Dressel (1961) and Paul B. Diederich (1974) in the United States. The new handbooks were alert to the limits of assessment, cautious about its use, and desirous to demonstrate that evaluation and instruction, when contextualized together, benefit students.

In 1977 the publication of *Evaluating Writing: Describing, Measuring, Judging*, edited by Charles Cooper and Lee Odell, heralded the fact that there was, indeed, a body of knowledge about writing assessment. Methods existed that had been used in a variety of instances, from providing a portrait of student ability through NAEP to identifying mature word choice through computer evaluation. Chapters by Cooper and Richard Lloyd-Jones covered, respectively, holistic and primary-trait scoring—and therefore covered forms of evidence related to construct, concurrent, and predictive validity. Chapters by Patrick J. Finn, Kellogg W. Hunt, and Odell linked writing ability to processes of maturity and critical thinking, thus providing discussions of conceptually related constructs. Mary J. Beaven provided a chapter on goal setting and peer review, thus calling attention to self-efficacy associated with the intrapersonal domain of writing and collaboration associated with the intrapersonal domain.

In many ways, the 1977 edited collection signaled a potential broadening of the field's understanding of the writing construct in ways that had not been established before. Topics of scoring were broadened by attention to the span of the writing construct and the varied ways writing ability could be investigated, from computer-generated lists of word frequency to asking students for self-evaluation of their writing processes and the effectiveness of their products.

The second handbook is discussed in chapter 2. As we note there, Miles Myers's *A Procedure for Writing Assessment and Holistic Scoring* (1980) is a practical, not a philosophical monograph. Whatever faults might be associated with the volume are overcome by its aim. As Myers urged in his 2014 interview with us shortly before his death, we should "remember that the 'procedure' book was intended as a proposal for teachers to try scoring sessions in their districts, and we did always require every step had to be taken. We wanted districts to fund teachers engaging in a collective examination of student writing in a school or district. BAWP had learned that collective efforts could become an ethical commitment to both reliability and validity, calling into question how grading typically worked" (email to authors, December 8–14, 2014). For Myers, assessment had a positive impact as teachers bonded together to form communities dedicated to moving beyond reductionist ways of teaching and assessing writing.

The third handbook, *The Evaluation of Composition Instruction* (1981), discussed earlier in this chapter, was authored by Barbara Gross Davis, Michael Scriven, and Susan Thomas but was essentially the creation of Scriven. With a PhD from Oxford University, Scriven held the rank of professor at the University of California, Berkeley, when he conducted his investigation of the BAWP from 1977 to 1978. According to Myers, "BAWP needed Scriven, a professor of philosophy, almost as much as Scriven needed BAWP" (email to authors, December 8–14, 2014). An external evaluation of the program by an eminent evaluator would lend credibility to the fledgling program; and an evaluation of BAWP, a fledgling but important educational-development program, would give Scriven the kind of momentum that would, in fact, earn him the rank of university professor and director of the Evaluation Institute at the University of San Francisco in 1978. With the publication of the program-evaluation handbook in 1981, it was clear that the work had paid off: examples from BAWP were the core of the book.

While evidence related to validity, reliability, and fairness are evident throughout the book, its design is structured around a checklist approach based on phases of the evaluation: previewing, designing, conducting, synthesizing, reporting, and evaluating. In turn, these phases are informed by "scientific design" with attention to test construction and comparison groups (Scriven 1981, 29). It is, in fact, just this orientation toward design that flummoxed Myers, as we note in chapter 7. In his analysis of BAWP, we can see the quintessential Scriven in action as he classifies gains in professional development as side effects—those "unintended good and bad" aspects of the instructional program that could be determined by brainstorming with program administrators, reviewing similar projects, analyzing the data at hand, observing instructional activities, and interviewing national leaders. Using these techniques, Scriven reports the side effects he observed in his program review of the BAWP: increased professional status of teachers; disciplinary integrity of writing instruction; pedagogical shifts to a process-based view of writing; increased collaboration among school districts and postsecondary institutions; improved monitoring of outcomes; and model use in other disciplines. Of course, to Myers these were the very basis of BAWP, which explains why the Scriven assessment model was quintessentially different from that needed to evaluate the project. As we observe in chapter 7, Scriven's program-evaluation model was the norm, and it stayed the norm for decades—but it was challenged by Harvard's Carol H. Weiss (1972), and her theory-based and action-oriented program-evaluation model is more aligned with the handbooks written by those for whom composition, as Louise Wetherbee Phelps would phrase it in 1988, was a "human science."

The fourth handbook exerted an important influence on researchers in both the United States and the United Kingdom. Content, organization, vocabulary, language use, and mechanics—these were the criteria that stood as the unifying framework for *Testing ESL Composition: A Practical Approach* (1981) and *Teaching ESL Composition: Principles and Techniques* (1983) by Holly L. Jacobs and her colleagues. Writing about the testing volume, the young reviewer Liz Hamp-Lyons (1984) noted that the volume had been influential in the United States but had, unfortunately, been ignored internationally. Observing that the trait-based approach was a milestone achievement, Hamp-Lyons praised the volume as the first time a review of assessment in first- and second-language writing had been provided between two covers. A generation of international assessment researchers would benefit from details of the method as used at Texas A&M University, College Station, as well as the practical advice for implementation.

The method proposed in *Testing ESL Composition*, the ESL Composition Profile, followed a classical rhetorical framework of inventio (content), disposition, (organization) and elocutio (vocabulary, language use, and mechanics). Each variable was categorized by four levels of proficiency, ranging from excellent to very poor. Hamp-Lyons praised the method for its combination of holistic evaluation with conscious attention to the range of specific criteria. Yet with the praise came her ever-rebellious caution: "Beside the strengths of such a fully defined test instrument must be set the disadvantage that, by using it, one is committing oneself to the test developer's construct" (1984, 243). Living in an era of protests and cautious by nature, she came down on the side of individual difference. Yet, despite Hamp-Lyons's James Britton-like objections to conformity, she had to acknowledge that Jacobs, Zinkgraf, Wormuth, Hartfiel, and Hughey had produced the first handbook for teaching and assessing English as a second language.

The fifth handbook, *Evaluating College Writing Programs* by Stephen P. Witte and Lester Faigley (1983), stood in opposition to the handbook by Davis, Scriven, and Thomas. For Witte and Faigley, there was no sense of scientific objectivity that could be achieved by bracketing the aims of the program and seeking information from comparison groups. Indeed, rather than follow any single approach, Witte and Faigley encouraged educational researchers to pursue choice and match method to aim. Theirs was a component-based approach based on five elements: cultural and social context, institutional context, program structure and administration, content or curriculum, and instruction. While aspects of validity and reliability are discussed through the volume, Witte and Faigley place emphasis on heuristics that derive from analysis of the five components and their interactions.

Finally—and here we end our handbook survey—we acknowledge the importance of Edward M. White's *Teaching and Assessing Writing* (1985). Along with the slim volume by Myers, White's book was likely to be on the shelves of those who found themselves responsible for large-scale assessments and needed solid advice from a knowledgeable researcher. The early reviews noted just that need. "It's about time," David Taylor wrote in his review. While a fifteen-year "flowering of research" may have caused a revolution in the ways writing was taught and evaluated, that information had been "trapped in journals, and scattered across one-issue research monographs and anthologies" (1984, 140). Praising the publication of a single-author guide, Taylor noted how the book's theme—that sophistication in assessment improves writing instruction—was both innovative and promising. Especially noteworthy was White's emphasis on holistic scoring that could be connected with all aspects of classroom teaching—a marriage White believed, according to Taylor, was heaven made.

A scholar of Jane Austen who recognized the importance of narrative and irony, White knew how to weave a handbook. While he covered fundamental principles of measurement involving validity, reliability, and fairness, these appeared in a chapter on evaluating writing programs and projects that came late in the book. More important were naturally occurring issues involving instruction and its relationship to assessment and the presentation of holistic scoring as a humanistic response to assessment. And, while poststructural theories of reading would appear, at first glance, to have no part in holistic interpretation, they were paradoxically a "resistance movement" against narrow analytic interpretations (1985, 92). The process of reading, especially in interpretative communities, was to be emphasized over what used to be considered the meaning of a text. By the time readers reached the last sentence of the last chapter, they had been inductively led to the very place they began: "The more we know, and the more we help our students know about assessing writing, the more effective our teaching will become" (289).

As we turn from the handbooks, another contemporary question about the validity of holistic scoring is the focus of the rest of this chapter. Can holistic scores record change in writing proficiency, whether conceived as personal growth or learning improvement or educational progress? There were already major doubts. Human development often manifested itself as regressive, a stream full of eddies, not friendly to unidirectional measuring devices like the hydrometer in an irrigation ditch. As we have seen, Lucas was one of the earliest composition experts to dwell on the issue. She had raised it in her 1977 memo to Scriven (see chapter 7). In 1980 she wrote, "Analytic error counts and even holistic responses may determine that writers-in-transition are less able performers than before, when actually each of these flaws can be seen in context as signaling movement toward a higher level of competency" (1982, 476). Learning during an academic span of time may be little different. Can a whole-essay measure with only three to six points on its scale detect the small, partial, stop-and-go, backsliding changes in student writing over the short span of one academic course, even over one or two years? As for progress within academic programs, as we have seen, Albert Lavin and a few other independent researchers had used holistic scoring to evaluate the curricular success of local English programs in bringing students along in their writing skills.

But long-term improvement of student writing skills across states? That was a different genre of research no handbook and few studies had considered. Could there be formed a research venture large enough to tackle that issue, and could holistic scoring help tackle it? The answers turned out yes and maybe not.

THE NATIONAL ASSESSMENT OF EDUCATIONAL PROGRESS, 1969–1984

The early history of the NAEP follows Hayden White's emplotment of tragedy, at least from the viewpoint of some who played a role in it. A flawed but more rigorous direct measure of writing gains control and then loses that control to a weaker but more clever measure of writing (Othello and Iago). Or maybe independent language investigators unwittingly bring about their own downfall when they sign away their independence (Michael and Luke). Whichever, the story of the early NAEP begins long before its first testing in the spring of 1969, in fact more than a century before.

In June 1867, fourteen months after General Robert E. Lee's surrender at Appomattox, the US House resumed its prewar debate over the establishment of a department of education. The National Association of State and City School Superintendents had petitioned for such a federal office, whose purpose they said would be gathering "the results of school systems in order to determine their comparative value" (Morgan 1985, 14). Those were alarming words to a Congress exhausted from war-time federal controls. But in presenting the bill, James A. Garfield of Ohio, future US president, assured the House that the department would have no power to interfere with schools anywhere. It would collect only "such statistics and facts as shall show the condition and progress of education in the several States and Territories" (*Congressional Globe* 1867, 2969, column 3).

Predictably, opposition to the bill was loud. Andrew Rogers of New Jersey, once a school teacher, lone Democrat in the House, delivered a thin-edge-of-the-wedge warning. Rogers predicted that the federal department might start by collecting "facts and statistics" but later, through amendments, would "inflict upon the country a centralization of power and influence" that would, in the end, "control and regulate the educational system of the whole country" (*Congressional Globe* 1867, 2969, column 1). But just as loud were believers in national progress through the gathering of scientific data. It took two votes, but the bill did pass, barely. The government, however, had more pressing matters, such as Reconstruction. Within a couple of years the new US Department of Education was reduced to an Office of Education buried deep in the US Department of the Interior, and for a century it never collected one fact or statistic.

One century later, 1966: déjà vu. In 1953, Eisenhower had established the US Department of Health, Education, and Welfare, and in 1962, Francis Keppel, the newly appointed Commissioner of Education, decided it was time for the government to take up its 1866 mission to "show the condition and progress of education" in the nation (Congressional Globe 1867, 2966). As Keppel (1966) would later write, "There was an information problem" (108). Expert and lay groups were formed to create testing objectives. In July 1968, a Committee on Assessing the Progress of Education assumed responsibility for the first examination cycle, to be given 1969–1970.[12] In summer of 1969, in the middle of the first testing, NAEP was turned over to the Education Commission of the States (ECS), a nonfederal interstate compact funded by the Carnegie, Danforth, and Ford foundations. ECS ran NAEP for the next two cycles: 1973–74 and 1978–79. Then an experiment in national testing run largely by independent researchers abruptly ended.

For its first three cycles, NAEP was *sui generis*, noble in its intentions. Directed by Ralph W. Tyler, one of the most respected educationists and influential researchers in the nation, NAEP used a matrix sampling design, as we note in chapter 5, to increase construct representation through group scoring. Academic subjects, ranging from citizenship to writing, were rotated so examination time for any student was no more than forty minutes. To protect students, teachers, school districts, and states, data was aggregated only by age, gender, SES, population density, and four main demographic regions of the United States. Implicitly, NAEP intended to honor James Garfield's 1866 promise to record facts and statistics and let schools, districts, and states profit as they wished from the information.

Nevertheless, as in 1966, even when NAEP was no more than a proposal, resistance to it was fierce—fiercest, not surprisingly, among educationists themselves. Harold Hand, professor of education at the University of Illinois, warned—shades of schoolteacher Andrew Rogers—that NAEP would eventually result in a "centrally controlled curriculum" (1965, 9). NEA and other educational associations recommended that their members take no part in the testing. NAEP countered by sending out its people to give speeches declaring that its intention was not federal control over teachers but teacher power through facts. Among the advocates was Diederich of ETS. At the NCTE annual convention in 1968, in a speech that was later printed in *Research in the Teaching of English*, Diederich went further and assured teachers and administrators that NAEP would be such a good and cheap test that it would *prevent* any political move toward federal standardized testing. The assurance contained a friendly caution. "If it is not shown a better way," Diederich said, "sooner or later Congress will adopt a national testing program" (1969a, 13). That would be a contract, Diederich said, even ETS would not want.

Diederich could have told his audience, but did not, that ETS had already received the contract to design and administer the 1969–70 NAEP tests of writing. He could not have told his audience, of course, that fourteen years later, ETS would take over NAEP from the Education Commission of the States and the assessment would begin morphing into just what its original academic critics feared, a national test of achievement comparing state with state.

Diederich also did not mention an enigma, latent ever since Congress's 1867 agreement to document the "progress of education." What exactly was the "progress" that the NAEP intended to assess? The designers of the new NAEP were determined not to measure individual student improvement. But then what kind of progress were they going to measure? They planned to test group performance every four years on academic subjects, including writing, at the ages of nine, thirteen, and seventeen. But how could "progress" be inferred from the outcomes? If a sample of nine-year-olds in 1973–74 wrote better than another sample of nine-year-olds in 1969–70, does that mean the later students grew up faster (maturational progress), their schools taught more efficiently (educational progress), or their times were more propitious (cultural progress)? Or was there an unknown spiral nebula of evolving intersectionality among variables of gender, race/ethnicity, student economic status, and individual maturation difference? And—an enigma within the enigma—what kind of testing could sort out and measure these changes? It was hard enough to measure writing proficiency at one point in time, as contemporary research was finding. Measuring it over time would be like wrestling Proteus or, following Heraclitus, placing one's foot in the same stream twice.

Actually, when NAEP started contemplating its first tests, educational psychologists had been wrestling with longitudinal intersectionality for years. They knew longitudinal designs (measuring the same people at different years) obscured historical or cohort effects, that cross-sectional designs (measuring different groups at the same point in time) obscured maturational effects, and that even designs investigating the interaction between longitudinal and cross-sectional data (e.g., Kessen 1960) obscured sociocultural, motivational, and learning effects. These problems can be seen in early cross-sectional studies of change in writing performance. In 1961, Albert Kitzhaber (1963) compared countable errors in first-year and fourth-year writing at Dartmouth College and found the seniors less proficient, and he attributed the change to teaching and curriculum without asking if the seniors were just less motivated to produce the writing. Kellogg Hunt (1965) numbered stylistic features, including T-units and sentence length, in open-topic writing produced in 1960 by twelfth, eighth, and fourth graders, attributing the differences to "maturity" without asking about possible historical cohort effects (the different birth dates would have been 1942, 1946, and 1950).

Both Hunt and Kitzhaber had been asked by the Committee on Assessing the Progress of Education to help develop the writing objectives for the first NAEP testing (Norris 1969). How could their bean counting measure the four objectives they and other academic scholars proposed: write to communicate adequately in (1) a social setting, (2) a vocational setting, (3) a scholarly setting, and (4) to appreciate the value of writing. Was a direct measure of writing the answer? No one, understandably, had tried to measure the "progress of education" nationwide with holistic scoring of essays. Yet that was what the first NAEP testing thought to do—and the method of measurement started NAEP on a very uneven road. There is no better way to introduce the problems of recording educational "progress" through holistic essay scoring than to watch how it fared in the first four NAEP writing tests: 1969-70, 1973-74, 1978-79, and 1983-84.[13]

How did holistic scoring play out in the early history of NAEP testing? A popular narrative—at least within composition circles—is that holistic essay scoring failed NAEP's purposes in its first testing, to be rescued in the second testing by a new-born hero, primary-trait scoring (e.g., Elliot 2005, 196-98; Lloyd-Jones 1977). Creditable enough, the tale, however, omits the part holistic scoring continued to play in NAEP. To anticipate, early on, holistic scoring failed to record dependable evidence of long-term educational progress, yet it outlasted primary-trait scoring and eventually helped turn NAEP into what its original critics had feared in 1866 and a century later—a mandated, federally controlled, and commercially run national assessment of "progress" in school education, measured by achievement levels that could be compared state by state.

1969–70. NAEP never operated totally free of testing organizations. In 1965, ETS was contracted both to create the writing objectives and to run the scoring of essays. ETS designed twenty-minute impromptu essays for the students, who were aged nine, thirteen, and seventeen, in stratified groups of 2,000 to 2,500.[14] To score the writing samples, ETS applied its Advanced Placement English holistic scoring system, discussed in chapter 5. The scale had eight points (not counting zero as a point). There was no rubric, and raters internalized a set of sample essays. An essay's score was the sum of two independent ratings. Discrepant scores were not adjusted, and single-rater reliability was estimated on a 10 percent sample of the scores. The topics were different for different age groups, with one exception. Some students aged thirteen and seventeen wrote on the same task, to describe an admired characteristic of a famous person, their choice. This allowed an "overlap study" (i.e., cross-sectional study) in which essays from the two age groups were mixed together and rated with age of writer hidden. The results gave a glimpse of something that might be called "progress." For instance, judging by holistic score, not many thirteen-year-olds, only 5 percent, wrote as well as 17 percent of the seventeen-year-olds (Brown 1980). But who was responsible for the progress—the students, the schools, or the culture? And of what writing accomplishments did this "progress" consist?

These were the very questions asked in the drubbing NAEP took soon after the outcomes of its first test were published. The critique from composition scholars was especially cutting. They charged that NAEP's measurement of language competency was probably confounded with maturation effects ("psychological development") and cultural effects ("regional mores"). The testing disregarded teachable writing traits such as organizational pattern, vocabulary, syntactic fluency, evidence of revising, and discourse mode. Critics especially noted that "personal and creative writing" was missing, even though a panel of specialists, gathered by ETS, had recommended it when the test was in preparation (Farrell 1971).[15]

It was the holistic scoring that took the worst hits. John C. Mellon at Boston University noted that its output was undiagnostic, "lean and of little use" (1972, 99). The procedure imposed a normal curve on raters and ended with only a "holistic rank-ordering." Such self-relative, norm-referenced scoring yielded hardly any significant differences according to age, community size, gender, or region of the country. It definitely did not tap into "the developmental schedule according to which children progress to adult competence in the production of verbal discourse" (103). In sum, "The 'overall-quality' method of evaluating compositions should be abandoned in favor of absolute descriptive measures" (105).[16] The first effort to use holistic essay scoring in a national test of US writing proficiency precipitated one of the earliest consolidated critiques of the method.

Yet this critique left unscathed the overlap study, despite its use of holistic scoring. To reviewers it seemed valid to compare the essay production of two age groups writing on the same topic. Even if learning could not be separated from maturation, changes in writing over time was a kind of "progress" the testing should investigate. In 1970 compositionists were keyed on human development much more so than later. When Mellon recommended that NAEP enlarge its focus on "utilitarian" modes of writing to include personal, creative, and expressivist genres, he was thinking of James Moffett's developmental sequence of modes based on rhetorical distancing and of Britton's developmental categorization of modes according to spectator role (Mellon 1972.). Henry Slotnick, who for NAEP had measured stylistic features such as sentence length with computer programs, went further. He recommended that the next examination should mingle essays from both testing cycles. "It should be possible to describe the improvement in writing that has occurred during the intervening years" (1971, 1115). That design, of course, would further confound variables because (unlike longitudinal studies) it would compare different people at different times. But the hope, a better score from the same academic grade at a later date—wasn't that what ordinary people imagined "progress of education" to be?

1973–74. For the second round of NAEP testing, now under the aegis of the Education Commission of the States, English specialists were asked to join the team. The newcomers included some highly accomplished scholars: compositionists Robert Gorrell, William Irmscher, and Richard Lloyd-Jones; linguists Louis Milic and Donald Sebold; an expert in analytical measurement of essays, Ellis B. Page. It also included William Coffman, who had helped validate Godshalk's pooled-rater holistic scoring for ETS's English Composition Test, discussed in chapter 6. These experts attended to the criticism of the first examination, and this time NAEP attended to them. The 1973–74 examination included expressive and personal writing. Students were given time to revise some essays. Nuts-and-bolts features were counted, among them agreement errors, sentence fragments, awkward syntax, misspellings, and paragraph and essay coherence. And, famously, the English specialists dealt with the charge that holistic scores were not diagnostic or criterion referenced by introducing primary-trait scoring.

Primary-trait analysis was developed by Carl H. Klaus and Richard Lloyd-Jones of the University of Iowa and Ina V. S. Mullis of NAEP. Rexford Brown says at first the method was called "holistic with a rubric," and that Mullis was the one to name it "primary trait" (interview with authors, September 9, 2014). It measures how well certain rhetorical strategies meet the rhetorical objectives set by the topic. For example, in the 1973–74 examination, all age groups were asked to look at a photograph of children jumping on an overturned boat and to narrate the action from the point of view of one of the children or of an unseen observer. Test developers decided that the primary trait, the one central writerly tactic for accomplishing this rhetorical task, was helping the reader enter into the writer's imaginary world. This primary trait was judged on a four-point rubric: 1—no real entry; 2—entry through an identifiable point of view but unstructured and inconsistent; 3—good entry with point of view realized but uneven development; 4—emotive and consistent entry.[17]

With primary-trait scoring, now educational progress could be metered by specific rhetorical criteria. Since, at the start, a few traits are selected for rating, primary-trait scoring is analytic at base, not holistic, and as with many analytic methods of rating essays, the results can be useful to teachers. That was always a major concern with the early NAEP assessors. "We were gathering data that could be educational, that could help improve teaching and learning, as opposed to ranking" (Brown, interview with authors, September 9, 2014). In a sense, primary-trait results were useful *because* they confounded learning and maturation. For instance, on the overturned-boat essays, 10 percent of age-nine students scored 3 on the primary trait of imaginative entry, compared to 29 percent of age-thirteen students and 44 percent of age-seventeen students. A third-grade teacher could teach point of view knowing that around a third of the students were capable of it. It is easier, for instance, than making pedagogical sense out of one age group's decline over four years from 5.12 to 4.85 on a holistic scale.

This decline was reported for age-seventeen students in the 1973–74 examination. NAEP had kept from public eye the essay topic used with age-thirteen and age-seventeen students in the 1969–70 testing, the task asking writers to describe something or someone impressive. Following Slotnick's advice, ETS administered the topics again to the same age groups. Papers from 1969–70 and 1973–74 were mixed and rated holistically, again using AP scoring procedures, perhaps so comparisons could be made of the scoring method itself. So, NAEP had data that was both cross-sectional and cross-time (although not longitudinal). The essays were also analyzed via a long list of stylistic traits elaborately defined. The description of "misspelling" extends for two pages (Brown 1975).

Alas, the new evaluation provided evidence for long-term educational progress that was debatable at best. There was some indication that the two older age groups might be writing worse in 1973–74 than their same age groups had been in 1969–70. Average holistic score for seventeen-year-olds, as we say, dropped two-tenths of a point. It also dropped for thirteen-year-olds, some three-tenths of a point. Neither decline was very much on an eight-point scale. (The large sample of test takers sometimes made tiny group differences statistically significant.) Trait analysis found a few differences, all miniscule, that might conceivably account for the drop: loss in paragraph coherence, loss in average letter length of words, increase in run-on sentences. These findings were cryptic. Any number of cultural-historical shifts over the four years could account for the changes. As was customary in early NAEP reports, experts were called in to explain findings. Two composition scholars, Ross Winterowd and Richard Lloyd-Jones, noted that "the declines in holistic scores reveal as much about scorers as they do about students. Language is always changing, and scorers may prefer standards of writing expression that are becoming outmoded" (National Assessment of Educational Progress 1975, 43).[18] The rank ordering of the holistic, of course, offered no concrete explanation.

1978–79. Yet NAEP did not give up on holistic scoring. In their third test of writing, they mingled age-thirteen and age-seventeen essays from the 1969–70, 1973–74, and 1978–79 cycles, essays all written on the old overlap topic, describing something that impressed the student writers. ETS, however, no longer was in charge of this testing. NAEP gave no official reason, but Brown, who at the time was involved with every aspect of the assessment, reported that ETS was too committed to norm referencing. "They were so into the paradigm of it doesn't make any difference what the content of the question is so long as it performs mathematically and enables us to achieve these generalized statements about the writing—well, that just seemed crazy." Brown added that "there was clear tension between those of us at the National Assessment and the people that we gave contracts to, like ETS. ETS thought it deserved any contract. They looked down on NAEP. . . . But, in fact, they didn't do a very good job" (Brown, interview with authors, September 9, 2014). This time the scoring was turned over to an independent academic, Edward M. White of California State University, San Bernadino, who had just finished directing a nine-year English Equivalency Examination using holistic scoring of essays for the California State University and Colleges system. For that program, White had been using AP scoring protocols, roughly the same as those ETS had used in the first two NAEP tests (Haswell and Elliot 2017). Again, he did so with the NAEP essays, though in a curtailed fashion. The AP scale was halved to four points, the scoring guide was minimal, and raters spent less than a minute per essay (Brown 1980, 65).[19]

Yet extending the cross-time study from four to eight years only further mystified the outcomes, old and new. With seventeen-year-olds, the previously recorded drop in holistic score from 1969 to 1974 disappeared, although the very same essays were rated. The drop from 1974 to 1979, about one-tenth of a percent, was not statistically significant. Cross-sectional results couldn't be compared because, inexplicably, the scoring guide for seventeen-year-olds was different than the guide for thirteen-year-olds, and the topic for the nine-year-olds was unique. All told, NAEP had little success in its third attempt to document long-term education progress in US schools, this time through holistic scoring run by an independent scholar. It is not surprising when, in their summary of this particular eight-year assessment, NAEP comments that the outcomes should explain why "National Assessment adopted the primary trait system and uses the holistic method so sparingly" (National Assessment of Educational Progress 1981, 14). It seemed that by 1980, when the holistic rage was at its height among schools and universities, NAEP holistic scoring was on its way out.

Yet a full turn to primary-trait scoring might have been hard to defend. The primary-trait maps of educational progress from 1969 through 1979 may have drawn a more specific picture, but it was a puzzle with only a scattering of puzzle pieces. Depending on the task and trait chosen, the picture mysteriously changed. With age-nine students, imaginative explanation, rated on four levels for a narrative based on a picture of a girl collecting fireflies, seemed to decline in 1974 and rise again in 1979. The same pattern appeared in age-seventeen students rated on storytelling prompted by a photograph of a stork. But age-nine students rated on their effort to enter into something other than themselves, such as a tree, showed no change with the years. And age-seventeen students rated on persuasiveness in a letter supporting a proposed recreation center declined dramatically over the eight years. Through the microscope of primary-trait rating, the long-term progress in composition teaching looked like Brownian motion, with micromovement in every direction.

1983–84. Then NAEP itself experienced a change. Ten years earlier, in 1973, funding for the second round of testing had been switched from private foundations to the National Center for Education Statistics, an office within the US Department of Education. Continued funding was much more assured, but it meant NAEP had become a standing, bipartisan, federal obligation. It was a switch with consequences that took a decade to unfold. In 1983, under a Reagan administration mission to privatize government, administration of NAEP was taken from ECS and handed over to ETS. No one ever expressed it openly, but the message seemed to say independent researchers had been given the oars and had lost the race.[20]

ETS did not take a long time to start shaping NAEP with an alertness to political forces attuned to accountability. Test takers were selected to represent school grades of four, eight, and twelve as well as ages nine, thirteen, and seventeen so achievement could more easily be attached to curriculum. The term *trends* replaced *progress* on the possibility that achievement levels might decline instead of growing year to year with the population and the GNP. In 1988, Congress legislated an NAEP testing schedule with mandated reporting of "long-term trends," every two years for reading and every four years for writing. Congress also charged NAEP's governing board, now politically appointed, with developing ways to compare achievement levels by state, which was done starting with the 1993 testing. Then, in 2001, the No Child Left Behind legislation required all states and school districts who received Title 1 funds to participate in NAEP reading and math tests, and a trial was begun of district-level comparisons. The number of student responses increased and, understandably, ETS introduced more online scoring. More significantly, NAEP had been transformed—despite Diederich's 1967 assurances—into a test of the educational system. ETS started calling its periodic reports on NAEP "The Nation's Report Card." Under scrutiny was the nation as a whole.

As for rating of student essays, the 1983–84 testing rejuvenated the use of holistic scoring. Essays were scored on a six-point holistic scale. Sample papers represented each of the six levels, which were divided first into "bottom half" and "top half" and then characterized as 1—response to topic, 2—undeveloped response to task, 3—minimally developed response, 4—developed response, 5—elaborated response, and 6—extensively elaborated response. Raters did not have a rubric but made a "global" judgment on "overall fluency," which presumably was "sensitive to a range of different skills, including organization, quality of content, grammar and usage, spelling, punctuation, and choice of words to express an idea" (Applebee, Langer, and Mullis 1986, 6; Ballator, Farnum, and Kaplin 1999, 37). Writing tasks from these same testing years were also scored by primary-trait methods, only now the four points had overtones of normative levels of achievement: "unsatisfactory," "minimal," "adequate," and "elaborated." Not by chance did the word "minimal," with its judgmental overtones, appear in both the holistic and primary-trait scales.

The 1983–84 results for "long-term trends" were, to use ETS's own word, "erratic." (Applebee, Langer, and Mullin 1986, 8). The writing of seventeen-year-olds went down and then back up, of thirteen-year-olds milled around and then rose a bit, of nine-year-olds just milled around all along. In sum, the nation's report card could only say that "achievement in 1984 seems to be no better than it was 10 years earlier" (6). But what did "no better" mean? The holistic score was especially uninformative.

On one topic, for instance, the percent of age-nine students in the top half of the "fluency scale" (using the holistic score) went from 30 in 1979 to 28 in 1984 (75). Those numbers tell us very little that is actionable in the classroom about how the learning of the nation's nine-year-olds was changing, if indeed it was. The language was enough, however, for newspapers around the land, who wrote headlines declaring two-thirds of the nation's school students were only "minimally competent" in writing. It seemed that was what many of their readers wanted to hear.

In 1986 we nevertheless see the full play of holistic and primary-trait scoring in *Writing Trends Across the Decade, 1974–1984*. Extending their study back to the 1973–1974 assessment, Arthur N. Applebee, Judith A. Langer, and Mullis used directly comparable assessments to file a ten-year report.

Their report models what would become, in the United States, the standard combined use of primary-trait and holistic scoring (Applebee, Langer, and Mullis 1986, 67–69). Described as "Task Accomplishment," primary-trait scoring was accomplished through scoring guides that isolated particular features of writing essential to task completion and then grouping those features into five levels of proficiency, from unrateable to elaborated. Described as a measure of "Overall Fluency," holistic scoring was accomplished through a chief reader and table leaders surveying the samples to be read and calibrating reader responses to the six-point scale. No rubric was used, and judgment was determined by the general impression of a writing sample relative to others.

In terms of validity, no specific construct model was provided. As the authors were careful to observe, "Very little is actually understood about the impact of various writing assessment methods on achievement, and this relationship needs to be researched further before drawing any conclusions based on the NAEP data" (Applebee, Langer, and Mullis 1986, 59). In the absence of a construct model, the designers focused on aligning task and scoring. The primary-trait and holistic scores were therefore aligned with the tasks—the very embodiment of criterion-based assessment. For the primary-trait scoring, the rubric was based on the three tasks eliciting informative, persuasive, and imaginative writing; for holistic scoring, the sample papers used for reader calibration were selected from the papers at hand. Technically, the strategy was brilliant in its desire to design an assessment that reflected writing as it was used at home, at school, and in the community.

Reliability was determined by having 20 percent of the papers scored twice. Results were reported innovatively and transparently. The two different types of scoring captured, as intended, related measures of

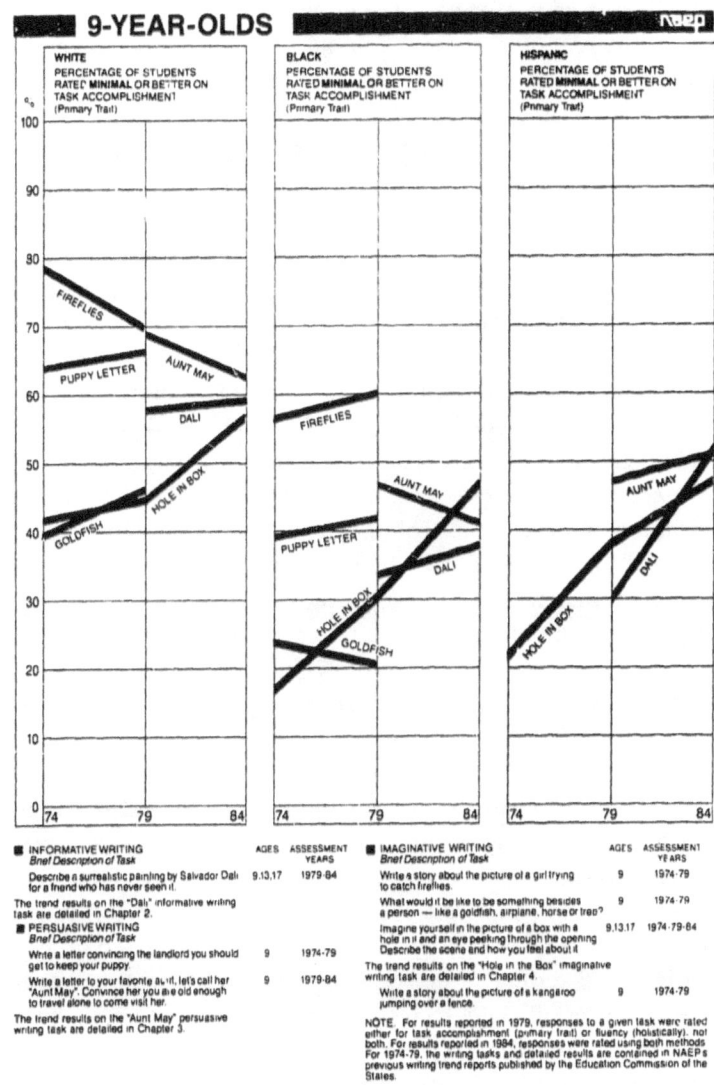

Figure 8.1. NAEP trends, based on inferences taken from primary-trait scoring, 1974, 1979, and 1984 (Applebee, Langer, and Mullis 1986, 50)

overall fluency and task-completion ability. Innovatively, evidence of fairness was demonstrated in terms of subgroup analysis by gender (male and female students), race/ethnicity (subgroups of black, white, and Hispanic students), and region (Northeast, Southeast, Central, and West). Figure 8.1 illustrates that white nine-year-old students showed mixed patterns of performance over time, while the performance of Hispanic nine-year-olds improved on all three writing tasks analyzed in 1984. In fact, in 1984 only the Hispanic nine-year-olds showed improvement on the persuasive task. To the best of our knowledge, this is the first time scores had ever been longitudinally reported for black, Hispanic, and white students in this manner on a national assessment

We can only scan ETS's changing attempts to score NAEP essay writing after 1984. In 1992 they tried combining primary-trait with holistic methods. They switched from their four-point primary-trait scale to what they called "modified primary trait scoring" on six points. According to NAEP, essays were still criterion referenced, rated against certain performance criteria (e.g., "elaboration" in argumentative tasks); "However, at their upper reaches, depending on the prompt, the 6-point evaluation guides also considered aspects of organization, elaboration, coherence, tone, style, and mechanics" (Applebee et al. 1994, 205). But raters found "the primary-trait dimension of the new guides was more hindrance than a help" (Persky 2012, 79). In 1996, to compare student writing at all three grades from 1984 to 1996, a study used straight-forward holistic scoring with a six-point scale and a four-criterion rubric (development, organization, syntax, and mechanics). In 1998 assessment designers would call this rubric a "focused holistic guide," stating confidently that the four traits "associated with overall quality writing" (National Assessment of Educational Progress 2000, 1). The traits themselves, however, were buried in the "overall quality" score and not reported. Primary-trait scoring was no longer on its way out, but out. Clearly, in trying to satisfy the call of Congress to record long-term trends in educational achievement ("progress"), ETS was shifting back toward a norm-based assessment of writing and away from a criterion-based trait system. The early NAEP testing of educational progress in writing 1969–1979 disappeared from official ETS reports of trends (e.g., Campbell, Voelkl, and Donahue 1998). In 2011 NAEP examinees did their writing exercises on computers. If it is true that constructs are mediated in digital environments (Katz and Elliot 2016), then assessment of writing trends in a longitudinal framework would have to begin anew.

Judging from the early NAEP testing of long-term trends, was there progress in student writing during the 1970s? Given the national anxiety over educational standards, the question seemed pressing at the time. Most of the public doubted there had been progress, most politicians seemed to yearn for proof of decline, and most writing teachers had seen neither one nor the other in their classrooms. Judicious historians of national testing have concluded that NAEP tests 1969–1984 agreed with the teachers and showed writing performance scores little changed over those years (e.g., Stedman 1998). Of course, maybe NAEP scoring methods missed the change. Maybe holistic-scoring procedures were too hyperopic to see progress in focus, and primary-trait procedures were to myopic to see it entire. Maybe the most convincing fact or statistic that emerges from NAEP's assessment of writing 1969–1984 is that correlations between holistic and primary-trait scoring run around a paltry 0.5, indicating that the two methods position scorers into seeing largely different constructs.

Both methods can be dissatisfying to raters, albeit in different ways. Primary-trait readers feel a tension between giving one score for an isolated trait when they sense a different score for the whole essay. Hilary Persky, an ETS primary-trait rater in the 1990s, remembers "puzzling over responses which had to be relegated to a level 3 in a 6-level guide despite overall high performance because they failed to address what struck me at the time as a fairly trivial demand" (2012n12). The tension was written into one of the very first primary-trait directions for 1973–74 readers: "A thank-you letter requires the adoption of writing strategies that result in an expression of gratitude. A thank you letter that does not do this is inappropriate [i.e., lowest-level score], *however well written it may be*" (Brown, Mullis, and Littlefair, xi; our emphasis). On the other hand, holistic readers may feel that scoring guides and rubrics exclude traits that are crucial. What are they to do when the instructions omit traits such as originality, humor, or cleverness, or when they read in their ELTS scoring manual that "candidates should not be heavily penalized for making factual errors" (Hamp-Lyons 1991, 134)?

Up to the present writing, it seems neither holistic nor primary-trait scoring has proved of much use to NAEP in recording long-term trends in school writing and offering causal inferences about those trends—despite generous amounts of money it has had to spend on the problem. At its height, in 2009 and 2010, congressional funding for NAEP was $130,121,000. Yet over the years, independent academic researchers, with their shoestring budgets and their tight focus on specific writing traits, have published significant information about trends, some of it using NAEP data (e.g., Gaies 1980; Sloan 1979; Smitherman and Wright 1984). Brown, who left NAEP in 1982, put it this way: "From the beginning, we felt that National Assessment was an *assessment.* It wasn't a test, but a broader, more concrete gathering of data useful on many different levels" (email to authors, 2014).

Does the early history of the National Assessment of Educational Progress follow Hayden White's emplotment of tragedy? From Brown's view, it seems to. From Persky's 2010 history, written from the perspective of an ETS researcher, it does not. Were we to step aside from both to look at the framework for the 2017 NAEP writing assessment ourselves—with tasks scored holistically to create profiles of student ability and the construct itself understood in terms of purpose and rhetorical flexibility—what would we think?

Seen from a past that does not stay there, is NAEP an emplotment of tragedy, romance, comedy, or satire? And, perhaps more significantly, is the accompanying ideological mode radical, anarchist, conservative, or liberal? Our hope is that, before giving an answer, you examine the evidence yourself—from archives and publications and reports and oral histories—and that, in doing so, you enact new narrative structures for a new generation of readers. We map how that might be done in the remaining two chapters.

A BIOGRAPHICAL CODA

In the histories of student-writing assessment, Rexford Brown deserves more recognition. Throughout the 1970s and 1980s, he was everywhere. His activities as a speaker and assessment consultant took him to schools and universities, state departments of education, federal agencies, educational laboratories, businesses, foundations, news outlets, and professional organizations. Throughout his life, as report writer, ghost writer, consultant, board member, policy analyst, program administrator, he often worked behind the scenes. On testing issues, however, he was at the forefront. His humanist bent did much to help early NAEP testing become perhaps the most original and most valid effort to assess President Garfield's "condition and progress of education" across the nation.

After earning his BA in American literature from Middlebury College in 1963, he taught high-school English for a year and then took up graduate work in literature at the University of Iowa. The attraction was the possibility of writing a novel for his dissertation, but he ended up doing a literary study of Anthony Burgess. His employment with NAEP (1971–1982) began by chance, as a graduate student reading composition and literature essays in 1970 for the first NAEP examination. In 1971 he was the eighth person hired by NAEP. There was "a director, an assistant director who knew something about assessment, four psychometricians who knew only about psychometrics but didn't know anything about writing or literature." He became their "token humanist" and wrote many of their reports (email to authors, 2014). Soon he was director of publications for NAEP and then for the Education Commission of the States.

Early at NAEP he was also involved with test construction, including primary-trait scoring. He helped resist inside pressure to score writing proficiency with multiple-choice questions. Yet he always distrusted holistic scoring and could be acerb in pointing out its problems, such as its difficulty in escaping norm referencing: "If the group of students who wrote the papers were all borderline illiterates, nothing in the scoring would have changed" (Brown 1979, 24). He wrestled long with the Proteus of writing "progress" and concluded that holistic scoring had proved "a very unsatisfying system for the evaluation of growth" (2). But he also recognized the original and irreplaceable virtue of holistic scoring and saw as a virtue its very inability to be "articulated objectively." Referring to Polanyi's notion of tacit knowledge, Brown said that "so vast is this tacit dimension of human experience that it can never be analyzed fully. . . . Upon such philosophical base rests holistic relational evaluation" (22). Consequently, he also had his doubts about trait-based scoring schemes such as primary-trait and holistic rubrics, schemes which "fragment the essay" (1979, 29). Nonetheless, in his later work educating teachers and directing teacher-education programs, he found the creation and application of holistic rubrics invaluable work for English instructors. His intricate grasp of language value making should not be forgotten in the historical reconstruction of early holistic scoring.

A HISTORICAL CODA

One of the problems with reconstructing history is that, as Jan Smuts suggested (1926), everything connects with everything. In 1866, during the June 5 congressional debate over whether a department of education should be established to collect "such statistics and facts as shall show the condition and progress of education," Andrew Rogers had his opposition speech interrupted. Josiah B. Grinnell, representing the 4th District of Iowa, wished to know whether Rogers had "ever opposed an appropriation for the purpose of collecting agricultural statistics, and whether this idea of collecting information in regard to education does not stand somewhat on the same basis." For Rogers it must have been a *bas d'escalier* moment. In the stress of the moment, he came up with a response that can be called trifling, beginning with "no resemblance whatsoever," concluding with "no analogy," and in between blustering that the collection of agricultural facts was "diffusion of knowledge" and the collection of educational facts was "interference with rights." At the end of the day, descending the Capitol steps, did he knock his forehead with the heel of his hand—thinking of a better answer? History would provide the best answer, but it would take a long chain of associated events (*Congressional Globe* 1867, 1866, column 1).

Grinnell's district included Iowa City and the University of Iowa, founded in 1847. Nine decades later, in 1935, the Education Department at the University of Iowa began administering its objective Iowa Tests of Basic Skill. In 1953 the ITBS had become so popular the university established its own corporation, the Measurement Research Center (MRC), to score the tests with high-speed scanning machines. MRC rapidly expanded, scoring other tests that were owned by Houghton Mifflin, Harcourt Brace and World, and the ETS. In 1970, however, ETS sent MRC boxes not of bubble sheets but of some 15,000 student essays. Needing live people to score the essays, MRC contacted Klaus of the University of Iowa Rhetoric Department. Klaus recruited ten graduate students, among them Rexford Brown. Brown spent two August weeks in an airplane hangar that was "hotter than hell," scoring essays holistically on an eight-point scale for five dollars an hour. At one point he had an insight, or as he wittily called it, an "inkling." Readers were passing around an essay written by a seventeen-year-old girl about her mother, her pick for a person "you most admire." She wrote how she had deceived her mother into thinking she was more popular in school than she actually was. Kleenex was being passed around with the essay (Brown 1986, 45). "The moment," Brown (email to authors, 2014) said years later, "just reminded me of this huge gap between what we were doing, which was simply to rank order papers, and what we were feeling as we were reading them."

It took more than a century, but Brown finally came up with the rejoinder Rogers needed. No, agricultural statistics are not the same as educational statistics because the second involves humans responding to humans with measures constructed out of something human. There is a mystery within the appraisal of acts of learning that itself can never be measured, not as you measure the weighing of cotton bales. In judging bales of students essays, "Holistic scorers need never explain what they are doing; and thus did holistic scoring achieve a certain amount of respect in our profession. Measurement got a foot in the door by pretending it was not measurement" (1978b, 2).

The same could be said of primary-trait scoring or any other contraption used by humans to fix a number or a grade to a piece of student writing. Researchers, both independent and entrepreneurial, were exploring that uneasy fact during the 1960s and 1970s. In years following, more and more were asking, should we give up on holistic scoring altogether or instead find ways to make it more workable?

NOTES

1. See Woodworth and Keech (1980); Gray et al. (1982); and Lucas (1988). With little doubt, Catharine Keech Lucas is responsible for popularizing the term *ecology* in writing studies. The earliest instance we can find is her coauthored study (Gray et al. 1982) published in *Properties of Writing Tasks*: "The fact that a substantial proportion of these students (72.7%) reported that they would have written very differently about the prompt if they had had more time to work on it raises questions about the ecological validity of holistic scores on a single sample as an assessment measure" (243). Her earlier term is "occasion" (Woodworth and Keech 1980). Today's sense of *ecology* emerged at the very end of the nineteenth century in connection with plant evolution but fairly soon was being applied to the interdependence of the human and natural environment. One major contributor was Jan Smuts and his concept of holism: "The creative intensified Field of Nature, consisting of all physical organic and personal wholes in their close interactions and mutual influences, is itself of an organic or holistic character—that Field is the source of the grand Ecology of the Universe. It is the environment, the Society—vital, friendly, educative, creature of all wholes and all souls" (1926, 352). So in writing research in the late 1970s, a whole-essay scoring method (holistic) was being reinterpreted by the principle that underlay it (holism).
2. In 1961, Congress established Project English within the Cooperative Research Branch in response to complaints from NCTE, MLA, and other groups that language and literature had been omitted from the original Cooperative Research charter. By 1963, Congress had made $13,000,000 available to Project English. Not long after, the same groups complained that now literature was being snubbed: "Evaluation, measurement, and research design were the bywords. Most English professors felt decidedly out of their element" (Steinberg 1963, 50). The record shows that a number of writing experts were happily aswim.
3. With the university research centers, again *independence* is a relative term. On the panel of reviewers for *The Evaluation of Composition Instruction* sat Paul B. Diederich of ETS. In 1996, UCLA's Center for the Study of Evaluation became the National Center for Research on Evaluation, Standards, and Student Testing (CRESST), which now partners with the Educational Testing Service, the RAND Corporation, and six universities.
4. From 1960–1980, over 100 dissertations were completed at US universities exploring issues of evaluation and assessment of student writing, the majority in the 1970s. Only a few studied commercial testing. Earlier, such dissertations were less common but not unusual. Of special note is Mary Luella Mielenz's 1939 dissertation at the University of Nebraska: *An Analysis of Background Factors and Their Possible Influence on Placement in Freshman English at the University of Nebraska-Lincoln.*
5. In his 1971 Florida State University dissertation investigating the effect of sentence-combining exercises on first-year college student essays, Frank O'Hare (1973) took the novel step of having a rater simply compare the pre and post essays of the same student (without knowing which was the earlier piece). Five salient essay traits were written on a blackboard in the view of raters, but the raters judged only which essay was better in terms of "overall quality." Statistically, the post essays were significantly better. By narrowing the comparison to two essays written by the same student, criterial noise was reduced, and distractions such as personality traits were cancelled out. The matched-pair design was adapted by a number of well-known researchers during the 1970s, among them William Combs, Donald A. Daiker, Andrew Kerek, Max Morenberg, and Lee Odell. They sometimes had raters judge individual criteria (e.g., concrete support) as better or worse, a method validated by Richard Haswell

6. Nold and Freedman's study had been completed in 1974, but it was held up for three years in the manuscript queue at *Research in the Teaching of English*.
7. For exceptions, see Marjorie Olsen (1956) and Frances Swineford (1956b). In their effort to validate the new ECT holistic scoring, Albert E. Myers, William E. Coffman, and Carolyn B. McConville (1966) factored the scores of readers and found only two dimensions, good and bad writing. They concluded that "it does not seem as though some judges rated the papers primarily upon grammar, while other judges rated the papers primarily upon style. Rather, this explanation suggests that the relative weighting between grammar and style is *roughly* the same for all judges" (52). That, of course, does not eliminate a possible halo effect in which the attention of the readers to grammar systematically overrode their attention to style despite the scoring guide's injunction to give the two equal weight. For more on this study, see chapter 4.
8. For a review of research on holistic scoring from a constructed response perspective, see Isaac I. Bejar (2017).
9. A year earlier at ETS, Gertrude Conlan had asserted that in the English Composition Test, minorities do better on essays than on objective items: "Among the students who score better on the essay section than on the multiple-choice section are many who are more familiar with other dialects and other languages than standard English" (1976, 6). Even earlier, local researchers were finding the same outcome—that majority students tended to score better than minority students—on the holistically scored essay of the rising-junior Georgia Regents' Examination (Hickman 1972; Prather and Smith 1975).
10. It seems the more popular holistic scoring became, the more it attracted extreme negative comments. Janny Griswold Tripp, language-arts teacher, compared it to "hog judging at the state fair" (1978, 385). Robert Mitchell, who called himself "the underground grammarian," likened holistic scorers to a "teacher club" (1979). Sharon Crowley, eminent composition scholar, called holistic reading "discursive gangbangs" (1985, 95).
11. For instance, one scale was

    The essay seems to be: *unimaginative*—:—:—:—:—:—:—*imaginative*.

    The rater marked one of the intervals. Psychological researchers had found semantic differential sets useful in probing unconscious attitudes such as stereotyping or authoritativeness.
12. The double dates reflect the rollout of the assessment. So in the first NAEP, seventeen-year-olds were tested in the spring of 1969, thirteen-year-olds in the fall of 1969, and nine-year-olds in the spring of 1970. Early NAEP testing deliberately selected groups by age rather than grade level to prevent hasty application of outcomes to curriculum.
13. Not to forget that in these years, NAEP researchers believed adamantly in multiple measures. They evaluated humanities education, including writing, in a multitude of ways ranging from error counts to surveys of family background and personal habits such as reading for fun. Rexford Brown, who was an NAEP insider, remembers the sometimes astonishing means of data gathering. "Music! We had a music assessment. Going to people's houses. Can you play an instrument? Yeah, I can. Play it for me" (email to authors, 2014). NAEP could afford labor-intensive investigations. As soon as Congress gave it permanent funding in 1973, it was awash with money. Brown notes that at one point, "Congress had withheld some money from us, some seven million dollars, because the program was so new. Nixon released

the funds, so suddenly we had seven million dollars. . . . Well, there is not a state department of education, even the most funded one like New York, that has that kind of money, to do the kind of assessments we did" (email to authors, 2014).

14. Also tested were over 800 nonstudents, adults aged twenty-six through thirty-five, who took the tests in their homes. On the 1969–70 essay assignment, nearly a third (29 percent) of this group turned in blank pages. A similar population was tested in 1973–74, but it seems motivation was still low. Thereafter, NAEP ceased testing out-of-school adults.

15. This may be the first recorded instance of what became a common complaint. Over the years, as institutional, state, and national mandated testing increased, scholars increasingly lamented that they had been consulted and sometimes paid by the test makers but in the end their recommendations had been ignored (e.g., Huot 2002, 52). One of the panelists was Lavin (see chapter 7). Did he talk holistic scoring with two other panelists, Paul B. Diederich and "Fred Fodshalk" [sic]? (NAEP 1973, 30)

16. Mellon was the most ardent critic of the first two NAEP examinations (1972, 1975). He thought the whole examination was "in most ways invalid and a sham" (1972, 106). In 1967 he earned his doctorate in education from Harvard with a dissertation (later published by NCTE) on the influence of sentence-combining exercises in making the syntax of students more mature. This work was prophetic in the sense that later scholars found sentence-combining performance to be one of the best indicators of writing maturation and holistic scores one of the worst. His opposition to holistic methods of essay evaluation ran deep. "I strongly believe, in education and in life, that comparisons pitting the quality one achieves solely against quality achieved by other members of one's group represent a most inhumane form of competition" (1972, 105).

17. See Ina V. S. Mullis (1976, 20). The rubric was further expanded for raters (Brown, Mullis, and Littlefair 1976, 24). Richard Lloyd-Jones recorded a later version of this rubric, with five levels (1977, 49–50).

18. Nowhere does the report bring up the obvious interpretation of the drop in holistic scores for thirteen- and seventeen-year-olds, namely the result of increases across the nation in students going to school and staying in school. That is, NAEP's later sampling might include less proficient students. SAT verbal scores also dropped during the early 1970s, causing great public concern until it was shown that the decline was almost entirely due to a shift in the population of SAT test takers (Beaton, Hilton, and Schrader 1977).

19. The rater's guide for level 2, for instance, notes: "These papers do describe something or someone but tend to be mere lists of details. They are often thin, loosely organized, and clichéd."

20. The Education Commission of the States suffered a loss of about half its staff. Among NAEP originators, bitterness about the change lasted. Some twenty years later, Ralph Tyler recalled that "the NAEP was given to ETS by a man briefly in the U. S. Office of Education. A man who resigned shortly afterward for using federal funds to pay for his private trips. He knew nothing about educational evaluation and did not understand that psychometricians do not learn much about educational objectives" (Finder 2004, 33). This narrative contradicts the extensive, competitive proposal planning at ETS and ETS's submission undertaken by Samuel J. Messick during the presidency of Gregory R. Anrig, documented in Norbert Elliot (2015) and available in the ETS archives.

9
WHAT DOES A SCORE MEAN?

All category systems are moral and political.
—Geoffrey C. Bowker and Susan Leigh Star, *Sorting Things Out*

In 1846, ten years after the HMS *Beagle* had docked home at Falmouth and thirteen years before *On the Origin of Species* would be published in London, Charles Darwin was sure of his theory of natural evolution but still could not defend it. He had good evidence that species evolved over time, but he had not discovered the mechanism through which that change was effected. So—it seemed the natural thing to do—he took up the systematics of barnacles. Giving barnacles scientific names turned out to be trickier than he had thought. Even within a species, or what might be conjectured as a species, individual barnacles differed one from another in characteristic after characteristic. How could you name an organism when no two were exactly alike? Did a category such as species actually exist in nature? "It is really laughable to see what ideas are prominent in various naturalists' minds when they speak of 'species,'" he wrote his friend and colleague Joseph Dalton Hooker. "It all comes, I believe, from trying to define the undefinable" (1887, 88). Although Darwin did publish his taxonomy of barnacles, four volumes' worth, he never solved the species enigma. Today, we still struggle with biological taxonomy and the definition of species. For instance, DNA analysis reveals an occasional horizontal or lateral transfer of genes from organism to organism, suggesting not a tree of life with distinctly different branches but rather a mosaic of interlaced threads, a web of variation (Quammen 2018; Woese 2005). It is by virtue of individual variation itself that evolution happens.

The desire for representations of complex systems forever carries the seeds of its own unraveling. Systematicists, who classify organisms, and compositionists, who classify essays—are not both trying to define the undefinable? If each new specimen is singular, what species do you call it? If each new essay is singular, what score do you give it?

DOI: 10.7330/9781607329121.c009

Let's put this last question another way, a better way according to current educational-measurement theory. What does a holistic score mean? The answer is that it depends. It depends on a lot. The meaning of a score is determined not by just the scoring guide. It depends also on the whole testing environment for assessing writing: world-view (the assumptions and intentions and background of the test maker); construct representation (the variables of written communication captured in the writing task); design (the reasons given and inferences intended in selecting the number of points on the scale); sampling plan (the race, gender, ethnicity, gender assignment, gender identification, and socioeconomic status of the test taker); and impact (the use of scores later by advisory boards, administration, faculty, parents, professional organizations, students, and the public). And this list covers only a fraction of the sociocultural and sociocognitive ecology by which the meaning of a score is set. Assessment is not simply the recognition of the value of an essay expressed in a number on a six-point scale (4) or in a qualifier (low medium). Assessment, any assessment procedure, is a nexus of assumptions, inferences, uses, and consequences, often unstated. Only by exposing the network of intention and belief can we find what a score means. When the student asks, "What does this score of 4 on my essay mean?" it is a good question, and the instructor has good reasons for not being able to answer.

This chapter spotlights some of the nexus of assumptions, inferences, uses, and consequences of scoring methods employed in holistic rating of essay writing. We do so at the risk of boring our reader. Geoffrey C. Bowker and Susan Leigh Star have been tireless divers into the deep-sea world of hidden classifications in, for instance, the naming of diseases, the cataloguing of books, and the practice of nursing. They say that "delving into someone else's infrastructure has about the entertainment value of reading the yellow pages in the phone book" (2000, 321–23). Maybe, or, we hope, maybe not. They agree, however, that building better systems requires a study of old systems because there is always a continuity from old to new.

Specifically, in this chapter we demonstrate it is indeed possible to unpack that nexus by attention to splitters (student writing that does not easily yield to a single score), rubrics (scores given meaning by language), and profiles (language used to create actions based on scores). While there are many ways to understand the interaction of belief systems and intentions with an assessment environment, attention to splitters, rubrics, and profiles is a useful way to shine light on that which is often hidden.

A note before we begin. Our perspective in this chapter is informed by what might generally be called a *framework of individual differences*. Often classified as differential psychology, the study of individual differences emphasizes cognition, personality, need, and attainment—why and how people differ. As William Revelle, Joshua Wilt, and David M. Condon (2011) write in their history of research in the field, modern individual difference studies began in the early twentieth century with Charles Spearman, continued through the factor analysis of L. L. Thurstone and the personality studies of Gordon W. Allport and Raymond Cattell at midcentury, waned in the mid-1960s under mounting desire for large-scale studies and situational explanations of behavior, and returned to the mainstream in the 1990s. Today, individual-difference researchers continue to study affect, behavior, cognition, and desire—the ABCD of personality. Adopting a perspective in which individual differences are examined in large-scale assessments allows us to examine the web of hidden structures tacitly implemented in the holistic assessment of writing. In providing measures of individual achievement, systemization too often takes command; as a result, the significance of difference is lost in the pressure for accountability. While there is no formal field of individual-difference studies in writing assessment, emphasis on difference nevertheless draws attention to concealed structures influencing the individual student. For two researchers who have spent their careers in classrooms, an individual-difference perspective allows us to appreciate the complexities of distributed assessments while understanding, to the extent that we can, the force of their impact on each life they touch.

HIDDEN STRUCTURES: INFERENCE, INTERPRETATION, AND USE

In 2013, Michael T. Kane of the Educational Testing Service proposed a system to validate the interpretation and use of scores. Central to his project was the interpretation/use argument (IUA). Once expressed, the IUA includes "all of the claims based on the test scores (i.e., the network of inferences and assumptions inherent in the proposed interpretation and use)" (2). In terms of writing assessment, we can extend his system in terms of four nodes in the "network of inferences and assumptions" that underlie a language test and construct the meaning of its output. Scoring inferences move from observed performance of the test taker through a value system embedded in a rating scheme to provide a score for the performance (such as a claim that an essay warrants a 4 on a six-point scale). Generalization inferences assume that a sample of observed performances of the test taker allows an estimation of future performance in tasks similar to ones performed in the test (such as a claim that high-school seniors with a score of 4 might earn a passing, though not remarkably high, grade in first-year-writing English). Extrapolation inferences carry this estimation further to include future performance in related domains (such as a writer who receives the highest score of 6 on the Analytical Writing Section of the Graduate Record Examination will make a strong law-school candidate). Decision inferences assume that test performances fix or support decisions about a test taker's future (such as a placement score of 2 puts the test taker into the first course of a basic writing sequence).

Of course, there are other inferences easily but not often identified. As Kane notes, each of these inferences contains a challenge: "Like scientific theories, IUAs can be challenged in various ways; one of the most effective ways to challenge an IUA (or theory) is to propose an alternative argument (or theory) that is more plausible given the evidence. The identification and evaluation of plausible competing interpretations is therefore a particularly useful strategy" (2013, 15). For example, a purely cognitive theory of writing would advance features of writing such as persuasion (critical-thought association with claims and qualifications). However, a domain-based theory emphasizing cognitive, interpersonal, intrapersonal, and neurological domains would challenge the value of the assessment itself in its failure to employ a rich construct model (White, Elliot, and Peckham 2015). Hence, construct inferences would be challenged. Gender inferences assume a simplistic relational effect of gender assignment on scores. It might be argued that grade-school female writers will outperform male writers in language tests—as they indeed tend to do (National Assessment Governing Board 2011; Willingham et al. 1997). Introducing distinctions between gender assignment and gender identity, as well as new categorizations based on intersectionality (Carbado and Harris 2019; Crenshaw 1991), confound this common classification. All these inferences are presumptive, as Kane rightly insists, in the sense that they are not definitive and are always challengeable (2013, 11–12).

Kane emphasizes that "the warrant for the scoring inference is a scoring rule or rubric" (2013, 25). With holistic scoring, underneath the rules or rubrics lie hidden orders. They are always operative and almost always unstated. They are the "invisible organizational structures [that] influence the design and use of systems" (Bowker and Star 2000, 323). Here, because of their complexity, biological systematics again provides a useful analogy. In 1735, Carl Linnaeus based his *Systema Naturae* (the system of the natural world) on a static hierarchical classification: nature has three kingdoms (plants, animals, minerals), each kingdom so many phyla, each phylum so many classes, and so on down through order, family, genus, and species. In 1859, Darwin toppled Linnaeus's structured order, basing his system of the living natural world on a dynamic, branching, evolutionary tree. For instance, over time animals diverged from plants, then fungi branched off from other plants. Linnaeus and Darwin—their two structured orders reflect their different underlying assumptions and inferences. Linnaeus assumed species were immutable, so his scheme is horizontal and synchronic. Darwin assumed species are mutable, so his scheme is vertical and diachronic. Again, these inferences are presumptive or interpretive. For many decades, even among groups of biologists, the Linnaean and the Darwinian structural orders coexisted.

In the years covered by this book, the mid-1930s to the mid-1980s, holistic-scoring schemes also were based on different subsurface structured orders, yet the schemes also coexisted, as we demonstrate in chapter 2. Had the constructors of the assessment wished, they had plenty of substructures from which to borrow. Thought leaders of the first eight decades of the twentieth century were in love with hidden subterranean systems—Sigmund Freud's map of the subconscious directing everyday desires, Max Wertheimer's gestalt law of closure by which an incomplete figure is unconsciously perceived as a whole, Claude Lévi-Strauss's implicit kinship structures, Jean Piaget's cognitive structures underpinning developmental stages, Noam Chomsky's deep structures of universal grammar, Talcott Parsons' invisible social structures that inform the way individuals behave and think, Gordon W. Allport's coordinated view of the structure of individuality, Eleanor Rosch's intuitive sense of centrality ordering prototypical categories, Hayden White's tacit emplotments shaping historical accounts, and Mary Douglas's ways that social institutions legitimize themselves with unstated analogies to the natural world—the list could go on and on.

As we have noted, those who built and led holistic-scoring sessions seemed aware of these structuralist theories on occasion, but only on occasion. Most of the holistic-scoring programs we have discussed seemed centered on workability and systemization—on input and output. Their developers focused on surface issues such as how the number of scale points (input) was associated with rater reliability (output). They largely left holistic scoring as they found it, a black box (Haswell 2006a, 67–73). The more holistic scoring worked, the more the developers left unattended controlling assumptions and inferences, including interpretation, use, and consequence. In this, holistic scoring joined the other behaviors studied by the century's structuralists: underlying structural orders functioned in unknown ways. Part of the usefulness of the structuralist thinkers—including the evaluation experts who *studied* holistic scoring—was their talent in finding ways to unearth those buried orderings.

Informed by individual-difference research and current measurement theory, we now turn to our structuralist analysis of holistic scoring, beginning with student writing that does not lend itself to a single score on a predetermined scale.

SPLITTERS: DIGGING INTO DIFFERENCE

One ready entry into holistic-scoring substructures can be found where the scoring fails to work, or seems to fail. Probably the most obvious fracture is when two raters independently give the same essay different scores that violate a predetermined range of difference. The act violates the main function of a classification, which is to sort stuff. If the classification is faulty or the classifier is bumbling, the same stuff ends up in different boxes. Just as the organism can't be at once a bacterium and a eukaryote, the essay can't be at once a 6 and a 3. The individual scorer or the scoring system or both fail.

Or do they? Among all sources of variation from task design to reader response, what if the problem lies with the essay itself? What if by nature the essay is anomalous—undefinable—and doesn't fit into the scoring system? This happens every day in biological systematics. A new plant doesn't fit any named species, so a new species is added to the taxonomy (currently about 2,000 new plant species are named each year). Or the classification is reconceived, and the organism is accepted as both a fungus and an animal.[1] Or the classification does not work at all and a new classification is needed, such as the archaea identified by Woese, which are fundamentally different from both bacteria and eukaryotes. In the case of holistic scoring, the essay is recognized as not just words on a page and the scale as not just boxes and labels on another page but both as operants within a reader's interpretation. Although they may violate the beyond-adjacency scoring rule in which a 6 and a 5 are adjacent and accepted but a 6 and a 4 are considered discrepant, the scores of 6 and 3 may also be understood as different perceptions, maybe both legitimate. Certainly they could be, according to gestalt theory. Consider the ambiguous figure-and-ground image shown in chapter 2. The viewer can switch interpretation back and forth from vase to faces or from figure to ground, and neither way is wrong—even though the lines on the page don't change.

Miles Myers called an essay that provoked divergent holistic scores a "splitter" (1980, 38). It is a good name because it directs attention to the essay itself as a factor in scoring agreement and interrater reliability—that is, in the horizon of understanding between the writing sample and the reader. Typically, poor reliability was blamed on the scorer. Scorers who didn't agree with other scorers were retrained and, if persisting in their self-centered and unruly ways, were kicked off the team. Occasionally disagreement was blamed on the scoring system, and if during training readers couldn't agree on an essay, the system itself might be changed to resolve the disagreement. Criteria describing a scale level might be rewritten to fit both interpretations.

Eventually, however, test makers and researchers identified splitter essays themselves as part of the problem. Splitters are not just results of a particular rating. They persist in drawing unalike scores with different sets of scorers (Haswell 1998, 237–44). Their disruptive textual properties can be winkled out: splitters tend to be uneven in accomplishment, to contain a profusion of slang, misspellings, emotion, fanciful creativity, or pure narrative; or—a fact of importance later in this chapter as we turn to profiles—essays to be written by English-language-learning (ELL) writers (Barkaoui 2011; for earlier studies, see Britton 1963; Daiker and Grogan 1988; Hake 1986; Haswell 1991, 334–46; Wolcott, Dovell, and Buhr 1988).

The way testing experts treat splitters is a good place to begin decoding the meaning of divergent scores. For instance, in his advice on scoring school essays, Myers approves of the "common solution" to splitters, which is to put them into the bottom half of the scale. "An upper-half paper," he reasons, "should not make the reader struggle to understand" (1980, 38). He also says that in deciding on a score, the rater should compare the splitter with the *anchor* essays above and below, not with other test essays. Earlier he had explained that when expert raters choose anchors, they should pick only papers "on which there is quick agreement for a particular score" (34).

This advice of Myers is alive with cryptic substructures. We will extract only three. First, there is the quality scale of communications in business or science settings in which at the top levels shine texts that are clear, single-minded, and quick to read—and at the bottom lurk texts that are obscure, complicated, and slow to read. His "primary emphasis is on what *works*" (1980, 4), what is the "most *productive*" (1)—god-terms in the technical and business world. When scoring splitters, it is most workable and productive just to put them in the bottom half, or to compare them with anchor papers that were picked for lucid and problem-free comparison—and then award a low score. Second, there is the tacit social ordering that places nonmajority people lower than majority people. Myers's phrase "struggle to understand" may be taken as code for a response to minority, disability, second-language writing, or intersectionality. We struggle to understand, and then place on lower levels, those different from majority stakeholders. Myers's own language gives this substructure away. The "upper" half of the scale should be "reserved" for papers that are "respectable" in mechanics (38). Third, the procedure quietly reinforces a social system that assumes the world will always have not only the poor but also the failing. The logic of Myers's holistic treatment of splitters begs a large question. It assumes society will always have a lower half, then creates a scoring system that forces raters to put some students into that very section of the scale, and then finalizes the reification with outcomes that confirm the initial assumption.[2]

In Myers's holistic-scoring procedure, what does a splitter's score (for example, 4 and 1 on a six-point scale) mean to the student? The score of 1 means more than below average. It means the score may have been the most efficient to give under the circumstances; that the writing cannot escape nonmajority status; and that the student is part of a failing group necessary for social stratification in a capitalist society. Also, discrepant scores are an empirical inconvenience and are associated with correlations falling below the 0.7 level considered the standard for timed-impromptu writing (Williamson, Xi, and Bryer 2012). How different might the meaning have been if the student had received an adjacent score conforming to the rubric? As for what the score meant *for* the student, that depended on another system not specified by Myers: local score use. Being placed into a basic writing class that yields no credit? Being prevented from matriculating from one course to another? Being denied timely graduation by means of a rising junior examination? Being denied admission to graduate school? Over generations of students, how many have received split scores (which they never learned about) that resulted in denial, in nonacceptance, in inequity?

By contrast, in 1981, Catharine Keech and Mary Ellen McNelly, Bay Area Writing Project consultants, deliberately trained their holistic scorers with anchor papers that included a few "chosen for their mix of good and bad qualities." During discussion of the anchors, a split vote by the raters was sometimes allowed to stand "since prolonged discussion or arbitrary rulings often serve to make the raters insecure about their category boundaries" (1982, 268). "Arbitrary"? The "arbitrary rulings" would have been issued by the question leaders. Inferred is a participatory democratic system in which every person's vote is equal. Keech and McNelly's scoring, in fact, averaged discrepant scores rather than have them adjusted by a more expert reader who would know the "right" score. Keech and McNelly, however, were not running a test of student writing. They were running an experiment to uncover the reasons that underpinned the decisions by different groups of raters—to expose "the values and criteria they hold most important" in awarding holistic scores (261). The groups were high-school students, UC Berkeley preservice graduate teachers in education, and BAWP experts. This study of splitters, therefore, offers insights into the substructural orders in which the IUA is structured by aim.

Figure 9.1 shows one anchor paper Keech and McNelly say is "typical of a 2/3 split judgment," (1982, 314) that is, a paper some raters put in the top half and others in the bottom half of the scale. It is a personal experience written by a high-school student in thirty minutes. This impromptu piece is uneven, no doubt: short but vividly detailed, lacking in introduction but ending with a nifty clincher, with simplistic organization but complex syntax. It was the language in the middle of the essay, however, that the open discussion of raters revealed contributed most to the split. Did the word choice of the author betray an immature writing style ("a lot of little rolled up pieces of paper with lipstick on them"), or was it a deliberate attempt to project the tone of a child in order to contrast with the grown-up tone in the last paragraph ("cigarette butts"). Did "slanted eyes" reveal an author with racial prejudice, or did "the people who were different I now see every day" show the author's growing awareness of that prejudice?

Self-history, awareness of changes in one's past, often becomes of salient interest in late adolescence (McAdams 1993; McLean and Pasupathi 2010). Perhaps it is not surprising that only 11 percent of the high-school scorers placed this piece in the bottom half of the scale, compared to 52 percent of the graduate-school apprentice teachers. For a majority of the author's peers, the score means *this piece speaks to me.* What might be surprising is that the criterion of *maturity* rarely if ever appears in holistic-scoring schemes. Although maturity is a pervasive cultural classification ("act your age"), it is usually erased from formal evaluation of school and college writing.[3] Yet as Keech and McNelly show, maturation surreptitiously operates in that evaluation, at least with this student essay. Keech could interpret unevenness in a student essay positively ("overall effectiveness of its unique combination of flaws and strengths" [1982, 268]) because she was attentive and sympathetic

Sample N

The first time I walked through an airport and watched the planes lift off while staring through the immense plate glass windows was really exciting. The hustle and bustle of the people, the noise of the jets an the slick floors of the terminal were just driving me crazy. There were so many different types of people, with slanted eyes. Some people couldn't talk correctly, the spoke in a jibberish sort of way. I saw more types of people then I could imagine while I was sliding back an forth across the slick floors. Mother thought they were dirty, but but she was wrong they weren't dirty but there sure were a lot of little rolled up pieces of paper with lipstick on them. the best was yet to come. With my nose pressed tightly to the window I could see the taxiing around the runways. I could even see a few taking off, first the front and then the back, floating through the air as easily as I could imagine.

The excitement of the airport is gone now, I've seen the planes take off a hundred times, and I've had my fill of slick floors and cigarette butts, and the people who were different I now see every day. The planes are still a little special though because they are the ticket to new firsts.

Figure 9.1. Sample N (Keech and McNelly 1982, 314) (courtesy of the National Writing Project)

to human development in students, development in which different cognitive and affective domains often progress concurrently at different rates.

In the 1980s the pressure accompanying the rise of minimum-competency testing grew noticeably in the United States—a process of accountability that, as we show in chapter 7, had begun in the 1960s. In 1979, as the pressure was mounting, Arthur Wise, senior scientist at the Rand Corporation, provided this list of strategies underlying such testing: "accountability, planning, programming, budgeting systems; management by objectives; operations analysis; systems analysis; program evaluation and review technique; management science; planning; cost-effectiveness studies; systems engineering; zero based budgeting" (546). As Wise noted, each was a management approach created outside of education, and each was emboldened by state law. Under such perspectives and legislation, US holistic essay scoring was engineered to tame splitters in order to increase rater agreement and thereby to yield stronger estimates of interrater reliability. Largely discarded were rating systems that embraced splitters and the subsystems that warranted them. Forgotten, for instance, was one maverick method that, amazingly, did what it could to increase rater disagreement. At McGill University, master's student Gwendolyn Pilkington tested a theory of her advisor, Norman France, that holistic rating should pair raters who most disagree with one another. The rationale was that random pairing of scorers would result in some raters who would "confirm each other's prejudices" (Pilkington 1967, 55). Two exceptionally lenient raters might pass a failing student, two harsh ones fail a passing student. In

Pilkington's method a field trial determined which pairs of raters were most divergent in their scoring. In actual rating, these pairs consulted on essays on which they disagreed, and if they could not come to an accord, the essay was turned over to a panel of five or six experienced teachers, and their pooled scores become the essay's final rate. Pilkington subscribed to the pooled-rater method of Stephen Wiseman (1949) and James Britton, Nancy Martin, and James Rosen (1966), which actively sought for a score "illuminated by beams from different angles" (Wiseman 1949, 206).

Underlying pooled holistic scoring is a social system, perhaps a worldview, that imagines every human as singular and possessed of a singular perspective. Pilkington admits the view presents problems for the measurement of human abilities and that most testing methods avoid it. But she found the view now and then as she read "through the maze of literature on examinations."

> Occasionally, we are led to catch a glimpse of the true pattern, through the genius of men like Galton who saw what now seems so obvious, that human beings are not carbon copies of one another. And then educators expound at length on the importance of taking into account "individual differences" in children, and the teacher training institutes pay lip service to the idea, while the children in many schools continue to be treated as though they were all cut like gingerbread men, from a common mold. (1967, 92–93).

Outside educational circles, of course, even in the 1980s, people in both the United Kingdom and the United States widely held individualism as a sacrosanct right, a system that tacitly assumed a scale, vaguely ethical, with weak conformists at one end and rugged individuals at the other. Wasn't even the smallest living creature, if nothing else, unique? As Edward White declared in his 1984 dithyramb, "Even the meanest bit of halting prose, even the most down-trodden of our fellow creatures, deserves to be taken as a living and vital unit of meaning, an artistic and human whole, not merely as a collection of scraps and parts" (409).

The barnacles Darwin brought back from the Galapagos, and among which he found none alike, were smaller than the period at the end of this sentence. Why shouldn't humans be measured in the same light? In a 1962 best seller, *Toward a Psychology of Being*, Abraham Maslow urged his fellow psychiatrists to slow down and treat each patient as a unique case. Yet no different than holistic scorers, psychiatrists are often driven by their circumstances to be in a hurry. That is when they are apt to lump their new patients into categories such as age, gender, and mental condition. Maslow called the tendency "rubricization."

RUBRICS: COLUMNS AND ROWS

Typically, holistic scoring dealt with splitters by trying to strategize them away. The basic underlying assumption was shared by census taking, that a single correct box exists for every citizen-essay the minute it is born. In the early 1980s the strategy tended to pursue three routes: through more controlled rater training, through more advantageous statistical calculations, and through what we are calling scoring rubrics. The strategy assumed that it takes experts to see the right category, no-nonsense training for nonexperts to see it, statistical inference testing to validate it, and a rubric to smooth the way from start to finish.[4]

Behind the push toward rubrics lay an ironic demographic imperative. As Thomas D. Snyder establishes in his statistical portrait of US education, the 1970s was a period of comparative slower growth in college enrollment than the 1950s and 1960s, when there were record numbers of young people of college age and increasing participation of older adults in college. Enrollment growth then slowed substantially during the 1980s, with only a 17 percent increase between 1979 and 1989 (1983, 66, fig. 15). However, steady growth in the accountability movement, as Wise (1979) noted, meant year by year more and more test essays needed to be scored—in K–12 education, between school and college, and in college. So, ironically, while US postsecondary enrollment did not grow comparatively, the presence of student work—never before seen in such numbers—expanded rapidly. By 1979 at least seventeen US states used direct evaluation of essays for statewide mandated testing (Frederick 1979). By 1983, 69 percent of colleges responding to a survey reported that they scored admissions essays for placement, almost all of them applying a local system of direct assessment (Greenberg, Wiener, and Donovan 1986, vii).

The numbers could be staggering. In the fall of 1978, the New Jersey Basic Skills Assessment Program began testing high-school students to place them into New Jersey postsecondary writing courses, and administrators found themselves with 24,984 twenty-minute essays, each needing to be scored holistically at least twice (Lutz 1980; State of New Jersey Basic Skills Council 1979). No wonder experts in writing assessment were in demand. One directory, published by the Regional Educational Laboratory Northwest in June 1980, listed around 250 consultants in writing assessment, some in testing firms such as ETS, ACT, National Evaluation Systems, and the Florida-based Planning, Development and Evaluation Association; some in regional educational laboratories; but most in school and college faculties operating as independents (Bridgeford 1981).

Under this increasing pressure of numbers, a majority of the testing experts held fast to holistic scoring. It remained costly, but to their honor they remained faithful to their belief that writing proficiency had to be tested with an essay and that an essay should be judged not by its parts but by its overall impression. The imperative of numbers, however, pushed that belief to its limits, perhaps into self-contradiction.

In rater training, experts had long operated under the Damoclean sword of rater reliability. Among other consequences, high disagreement led to increased costs in dollars and time since discrepant essays required a third reading. The pressure can be seen even with Fred I. Godshalk, who normally backed pooled rating and its amiable embrace of a diversity of rater perspectives. But in 1965 he agreed to run the scoring of essays in a research project that would demand stringent reliability parameters. In their preliminary report, researchers Ross M. Jewell, John Cowley, and Gordon Rhum of the State College of Iowa provide a rare look inside one of Godshalk's actual training sessions.

> As the rating session progressed, Mr. Godshalk would note whether any particular rater seemed to judge consistently in a way different from the other raters. At relatively frequent intervals, he would interrupt the reading to allow the readers to relax and would read aloud papers which had been passed on to him by individual readers. Frequently, these papers posed special problems which Mr. Godshalk would have the group discuss, always making clear his own judgment. The goal of the initial orientation and of the subsequent breaks in the reading was for Mr. Godshalk to convey to the readers his criteria and to get them to standardize their scoring so that they would agree in their ratings. The reading would be most "perfect" when all of the readers rated all the papers in the same way that Mr. Godshalk would rate them. (1966, C1–C2)

During rater training, new workers could locate the correct scoring category most reliably by noting the eye direction of one person: the scoring leader in charge. Once a system was in play, figuring it out became more important than the reason that system was initially established. The Godshalk scene was prophetic. As the number of essays burgeoned into the thousands, rating groups became larger, rater qualifications lower, and the rater corps less uniform. All tended to make rating sessions more controlled and authoritarian. The need for standardization spilled over and, at least potentially, extinguished curiosity.

There was also a tendency to improve interrater agreement with a bit of pretesting legerdemain that didn't cost a penny. That was the decision on what would count as a rater agreement. By 1980 it was a custom of long-standing to stipulate adjacent scores (for instance, a score of 6 and a score of 5) as a match. Three decades earlier, in 1951, Paul

B. Diederich had protested the practice in the College Board's newly revised English Composition Test, pointing to the tradition of psychometricians to count only exact matches as an "agreement." But no one could afford to listen. By the early 1980s test makers rarely even felt the need to defend their use of adjacent scores (actually there was no way to do that except on the grounds of expediency). By then, some had gone rather farther down that road. In 1980 the Regional Educational Laboratory Southwest tested a holistic scoring in which criteria were each rated on a three-point scale. They boasted that 96 percent of the time, at least two of the three independent readers had matching scores (Cronnell 1980). A little calculation shows there are only ten combinations of the numbers 1, 2, and 3, and 1-2-3 is the only one of them in which two of the numbers are *not* the same. By mere chance, 90 percent of the time two of three readers will agree. In some holistic ratings, agreement was defined as two and even three points apart on a six-point scale (e.g., State of New Jersey Basic Skills 1982).

Mounting pressure of the raw numbers of test takers and their essays may have affected the growing preference during the 1980s of a rubric over a scoring guide. A rubric arranges the selected criteria and numbered scale in a table format so each criterion is described and scaled in the same way. A scoring guide describes the selected criteria in a way that connects to the holistic scale, but the connections are not uniform across the criteria.[5] The difference between the two schemes is not minor in terms of underlying assumptions and public consequences. According to our definition, a rubric names two or more criteria and systematically applies each of them to a scale of two or more value levels. Graphically, this system of coordination takes the form of a grid. For instance, in Richard M. Bossone's early rubric used in his study of basic writing students enrolled in community colleges in the City University of New York system (1969, 61), the criteria are ideas, organization, sentence structure, wording, and punctuation/mechanics/spelling, spread across the horizontal rows of the grid. The vertical columns provide the scores of superior, average, and unacceptable. The interaction of row and column lends precision to the score.

Compare the scoring guide shown in figure 5.3. As with other scoring guides modeled after the Advanced Placement program guides, there is only one description for each scale category, and criteria are not uniformly distributed through these descriptions. Proponents of one scheme often disliked the other. Diederich (1969b), whose scale clearly influenced Bossone's scoring rubric, considered the AP-style scoring guide a "blunt instrument." In holistic evaluation, of course, with either

COMPOSITION SCALE: GRADING STANDARDS

	Ideas	Organization	Sentence structure	Wording	Punctuation Mechanics Spelling
Superior (A - B)	Thesis statement is significant and clearly stated, supported by concrete and substantial points clearly related to the thesis statement	Plan of the paper is easy to follow, developed with originality and consistent attention to unity, coherence, emphasis	Sentences are well constructed even in varied and complicated sentence patterns	Words are used with correctness and distinctiveness; precisely, economically, imaginatively.	Rules of standard English have been observed; clarity and effectiveness of expression are enhanced accordingly
Average (C)	Thesis statement is apparent but insignificant or general, supported by points which are not fully explained and which are occasionally repetitious and irrelevant	Plan of paper is apparent but not consistently fulfilled. Somewhat inconsistent in attention to unity, coherence, emphasis	Sentences are usually correct in more familiar patterns but lack distinction	Words are generally appropriate but lack imagination and economy	Rules of standard English are violated occasionally which tend to weaken clarity and effectiveness of expression
Unacceptable (D - F)	Thesis statement is lacking or confused and points, if any, not explained or are repeated or irrelevant	Plan of paper is not apparent and is undeveloped. No attention is paid to unity, coherence, emphasis	Sentences reflect major errors, such as fused and incomplete and tend to be monotonous or childish	Words are used carelessly or inexactly and reflect substandard and childish quality	Basic rules of standard English are violated to a degree that communication is obscured

Figure 9.2. Holistic scoring rubric (Bossone 1969, 62) (courtesy of the City University of New York)

rubric or guide, the result of the scoring is the same: the essay is placed in one and only one of the scale levels.

Historically, early on in formal large-scale testing, use of the holistic rubric was scattered. That use has the hallmarks of spontaneous generation. It seems some early applications were by researchers, as with Bossone's 1969 trial, or Marlene Moslemi's research study in 1975 that rated school stories for creativity. In formal accountability testing, schools started applying holistic rubrics here and there in the 1970s. In Colorado, for instance, the Jefferson School District tried an elaborate eight-criteria rubric in 1976 (see Myers 1980, 50). As the years passed, holistic rubrics became simpler and more popular for state-mandated testing and for use in composition classrooms. It seems that for researchers and educators, a model lay close at hand. For decades, researchers in composition had been using analytic scales, that near cousin of the holistic rubric. And for much longer, writing teachers had been using what we call scaled criteria and what other researchers called "schedule of marking" (Wallis 1927), "analytic schedule" (Wiseman 1949), or "scoring grid" (Harris 1966), with a list of criteria coordinated on a scale, each criterion awarded a point or letter grade.[6] These are William Boyd's grading systems by which teachers are wont "to break up the essay into its unit characters and to assign marks to each on some definite principle" (1924, 58). The intent of teachers was to provide feedback so students could see where the strengths and weaknesses lie in a submitted paper. Usually the scaled criteria of teachers were diagnostic. But sometimes teachers added up the points on the grid to produce a final grade for the whole paper, in which case their scheme was purely analytical.[7]

It was a thin line. The proximity of holistic and analytical made scoring rubrics a double-edged sword. The rubric helped raters recognize, accept, and handle uneven essays, doing its part in countering halo effects. With a splitter, the scorer marked different criteria at different scale levels and then, with that unevenness graphed, decided on the most fitting level for the entire essay. The itemizing of criteria along one axis of the grid served as a kind of mnemonic, like a grocery list. At a more profound level, the rubric operated as a checklist, little differently than a census form or an auto mechanic's worksheet. Test makers could adapt the rubric to different topics or different test populations simply by changing criteria. Criteria could be limited to a few of special importance, resulting in "focused holistic" or "modified holistic" schemes (Sachse 1984; Texas Education Agency 1980).[8] While we note in chapter 8 that early NAEP researchers were careful to align task and scoring guide, this was not often the case, as the demands of large-scale assessment compromised the painstaking work of task and rubric synchronicity.

On the other hand, by systematically itemizing criteria for consideration, the holistic-scoring rubric created its own kind of halo effect. It discouraged and sometimes forbade raters to count any other criteria (e.g., writer content accuracy). By contrast, the scoring guide countenanced a myriad of unnamed writing traits that might form part of an individual scorer's gestalt of an essay's merit. The rubric's systematic isolation of a few criteria encouraged an instructor to teach and a student to write to those traits and only those traits. The holistic rubric was thus potentially friendlier to pedagogically constrained systems such as the five-paragraph theme. And the array of a certain number of criteria took on that aura of unquestionable expertise a checklist often projects. Who challenges the mechanic with a worksheet, the census taker with a form, the medical doctor or airline pilot checking off items on a clipboard?

It is worth issuing the challenge. Where do the criteria, each honored with a column of its own, come from? Why these few chosen and not the many others omitted? Michael Scriven, master of checklists (see chapter 7), did not waver in his answer to these questions. The criteria or checkpoints in a checklist are "a priori" (1974, 8). They do not lend themselves to logical explanation or proof. In his word, they are "self-referent" (10). Scriven explored the point in an early essay called "Logic of Criteria," in which he laid out the philosophical difficulty with definitions. What, he asks, "is the relation between being a lemon and the various properties of a lemon?" (1959, 859). He concludes that a lemon cannot be defined by a single property (e.g., sourness) but by a set of properties, a "cluster-concept" (862), and further that the properties that make up a cluster concept are always provisional. A definition must always await evidence that it is sufficient for its particular use (Darwin might have agreed). Even each property selected is always a "presupposition involved, namely that there is such a property" (867). The same with checklists, Scriven would say later. No matter the experience and expertise that may have selected the criteria for the final version of a checklist, the proof remains in the pudding, and designers must wait for "direct empirical evidence that the present version is worthwhile" (1974, 11).

Nonetheless, other thinkers at the time were arguing that criteria for classifications such as checklists and scoring rubrics are not self-referential. For instance, Christopher Peacocke, a British philosopher specializing in epistemology, argued that any concept appearing to be a self-sufficient whole is actually supported by explanatory systems outside it: "The verification of the application of a scheme of holistic explanation is itself holistic" (1979, 216). The background system is usually unstated. Sociologist Mary Douglas argued that covertly a classification is shaped by the social institution within which it functions. Behind the selection of criteria lies a hidden structure, which she called "naturalization." Naturalization serves as a legitimizing step in a feedback loop. The loop involves a social institution (1) favoring a social order, (2) creating a classification that fits the order, (3) naturalizing the classification by analogy with "formal structures in non-human realms," and then (4) using the outcomes of the classification to legitimize the social order (1986, 55). The nineteenth-century US social institution of slavery imposed a classification of people into human and subhuman, the classification tacitly assumed an analogy with the natural biological order of humans and higher apes, and then the classification was used to support the institution of slavery. As for the naturalizing analogy, that institution did not lack scientists who argued from physiological features that Africans and African Americans were apes, not humans. With some justification, Douglas calls such a feedback loop "self-policing" (46).[9]

Scoring rubrics are two dimensional, and either dimension illustrates Douglas's theory of the naturalization of social classifications. We have already seen how the interaction of the vertical column of merit with the horizontal row of attributes can create a classification that justifies an ordering of writing students into ready and not ready, an ordering that seems to be an integral part of the institution of US public education. The scale classifies test takers into top and bottom, the division is naturalized by describing it as fitting a "normal curve," and then the outcomes of the testing confirm the institutional order of "remedial" and "regular."[10] The theory can also apply to the horizontal axis, the list of writing traits. Just as Scriven sees criteria that are "self-referent," Douglas sees criteria that are part of a "circle of self-reference" (1986, 109), part of her naturalization loop. But with Douglas, they are not a priori but a posteriori, derivable from an already existent social institution. But which institution do they come from?

Let's argue that writing traits can be self-serving functions within the social institution of composition teaching. There are some dimensions of composing teachers find more teachable than others. Knowledge of writing conventions (from grammar, mechanics, and usage to document formatting) are teachable because the aberrations from them are easy to detect in student writing and easy to debunk, and the correct forms are easy to make students practice. The same could be said of support—readily seen and readily taught (e.g., the five-paragraph essay). Not so with dimensions of writing such as truth (writer content accuracy) or joy of writing (attitudes toward writing). How many past scoring rubrics set the criteria of conventions and support, and how many truth or enjoyment?[11] According to its ideology, holistic scoring kept teachers—and students—from judging a paper by its superficial, countable parts; hence, scoring ideology specified general impression, yet scoring guides identified traits such as conventions or support. Indeed, often the holistic rubric pushed the scoring guide in the direction of analytic scoring. In such ways did holistic scoring work against its own good intentions.

How then are the chosen criteria naturalized? In many ways. Scriven (1978) himself, in defending his own rubric (described in chapter 7), claimed the dimensions were factor analyzed in the scientific experiment of Diederich, French, and Carlton (1961), as if these particular traits occur naturally in all essay writing and could be generally used as a source of evidence across students and genres. (Student Keech [1978, appendix A6] corrected teacher Scriven, pointing out that, no, the traits were *factored in* from reader *response* to student essays.) But dozens of other empirical experiments studied classroom interventions through these familiar scoring-rubric criteria, and, whether or not the intervention improved the student writing, left the criteria unquestioned. As we are learning today from corpus analysis of scoring rubrics (Dryer 2013), the most powerful naturalization of standardized rubrics—that is, of systematic underrepresentation of student individual ability on varied tasks—may have been the employment of independent testing firms such as ETS or ACT to run the testing. During that period of our history, no doubt many teachers wondered, at least in their inside voice, where on earth the scoring criteria came from in the first place.

In the history presented in this book, we have come to realize that the identification of scoring criteria—in reality, the variables of written communication—reveals seven research traditions that are today realized in writing studies: latent variable models; corpus analysis; meta-analysis; experimental research; expert-panel recommendations; consensus statements; and teacher knowledge. Derived from a line of thought begun by Spearman (1904), latent variable models identify correlations among variables of a given construct that is examined under uniform conditions. We see latent variable modeling in the factor analysis of Diederich, French, and Carlton (1961), discussed in chapter 6. Defined as examination of textual patterns in a specific body of text produced under naturalistic conditions, corpus analysis was used by Albert R. Kitzhaber (1963) in his study of first-year writing syllabi discussed in chapter 8 (Aull 2015). Meta-analysis, a statistical method in which results from independently conducted, comparable studies are combined and analyzed to determine relationship among variables and effect size, began with the British researcher Ronald Fisher (1935). In writing studies, that technique was first used by George Hillocks Jr. (1986), analyzed in chapter 8. Experimental research—in which hypotheses are set, random assignment is employed, variables are modeled, measurement is taken, intervention is enacted, and measurement is taken again—is found in the work of Eva L. Baker and Edys Quellmalz (1979) and in Quellmalz (1981a, 1981b, 1891c), also described in chapter 8. Provided by researchers known for their scholarship of a given field of study, expert-panel recommendations are made based on adherence to predetermined standards. Expert-panel recommendations in measurement find their origin in the American Psychological Association's Committee on Test Standards (1952) that is discussed in chapter 10. In writing studies, such recommendations were late to arrive, with standards-based recommendations for writing appearing in the United States for elementary school in 2012 (Graham et al., 2012) and for secondary school in 2016 (Graham et al., 2017). Consensus statements, those panel recommendations based on the collective wisdom of scholars, were also quite late to appear in the United States. The *WPA Outcomes Statement* (Council of Writing Program Administrators 1999) and the *Framework for Success in Postsecondary Writing* (Council of Writing Program Administrators, National Council of Teachers of English, and National Writing Project 2011) are examples of such statements. Today, we no longer must wait for results, as Scriven advised, to gain confidence in the variables expressed in our rubrics. As to traditions of teacher research, these are everywhere apparent in this book, from the UK work of James Britton and his colleagues (1966) to that of James Gray and the BAWP team (1982) in the United States. As our study of genre of holistic scoring has illustrated, emphasis on assessment has helped lead to the identification of research traditions dedicated, from the mid-1930s to the mid-1980s, to the variables of written communication.[12]

However, if the substantive body of knowledge drawn from these seven traditions is jettisoned and emphasis is placed on a restricted form of reliability concerning consensus between two readers, then things fall apart.[13] The link between the impulse for standardized rubrics and the obsession with interrater reliability is clear: one fuels the other. And so it is that, when taken in isolation, evidence related too strictly to interrater reliability can diminish research traditions and have adverse consequences for students. Within a narrow framework of reliability, it is therefore no wonder algorithms did a better job that humans. By the late 1990s, testing organizations began to use machines to score student essays, with evidence arguing that the machines were more reliable than human raters.[14] While the rubrics have long been removed from the Criterion® Online Writing Evaluation Service, during the early days of the e-rater® scoring engine, rubrics were used to help students and instructors interpret scoring levels. The score was described as "holistic." As such, ETS researchers implied that the scores, expressed in the rubric, were a generalized classification of "writing" based on "variables" while, in fact, the scoring engine classified particular instances of student writing (a limited corpus) based on teacher-sanctioned merit (inferred from a given group of readers) through general linear modeling (in which a holistic framework was literally impossible because the scores were derived through regression analysis). In the early days of automated scoring, generalization inferences were often advanced while qualifications were minimized.[15] So much, it appears, depends on the design of a rubric.

What then does a rubric score mean to the teacher? Bossone's 1969 study—"to make a diagnosis of the writing problems which are typical of the junior college student who has been assigned to a non-transferable remedial English class" (4)—offers a unique insight into that question. He had fourteen two-year college composition teachers and four department chairs at four New York City community colleges apply his holistic rubric (fig. 9.2) to seventy-eight essays written by students who had failed a placement test and had been assigned to basic writing. Then he studied the rubric response sheets. He was appalled. About 85 percent of the teachers

> did not engage with the analytic method of rating compositions. Rather, they seem to prefer the general impression method. With the majority of teachers, comments based on the five factors listed on the evaluation form were either non-existent or so brief as to be of no value at all. Instead of individual comments based on the five factors, more frequently a general comment, vague about suggestions for revision and negative in tone, indicated that the papers was a "D" or "F."

The other 15 percent of teachers attended to the criteria, were more positive in tone, and passed more of the papers (18).

Bossone had found what other researchers had observed: writing teachers prefer general-impression scoring to analytic-grid scoring (e.g., Cast 1940, 59; Lamb 1953, 133). But he did not belong to that majority. He was a teacher himself, with an intense sympathy for students who had been deemed remedial, by whatever bureaucratic means. As he said, the students themselves had prompted his remarkable 1969 study: "The bewildered looks of many remedial English students (which I came to know as I visited classrooms) haunted me" (2). For their sake, he saw a holistic-scoring rubric, properly filled out, as more useful than a scoring guide without separable criteria. He was a trait person.[16]

In following years, many teachers who worked and sympathized with another disadvantaged group of students, English-language learners, also turned out to be trait people. Some of them crossed over the thin line and rejected holistic scoring completely. Many realized that unless the rubric is based on the task at hand, its value is limited—and scores resulting from standardized rubrics may, when used on diverse student populations, result in more harm than good.

PROFILES: ASSESSMENT AIM

So often, our research interests begin in our families—a mother who teaches us to read, a grandmother who sits by us as we learn our alphabet. Before we know it, we are studying literature or teaching writing. If our fathers and grandfathers are factory workers and carpenters, we are forever drawn to those for whom school stood as a democratic ideal. For Liz Hamp-Lyons, perspective began at home. Her father was an educator of deaf and hard of hearing students. When she was in college, his own research focused on assessing the reading level of deaf and hard of hearing children, developing a test that was widely used in the United Kingdom in the 1970s. She hand calculated the statistics for him.

Influenced by her father, here is how she described her own perspective:

> I learned that it is essential to solve problems for people who are not the "norm"—and that most tests only report in any really "true way" for "normal" people. Add this to the hippie tendencies and you can see that it wasn't my nature to accept simple answers to big questions. People like Wiseman were looking into fine detail and getting good answers, but didn't have quite the right questions; Britton and others were asking the right questions but could only see levels, starting as they were from a "vertical world view." I don't know why I saw a "parallel world view" (or should that be "horizontal"?). (email to authors, August 10, 2014)

That parallel world-view—one that would characterize her career—was also derived from her school experiences. Her early life did not suggest any likelihood that she would end up working in education. As she told Yan Jin in 2014,

> I was a very naughty pupil at school and an even worse one once I became politically aware. I was a scholarship child at a Roman Catholic grammar school back in the 1960s, and once I started campaigning for nuclear disarmament through the CND (Campaign for Nuclear Disarmament) and playing truant from school, I was always in trouble with the nuns. (339)

She completed teacher training and began working in a technical college. She recalled, "I taught English to nursery nurses, panel beaters, motor technicians, and hairdressers" (Jin 2014, 340). She learned she had been accepted in the advanced diploma in English-language teaching at the University of Exeter. There were students from Australia, Egypt, Turkey, Taiwan, Japan, and Nigeria. Her world-view opened and her fascination with language emerged. She earned her advanced diploma as well as a master of education, both from Exeter. She taught in Greece, Iran, and Malaysia. She and her husband moved to downstate Illinois and back to Europe to begin a post at the Institute for Applied Language Studies at the University of Edinburgh. In 1987 she received her PhD in applied linguistics and language testing from Edinburgh. She completed the final submission just after she returned to the United States to take a post at the University of Michigan. There she served as associate director of assessment on the English Composition Board under Debby Keller-Cohen and also worked with John Swales in the English Language Institute.

The British Council embargoed her dissertation, *Testing Second Language Writing in Academic Settings*, for five years because the instruments she had developed were confidential. Working with Alan Davies, she had undertaken a validation study of the English Language Testing System (ELTS). Begun in 1980 by Cambridge English Language Assessment and the British Council, ELTS was the parent assessment of today's International English Language Testing System (IELTS)—one of the world's largest English-language test batteries, counterpart to the US Test of English as a Foreign Language® (TOEFL). ELTS was designed to provide information on the language-skills performance of English-language learners entering UK universities.

During the period of Hamp-Lyons's dissertation, ELTS was a two-tier test. The first consisted of two multiple-choice tests, one in reading and the other in listening. Every candidate took these tests. In the second tier there were three tests: a multiple-choice assessment of study skills, a direct writing assessment, and an oral interview. In the second tier students could choose one of six modules: general academics, life sciences, medicine, physical sciences, social studies, and technology. The first was for candidates who had not selected a disciplinary field, and the remaining five were based on the largest applicant groups for British Council scholarships. When first administered, 4,000 candidates sat for the test. By 1985 the test was administered to 10,000 candidates. As of the publication date of this book, the current IELTS is taken by more than 1 million candidates around the world every year.

The ELTS tests, Hamp-Lyons wrote in her dissertation, were based on three "theoretical positions, or constructs, of how language proficiency is composed" (1987, 180). First, language is divisible according to skills demonstrated in reading, listening, writing, and speaking. Second, language is divisible into general and disciplinary areas; hence the assessment of general academics and of specific disciplinary areas. Third—and "most contentiously," as she described it—language proficiency is associated with a specific area of study as identified in the six modules. The new test was first given in 1979, and the validation study—the Edinburgh ELTS Validation Project—was commissioned the following year under the direction of Davies and Clive Criper. The project ran from September 1981 to March 1986. Hamp-Lyons was a half-time research associate from October 1982 to September 1984 and from October 1985 to March 1986.

In her part of the validation study of ELTS, she focused on the writing component and its impact: "What are the effects on writing scores of overseas non-native postgraduate students at British universities when these testees are asked to write on topics closely related to the content of their own academic disciplines (a 'specific academic purpose'—SAP topic) compared to a topic accessible to all members of the university community (a 'general academic purpose'—GAP topic)? How can these effects be accounted for?" (Hamp-Lyons 1987, 192). Her sampling plan consisted of 111 postgraduate students, of whom 103 were Edinburgh University students, with the remaining students at other universities who had attended courses there. While the design of the study is deserving of more extended treatment as a model of UK awareness of empirical methodology, it is important to understand two findings.

The first was that there was neither an SAP nor a GAP "factor," as Hamp-Lyons phrased it, "which causes students to perform differently across writing tests" (1987, 235). Simply put, the data did not allow clear distinctions to be made between a disciplinary associated topic and a generalist topic. That could be no surprise, as she understood, when the entire sample size was so small, with subgroup differences even smaller.

The second—that there was a need for an alternative to holistic scoring—would remain a touchstone to writing assessment researchers long after the dissertation was completed in 1983 and the five-year embargo of it. What was "urgently needed," as Hamp-Lyons reminded her readers after reviewing the results, "was a scoring procedure which could provide scores of adequate reliability with only one rater" (1987, 343). That problem had been substantively addressed in the profile scoring method. Since its initiation in 1979, it had been clear that multiple

```
                    Figure 5.1.5.: Profile Method

1.  Skim the script again as many times as you need to, but
    very quickly each time, until you have been able to
    circle a 3-band range on each line of the profile grid
    below:

    linguistic accuracy       9  8  7  6  5  4  3  2  1

    linguistic appropriacy    9  8  7  6  5  4  3  2  1

    argumentation             9  8  7  6  5  4  3  2  1

    organisation              9  8  7  6  5  4  3  2  1

    communicative quality     9  8  7  6  5  4  3  2  1

2.  Now there are two ways to reach a final band, and you
    may choose whichever seems appropriate:
(i) if you see a clear pattern on the grid which enables
    you to make up your mind on the best band, do so. For
    instance, if you found you had this pattern:
```

Figure 9.3. Profile method (Hamp-Lyons 1987, fig. 5.1.5) (courtesy of Liz Hamp-Lyons)

markings of a single writing sample were not possible because the test was on-demand and offered in countries wherever British Councils were located.[17] "The procedure that was developed," she noted, "required the same rater to read several times, looking at different features each time, thus attempting a multiple response from a single rater" (254). Her contribution asked readers to focus attention on dimensions of writing: linguistic accuracy, linguistic appropriateness, argumentation, organization, and communication quality. Scores were awarded on nine levels, from the highest (9, described as giving the reader "full satisfaction") to the lowest (1, a "true non-writer"). A substantial advancement over earlier uses, the profile method and profile scale are shown in figures 9.3 and 9.4, respectively.

Understanding the significance of score use, Hamp-Lyons had dismissed holistic scoring as unsuitable in contexts where specific information was needed to create a profile of the writer and where the information arising from the test outcomes was used diagnostically in on-arrival language-teaching programs. The global quality of holistic scoring—"that the quality of any piece of writing is greater than any of its directly observable parts" (1987, 97)—was unsuited to the feedback needed to make admission decisions based on language ability. Described by Hamp-Lyons as yielding "imprecision" (102), holistic scoring stood in

What Does a Score Mean? 251

COMMUNICATIVE QUALITY	ORGANISATION	ARGUMENTATION	LINGUISTIC ACCURACY	LINGUISTIC APPROPRIACY
9. The writing displays an ability to communicate in a way which gives the reader full satisfaction.	The writing displays a completely logical organisational structure which enables the message to be followed effortlessly.	Relevant arguments are presented in an interesting way, with main ideas prominently and clearly stated, with completely effective supporting material; arguments are effectively related to the writer's experience or views.	The reader sees no errors of vocabulary, spelling, punctuation or grammar.	There is an ability to manipulate the linguistic systems with complete appropriacy.
8. The writing displays an ability to communicate without causing the reader any difficulties.	The writing displays a logical organisational structure which enables the message to be followed easily.	Relevant arguments are presented in an interesting way, with main ideas highlighted, effective supporting material and they are well related to the writer's own experience or views.	The reader sees no significant errors of vocabulary, spelling, punctuation or grammar.	There is an ability to manipulate the linguistic systems appropriately.
7. The writing displays an ability to communicate with few difficulties for the reader.	The writing displays good organisational structure which enables the message to be followed without much effort.	Arguments are well presented with relevant supporting material and an attempt to relate them to the writer's experience or views.	The reader is aware of but not troubled by occasional minor errors of vocabulary, spelling, punctuation or grammar.	There are minor limitations to the ability to manipulate the linguistic systems appropriately which do not intrude on the reader.
6. The writing displays an ability to communicate although there is occasional strain for the reader.	The writing is organised well enough for the message to be followed throughout.	Arguments are presented but it may be difficult for the reader to distinguish main ideas from supporting material; main ideas may not be supported; their relevance may be dubious; arguments may not be related to the writer's experience or views.	The reader is aware of errors of vocabulary, spelling, punctuation or grammar, but these intrude only occasionally.	There is limited ability to manipulate the linguistic systems appropriately, but this intrudes only occasionally.
5. The writing displays an ability to communicate although there is often strain for the reader.	The writing is organised well enough for the message to be followed most of the time.	Arguments are presented but may lack relevance, clarity, consistency or support; they may not be related to the writer's experience or views.	The reader is aware of errors of vocabulary, spelling, punctuation or grammar which intrude frequently.	There is limited ability to manipulate the linguistic systems appropriately which intrudes frequently.
4. The writing displays a limited ability to communicate which puts strain on the reader throughout.	The writing lacks a clear organisational structure and the message is difficult to follow.	Arguments are inadequately presented and supported; they may be irrelevant; if the writer's experience or views are presented their relevance may be difficult to see.	The reader finds the control of vocabulary, spelling, punctuation and grammar inadequate.	There is inability to manipulate the linguistic systems appropriately, which causes severe strain for the reader.
3. The writing does not display an ability to communicate although meaning comes through spasmodically.	The writing has no discernible organisational structure and a message cannot be followed.	Some elements of information are present but the message is not provided with an argument, or the argument is mainly irrelevant.	The reader is primarily aware of gross inadequacies of vocabulary, spelling, punctuation and grammar.	There is little or no sense of linguistic appropriacy, although there is evidence of sentence structure.
2. The writing displays no ability to communicate.	No organisational structure or message is recognisable.	A meaning comes through occasionally but it is not relevant.	The reader sees no evidence of control of vocabulary, spelling, punctuation or grammar.	There is no sense of linguistic appropriacy.
1. A true non-writer who has not produced any assessable strings of English writing. An answer which is wholly or almost wholly copied from the input text or task is in this category.				
0. Should only be used where a candidate did not attend or attempt this part of the test in any way.				

Liz Hamp-Lyons for the British Council ©British Council 1986

Figure 9.4. Profile scale (fig. 5.1.11, Hamp-Lyons 1987) (courtesy of Liz Hamp-Lyons)

contrast to that which was needed for ELTS. Wisely, she saw that reliability evidence was related to the construct validity of the assessment. When the dimensions of writing are clearly defined for writers and scorers,

> the validity problems centre on the critical need to ensure that the purpose and values in the writing context are fully clear to the writers and that the criteria for assessment and the guidance for the recognition and evaluation of the characteristics of the writers writing are appropriate and accurate. When these requirements are satisfied, analytic scoring and primary trait scoring [both informing the profile method] lead to the empowerment of writers who create successful texts for the defined

context, and also to the empowerment of readers who understand what it is they are asked to do and why. (110)

In 2016, Hamp-Lyons was still continuing this line of thought. In an editorial entitled "Farewell to Holistic Scoring?" (2016a), she advocates multiple-trait scoring in favor of either global information obtained from holistic scoring or reductionist scores of analytic observation. Multiple-trait scoring, she argues, can make sense to students, teachers, and testing agencies. Later that same year, she continued her call for the end of holistic scoring.

> In my view, multiple trait rubrics are tools that can make sense to teachers and to test agencies. They open up tremendous possibilities for giving feedback to students based around a publicly available rubric that can be understood by learners as well as their parents. . . . Multiple trait approaches are also beginning to find links with the proponents of automated scoring, since the process of creating a local rubric applies some language-based principles and processes that the developers of automated systems aim to emulate in their programmes. (2016b, A4)

Hers is the enduring theme of equity. As she says about the nursery nurses, panel beaters, motor technicians, and hairdressers whom she taught early in her career, there is still much at stake involving their futures.

THE END OF HOLISTIC SCORING?

Splitters, rubrics, and profiles bring to the surface the contradiction that lies buried at the nucleus of holistic scoring. From a philosophical perspective based on gestalt holism, if the perception of the relative quality of an essay is other than the sum of its traits, a unitary score representing that quality cannot be completely known through trait analysis. If the perception is unanalyzable, the source of the perception is unanalyzable. From an operational perspective based on individual differences as a differential psychology, if information is imprecise, information on affect, behavior, cognition, and desire cannot be gathered systemically to advance individual student learning. While the individual perspective we have adopted in this chapter allows us to identify the concealed structures surrounding holistic assessment, it also has allowed us to draw attention to the need for actionable information necessary to help a student gain proficiency in the multiple domains and varied genres of writing.

The contradiction between obtained score and writing sample is especially clear to K–12 or first-year college writing students who want to improve their writing and, at least implicitly, find writing traits meaningful, useful, and consequential. What can a score produced by a holistic scheme mean to those students? If it is a pooled rate, it means this is the averaged vote of several experts, but the vote by itself is no more useful than the single grade left by the instructor at the bottom of an essay. The score leaves a student with no grounds to question or contest the consequences—denied course credit, held back a grade, denied a certificate because they left school, refused admission. If the score comes with a scoring guide or rubric, as many in testing encourage, it means the writing sample was judged according to the named criteria, but how well the student performed on them is left up in the air: only a single score is given. Better for both student and teacher if a returned sample comes with a profile since the level of performance on separate traits is described more fully and designed for the student and instructor to work together to improve writing.

But wait, haven't we left holistic scoring and crossed the line into analytic scoring? And in doing so, what have we left behind? Read again Keech and McNelly's "Sample N" in figure 9.1. Isn't there a quality about it that defies classifying? Isn't there some shaping or sensing of words and ideas not often found in high-school impromptu writing? But what do you call that accomplishment—deftness, verbal luminescence, potential, *joie d'esprit, joie d'écrire*? No name seems right. Maybe the effort to find the right word is, as Darwin said, trying to define the undefinable. If so, do we not still have a need for holistic scoring?

And isn't that need ethical? Are we not, following the philosopher James Rachels (1986), compelled to give equal weight to each individual, who might otherwise be affected by decisions to abandon that which can capture the "other than"—the very element of writing that may, in fact, be the very thing the student needs to succeed? As current researchers in educational measurement (American Educational Research Association, American Psychological Association, and National Council on Measurement in Education 2014) and writing studies (Poe, Inoue, and Elliot 2018) remind us, a score fully understood requires an appreciation of fairness.

Bossone is no longer with us, but we are still haunted by those bewildered looks of students nearly fifty years ago, students put into remedial writing classrooms in the community colleges of Manhattan, New York City, Staten Island, and the Bronx. Was it fair to these students for a majority of their teachers to avoid trait-based holistic scales and instead evaluate their papers with an unadorned D or F and a peppering of circles around misspellings and mispunctuations and only the vaguest indications of how to improve? Just because "it is easier to be a proofreader than a critic," as Bossone noted (1969, 34), does that mean writing evaluation should always take the easier way? The easiest way to score a student essay is to have a machine do it, but computer algorithms can perceive only parts of language and therefore can never, by any stretch of the imagination, score holistically. Evidence suggests that humans can score more reliably holistically than analytically, but which way is better for the student—impression based or trait based? The question, like the species question, is yet to be answered.

Or is it a question of consequences that has become moot, not worth trying to answer because of the complexities at each turn? That depends on perspective derived from standpoint. If one is interested in individual differences, the question remains important. If one is interested in distributed assessment, the question is already resolved.

Hamp-Lyons's dissertation study of ELTS scoring—largely finished by 1984 because implementation with a completed rater-training manual was needed for test administration in April of that year—demoted holistic scoring and promoted profile scoring, but it did not mark the end of holistic scoring. At least in the United States, although the method remained contagious, probably its most widespread use among researchers as a sole measurement of writing began to decline somewhere between 1985 and 1990. (Our social-contagion model shown in chapter 2 predicts a complete exposure to holistic scoring in 1987–1989 but, even during that period, criticism was building.) Hamp-Lyons's study does hand the method one of a series of damaging blows, both theoretical and pragmatic. In the 1980s, profile and primary-trait methods—increasingly applied in local assessments around the nation—challenged the thin information offered by a holistic score. More blows followed. In 1984, Davida Charney published her widely read critique, charging that experts had often begged the question of "whether holistic ratings produce accurate assessments of 'true writing ability'" (1984, 68). Portfolio scoring, famously installed in 1986 for end-of-course assessment at SUNY Stony Brook by Peter Elbow and Pat Belanoff, challenged the validity of a single, impromptu sample. In 1988, in another widely read piece, Catherine Keech Lucas questioned whether holistic scoring could ever be faithful to an "organic model of learning as growth" (Lucas 1988, 10). In the early 1990s university placement systems relying on teacher knowledge rather than preset rubricized criteria were independently studied and applied at Washington State University and the University of Pittsburgh (Haswell, Wyche-Smith, and Magnuson 1992; Smith 1992). In 2003, Bob Broad argued that the typical holistic rubric is a radical simplification of teacher value systems. Most devasting for traditional holistic scoring, beginning in the late 1990s, automated scoring of essays proved more efficient and cost effective than using two human raters. Yet, even this kind of "holistic" scoring was challenged by the measurement community itself. In a 2006 study conducted by the Graduate Management Admission Council, researchers found that the automated scoring method—launched in 1999 and producing only a holistic score—masked variation in the traits of support and language that had been identified by analytic scoring. Further, as the authors concluded, information "provided by the analytic scores would indeed offer more information to admissions officers about each examinee's varying levels of ability on the four key writing criteria of the ARG [argument] analytic scoring rubric" (2006, 8).

In sum: approval and use of holistic scoring followed a classic trajectory for those researchers interested in individual difference, almost in a physical sense. It continued to rise, but the impetus did not hold among many in writing studies. While 1987 is a convenient date of periodization, subsequent decline, though stormy and erratic, appeared unstoppable. If one is interested in individual difference, the question of the information provided by a holistic score remains significant in two ways. If the score does indeed provide information about ability akin to deftness, verbal luminescence, potential, *joie d'esprit*, *joie d'écrire*, the holistic score is important. But if not, trait scores are preferable because the information these scores provide is actionable for individual students. As some quantitative researchers have concluded in both the United States (Elliot et al. 2016) and Europe (Zlatkin-Troitschanskaia et al. 2019), rejecting an either/or approach allows a combination of trait and holistic scores to be used as a rich basis of evidence related to validity, reliability, and fairness tied to assessment aim. Used alone, however, direct scoring of student essays by human raters using holistic methods seems a relic of the past, a fashion our profession is managing to shed in preference for information that provides actionable feedback and advances student learning.

True, if one is interested in distributed assessment, on the other hand, the value added by holistic scoring has never lost favor. In the 2011 NAEP Writing Assessment, the scoring rubric was defined with citation of Myers (1980), at that time a reference over three decades old: "The use of a holistic rubric is recommended as the basic tool for evaluation of responses on the 2011 NAEP Writing Assessment. The holistic approach to scoring focuses on an evaluation of the whole response rather than on its individual parts (Myers 1980). That is, a response will not be evaluated with a separate score for each writing feature, and an overall score will not be derived by adding together scores for each separate feature. Instead, a response will be scored by assessing performance across multiple criteria—development of ideas, organization of ideas, language facility and conventions—to evaluate overall performance" (National Assessment Governing Board 2011, 40). In a 2018 analysis of US state testing plans submitted for the 2016–2017 assessment cycle, twenty-one states used holistic assessments as part of either the Partnership for Assessment of Readiness for College and Careers (2016) or the Smarter Balanced Assessment Consortium (2014). These numbers suggest that, at the present writing, a majority of the 50.7 million students in US public schools will have their writing scored holistically by either a national or state-based test. Used in distributed assessments, direct scoring of student essays by human raters applying holistic methods seems a part of our present and immediate future.

As we conclude our analysis of the nexus of assumptions, inferences, uses, and consequences of holistic scoring revealed through attention to splitters and rubrics, we must make two observations. They will lead us into the next chapter. First, challenges to holistic scoring had been raised by teachers and researchers long before 1987, as previous chapters show. Profile-like analytic scoring had been supported as preferable to general-impression scoring as early as 1917 (Burt 1917). A portfolio ("folio assessment") was used to evaluate Scottish students writing in O-level examinations in 1974 (Spencer 1979). Critique of the construct validity of short impromptu essays was common before the 1980s (e.g., Nystrand 1977). So was critique of its ability to measure writing growth (e.g., Diederich 1963) and its reliance on individual teacher value systems (e.g., Wise 1953) and on teacher expertise (e.g., Cast 1939, 1940). And computer scoring of essays had been competing against teacher scoring at least since 1965 (Page and Paulus 1968).

Second, essay scoring in examination settings has long been investigated by empirical study and often has not passed the smirk test (e.g., Edgeworth 1888, 1890). Over the long historical run, such study may not have been good news for holistic essay scoring, whose defensible manifestations teeter on the edge of folly when the method is placed in context. How sane is it to give a student twenty minutes to write impromptu on a novel topic, then give raters only a few minutes to put a score of 1 to 6 on the essay—and then, if two raters come close in their scores, to declare the student's writing proficiency as one of those six numbers? The narrator of Joseph Conrad's *The Shadow-Line* suggests a mad carpenter can make a sane box (1917, 83). Can sane carpenters make an insane box? To their honor, many users of the black box of impressionistic scoring demanded probing of the box. And as we have seen, the findings of the probes helped question the use. Bruno Latour has argued that in technology, the uncritical reliance upon black boxes increases over time (1987, 21–62). In some ways that proved true with holistic scoring of essays. But in other ways, even the early history of that technology offers exceptions to Latour's rule.

Who can say, however, that the origin, development, and decline in the status of holistic scoring among many writing researchers may not turn out to have been a story still worth our attention? Over the decades, the investigations into holistic scoring played a major role in increasing professional understanding of evaluating written communication. Methodologically, that which we know about research in the teaching of English is deeply indebted to the study of holistic scoring. Seen in this light, it turns out that Clay Spinuzzi (2003) was correct: we can map genres and, in doing so, we are able to observe patterns—in this case, as we have recorded in this book, of a profession creating itself. As Carolyn R. Miller (1984) would have us remember, tracking genre is tracking discourse communities. If today we understand the significance of fairness and the centrality of equity in educational assessment, a volume of past investigations into holistic scoring provides an important boost to that understanding.

In chapter 4 we offer eight postulates, some based on our observation that there is a one-way relationship between political interest and test construction. To those postulates (derived from our analysis of UK studies) we now add five more (based on US studies):

9. *Innovations in large-scale assessment programs often come from independent practitioners.* When assessment is at its best, it does not run along solipsistic methodological lines. Since 1969, NAEP stands as the obvious model here, but others—less well known—are to be found, such as the role played by George Gadda at the University of California in the 1980s. While opposition is often noted between large-scale and local assessments, when both follow the same pattern of principled inquiry, programs are developed that benefit all through the inclusion of multiple points of view and the resulting transparency.

10. *Outside evaluation of a writing program tends to offer unwarranted critique due to misaligned methodology, while in-house study suffers from confirmation bias.* Scriven's external assessment of the Bay Area Writing Project interpreted the core of the program—teacher development—as an unanticipated consequence. Self-evaluation such as that reported by Edward M. White justified the California State University English Equivalency Examination with little reservation. While Carol Weiss (1972) and Stephen P. Witte and Lester Faigley (1983) offered alternative models of action and heuristics, these were not widely accepted during the period of our history—and may not be accepted by many program evaluators today.

11. *Within any given institution or assessment program, multiple forms of assessment with distinctly different theoretical bases operate concurrently.* While hegemonic forces exist, variety nevertheless emerges as we look to specifics. While the Educational Testing Service and the Bay Area Writing Project had clear aims during their early histories, on any given day Diederich was working on vastly different problems than was Godshalk, and, across the country, James Gray and Leo Ruth worked alongside each other while maintaining different referential frames. The more we examine detail, the less we are likely to make claims regarding research traditions based on totalizing premises.

12. *Assessment practices do not necessarily improve over time.* Recall our claim in chapter 5 that the 1945 study by Diederich surpasses most of today's assessment of undergraduate writing proficiency in providing evidence validity, reliability, and fairness. As Richard H. Haswell (2005) has argued, the scholarship practiced in the United States and the United Kingdom between 1936 and 1987 was more rigorous than that which followed. In terms of the impact of assessment, the examination of disparate impact we see in Hunter Breland (1977) and Edward M. White and Leon L. Thomas (1981)—undertaken years after the assessments had high-stakes consequences for students—does not necessarily accompany distributed and local assessments. At the present writing, the validity of this claim may be demonstrated by looking for subgroup analysis on the website of any purchased local assessment.

These postulates extend, as we will see in our final chapter, to the approach we offer to evidence gathering. So, a final postulate:

13. *The trouble with historical postulates is that they are summative, not formative. As such, they tend to be reactive.*

Is it possible this particular history may eventually trace a circle, even a spiral, that allows us to see emerging and reemerging patterns? Since history is imagined and made by language-using individuals, it can be reimagined and remade by them. The past is more malleable than we think. Can a knowledge of the successes—and the failures—of holistic scoring, combined with new knowledge about fairness and evidence, lead to enriched evaluative methods in which individual differences are as honored as systematic precision? Could that mosaic mandala map a way to make history actionable?

NOTES

1. In the 1990s, molecular biologists rearranged this part of the evolutionary tree. They discovered by DNA comparison that fungi were closer to animals than to plants. So in evolutionary history, first plants and animals diverged, and later fungi branched off from animals. You, human reader, are more nearly allied to the mildew growing on your African violet than to the violet.

2. Note that the scale chosen by Myers has six points (of which 6 is high) and that he stipulates a splitter as an essay that elicits two scores divergent by more than one point. If the scores differ by more than one point (6 and 4, 6 and 3, 6 and 2, 6 and 1; 5 and 3, 5 and 2, 5 and 1; 4 and 2, 4 and 1; 3 and 1), any split score except the 6 and 4 would place the essays into the lower half of the scale because each shows signs of weakness. Another common way holistic projects assure failures is to tell scorers to use all points of the scale, and if, as Myers informs readers, the final scores approximate a bell curve, "the reading did an adequate job of distributing the range of writing ability" (1980, 44). Such a distribution, the project's statistician might declare, without noticing the pun, will further statistical discrimination. These scores will then be subjected to a cut score. Often, the cutoff is picked to fill seats available in noncredit and credit courses, in which case the test outcomes appear as evidence for a curricular need—when actually the curricular need (to fill available seats) determined the test outcomes.
3. The closest writing experts come is with their notion of sophistication. But a less divisive construction can hardly be found in their ranks. Sometimes they resort to *sophisticated* as a term to define their top holistic category (e.g., Grabar, Hines, and Miranda 1974, 485). Other times they equate sophistication with attempts of students to copy the artificial style of textbooks (e.g., the "sophisticated phoniness" that Thomas Newkirk found awarded in NAEP writing tasks [1979, 7]).
4. This process is no different than with botanical identification. Anyone on a wildflower listserv knows the way members assume that an unidentified specimen has a correct scientific name and that flower manuals and flower experts can provide it. Polymorphy or species complex is sometimes considered the last refuge of a scoundrel. The rage for order can be found in every preoccupation shared by humans.
5. In the history of US essay testing, rubric often referred to what this book calls scoring guide. The earliest date we can find of the term "rubric to mean a holistic scoring device"—one that predates a 1978 use of the term as an explanatory or descriptive part of an examination (definition 1C) in the *Oxford English Dictionary*—is 1956, when Earle G. Eley wrote that readers for ETS's English Composition Test do not "memorize a comprehensive rubric" (313). He continued: "It is the richness of the teacher-reader as a critic of student performance that we seek: to over-mechanize the reader's task is to deprive it of significance for the sake of statistics" (313). The term "rubric" did not catch on very readily. Gerhard Friedrich, who had been an AP scorer from its start, uses "rubric" in scare quotes in his description of the 1973 California State University and College's English Equivalency Examination (White 1973, 36). In her 1976 description of AP English readings, Ruth F. Smith was still using the term in scare quotes (Advanced Placement Program of the College Board 1980, 10), and so were AP staff members Christopher Modu and Eric Wimmers in 1981 (611). This meaning of rubric must derive from the late nineteenth-century use of the word to mean a section heading of a piece of discourse (definition 2C— "a descriptive heading; a designation, a category"—in the *Oxford English Dictionary*, s.v. "rubric," 2018). In 1918, Philip Hartog used rubric in this way to refer to a list of tasks in an examination (12). And that usage of rubric, of course, derives from the centuries-old letterpress practice of rubrication, indicating major sections of a text by printing the first word or sentence in red. The language in red was called the *rubric* (definition 1 in the *Oxford English Dictionary*, s.v. "rubric," 2018). And that practice goes back to Roman Catholic Church liturgical texts scribed in the late Middle Ages, which were indebted to earlier Roman law books. A long journey, from Roman law to holistic rule.
6. Confusion between scores and grades continues to the present. While a score can be used for both formative and summative purposes, a grade is often associated

with a summative judgment. For example, while a score based on a rubric applied by a peer may provide formative feedback for a draft in a classroom setting, use of the rubric to assign a grade causes confusion. Scores and grades are two distinctly different judgments of student proficiency. Scores are limited to one observation made on a single day; conversely, grades are given by a student's instructor and are informed by a longitudinal, robust concept of the writer as engaged in the writing process.

7. Confusion between individually reported traits and summed traits continues to the present. Summing of points masks the variation in score levels for different variables in which, for example, a student can score low on organization and high on knowledge of conventions.

8. The proliferation and easy malleability of holistic rubrics may have helped generate the circus atmosphere of holistic scoring at its peak in the 1980s. It is worth noting again the July 1981 New Orleans conference on holistic scoring, called "Feasibility of Assessing Writing Using Multiple Techniques," in which school and university test administrators bragged of their "unique" systems of holistic scoring and could not agree on terminology or methods (McCready and Melton 1981, 80–81).

9. Peacocke and Douglas, the first philosophically and the second sociologically, expose the temptation of the holistic essay-scoring enterprise to drift toward self-explanation or self-sufficiency. That temptation can be seen most clearly, perhaps, in rater-training sessions, where fledgling teacher-raters are edged away from their local, individual, classroom-based standards toward a unified, self-contained group standard. Again we are reminded that holistic essay scoring was born in decades when, in US and UK English departments, New Criticism and Formalism reigned, with their belief that criticism was practical (Richards 1929). After WWII, in intellectual circles the most fundamental battle was contextualism versus holism.

10. Confusion between the origin of Gaussian distribution and the application of the normal curve continues to the present. A mathematician and astronomer, Carl Frederick Gauss observed that repeated independent measurements varied due to error, but variances (that is, deviations) were consistent. Gauss established that the probability of error was distributed according to a curve that was unimodal. In addition, Gauss observed that about 68 percent of observations in a one-humped curve lie one standard deviation above and one standard deviation below the mean; that about 95 percent lie at two standard deviations on either side of the mean; and that about 99 percent lie at three standard deviations. While the Gaussian distribution is enormously helpful in understanding error and its distribution, the prevailing concept that student writing performance must fall within a normal curve is incorrect. Depending on sample size and population at hand, there is no reason a distribution must be unimodal. As biostatistician Bart K. Holland reminds us, "We can never remove uncertainty from life, of course, and it can be unnerving to think that there is substantial uncertainty in such processes as the measurement of aircraft parts or the testing of drugs' effects in medical experiments" (2002, 50). So, too, it is in the measurement of writing ability where, in many cases, assumptions of a normal distribution—or even worse, rigging scoring to fit a normal distribution—are flat-earth wrong.

11. For the costs of ignoring content in distributed assessments, see Les Perelman (2012). For a research bibliography on distributed evaluation, see Whithaus (2010). For large-scale assessment involving attitudes toward writing, see Karen S. Nulton and Irvin Peckham (2017).

12. It is important to remember, as we note in chapter 10 regarding our category-of-evidence (CoE) approach, that the development of innovative methods should be accompanied by new forms of contextualization. An example is the use of latent

variable models to develop criteria for writing assessment. Is it possible to create a latent variable model of writing? In one sense that is precisely what Diederich, French, and Carlton attempted in 1961 using holistic scoring and factor analysis. Perhaps that impulse—to come to terms with one variable model that can be used across time and circumstances—is why that study is so often referenced. However, based on what we know today about the significance of genre, it is important that we not frame variable modeling as an effort that will allow us to identify elements of writing that will work across all imaginable contexts. Further, it is important to acknowledge that race, gender/ethnicity, socioeconomic factors, and the intersectionality of these and other factors require that we attend to subgroup analysis in terms of the writers themselves. To approach latent variable modeling today, researchers would have to obtain varied genres of writing important to school and workplace settings. Further, researchers would need to obtain group and subgroup sizes sufficient to make generalization inferences to the larger population of interest about how various subgroups of writers deal with specific genres. While we could not, at least at first, speak of a single latent variable model, we could begin with genre specific models used by different subgroups. Then, perhaps over time, a variable model could be developed that had cross-genre and cross-group usefulness. Lest this program of research appear too daunting, researchers can begin at once to develop campus-specific models that will be of use. Attention to genre and sampling plan would allow variable models to be created that would be of use at specific sites in helping students, instructors, and administrators identify specific elements of writing that were derived by latent variable modeling. Latent variable modeling, of course, is only one approach to understanding the nomothetic span of writing. Other approaches, such as structural equation modeling and its use at the level of task and item, would yield evidence of covariation and multidimensionality in the given construct (Debeer, Janssen, and DeBoeck 2017).

13. In a landmark study of reader reliability in writing studies discussed in chapter 1, Edward W. Wolfe, Carol M. Myford, George Engelhard Jr., and Johanna R. Manalo (2007) identified three types of evidence related to DRIFT (readers as differential reader functioning over time): differential severity (becoming more or less severe as a reading proceeds); differential accuracy (becoming more or less accurate as a reading proceeds); and differential scale category use (using the full range of categories included in the scoring guidelines at the beginning of a reading, but later showing a restriction in the range of categories employed). In light of these three categories of evidence, each related to changes over time, views of interrater reliability focusing only on episodic agreement are restricted. Limited view of reader reliability may neglect evidence that, in turn, has consequences for validity and fairness.

14. All involved sometimes forget that the computer algorithms were designed by humans to approximate writing-teacher response, even to approximate traditional teacher-friendly criteria. The personnel involved in creating ETS's e-rater® were quite explicit about this, describing it as "a software application designed to produce holistic scores for essays based on the features of effective writing that faculty readers typically use: organization, sentence structure, and content. The e-rater software is 'trained' with sets of essays scored by faculty readers so that it can accurately 'predict' the holistic score a reader would give to an essay" (Burstein, Leacock, and Swartz 2001).

15. A history of automated writing evaluation (AWE) has yet to be written (Hammond 2019), but the context in the early twenty-first century is provided in Ericcson and Haswell (2006). Following the publication of that volume, a milestone debate on the limits of such scoring arose between Mark Shermis (Shermis and Hammer

2013) and Les Perelman (2014). Emphasizing the role of genre in AWE, Jill Burstein, Norbert Elliot, and Hillary Molloy (2016) established a new direction for AWE when an innovative formative assessment platform was launched in 2017 (Burstein et al. 2018). At the present writing a hard left turn for AWE is resulting in actionable, formative feedback to students.

16. Bossone was born in 1924, graduated from UC Berkeley, taught reading at Portola Junior High School in the Sierras northwest of Sacramento, joined the education faculty at UC Riverside in 1962, and then in 1968 moved east to Richmond College in Staten Island (which soon merged with Staten Island Community College to become the College of Staten Island). His interest was always basic reading and writing, in which he quickly made himself a national authority. Best known for textbooks, pedagogy, and theory of basic writing, his data-based studies can still inform. In 1966 he investigated California community colleges and discovered that 70 percent of the students had been placed in basic English and, of those, only 30 percent went on to regular first-year English (Bossone 1966).

17. This on-site scoring necessitated the use of a "huge training manual," Hamp-Lyons recalled (email to authors, August 7, 2017).

10
RECONSIDERATIONS

And all their minds transfigured so together
More witnesseth than Fancy's images,
And grows to something of great constancy,
But, howsoever, strange and admirable.
  —William Shakespeare,
    A Midsummer Night's Dream

True ease in writing comes from art, not chance,
As those move easiest who have learn'd to dance.
'Tis not enough no harshness gives offence,
The sound must seem to echo to the sense.
  —Alexander Pope, An Essay on Criticism

How curious that James N. Britton, Nancy Martin, and Harold Rosen opened their report, *Multiple Marking of English Compositions*, with a quote from William Shakespeare's *A Midsummer Night's Dream* (1966, vi). Equally curious is that Arthur N. Applebee, Judith A. Langer, and Ina V. S. Mullis opened *Writing Trends across the Decades, 1974–1984*, with a quote from Alexander Pope's *An Essay on Criticism* (1986, preface).

Surely Britton, Martin, and Rosen knew what they were doing in selecting Act V from a Renaissance comedy in which reality itself is questioned. The speaker is Hippolyta, intellectually challenging Theseus, the patriarchal duke of Athens, who has just declared that the woodland events he has witnessed are more strange than true. The poet's pen, he cautions, is full of tricks—airy nothings are given names, and cool reason vanishes. But, Hippolyta counters, when all the story of the night is told over, and all is taken together, more arises than the sum of the plot—something other than actions, something strange and admirable. An Amazon, Hippolyta takes interpretative control and reminds Theseus that the plot is not the only thing that matters. Instead, it is the great constancy that matters—the plot and the language and the way that both, taken as one, transfigure the minds of the audience (Guite

2010, 61–63). Interpreted holistically, something strange and admirable can be understood if only the audience is willing.

Applebee, Langer, and Mullis were having none of Shakespeare's fairyland. Pope's closed couplets, meticulous in precision indicative of the Enlightenment, provided the setting of a report in which everything must work. Both student writing and the psychometric mechanisms used to describe it must operate in measured ways, form fitting function. Whatever effort is required behind the scenes, easy vigor must be the result. How odd that the quote, taken from *An Essay on Criticism*, is wrongly attributed to *An Essay on Man*. But, then again, perhaps the emphasis on harmony really does suggest a deeper meaning, expressed in the later poem: "One truth is clear, / Whatever is, is right."

In the work of Britton, Martin, and Rosen, it is not hard to hear the laughter from the tavern, the hope that, just around the corner, something magic might appear. In that of Applebee, Langer, and Mullis, Enlightenment engineering is the order of the day. Listen carefully, and you can hear the whirr of the machine.

As we turn to the final chapter of our history, we say farewell to the broad sweep of history and turn to a precise analysis of the major studies and handbooks that rest at the heart of our book. With a focus on interactions among categories of evidence, we hope we maintain the fluidity of the Renaissance with the precision of the Enlightenment. The future, we hold, must be understood in terms of synthesis.

WHAT WORKS: A CATEGORY OF EVIDENCE INTERPRETATIVE FRAMEWORK

In the history we present in chapter 1 through chapter 9, the most theorized study is that by James Gray and his colleagues (1982). To provide a firm knowledge base for the study of writing tasks, Leo Ruth targeted four sources of knowledge: the psychometric tradition described above; professional wisdom, historically presented in "Philosophy of the Assignment" by George R. Carpenter, Franklin T. Baker, and Fred N. Scott (1903); discourse theory from Alexander Bain (1890) to James Kinneavy (1971); and a review of writing research revealing distinct areas of study. In this section Catharine Keech (1982, 132-213) surveyed research related to topic selection and prior knowledge, task wording and comprehension, selection of discourse mode, specification of rhetorical context, and contextual influences such as motivation and access to genre. Even the individual studies of response analysis were based on Wallace Chafe's (1980) concept of idea units (a chunk of spoken words representing a conceptual unit) and William Labov's (1972) emphasis on the role of evaluation within narrative (a speaker's self-reflection on the raison d'être for the narrative itself).

In their presentation of sources of knowledge, Gray, Ruth, Sandra Murphy, and Keech (1982) demonstrate the power of identifying categories of evidence in advance of an assessment. It is no accident that the first section of their report to the National Institute of Education is devoted to grounding the research in traditions, and we may usefully advance our notion of actionable history by attending to evidence-based practice.

In her review of the history and basis of such practice, Norwegian researcher Tone Kvernbekk (2017) notes the pervasive presence of an evidential basis for practice in healthcare, psychiatry, and social policy, as well as education in the decade following the end of our history. In terms of a definition, Kvernbekk offers the following: evidence-based practice "involves the use of the best available evidence to bring about desirable outcomes, or conversely, to prevent undesirable outcomes" (1). Practical as well as causal, evidence-based systems are epistemological in nature and, as such, are accompanied by the claims and qualifications famously explicated by Stephen Toulmin in his uses of argument. Debates accompanying evidence-based practice range from the design of randomized controlled trials in assembling evidence to the generalizability of inferences across diverse populations.

Commonly known as the *what works agenda* in education, the evidence-based practice movement in education was instantiated in the United States in 2002 at the federal level as the What Works Clearinghouse, a division of the Institute of Education Sciences within the US Department of Education. Working under a uniform framework documented in the *Standards Handbook* (US Department of Education 2017b) and the *Procedures Handbook* (US Department of Education 2017a), the Institute of Education Sciences reviews evidence of programs, policies, and practices and produces a variety of reports and practices guides. Taken together, the two handbooks explain the range of activities involved in the collection of evidence regarding educational effectiveness—from the basis of review protocols to the dissemination of findings. The approaches we now describe are deeply informed by IES practices (US Department of Education 2017a, 2017b) that arose in the United States, as well as healthcare research (Whelton and Carey 2017, table 1, e132).

For purposes of precision, we extend an evidence-based approach to a category-of-evidence (CoE) interpretative framework that allows us to understand, with some precision, the evidential basis for the writing-assessment studies we have examined thus far in our history. While we turn in detail to the evidence-based-practice movement at the end of this chapter, we encourage readers to review table 10.1 in terms of three categories of evidence related to validity, reliability, and fairness. As demonstrated in previous work, this interpretative-framework approach allows navigation of complex information by focusing on foundational research evidential categories (Elliot, Rupp, Williamson 2015). And, as we demonstrate at the end of the chapter, this approach is equally useful in charting future research directions in which the categories maintain their force, with some justified modification.

These three categories of evidence are used repeatedly in the history we have presented. In the United States, the categories take their origin in a 1906 committee of the American Psychological Association (APA) that was charged with standardizing measurement techniques associated with experimental research (American Psychological Association Committee on Test Standards 1952). In the United Kingdom, the founding of the British Psychological Association in 1901 may be taken as a related origin date for an evidence-based view of research (Edgell 1947). In language use the *Oxford English Dictionary* provides a much earlier origin date of 1851 for validity (as related to soundness of argument, in def. 2), a comparable date of 1909 for reliability (as the degree to which repeated measurements yields consistent results, in def. 2), and a much earlier date of 1450 for fairness (as equitableness and justness, in def. 6). It is probably safe to say that these earlier concepts were first brought into the precise service of measurement in 1879 by Frances Galton, who defined psychometry as "the art of imposing measurement and number upon operations of the mind" (def. 2). Galton wrote just before a time when the first generation of what Adrian Wooldridge refers to as "hard-core members" of educational researchers were beginning to make their presence felt in both the United Kingdom and the United States (1994, 2).

However, it is important to remember that, while these categories are in play during the history we present in our book, these terms are fluid and, especially in the case of *validity*, contested. In using these categories we therefore realize that some may level a charge of presentism and hold us methodically accountable. Yet, as Wai Chee Dimock has noted in her caution about those who would hold others morally complicit, "A cautiously adopted presentism might allow humanists to bracket the nontrivial differences among historical periods and act as a cumulative force under conditions no less adverse" (2018, 257–58). So we turn to our conceptual system, an extension of evidence-based approaches used in *Writing Assessment, Social Justice, and the Advancement of Opportunity*

(Poe, Inoue, and Elliot 2018), firm in our belief that the past is interpretatively fluid—and most useful if we can manage to focus on purposeful engagement that is equally beneficial to all.

A LOOK BACK: CONCEPTUALIZING THE STUDIES AND HANDBOOKS

In table 10.1 we present the major studies examined according to the categories of evidence used to make research claims. While we provide only brief details of each study demonstrating the CoE used, we ask that readers return to earlier chapters for contextualization and detail.

Using the CoE framework, we can also examine the handbooks in the same systematic way. While the sources of evidence vary among each, common among all is that these are tales from the field. Beginning with William Boyd, who served on the Research Committee of the Educational Institute of Scotland in 1919, and continuing to Edward M. White, who directed the English Equivalency Examination in the United States beginning in 1973, these handbooks are united by their singular emphasis on helping classroom teachers.

The overview of research studies and handbooks identified in tables 10.1 and 10.2 illustrates the various levels of evidence used to support findings and offer advice. Four conclusions may be reached.

First, our approach allows us to see that holistic scoring was intimately involved with a wide variety of research aims. Especially notable here is the study by Paul B. Diederich, John W. French, and Sydell T. Carlton (1961), as well as that by Sarah Warshauer Freedman (1979), in which holistic scoring served as the basis for establishing elements of writing ranging from organization to knowledge of conventions. These varied uses of holistic scoring demonstrate that the genre was used for a variety of purposes, ranging from the traditional (offering a basis for inferences about student ability) to the innovative (deriving a construct model).

Second, table 10.1 reveals that, in most cases, there is both a homogeneous and a restricted range of evidence in the studies themselves. While the significance of forms of evidence in assessment has been provided elsewhere (Elliot, Rupp, Williamson 2015), researchers in both the United Kingdom and the United States had access to these forms of validity: concurrent, construct, content, criterion, and predictive. In terms of reliability, common forms of evidence included interrater reliability, intrarater reliability, test reliability, and writer reliability. In terms of fairness, evidence was inferred from validity and reliability, and differential prediction techniques appeared quite late. Specifically,

Table 10.1. Research studies, 1936–1987

Authors	Date	Validity Evidence	Reliability Evidence	Fairness Evidence
Hartog, Rhodes, and Burt	1936	construct	interrater reliability intrarater reliability	consistency consequence
Cast	1940	construct	interrater reliability	consistency consequence
Diederich	1946b	construct	interrater reliability intertopic reliability	consistency consequence
Wiseman	1949	construct predictive	interrater reliability	consistency consequence
Coward	1950	construct	interrater reliability	consistency consequence
Finlayson	1951	concurrent construct predictive	interrater reliability intrarater reliability	consistency consequence
Anderson	1960	construct	interrater reliability intertopic reliability	consistency consequence
Diederich, French, and Carlton	1961	construct concurrent	interrater reliability	construct consistency consequence
Godshalk, Swineford, and Coffman	1961	criterion	interrater reliability test reliability	consistency consequence
Britton, Martin, and Rosen	1966	content concurrent	interrater reliability	consistency consequence
Diederich	1966	construct	interrater reliability	consistency consequence
Myers, McConville, and Coffman	1966	construct	interrater reliability	consistency consequence
Percival	1966	construct concurrent	test reliability	consequence
White	1973	concurrent construct predictive	interrater reliability	consistency consequence
Breland	1977	differential prediction	test reliability	group and subgroup analysis; differential prediction
Nold and Freedman	1977	predictive	interrater reliability	consequence
Freedman	1979	construct	interrater reliability	consequence
Woodworth and Keech	1980	construct	interrater reliability	group and subgroup analysis; consequence
White and Thomas	1981	differential prediction	test reliability	group and subgroup analysis

continued on next page

Table 10.1—continued

Authors	Date	Validity Evidence	Reliability Evidence	Fairness Evidence
Gray et al.	1982	construct theorization	interrater reliability intertopic reliability	group and subgroup analysis consequence
Applebee, Langer, and Mullis	1986	construct discriminant	interrater reliability interrater reliability	group and subgroup analysis
Hamp-Lyons	1987	construct	interrater reliability	group and subgroup analysis

Table 10.2. Practitioner guides, 1924–1985

Authors	Date	Validity Evidence	Reliability Evidence	Fairness Evidence
Boyd	1924	construct	pooled scoring	standard scale
Vernon	1957	construct predictive	pooled scoring	intended consequences unintended consequences
Dressel	1961	construct concurrent predictive	test reliability	intended consequences
Diederich	1974	construct	interrater reliability	bias
Cooper and Odell	1977	construct concurrent predictive	interrater reliability intertopic reliability	consequence
Myers	1980	construct concurrent predictive	interrater reliability intertopic reliability	intended consequences unintended consequences
Davis, Scriven, and Thomas	1981	construct content concurrent predictive	interrater reliability intertopic reliability	consequences
Jacobs et al.	1981	construct	interrater reliability	consequences
Witte and Faigley	1983	construct concurrent predictive	interrater reliability intertopic reliability	consequences
White	1985	construct content concurrent predictive	interrater reliability intertopic reliability	consequences

concern for fairness could be inferred from discussions of consistency and consequence.

In terms of homogeneity, emphasis on the writing construct is shared among nearly all the studies, even if that terminology is not directly used. Emphasis on construct validity is historically well established in writing assessment (Elliot 2005), with its evolution transforming from a mechanical conception in the early 1900s, to a content-oriented definition by midcentury, and most recently to sociocultural definitions (Behizadeh and Engelhard 2011). However, in the majority of studies, the designs do not seek concurrent and predictive evidence. In that most, but not all, of the studies are designed to justify the use of scoring procedures, and the resultant scores to make inferences about student ability, absence of other forms of validity (especially criterion and predictive forms) is notable. Similar restrictions are associated with reliability evidence. Because of problems associated with score precision, focus on interrater reliability is to be expected and has also been historically well established (Elliot 2005). Nevertheless, challenges to intrarater reliability were noted in 1936 by the United Kingdom's Philip Joseph Hartog, Edmond Cecil Rhodes, and Cyril L. Burt; and in 1960, Canadian researcher C. C. Anderson used two topics, with a combined twelve essays written per student, in his factor-analysis study of writing fluctuation, topic and writer limitations, and rater discrepancy. Although these forms of reliability evidence were in use, focus remained on interrater reliability—in many ways, a proxy for fairness in the studies we examined.

Third, our approach allows us to chart the emergence of fairness as a CoE. While we have included a category of fairness in the earliest studies, however, it is often an inferred form of evidence in the studies examined. Robust construct representation, as well as consistency, are both related to fairness, but the word itself is rarely used in the studies. Table 10.2, categories used in the handbooks, displays a wider range of forms of evidence, as would be expected for practitioner guides introducing readers to assessment-related procedures. However, again, the term *fairness* is rarely, if ever, mentioned. With the Civil Rights Act of 1964 in the background, the first fairness study by Hunter Breland (1977) and then one by Edward M. White and Leon L. Thomas (1981) both seem historically tardy. Technically, as early as 1977 we see regression analysis used to identify differential prediction—a technique that would become standard in legal cases to determine disparate impact (Poe and Cogan 2016; Poe et. al. 2014). Similarly, we see in the study by White and Thomas (1981) evidence of an early use of differential validity analysis in which the assessments produced different score distributions for different student groups.

Fourth, our approach allows us to see the value of a broad range of evidence. While our narrative has been focused on the origin and development of holistic scoring, our CoE approach allows us to take a second look at those studies that used the most comprehensive approaches, such as Douglas S. Finlayson's 1951 study at the University of Edinburgh.

As early as that study, we find a full-range of forms of evidence accompanied by sophisticated analytic techniques. We see what can be gained by a comprehensive design in a key paragraph in Finlayson's summary: "In correlating the essay with an outside criterion, it is found that it is measuring something different from the IQ, EQ, and scaled teacher's estimate in English of the existing qualifying battery. A follow-up investigation is necessary to ascertain if this something is relevant to secondary school success" (134). Perhaps that vague reference to "this something" was deliberate, a suggestion that the writing construct was something other, something different, than what was measured by the other criterion variables.

Range and restriction of evidence, emergence of foundational categories, value of research approaches, and variety of research aims—each conclusion follows from a focus on evidence. Viewed in this way, tables 10.1 and 10.2 lead to a different conclusion than that reached by Brian Huot in concluding that the research he reviewed seemed "fragmented or ad hoc"—a reflection of the "current nature of the condition of much of the writing assessment literature" (1990, 239). In contrast, we find that literature unified by a common interest in evidential categories pursued internationally by a community of researchers. As we note in the introduction to this book, the work of one of the authors of the present volume (Elliot 2005) must also be reconsidered in light of our study.

Proven intercreatively useful, our CoE approach can be enhanced by the use of typologies. That is, determination of categories may be enriched by demonstration of a continuum for each category.

Helpful here is the use of typology figures and what they allow regarding conceptualization, precision, insight, and measurement. Well established in the social sciences, as David Collier, Jody LaPorte, and Jason Seawright (2012) point out, conceptual typologies yield insight into underlying dimensions that, in turn, strengthen empirical research design and interpretation. Defined as a system of categories, figures 10.1, 10.2, and 10.3 allow us to map out specific dimensions one at a time of the categories of evidence used in tables 10.1 and 10.2.

In terms of evidence relating to reliability, for example, we can use figure 10.1 to interpret the range of interrater reliability evidence related to general impression, holistic scoring along a continuum leading to trait-based scoring. Similarly, we can then use pooled and adjusted-scoring categories—ways of resolving discrepancy—to create four quadrants into which we can locate our studies.

The prewar work of Hartog, Rhodes, and Burt (1936), for example, fits nicely into quadrant 3. Their advocacy of general-impression scoring

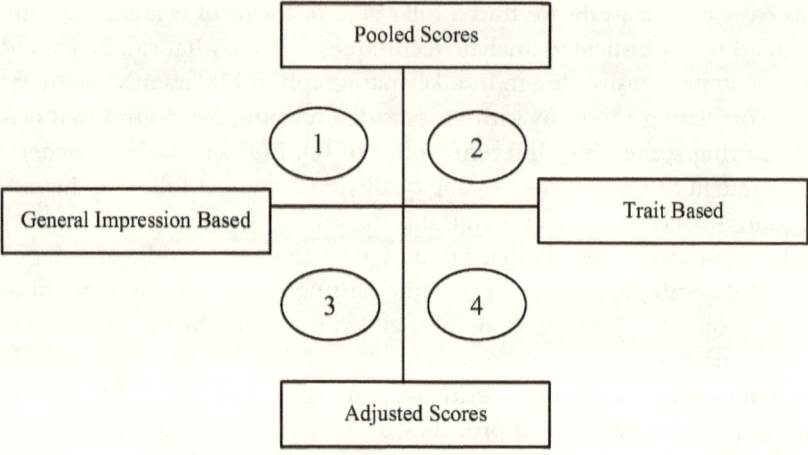

Figure 10.1. Conceptualizing reliability: Interrater evidence

was accompanied by score adjustments—made in an office by using techniques involving percentages, standard deviations, and standard errors—to ensure a level of standardization. In the postwar environment, Stephen Wiseman's 1949 study indicated the value of pooled judgments in assuring reliability based on a general-impression score. Here, quadrant 1 provides a useful location of the study. In the United States, the factor analysis study of Diederich, French, and Carlton (1961), located in quadrant 3, illustrates how the adjusted scores of fifty-three readers were used to derive the five-factor trait model. Once formed, we can see how the use of that scoring model is described by Diederich in his 1966 *English Journal* article. This study can be located in quadrant 4.

In terms of evidence related to validity, a range of construct-related evidence can also be interpreted along a continuum, as shown in figure 10.2. Emphasis on the writing task allows identification of a task aligned with a specified view of the writing construct, often tailored to the study at hand, to a task that is standardized. Similarly, we can look to a specified view of the writing construct (with variables carefully defined) and to one that is implied (with variables often noted but not justified).

The UK study by B. M. D. Cast used standardized writing tasks that would yield "typical compositions from pupils in school and typical specimens of marking from examiners" (1940, 258). Focusing on the essays scored analytically according to mechanics and literary traits, we can locate the study in quadrant 2. Also, focusing on the general-impression scoring used by Cast—an implied, though not articulated, construct model—we can locate elements of the study in quadrant 4. In

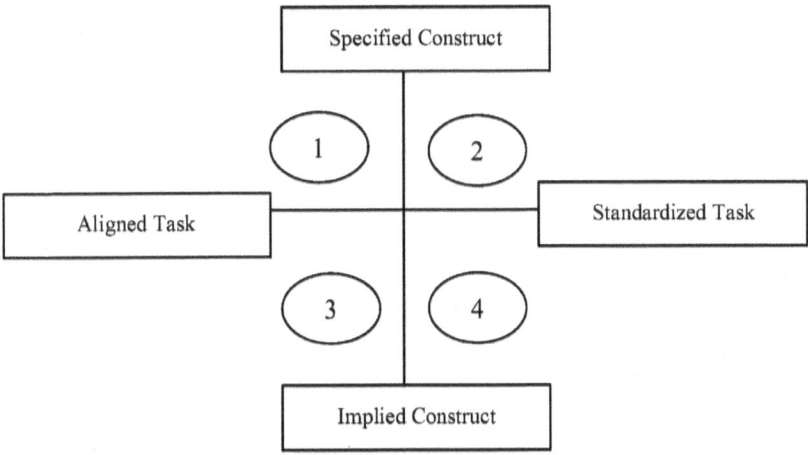

Figure 10.2. Conceptualizing validity: Construct evidence

the case of the English Equivalency Examination first used in California in 1973, we can place the study in quadrant 3. In terms of research in which a specified construct and writing task are aligned, the study of student audience awareness by Patrick Woodworth and Catharine Keech (1980) can be placed in quadrant 4. The writing task, based on classroom assignments allowing students to speak with authority, was scored analytically on a scale including genre and stance. As is the case with the Cast study, we note that the study can also be placed in quadrant 3 due to its use of holistic scoring.

In terms of evidence related to fairness, a range of consequences can similarly be interpreted along a continuum, as shown in figure 10.3. Emphasis on impact yields emphasis on a range of unintended positive and negative consequences, as well as a continuum of intended positive and negative consequences. Because they are based on the experience of the authors and provide guidelines, the handbooks provide an especially useful way of conceptualizing the interplay of intention and consequence.

In the United Kingdom, Phillip E. Vernon was especially candid about "the bad effects of selection on the mental health and personality development of children and on junior school teaching, while also pointing out exaggerations that often receive undue publicity" (1957, 169–70). Increasingly doubtful about the cost-benefit logic that accepted the negative impact of streaming students into school based on tests—a process that would determine their future lives—he posited that the majority of psychologists "would gladly abolish the selection

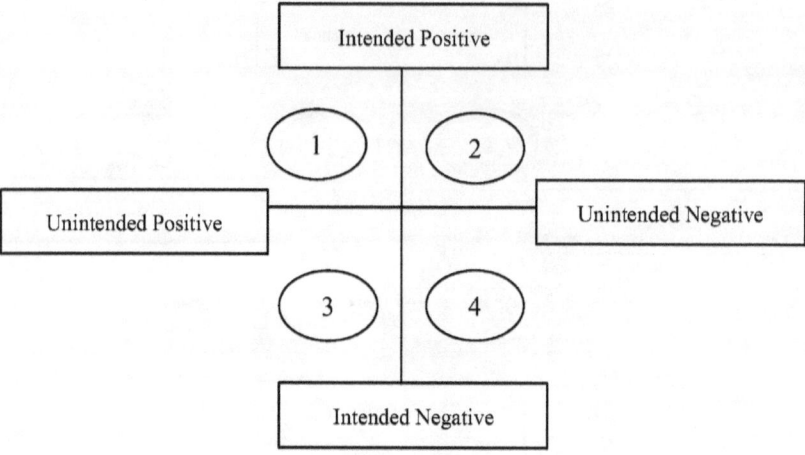

Figure 10.3. Conceptualizing fairness: Consequence evidence

system if there were a practicable and just alternative" (35). As such, we may place the study in quadrant 2 as a way to conceptualize how intended positive consequences may be in conflict with unintended negative consequences. In terms of unintended negative consequences of test use as they interact with intended negative consequences, Vernon identified the dangers of special preparation and impact of limited-response item types in classroom instruction. The study may, therefore, also be placed in quadrant 4. Read in the context of its publication, his *Secondary School Selection* may be interpreted as a document emblematic of a time when the risks of tests used to stream students, especially IQ tests, were overcoming their benefits. In the United States, the handbook by Barbara Gross Davis, Michael Scriven, and Susan Thomas used the Bay Area Writing Project evaluation to identify what the authors described as side effects, ranging from increased professional status of teachers to model use in other disciplines. In this interaction the study may be located in quadrant 1. In the interaction of intended positive and intended negative consequences, Davis, Scriven, and Thomas also recognized that cost models for the study had to be built from "data readily available," such as salaries (1981, 141). Costs of inservice and curriculum development—which Miles Myers recognized were the heart of the program—were determined in "rough figures" (141). Identifying the intended negative consequences in which costs were determined that were easily researched has an unanticipated positive benefit: we can see the disjuncture that occurred between the aim of the Bay Area Writing Project and the elementalist model used to assess it. Placement of the study in quadrant 3 thus helps us see *The Evaluation of Composition Instruction* as a handbook published during a time when decontextualized program-assessment models had reached their limit.

Before leaving these three taxonomies, it is important to note that they can also be used to reconceptualize value dualism—those killer dichotomies (Berthoff 1990) in which disjunctive pairs are framed as oppositional rather than complementary (White, Elliot, and Peckham 2015). The 1986 report of Arthur N. Applebee, Judith A. Langer, and Ina V. S. Mullis is useful here. Using figure 10.1, we can see how complementarity can help us identify the value of a study. In their use of both primary-trait scoring (used to identify student success in accomplishing specific-information, persuasive, or imaginative writing tasks) and holistic scoring (used as a measure of overall fluency in accomplishing these tasks), Applebee, Langer, and Mullis found a way to assess student writing in order to provide performance information through methods often seen as diametrically opposed. In addition, taxonomic thinking can help us understand the relationship between standardization and localization. While NAEP required tasks that had to be standardized to be useful in comparing performance information across US settings, the tailoring of the rubrics to constructed response tasks, as described by Richard Lloyd-Jones in his appendix (1977, 47–66), makes us rethink criticism about rubrics. The resonance between task and rubric provided an excellent way to evaluate writing before meta-analysis methods provided an empirical variable model of writing.

Taken together, figure 10.1, figure 10.2, and figure 10.3 allow us to conceptualize evidence related to interrater reliability, construct validity, and consequences related to fairness. While we have focused on quadrants, equally important is the continuum on which each category exists. This sense of evidence span should lead to the firm conclusion that it is unwise to think about any evidential category in absolute terms, let alone think of a form of writing assessment as invalid, unreliable, and unfair without evidence. Because of the complexities of the phenomenon under investigation and the varied means used to capture written communication, it is far more accurate to focus on specific evidential forms conceptualized along a continuum and in interaction with each other.

AN ACTIONABLE HISTORY: EXTENDING THE COE APPROACH

As we close our history in the early 1980s, we can see the road rising ahead of us. Forthcoming was White's defense of "holisticism" (1984) and of controlled adjusted-rater holistic scoring procedures in *Teaching and Assessing Writing* (1985). Five years later, a handbook was published to support postsecondary-educator use of holistic scoring for junior-year credentialing assessments (Elliot, Plata, Zelhart 1990). To come was Huot's masterful summary of trends in writing assessment in *Review of Educational Research* (1990); the edited collection *Validating Holistic Scoring for Writing Assessment* (Williamson and Huot 1993) with its comprehensive introduction to measurement issues by Michael M. Williamson (1993); and the first issues of *Assessing Writing* (1994) and *The Journal of Writing Assessment* (2003). By the early twenty-first century, specialized research in writing assessment had come into its own.

As our early history of holistic scoring illustrates, the record invites us to challenge many of our assumptions, especially those related to origin, community, and genre. Our approach to genre as a constitutive force has led us to identify a UK origin in 1936 and a fluid international research community working on a defined program of research. Further, our emphasis on genre has allowed us to see how a community dedicated to principled research learned how to investigate empirically written communication in academic settings.

In closing our history, we return to our promise to make it actionable: to take the principles of the past and demonstrate how they have relevance to the present. Emphasis on action allows us to answer the fundamental question that drove this volume: What is the use of history?

To articulate our actionable directions, we begin with attention to current demographic shifts that will impact educational conditions in the United States and abroad. As a 2018 report from the US Census Bureau skillfully explains, "Beyond 2030, the U.S. population is projected to grow slowly, to age considerably, and to become more racially and ethnically diverse" (Vespa, Armstrong, and Medina 2018, 1). Between 2030 and 2040, population growth is expected to fall to 1.8 million per year—and to continue falling to 1.5 million per year between 2040 and 2060. The nation's sixty-five-and-older population is projected to nearly double in size in coming decades, from 49 million in 2018 to 95 million people by 2060. In terms of diversity, international migration will overtake natural population growth. While the non-Hispanic white population will shrink, the population of those who are two or more races will be the fastest growing racial or ethnic group, followed by members of Asian and Hispanic groups. Also, the nation's foreign-born population—expanding from 14 percent to 17 percent of the population—is projected to grow from 44 million people in 2018 to 69 million in 2060.

From an international perspective, by 2028 the foreign-born cohort of the US population is projected to be higher than at any time since

1850. As the United Nations Department of Economic and Social Affairs, Population Division (2017) observes, the number of international migrants worldwide continues to grow rapidly, reaching 258 million in 2017, an increase from 220 million in 2010 and 173 million in 2000. India has become the nation with the largest number of people in diaspora, followed by Mexico, the Russian Federation, and then China. North America has become one of the fastest-growing destinations for migrants from Africa, with an annual average growth rate of 4.9 percent, representing an increase of 1.5 million migrants. In 2017 the largest bilateral corridor—migratory movements between pairs of countries—was that between Mexico and the United States. At the present time, the United States hosts 98 percent (12.7 million) of all Mexican-born individuals living abroad.

As these shifts reveal, fixation on sharply divided geographic and population categories does not well serve histories of ideas such as ours, especially when we are investigating ways to understand how that most essential human activity—written communication—is assessed. Better, we think, to advance a call for cosmopolitanism. As Kwame Anthony Appiah (2007) demonstrates in his plea for a new ethics in a world of strangers, the origin of the term *cosmopolitanism* dates to the fourth century BCE. Today, there are two standpoints that inform the concept of cosmopolitanism. He writes,

> One is the idea that we have obligations to others, obligations that stretch beyond those to whom we are related by the ties of kith and kind, or even the more formal ties of shared citizenship. The other is that we take seriously the value not just of human life but of particular human lives, which means taking an interest in the practices and beliefs that lend them significance. (xv)

Universal concern and respect for difference: as we have demonstrated, sometimes these clash and sometimes they align. In terms of writing assessment and the actionable history promised in the introduction to this volume, just how far the concept of cosmopolitanism can be taken is illustrated by our threefold proposal for a renewed attention to evidence, a reconceptualization of fairness, and an ecological approach to assessment.

With these shifts in mind, we can now return to our CoE approach and emphasize the need for integration, as shown in the fairness-first approach of figure 10.4. These dramatic shifts will require that, on an international basis, we rethink what we know about writing assessment in order to advance opportunities to learn for those we have met but know little about.

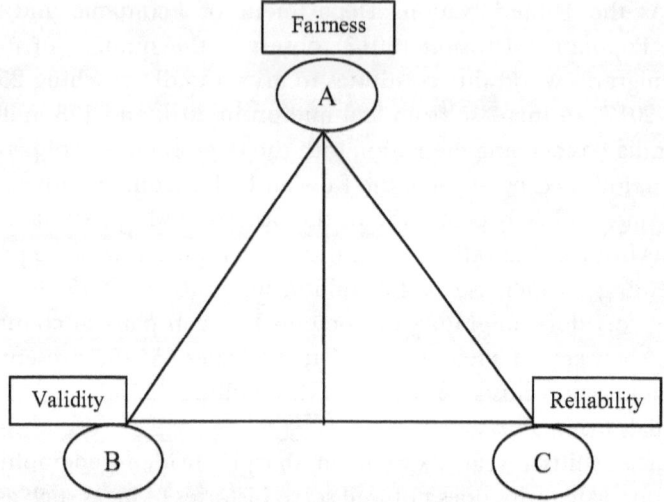

Figure 10.4. Conceptualizing fairness, validity, and reliability evidence: An integrated model

Historically, most of the studies analyzed in this book fall along the continuum from B to C. Only the Breland (1977) and the White and Thomas study (1981) encompass the isosceles triangle. As colleagues have shown in a number of recent historical and conceptual studies summarized by Mya Poe, Asao B. Inoue, and Norbert Elliot (2018), attention to subgroup analysis in writing assessment has not advanced in the past four decades and is only now beginning to get the attention it deserves. Even the most elementary questions related to differential validity and differential prediction are not addressed in studies that aim to make interpretative statements about students and to justify score use (Elliot et. al. 2016). We rarely know if writing samples were read reliably for subgroups (Kelly-Riley, Elliot, and Rudniy 2016). And, while fairness is often mentioned, studies linking history, definition, and empirical practice are only now beginning to emerge in new concepts related to pluralism. Indeed, figure 10.4 is well suited to help us understand the span of issues raised by Paul Newton (2017) in his call for attention to central issues for "purpose pluralists" drawn to the principle that assessment should be driven by aims rather than concessions: perspectives used to justify the existence of an assessment; design of the assessment specifications themselves used to assess a given construct; and trade-offs and consequences arising from multiple perspectives. Newton urges purpose pluralists to consider the deeply contextual nature of all assessment. If we take that aim and consider it in terms of the rapidly shifting demographic profiles defined above, we can better understand that fairness can serve as an integrative principle for evidence gathering. Points B and C must be integrated with point A in order for writing assessment to meet challenges posed by, to put it straightforwardly, a new kind of sampling plan.

While figure 10.4 may be well positioned to help us understand the span of issues related to evidence, detailed conceptualization of these issues is required to complete the CoE approach we advance in concluding our volume. We thus turn to an extension of the RAD model based on our CoE approach.

For writing studies, the specifications of RAD research—that which is replicable, aggregable, and data supported—were first offered in 2005 by Richard H. Haswell. As Karen J. Lunsford notes, while his call for a data-driven approach to systematic knowledge production has been largely embraced, "the aggregable and replicable aspects are still being considered, adopted, and adapted" (2017, xiii). Because of unique contexts, replication is difficult, and, because of that uniqueness, aggregation is equally challenging. "What, exactly," she asks, "does it mean to replicate a study and to aggregate data?" (xv).

In 2014, Mark J. Brandt, Hans IJzerman, Ap Dijksterhuis, Frank J. Farach, Jason Geller, Roger Giner-Sorolla, James A. Grange, Marco Perugini, Jeffrey R. Spies, and Anna van 't Veer offered what they termed a "replication recipe" for empirical studies based on five ingredients: defining the effects and methods the researcher intends to replicate; following as precisely as possible the methods of the original study; establishing adequate statistical power; providing complete details about the replication available; and evaluating replication results while comparing them critically to the results of the original study. While an admirable guide, the recipe focuses on what constitutes similarity, not what may constitute difference. Even following these procedures, it would not have been possible to replicate most of the studies noted in this book because of the unique contexts of the sites and their students. What occurred in Devon when children were evacuated to that city during World War II would surely not be replicable in the children sampled by Britton, Martin, and Rosen in 1966. And the student writing used by Diederich, French, and Carlton to build their factor-analysis model in 1961was radically different from that used by Freedman to build hers in 1979.

Yet the research aim of replication and the aggregable data to follow is only problematic if we think in terms of systems rather than sampling plans. Here, Kvernbekk (2017) is again helpful. She does not attempt to resolve debates involving standardization and localization. Rather, she emphasizes that evidence-centered approaches must acknowledge the importance of context, the role of process, the identification of enabling factors, and the consequences of adoption. As she wisely cautions, "The intervention is not solely responsible for the result; one has to take both the target group (whatever the scope) and contextual factors into consideration." Equal caution is raised regarding the nature of enabling factors associated with replication. As she notes, "There is no reason to assume that one needs exactly the same contextual support factors. The enablers that made X work there need not be the same enablers that will make X work here. What is important is that the practitioner carefully considers how X can be made to work in his or her context" (16). The research story and the local-practice story, she reminds us, must be brought together. Again, we see the need to be ever alert to the sociocognitive ecology in which written communication is embedded (Flower 1994; Mislevy 2017).

In writing assessment, the aim of the RAD model has been given agency by program-assessment models such as design for assessment (DFA). Intended to unify the research narrative with the local narrative, DFA provides a nine-component model, with categories of evidence including consequence, theorization, standpoint, research, documentation, accountability, sustainability, processes, and communication (White, Elliot, and Peckham 2015, 155, fig. 5.1). Because our focus is on an expansion of RAD that may be used for broad purposes, we place our CoE approach in the fourth component: research.

To the list, this book adds a much-needed tenth component: history—an awareness of the ways the past has shaped and continues to shape all elements in the assessment ecology, accompanied by efforts to use that awareness to conceptualize and reshape an ecology reflecting known complexities of language use.

In essence, an historically informed DFA yields a step-by-step process that can be used in those assessments for which the aim is the local, site-based understanding of student capability. It is a process intended to be of use to those who favor mosaics. Such planned approaches to writing assessment hold the power to transform both research and theory in our field. Combined with a renewed attention to evidence and a reconceptualization of fairness, this ecological approach to assessment provides an actionable sense of history—one in which the research and understanding of the past is used to structure opportunities for us all when visible language is the object of our care. While additional categories of evidence may be needed to capture specific assessment genres, our three categories of fairness, validity, and reliability provide a just-qualified model for principled evidence collection.

Used before the assessment begins, CoE allows exacting questions to be posed and details to be addressed before the assessment is undertaken in order to provide a safeguard ensuring demands are met before inferences are made, use begins, and narratives are shaped.

Consider, then, table 10.3—part of our actionable history in which we use evidential categories from the past to plan a common future. The model is clearly based in writing-assessment methodology, but—as we have demonstrated—extension to writing research in general is appropriate and warranted.

Here we provide the three evidential categories in column 1 grouped under aims associated with research genres, represented in row 1, ranging from basic foundational research to the monitoring that accompanies large-scale projects. In this way precision can be obtained in research design, with the CoEs understood as facilitating a continuum of research. Rather than risk lack of alignment between research aim and CoE demand, we introduce process as a way to anticipate demands as they arise.

There are three features of table 10.3 that are intentionally provocative and designed to emphasize the need for principled research design in light of the shifting demographics we have noted above.

First, initial emphasis is placed on theory building as a primary consideration of each category. Following Andrew Morton (1980), we acknowledge the plurality of theory and recognize that theory building works on the principle of "as if" thinking in which we suspend our disbelief and work on the basis that what we are describing will increase truth. Following Andrew Cole (2015), we also realize that theory, as found in Hegel, must capture the difficulties of thinking, conceptualize thought through language, enact this materiality, and historicize that very materialization. Following Kant, however, we continue to see the value of constitutive concepts which are at the core of the CoE approach. Led by Timothy W. Crusius (1989), we hold that approach must also offer a typology; determine arrangements in which each construct sample allows for construct representation; demonstrate a sequence that explains how students learn; offer evidence of how the writing construct is related to how students actually compose; offer evidence of how writing construct use creates identity and serves the needs of audiences; and offer evidence of how the writing construct, as understood in a particular instantiation, relates to other learning models operating in other fields across the university. We also hold that theory-building

Table 10.3. Replicable, aggregable, and data-supported scholarship: An extended category-of-evidence model

Research Genre

	Foundational →	*Developmental* →	*Efficacy* ↔	*Effectiveness* ↔	*Scale-Up* ↔	*Monitoring* ←
Aim	to gain basic knowledge through thought experiment and/or limited field testing	to determine knowledge span through initial field testing	to use knowledge under ideal conditions	to use knowledge under typical conditions	to use knowledge in large-scale conditions	to monitor and refine knowledge longitudinally
Evidence						
Fairness ↓						
Theorization	adoption of fairness principles	initial articulation of fairness principles	implementation of fairness principles under ideal conditions	implementation of fairness principles under typical conditions	implementation of fairness principles under large-scale conditions	continuous monitoring of fairness principles
Consequence Modeling	identification of bias analysis techniques, with special attention to differential functioning	initial articulation of bias analysis techniques, with special attention to differential functioning	bias analysis under ideal conditions, with special attention to differential functioning	bias analysis under typical conditions, with special attention to differential functioning	large-scale analysis using bias analysis, with special attention to differential functioning	continuous monitoring of bias analysis, with special attention to differential functioning
Sampling Plan Design	sample size determined with attention to effect size and commitment to group and subgroup reporting on all evidential categories	sample size determined sufficient with attention to effect size for initial evidence collection, with reporting on all evidential categories for group and subgroups	study implemented under ideal conditions with attention to effect size and reporting for all evidential categories for group and subgroups	study implemented under typical conditions with attention to effect size and reporting on all evidential categories for group and subgroups	large-scale study implemented, with attention to effect size, and reporting on all evidential categories for group and subgroups	continuous monitoring, with attention to effect size of all evidential categories for groups and subgroups

continued on next page

Table 10.3—continued

Research Genre

	Foundational →	Developmental ↔	Efficacy ↔	Effectiveness ↔	Scale-Up ↔	Monitoring ←
Universal Design	identification of universal design approach and anticipate challenges and benefits for all participants	initial articulation of universal design approach	implementation of universal design implemented under ideal conditions	implementation of universal design implemented under typical conditions	large-scale implementation of universal design	continuous monitoring of implemented universal design
Validity ↕						
Theorization	domain-based hypothesis building	initial domain-based hypothesis testing	domain-based hypothesis testing under ideal conditions	domain-based hypothesis testing under typical conditions	large-scale domain-based hypothesis implementation	continuous monitoring of domain-based hypothesis building
Construct Modeling	identification of domain-based construct model	initial field testing of domain-based construct model	domain-based construct model implemented under ideal conditions	domain-based construct model implemented under typical conditions	large-scale implementation of domain-based construct model	continuous monitoring of implemented domain-based construct model
Response Processes	identification of principles for response processes analysis	initial field testing of response processes	examination response processes under ideal conditions	examination of response processes under typical conditions	large-scale examination of response processes	continuous monitoring of response processes
Criterion Measures	identification and justification of relationships to other variables	initial field testing of relationships to other variables	examination of relationships to other variables under ideal conditions	examination of relationships to other variables under typical conditions	large-scale analysis of relationships to other variables	continuous monitoring of relationships to other variables

continued on next page

Table 10.3—continued

Research Genre

Reliability ↑	Foundational →	Developmental ↔	Efficacy ↔	Effectiveness ↔	Scale-Up ↔	Monitoring ↔
Theorization	identification of precision principles and replication goals	initial field testing of precision principles and replication goals	implementation of precision principles and replication goals under ideal conditions	implementation of precision principles and replication goals under typical conditions	large-scale implementation of precision principles and replication goals	continuous monitoring of precision principles and replication goals
Precision Modeling	identification of reliability coefficients and their interpretation	initial determination of reliability coefficients and their interpretation informed by initial context	determination of reliability coefficients and their interpretation under ideal conditions	determination of reliability coefficients and their interpretation under typical conditions	large-scale determination of reliability coefficients and their interpretation	continuous monitoring of reliability coefficients and their interpretation
Replication Modeling	identification of design elements required for replication	initial determination of replicability for the study at hand	determination of replicability under ideal conditions	determination of replicability under typical conditions	large-scale replicability	continuous monitoring of replicability
Decision Consistency	identification of classification across assessment episodes	initial determination of precision of classification	determination of precision of classification under ideal conditions	determination of precision of classification under typical conditions	large-scale decisions based on classification	continuous monitoring of decision consistency

regarding the CoE approach will benefit by association with social exploration scholarship. Ellen Cushman (2016) has already begun this work by using a decolonial approach to validity in writing assessment. More broadly, Cheryl Glenn (2018) has used rhetorical feminism—with emphasis on the histories, rights, contributions, expertise, and opportunities of martialized groups—to further advance the scholarship of social exploration. Historical recovery projects such as ours appear aligned with incisive research employing decolonial perspectives and rhetorical feminism. While all of this may seem like a heavy lift, when research is used to make inferences about student ability, we hold that theorization is the first step.

Second, elements of fairness, validity, and reliability are not meant to be exhaustive but, rather, intended to provide a just-qualified approach to research designed for engagement. Here we recall Newton's 2017 observation that we must justify the existence of assessment in the first place. As he writes, "The expertise perspective, in isolation, provides insufficient justification for the existence of an assessment" (9). Meant to be discussed by a variety of stakeholders, the research at hand benefits from the carefully selected elements of the three categories. For example, we have provocatively included determination of sampling plan under fairness and not, as traditionally understood, as a way to determine threats to validity. As stakeholders gather to design research, especially assessment research in which claims will be made about student ability, exact determination of subgroup size and commitment to reporting becomes prerequisite to further research planning. In addition, sample size determined with attention to effect size so the sample has sufficient power becomes a primary consideration (Maxwell 2000), and commitment to group and subgroup reporting on all evidential categories is established initially as a commitment. While seemingly a technical concern, insistence on well-designed sample-size determination is critical to the inferences we make about our students.

Third, as the arrows suggest, there should be interaction among the categories and genres so each cell in table 10.3 leads to important information about another cell. Thus, for example, the commitment to subgroup analysis in the design of the sampling becomes associated with examination of response processes for these subgroups to ensure a task is interpreted in similar ways by all participants as a safeguard to validity. In terms of reliability coefficients, attention to subgroup analysis also compels readers to present, say, quadratic weighted Kapp coefficients for the overall group and for all subgroups. As a research program progresses, column and row interactions become especially important.

While seemingly an obvious concern, insistence on analysis of category interactions prevents the siloed approaches too often found in many of the evidence-gathering approaches documented in this book.

Now consider table 10.4, a model for both research design and use of research information. Table 10.4 uses the CoE approach provided in table 10.3. Here we demonstrate how the research model can be transformed in a hierarchy of high-quality evidence, moderate-quality evidence, and emerging evidence based on the CoE framework. In unifying research design and information use based on such research, stakeholders can decide what kind of information may be adopted into a curriculum with little reservation, with some reservation, or with some hesitancy. While we understand the hesitancy to accept a hierarchical research model, in cases in which, for example, a curriculum is to be revised according to new research findings, it is best to ensure the reported research has sufficient evidential categories before students feel the consequences of the decision.

Both tables 10.3 and 10.4 have the benefit of transparency, integration, and interaction. Whether one agrees or not with a given research design, the principles that drive that design—and its possible curricular adoption—are transparent. Stakeholder agreement can then be extremely precise, and any disagreement can be addressed in equally precise ways. As the arrows in both tables suggest, ours is an integrative model in which classifications are unified under the fairness-first principle shown in figure 10.4. Ultimately, the typology is designed to yield interaction between and among cells. As such, a program of research may emerge over time as its sponsors seek regularly to determine one CoE in terms of another.

Despite its appearance, a CoE approach is not intended to be structuralist: the approach must be contextualized. Let's take a basic formulation of assessment *of*, *as*, and *for* learning as first offered in the United Kingdom by the Assessment Reform Group (1999) and continued in terms of formative assessment (Bennett 2011) and achievement, identity, and equity (Heritage and Wylie 2018). In assessment *of* learning, we can include the studies presented in the present volume in which student writing is assessed. In assessment *as* learning, we emphasize the varied ways stakeholders encounter research and the information it yields as a form of learning itself that produces a valuable learning experience. In assessment *for* learning, the research process helps stakeholders plan curricular innovation and future research programs. While assessment *of* learning is traditional, the Assessment Reform Group notes, assessment *as* and *for* learning "calls for different priorities, new procedures and a

Table 10.4. An evidence model for research and recommendations

Categories of Evidence			
High Quality Evidence	Fairness Evidence →	Validity Evidence ↔	Reliability Evidence ←
	Theorization: Authors provide definitions of fairness which are operationalized.	Theorization: Authors define construct domains, identify those domains under examination, and offer study hypotheses.	Theorization: Authors define principles of precision and replication.
	Consequence Modeling: Authors identify bias analysis techniques that are operationalized, with special attention to differential functioning.	Construct Modeling: Authors use a domain-based model that is operationalized.	Precision Modeling: Authors systematically use and interpret reliability coefficients.
	Sampling Plan Design: Authors demonstrate that power is sufficient to allow group and subgroup analyses, use effect size, and report on all evidential categories for group and subgroups.	Response Processes: Authors report principles for group, subgroup, and selected individual response processes analysis and conduct analyses based on these principles.	Replication Modeling: Authors identify design elements required for a replication.
	Universal Design: Authors adopt a universal design approach and report anticipated challenges and benefits for all participants.	Criterion Measures: Authors justify and report criterion measures.	Decision Consistency: Authors identify and justify the classification processes used and reveal their consistency over time.
Moderate Quality Evidence	Fairness Evidence →	Validity Evidence ↔	Reliability Evidence ←
	Theorization: Authors imply fairness principles and use techniques related to fairness.	Theorization: Authors offer hypothesis based on a generalized model.	Theorization: Authors infer principles of precision and replication and employ related techniques.
	Consequence Modeling: Authors use bias analysis techniques, but the basis for their use is not identified.	Construct Modeling: Authors imply a domain-based model that is operationalized.	Precision Modeling: Authors unsystematically use reliability coefficients and interpret them without justification.
	Sampling Plan Design: Authors provide sample size but do not demonstrate that power is sufficient to allow group and subgroup analyses and do not report effect size. Authors do not report on all evidential categories for group and subgroups.	Response Processes: Authors report response processes, but the principles for subgroup and individual selection are not clear.	Replication Modeling: Authors imply design elements required for a replication.

continued on next page

Table 10.4—continued

Categories of Evidence			
Emerging Quality Evidence	Fairness Evidence →	Validity Evidence ↔	Reliability Evidence ←
	Theorization: Authors offer no definitions of fairness and use no techniques related to it.	Theorization: Authors do not define a construct model and do not offer study hypotheses.	Theorization: Authors do not identify principles of precision and replication and do not use related analyses.
	Consequence Modeling: Authors do not use bias analysis techniques.	Construct Modeling: Authors infer a construct model.	Precision Modeling: Authors do not use reliability coefficients, or use them inconsistently, and offer little or no interpretation.
	Sampling Plan Design: Authors provide, but do not justify, sample size. Authors do not report power or effect size for either group or subgroup analysis. Authors do not report on all evidential categories for group and subgroups.	Response Processes: Authors do not systematically report response processes or do not report them at all.	Replication Modeling: Authors do not offer design elements required for replication.
	Universal Design: Authors do not adopt a universal design approach.	Criterion Measures: Authors do not report criterion measures.	Decision Consistency: Authors report the classification processes used but do not provide estimates of classification reliability over time.

new commitment" (1999, 2). When focus is narrowed to assessment for learning (AfL), the aim becomes increasingly formative. As Randy Elliot Bennett suggests, "Well-designed and implemented formative assessment should be able to suggest how instruction should be modified, as well as suggest impressionistically to the teacher what students know and can do" (2011, 8). To lend specificity to this aim, Margaret Heritage and Caroline Wylie (2018) identity four applications of AfL: communicating learning goals to students; intentionally obtaining evidence of learning while learning is taking place; student self-assessment; and shortened feedback cycles. A moment's thought reveals that AfL aims and practices can break the link between high-stakes testing and summative assessment and allow opportunity to be advanced formatively.

In order to generate research questions based on this three-part formulation of assessment, we note there are at least seven categories of key stakeholders in any given assessment: advisory boards, administration, faculty, parents, professional organizations, students, and the public. Now, if we take our three distinct forms of assessment one at a time in our seven categories, we find there are thirty-five possible combinations. These could range from investigations of student performance by group as related to self-efficacy measures (assessment *of* learning), to studies on effective ways of reporting research to advisory boards (assessment *as* learning), to research demonstrating effective ways of presenting curricula to the general public (assessment *for* learning). As we begin to understand these questions in terms of new sampling plans and the new stakeholders that will soon be involved, we readily see just how much we do not know.

In our introduction we wrote that the history we have told is a story of genre in context. As we conclude the book, we remain alert to the fact that history as social exploration—part of interpretative maps identified in chapter 1 and noted above as part of theory-building—may well be the perspective that many will bring to this volume. As the book goes to press, two presidential addresses—one at the Conference on College Composition and Communication (Inoue 2019) and the other at the American Educational Research Association (Wells 2019)—point to the disjuncture between student social experiences and educational assumptions. We realize the gravity of such charges, just as we recognize those leveled at appropriating the past for present aims when the past is treated as a series of objects fixed by an elite, white, male gaze. While we have not written from a social justice historiographic perspective (Hammond 2018), we recognize that authors of the studies we have selected often made inferences that could only be interpreted as cruel.

Examples of injustice are present through the history we present. While it is true that Cast was among the first researchers to examine the relationship between writing and personality, it is equally true that she observed that a child who relied on broad impressions rather than a defined analytic method had "not an idea in her head" (1940, 57). We note the callous nature of Boyd's use of a writing sample, classified as unsatisfactory, in his 1924 handbook without even a glance back at the impoverished child who recalled a day at a pond in winter: "We make snow men and we make weman. When we go to School my Mother wrappes me up as well as she can and sends me off to School" (84). We are troubled at Paul B. Diederich's (1946) suggestion that student papers for large-scale assessment could be read at home with children and other distractors kept firmly out of the male gaze. We are horrified that his Rutgers Plan for reducing the teaching load (1961) was based on college-educated wives that he described as "good wenches" (4)—the "hundreds of thousands of these bright, well-educated women sitting at home in the morning watching television and growing increasingly restless and neurotic" (5). We shudder at the confidentiality violations of Louie Crew (1977), who published a student examination from the Board of Regents of the University System of Georgia to make a point about "one who flunks blacks and rednecks" (709). In all the analyses we have recorded in this book, we surely must remember the little girl described as brainless, the women described as neurotic, and the student whose essay was stolen. We must never excuse these injustices as representative actions of historical periods, and we must promise to do better this time around.

In the histories of writing assessment that are to come, we hope acknowledgment of cruelty is accompanied by the achievement of justice. There is much that can be done and better ways to do it. Assessment scholars are only now insisting on fairness as first among foundational principles of evidence. We are only now exploring assessment as a way to advance opportunity for all. Imagine what can happen if such ideas hold.

And so we end where we began, with a question: What is the use of history?

Why, of course, to make it.

There is much to do. Together, let us begin.

Glossary
TECHNICAL TERMS CONNECTED WITH EARLY HOLISTIC SCORING OF WRITING

The specialized vocabulary used in this book follows standard usage of the period from the mid-1930s to the mid-1980s in the United Kingdom and the United States. This glossary does not include significant change in terms beginning in the late 1980s, as is the case with evidence related to validity (Messick 1989). The definitions are bound to their time, and so they are deliberately closer to those found in the 1952 "Technical Recommendations for Psychological Tests and Diagnostic Techniques: Preliminary Proposal" (American Psychological Association Committee on Test Standards) than they are to the 2014 *Standards for Educational and Psychological Testing* (American Educational Research Association, American Psychological Association, and National Council on Measurement in Education). Terms are alphabetized, and representative UK and US studies are identified in which the terms are used. We hope that the definitions are useful to readers of the present book as well as our WPA-CompPile Research Bibliography, no. 27 (Haswell and Elliot 2019).

adjusted-rater scoring. Assignment of scores through adjunction or averaging. When two independent reader scores are discrepant, a third reader is called in to resolve the issue. Sometimes the third reader independently scores the essay, and all three scores are averaged; sometimes the third reader's score is declared the final score if it matches or is adjacent to one of the first two scores (Myers 1980); and sometimes a third reader adjudicates by talking the two original scores into an agreement.

analytic scoring. Assignment of separate scores to different dimensions of writing (Wiseman 1949). Related to trait scoring, criterion scoring, or schedule scoring, in analytic scoring raters use a checklist identifying the parts to be scored with scales for dimension of writing. The scales are commonly termed analytic scales, scaled criteria, or schedules of marks.

anchor. A writing sample used to define a scale value. Equivalent terms are sample, model, benchmark, exemplar, range finder. Ideally taken from the set of papers to be scored, the anchor is used for rater training and sometimes for comparison in actual scoring. Sometimes the anchor marks the boundary between scale points but more often illustrates the score level in general. When the latter, it may be called a prototype (Myers 1980).

authenticity. The degree to which a test of writing allows writers to demonstrate their actual abilities. A portfolio of writing samples taken over time under actual writing situations would be more authentic than an impromptu essay written on an unfamiliar topic in twenty minutes. In this sense, the term authentic/authenticity appears late in our history due to delayed attention to construct validity as captured in the prompt (Nystrand 1977; Stiggins 1982).

bias. Systematic error in a score. Due to diminished construct representation or construct irrelevant assessment elements, scores may differentially affect certain groups. Breland (1977) investigated bias in the Test of Standard Written English by using differential prediction to see if the test predicted writing-course grades differently among groups of students.

calibration. Rater training to achieve desired level of consensus. Training of raters so they all agree to procedures and standards to be followed by the corps of raters as a whole. Sometimes called *norming* in writing assessment, calibration leads to a desired level of interrater agreement and interrater reliability.

chance. Mathematical probability that grounds probabilistic reasoning. Elimination of chance, or error, is an aim of holistic scoring. Early writing-assessment scholars were transparent about the role of chance in their scoring processes (Edgeworth 1890; Hartog, Rhodes, and Burt 1936).

concurrent validity. Evidence of validity in which the information on a targeted performance and a related outcome are collected as close together in time as possible. Huddleston (1952) examined the relationship between essay scores (targeted performance), objective item scores (related outcome), and on the College Board's English Composition Test.

connoisseurship. Specialized knowledge assumed when a single teacher's score was determined to be reliable for external examination decisions. The term was coined by Weir, Vidakovic, and Galaczi (2013, 208). Connoisseurship was assumed in early UK examinations (Hartog, Rhodes, and Burt 1936) and early US College Entrance Examination Board tests (Commission on English 1931).

consequences. Outcomes of using tests in defined contexts. While consequence was often a broad concern in terms of decisions (Hartog, Rhodes, and Burt 1939), specific group comparisons associated with fairness appeared quite late (Breland 1977).

consistency. Efforts aimed at the reduction of error in testing. As Hartog, Rhodes, and Burt note, "In the present series of investigations we are dealing only with the question of consistency. To say that the 'consistency' is low, is another way of saying that the element of chance in the examination is great" (1936, 68). The more consistent independent raters are, the more their interrater reliability increases.

construct. A postulated attribute that an assessment is designed to measure (Cronbach and Meehl 1955).

construct validity. Evidence that a postulated attribute (e.g., writing ability) is present in a given context (an actual sample of student writing performance). Evidence is used to support a proposed interpretation based on theoretical implications associated with the construct. White and Thomas (1981) examined differential impact on groups of students due to the ways that multiple-choice testing and holistic scoring captured the writing construct.

consulted-rater scoring. Assignment of scores through consultation. Two or more raters discuss essays to which they have, independently, given discrepant scores. The final score awarded is not an average of the independent scores but the mutually agreed-upon score arrived at during consultation (Pilkington 1967).

content-scheme scoring. Assignment of points from a predetermined system. In the United Kingdom the term refers to a method of scoring examination essays—paragraph size or longer—on academic subjects. The content scheme identifies the amount of credit the rater (or marker in Britain) should award for each correct point the writer makes. Points awarded by the examiner but not on the content scheme often are left uncredited (Mather, France, and Sare 1965).

content validity. Evidence that demonstrates the degree to which the content domain of a test is appropriate relative to its intended purpose. Britton, Martin, and Rosen provided a detailed appendix of writing tasks intended to obtain a cross-section of candidate writing ability based on classroom practice (1966, 35–38).

controlled holistic scoring. Assignment of scores determined through guidance. Readers are guided in various ways, with the use of anchor essays, scoring guides, rubrics, preset distribution of scores, and often fairly lengthy rater training and recalibration (Godshalk, Swineford, and Coffman 1966).

criterion-referenced score. Evidence based on defined performance levels. White (1973) interpreted scores on a six-point performance scale in terms of a cut score referenced to the earning of credit for a particular course.

criterion measure. An indicator of an agreed-upon performance outcome. Page and Paulus (1968) compared their computer scoring of a set of essays with a criterion measure consisting of the pooled rates of the same essays scored by thirty-two humans (the performance outcome). Course grades and grade-point averages are common criterion measures used as evidence for the validity of holistically scored essays.

dichotomous query scoring. Assignment of binary scores. Any number of individual essay achievements are posed, and the rater responds yes or no to each (e.g., Is there a single thesis?). For a total score, the number of affirmative answers is tallied (Cohen, Sheldon, and Chadbourne 1971).

direct evidence. In writing assessment, direct evidence is gathered from writing performances (often essays) and the scores given to them (Hartog, Rhodes, and Burt 1936).

discrepancy. Difference between the scores given independently by two or more raters other than a match. In adjusted-rater scoring, the test developers establish a discrepancy level that will trigger a third reading to resolve the disagreement. On a six-point scale, adjacent scores (3 and 4) may be treated as a match, and scores more than one score apart (3 and 5) are considered discrepant and adjusted by a third reader. Diederich (1946b) used resolution of discrepant scores in the Comprehensive Examination in English.

distributed ranking. The sorting of essays in a set into a small number of categories (e.g., top, middle, bottom) and then sorted from highest to lowest value in each category, usually with some essays moving from one category to another in the process (Palmer 1961, 211–13).

distribution. Dispersal of scores across a defined score range. Coward (1950) used a given distribution. Britton, Martin, and Rosen (1966) used an open distribution.

ecology. The whole physical and mental context connected with an act of writing. In composing an examination essay, recognition of the ecology of the assessment includes familiarity with the issues in the prompt, knowledge of writing processes, anxiety about writing, temperature of the examination room, distracting noises, hours of sleep before the examination, and other elements that might impact the assessment (Lucas 1988).

error. Difference between approximation and determination. In classical test theory, an error of measurement is the difference between observed and true score. In writing assessment, error often is attributed to two forms: measurement error and rater error.

evidence. Information presented to draw an inference or make a claim. In writing assessment, two types of evidence are often used: direct evidence and indirect evidence.

formal holistic scoring. Use of a scale to assign a single value mark to a whole essay and not separately to individual aspects, with scorers trying to apply the scale consistently, and with the final score for each essay derived from two or more independent ratings (in earliest UK use, Hartog, Rhodes, and Burt [1936]; in more common UK use, Britton, Marten, and Rosen [1966]; in early US use, Diederich [1946b]; in more common US use, Godshalk, Swineford, and Coffman [1966]).

formality. Amount or degree of regulations or preset procedures that govern the scoring of essays. In holistic scoring, two types of formality are often used: formal holistic scoring and informal holistic scoring.

general-impression scoring. Assignment of scores based on overall performance. Holistic scoring without much training, and therefore open, is performed at the rate of two minutes or less per essay. Also called rapid-impression marking (Britton 1963) or rapid-impression reading (Godshalk, Swineford, and Coffman 1966). In both the United Kingdom and the United States, the term was used loosely to refer to practically any sort of holistic scoring.

given distribution. Mandated score dispersal. Before actual scoring, raters are told to approximate their scores to some preset distribution before actual scoring. As Coward (1950) instructed raters, on a 1–10 scale, at least one essay should be scored 1 and one essay should be scored 10. Instructions may also be given so the number of essays in the scoring pool reflect a Gaussian distribution (68 percent of observations in a unimodal curve lie one standard deviation above and one standard deviation below the mean; about 95 percent lie at two standard deviations on either side of the mean; and about 99 percent lie at three standard deviations).

grading. Assignment of value with the use of established parameters. Grades are assigned with the use of a rubric or scoring guide to a preexisting numeric scale, usually academic (e.g., 100 to 1; or A to F) (Valentine and Emmett 1932).

halo effect. As used in early writing-evaluation research, a kind of rating error that occurs when one trait of a writing sample influences the rater's judgment about other traits (Braddock, Lloyd-Jones, and Schoer 1963). Mistakes in grammar, for instance, may lower the reader's judgment about the writer's ability to make an argument. The term was coined by Thorndike (1920).

holism. The tendency in nature to produce wholes from ordered groupings. Philosophically, a whole cannot be defined as a mere collection of its parts, and parts and wholes are interdependent to the extent that change to one part changes everything else. The concept of holism long predated the word coined by Smuts in 1926. The opposing concept has many names, including atomism and Cartesian rationalism.

holistic. The perceptual tendency to organize into wholes. Originally the adjectival form of Smuts's term holism, the term perhaps was first applied to formal holistic scoring by Ann Coward, spelling it "wholistic" (1950, 3; 1951, 83).

holistic scoring. Use of a scale to assign a single value mark to a whole essay and not separately to individual aspects, with scorers trying to apply the scale consistently, and with the final score for each essay derived from two or more independent scorings. As is the case with general impression scoring, the term holistic scoring was used loosely. To focus our analysis in this book, we use the term formal holistic scoring.

indirect evidence. In writing assessment, indirect evidence is gathered from limited responses (often multiple-choice questions) based on elements such as knowledge of conventions, vocabulary recognition, and the ability to revise.

informal holistic scoring. Use of only one reader per essay and reliance chiefly on individual internalized standards (Gray et al. 1982).

interrater agreement. Degree to which two or more independent raters consistently score a writing sample. This measure of consistency targets two or more raters (Myers 1980).

interrater reliability. Degree to which rank ordering of writing samples is consistent across raters. This measure of consistency targets two or more raters (Morrison and Vernon 1941).

interval scale. Scale with equal intervals (Piché et al. 1978). In formal holistic scoring as well as related forms, scales are usually treated as if they were interval.

intrarater reliability. Degree to which the same rater rates the same essay consistently over time. This measure of consistency targets a single rater (Advanced Placement Program 1980).

jangle fallacy. Different words that may or may not refer to the same concept. Defined by Kelley (1927), this problem poses unique and substantial challenges to educational measurement in which different words for the same construct may, in fact, be unwittingly measuring different constructs.

marking. Scoring or grading. The name most commonly used in the United Kingdom (Hartog, Rhodes, and Burt 1936).

matched-criteria ranking. Fitting an essay into a set of exemplar essays already rank ordered according to selected criteria (e.g., style and form in Willing [1918]; or content, structure, and mechanics in Van Wagenen [1923]).

measurement. A dimension obtained by systematic judgment. For Burt, "An approximate estimate on an arbitrary scale of an individual's capacities or attainments" (Hartog, Rhodes, and Burt 1936, 246).

measurement error. Technically, the difference between an observed and true score. More broadly, degree to which a procedure introduces a consistent error. Hughes, Keeling, and Tuck (1983) examined the way that the use of a scoring rubric may be affected by the instructions given to raters, or the order in which raters received and read essays.

nominal scale. Scale with categories that serve as labels (Applebee, Langer, and Mullis 1986).

normal distribution. A unimodal distribution. The normal curve was first defined using errors in attempts to measure an astronomical event by Carl Friedrich Gauss in 1809 and used in 1917 to record chest measurements of Scottish soldiers. As Applebee, Langer, and Mullis note, "In general, holistic scoring produces a roughly normal distribution of scores for the total sample of papers, with scores equally distributed around the center of the scale" (1986, 68). However, actual graphing of a particular holistic scoring often reveals a non-normal curve, with the most frequent score occurring in the 6s on an eight-point scale (Haswell 1998, 241).

norm-referenced score. Evidence based on comparison of an individual test taker's scores with scores from a specific reference group taking the same test. As White noted, "A test normed on Eastern prep school students will probably distort the results when used on a less-advantaged group of students, whatever their writing ability, if the test contains the usual number of questions calling for cultural advantages and an ear for the privileged dialect" (1985, 64).

office-adjusted scoring. Assignment of scores through post-hoc adjustment. Statistically, independent-awarded scores are adjusted after the scoring is over. The scoring of raters can be compared and a leniency/severity "handicap" calculated for each rater, which is then added or subtracted from scores (Hake 1978). Hartog, Rhodes, and Burt (1936) also examined the use of the standard error of measurement as a way to adjust scores (292).

open distribution. Free score dispersal. Raters are allowed to assign any number of scores to any point on the scale (Britton, Martin, and Rosen 1966).

open holistic scoring. Assignment of general impression scores with few constraints. Raters experience relatively few constraints in the form of training, anchor essays, imposed distribution of scores, scoring guides, or rubrics (Hartog, Rhodes, and Burt 1936). Open and controlled mark end points on a continuum of holistic reading procedures.

open ranking. Comparison of essays in a set until all are rank ordered from highest to lowest value (Palmer and Nelson 1958). Usually ties are not allowed.

ordinal scale. Scale with rank-ordered differences in which the degree of difference is not known (Diederich 1949a).

pooled-rater scoring. Assignment of scores from three or more raters relying solely on a shared scale. Also called consensus scoring, collective judgment (Boyd 1924), or multiple marking (Head 1966). In pooled rating, a rater's score represents the perspective of one reader and is taken as no better or worse than another reader's score. The best approximation of the value of an essay is the sum or mean of all scores independently awarded to it (Britton 1963; Hartog, Rhodes, and Burt 1936).

predictive validity. Evidence in which criterion measures are observed at a later date. Breland and Gaynor (1979) examined the relationship between an essay written for the Test of Standard Written English in high school with end-of-the-course grades in first-year college composition to determine the ability of the test to predict course grades.

primary-trait scoring. Assignment of separate scores to different dimensions of writing unique to the writing task. Criteria, each scored on its own scale, are limited by their relevance to the rhetorical requirements established by the writing task. Scores for the criteria may or may not be added for a summative score (Mullis 1976).

profile scoring. Assignment of summed scores using a point-based checklist. Also called multiple-trait scoring, a form of analytic scoring in which raters score an essay using a tabled checklist of specific writing traits that have points assigned for each trait at each scale level, with the final score the sum of those points. The scores on individual traits are retained for post-test use (Hamp-Lyons 1987).

prompt. The specific assignment given to writers. The wording of the prompt, as distinct from the topic upon which the prompt is based, may have distinct effects on the writer (Ruth and Murphy 1988).

ranking. Sorting a set of essays from highest to lowest without the aid of a scale. Ranking is divided into three categories: distributed ranking, matched-criteria ranking, and open ranking.

rater error. Failure of rater consistency. Such failures are classified into two forms: interrater agreement and interrater reliability (Hartog, Rhodes, and Burt 1936).

referencing of scores. Evidence showing scores are related to a criterion measure or reference population. Score referencing falls into two categories: criterion-referenced scores and norm-referenced scores.

reliability. Degree to which a scoring procedure yields consistent and error free results upon repeated application. In writing assessment, evidence of reliability takes five forms: interrater agreement; interrater reliability; intrarater reliability; test reliability; writer reliability.

rubric. Arrangement of selected criteria in an isomorphic tabular format. A rubric is a visual presentation of each criterion, described and scaled in the same way. The scale for organization, for instance, is isomorphic with the scale for ideas (Bossone 1969). When used with holistic scoring, the method is sometimes called focused-holistic (National Assessment of Educational Progress 1998).

sample matching. A process in which essays in a set are assigned a value by fitting them one at a time to a preexisting set of essays arranged from highest to lowest (Hillegas 1912).

scale. A numeric system by which a value or characteristic is reported. Scales fall into three categories: interval scale, nominal scale, and ordinal scale.

scaled criteria. Assignment of scores to individual essay components. Also called schedule of marking (Wallis 1927), analytic schedule (Wiseman 1949), or scoring grid (Harris 1966), raters score using coordinated criteria for each writing component (Boyd 1924).

score. A specific number on a scale used to assess construct proficiency (Diederich 1946b). Also called mark in the United Kingdom.

scoring calculation. Principled method of adjusting or combining scores. Since formal holistic essay scoring has two or more raters independently rating each essay, scoring calculation is used to determine a final score. Scoring calculations fall into four categories: adjusted-rater scoring; consulted-rater scoring; office-adjusted scoring; pooled-rater scoring.

scoring guide. Arrangement of selected criteria in a non-isomorphic tabular format. As an aid for holistic raters, the scoring guide describes the selected criteria in a way that connects to the holistic scale but the connections are not uniform across the criteria (White 1973, 34–35).

test reliability. Degree to which a task achieves the same outcomes (equivalence of forms) when given again with similar test takers under similar testing conditions. This measure of consistency often targets the writing prompt (Davis, Scriven, and Thomas 1981).

topic. Area of inquiry upon which the prompt is based. Examinees may have a strong or weak understanding of the topic, or personal experience with it, introducing the likelihood of topic effects in the scoring of their essays (Braddock, Lloyd-Jones, and Schoer 1963, 9).

trait. Discernible and definable elements of an essay that are scored separately. As discourse features, traits range from forms of argumentation to syntactic variety. Beloved of empirical researchers, traits can be scored on a scale, as well as categorized, although often with some difficulty, as is the case for syntactic forms such as the final free modifier (Faigley 1979).

true score. In classical test theory, the average of the scores that would be earned by a test taker on an unlimited number of parallel tasks (Lord 1980). It goes without saying that the nature of true score varies with the conceptual basis of the task. Breland and Gaynor (1979) provide an estimate of the correlation between an indirect and direct measure of writing by using test-retest alternate-form reliabilities that can, in turn, be used to estimate composite score reliabilities and thus true-score correlations.

validity. "The degree of agreement of a measurement with the thing measured" (Hartog, Rhodes, and Burt 1936, xiv). In early holistic scoring research, this definition—an early form of judging the degree to which an inference based on a score is meaningful—was often parsed into four categories: concurrent validity; construct validity; content validity; and predictive validity.

writer reliability. Degree to which a writer performs consistently on different tests. This measure of consistency targets the writer (Diederich 1946b).

REFERENCES

Advanced Placement Program of the College Board. 1980. *An Informal History of the AP Readings, 1956–76*. New York: College Board.
Allport, Gordon W. 1937. *Personality: A Psychological Interpretation*. New York: Henry Holt.
American Educational Research Association, American Psychological Association, and National Council on Measurement in Education. 2014. *Standards for Educational and Psychological Testing*. Washington, DC: American Educational Research Association.
American Psychological Association Committee on Test Standards. 1952. "Technical Recommendations for Psychological Tests and Diagnostic Techniques: Preliminary Proposal." *American Psychologist* 7 (8): 461–75.
Appia, Kwame Anthony. 2007. *Cosmopolitanism: Ethics in a World of Strangers*. New York: Norton.
Anderson, C. C. 1960. "The New STEP Test as a Measure of Composition Ability." *Educational and Psychological Measurement* 20 (1): 95–102.
Anderson, Harold A., and Arthur E. Traxler. 1940. "Reliability of the Reading of an English Essay Test: A Second Study." *School Review* 48 (7): 521–30.
Applebee, Arthur N., Judith A. Langer, and Ina V. S. Mullis. 1986. *Writing: Trends across the Decade, 1974–84*. Report No. 15-W-01. Princeton, NJ: Educational Testing Service. Web.
Applebee, Arthur N., Judith A. Langer, Ina V. S. Mullis, Andrew S. Latham, and Claudia A. Gentile. 1994. *NAEP 1992 Writing Report Card*. Washington, DC: National Center for Education Statistics. Web.
Armstrong, Sharon Lee, Lila R. Gleitman, and Henry Gleitman. 1983. "On What Some Concepts Might Not Be." *Cognition* 13 (3): 263–308.
Ash, Mitchell G. 1998. *Gestalt Psychology in German Culture, 1890–1967: Holism and the Quest for Objectivity*. Cambridge: Cambridge University Press.
Assessment Reform Group. 1999. *Assessment for Learning: Beyond the Black Box*. Cambridge: University of Cambridge School of Education.
Aull, Laura. 2015. *First-Year University Writing: A Corpus-Based Study with Implications for Pedagogy*. London: Palgrave Macmillan.
Bain, Alexander. 1890. *English Composition and Rhetoric*. New York: D. Appleton.
Baker, E. L., & Quellmalz, E. (1979). Results of Pilot Studies: Effects of Variations in Writing Task Stimuli on the Analysis of Student Writing Performance. Studies in Measurement and Methodology. Work Unit 1: Design and Use of Tests. University of California, Los Angeles: Center for the Study of Evaluation Retrieved from ERIC database (ED 213 728).
Ballard, Philip Boswood. 1923. *The New Examiner*. London: University of London Press.
Ballator, Nada, Marisa Farnum, and Bruce Kaplan. 1999. *NAEP 1996 Trends in Writing: Fluency and Writing Conventions: Holistic and Mechanics Scores in 1984 and 1996*. Washington, DC: National Center for Education Statistics.
Barkaoui, Khled. 2011. "Effects of Marking Method and Rater Experience on ESL Essay Scores and Rater Performance." *Assessment in Education: Principles, Policy & Practice* 18 (3): 279–93.
Barsalou, Lawrence W. 1981. "The Instability of Graded Structure: Implications for the Nature of Concepts." In *Concepts and Conceptual Development: Ecological and Intellectual Factors in Categorization*, edited by Ulric Neisser, 101–49. Cambridge: Cambridge University Press.

Beaton, Albert E., Thomas L. Hilton, and William B. Schrader. 1977. *Changes in the Verbal Abilities of High School Seniors, College Entrants, and SAT Candidates between 1960 and 1972.* New York: College Entrance Examination Board.

Behizadeh, Nadia, and Engelhard, George. 2011. "Historical View of the Influences of Measurement and Writing Theories on the Practice of Writing Assessment in the United States." *Assessing Writing* 16 (3): 189–211.

Behm, Nicholas, and Keith D. Miller. 2012. "Challenging the Frameworks of Color-blind Racism: Why We Need a Fourth Wave of Writing Assessment Scholarship." In *Race and Writing Assessment*, edited by Asao B. Inoue and Mya Poe, 127–38. New York: Peter Lang.

Bejar, Isaac I. 2017. "A Historical Survey of Research Regarding Constructed-Response Formats." In *Advancing Human Assessment: The Methodological, Psychological and Policy Contributions of ETS*, edited by Randy E. Bennett and Matthias von Davier, 565–633. New York: Springer.

Bennett, James R. 1974. "Holistic Criticism." *Style* 8 (2): 287–88.

Bennett, Randy Elliot. 2011. "Formative Assessment: A Critical Review." *Assessment in Education: Principles, Policy & Practice* 18 (1): 5–25.

Berg, Harry D. 1961. "Evaluation in Social Science." In *Evaluation in Higher Education*, edited by Paul L. Dressel, 79–112. Boston: Houghton Mifflin.

Bernstein, Ruby S., and Bernard R. Tanner. 1977. *The California High School Proficiency Examination: Evaluating the Writing Samples.* Curriculum Publication No. 1. Berkeley, CA: Bay Area Writing Project.

Berthoff, Ann E. 1990. "Killer Dichotomies: Reading In/Reading Out." In *Farther Along: Transforming Dichotomies in Rhetoric and Composition*, edited by Kate Ronald and Hephzibah Roskelly, 15–24. Portsmouth, NH: Boynton/Cook.

Bestor, Arthur Eugene. 1953. *Educational Wastelands: The Retreat from Learning in Our Public Schools.* Champaign: University of Illinois Press.

Bhatia, Aban Tavadia. 1977. "Theory of Discourse and the Teaching of English Composition to Undergraduate Students." *CIEFL Bulletin* 13 (2): 59–70.

Black, E. L. 1962. "The Marking of GCE Scripts." *British Journal of Educational Studies* 11 (1): 61–71.

Blickhahn, Kate. 1973. "The Test Takers." *English Journal* 62 (5): 723.

Bloom, Benjamin S., Jane M. Allison, and Paul Diederich. 1950. "Examining." In *The Idea and Practice of General Education: An Account of the College of the University of Chicago*, edited by F. Champion Ward, 273–324. Chicago: University of Chicago Press.

Bolton, Paul. 2012. *Education: Historical Statistics.* House of Commons Library. Web.

Bossone, Richard M. 1966. *Remedial English Instruction in California Public Junior Colleges: An Analysis and Evaluation of Current Practices.* Sacramento: State Department of California.

Bossone, Richard M. 1969. *The Writing Problems of Remedial English Students in Community Colleges of the City University of New York.* New York: CUNY Research and Evaluation Unit for Special Programs.

Bourdieu, Pierre, and Jean Claude Passeron. 1990. *Reproduction in Education, Society, and Culture.* 2nd ed. Thousand Oaks, CA: SAGE.

Bowker, Geoffrey C., and Susan Leigh Star. 2000. *Sorting Things Out: Classification and Its Consequences.* Cambridge, MA: MIT Press.

Boyd, William. 1924. *Measuring Devices in Composition, Spelling and Arithmetic.* London: Harrap.

Boyer, John W. 2011 *"Teaching at a University of a Certain Sort": Education at the University of Chicago over the Past Century.* Occasional Papers on Higher Education XXI. Chicago, IL: The College of the University of Chicago.

Braddock, Richard, and Charles R. Statler. 1968. *Evaluation of College-Level Instruction in Freshman Composition, Part II.* US Office of Education, Cooperative Research Project No. S-260. Iowa City: University of Iowa.

Braddock, Richard, Richard Lloyd-Jones, and Lowell Schoer. 1963. *Research in Written Communication.* Champaign, IL: NCTE.

Brandt, Mark J., Hans IJzerman, Ap Dijksterhuis, Frank J. Farach, Jason Geller, Roger Giner-Sorolla, James A. Grange, Marco Perugini, Jeffrey R. Spies, and Anna van 't Veer. 2014. "The Replication Recipe: What Makes for a Convincing Replication?" *Journal of Experimental Social Psychology* 50: 217–24.

Braungart-Bloom, Diane S. 1984. "Measuring Writing Proficiency: A Registered Holistic Scoring Plan." Paper presented at the Annual Meeting of the American Educational Research Association, New Orleans, LA. ERIC Document No. ED 270 488.

Breland, Hunter. 1977. *Group Comparisons for the Test of Standard Written English.* CEEB Research and Development Report 77–78, No. 1. Princeton, NJ: Educational Testing Service.

Breland, Hunter, and Gail H. Ironson. 1976. "DeFunis Reconsidered: A Comparative Analysis of Alternative Admissions Strategies." *Journal of Educational Measurement* 13 (1): 89–99.

Breland, Hunter, and Judith L. Gaynor. 1979. "A Comparison of Direct and Indirect Assessment of Writing Skill." *Journal of Educational Measurement* 16 (2): 119–28.

Breland, Hunter, et al. 1987. *Assessing Writing Skill.* Research Monograph No. 11. New York: College Entrance Examination Board.

Breland. Hunter M., Melvin Y. Kubota, and Marilyn W. Bonner. 1999. "The Performance Assessment Study in Writing: Analysis of the SAT® II: Writing Subject Test." College Board Report No. 99-4. ETS Research Report No. 99–24.

Bridgeford, Nancy J. 1981. "A Directory of Writing Assessment Consultants." Portland, OR: Northwest Regional Educational Laboratory. ERIC Document No. ED 209 325.

Bridgeman, Brent. 2013. "Human Ratings in Automated Essay Evaluation." In *Handbook of Automated Essay Evaluation: Current Applications and New Directions,* edited by Mark D. Shermis and Jill Burstein, 221–32. New York: Routledge.

Britton, James N. 1955. "The Paper in English Language." *Use of English* 6 (3): 176–84.

Britton, James N. 1963. "Experimental Marking of English Compositions Written by Fifteen-Year-Olds." *Educational Review* 16 (1): 17–23.

Britton, James N., Nancy C. Martin, and Harold Rosen. 1966. *Multiple Marking of English Compositions: An Account of an Experiment.* Schools Council Examinations Bulletin No. 12. London: Her Majesty's Stationery Office.

Broad, Bob. 2003. *What We Really Value: Beyond Rubrics in Teaching and Assessing Writing.* Logan: Utah State University Press.

Brooks, Val. 1980. *Improving the Reliability of Essay Marking: A Survey of the Literature with Particular Reference to the English Language Composition.* CSE Research Project Report 5. Leicester: University of Leicester.

Brown, Rexford. 1975. *Writing Mechanics, 1969–1974: A Capsule Description of Changes in Writing Mechanics.* NAEP Writing Report No. 05-W-01. Denver, CO: Education Commission of the States.

Brown, Rexford. 1978a. "Choosing or Creating an Appropriate Writing Test." In *Basic Writing: Essays for Teachers, Researchers, and Administrators,* edited by Lawrence N. Kasdan and Daniel R. Hoeber, 105–16. Urbana, IL: NCTE.

Brown, Rexford. 1978b. "What We Know Now and How We Could Know More about Writing Ability in America." *Journal of Basic Writing* 1 (4): 1–6.

Brown, Rexford. 1979. *Approaches to the Evaluation of Writing: Some Theoretical Considerations and Practical Suggestions.* Unpublished manuscript. Mimeographed pamphlet.

Brown, Rexford. 1980. *Writing Achievement, 1969–1979: Results from the Third National Writing Assessment, Volume 1: 17-Year-Olds.* NAEP Report No. 10-W-01. Denver, CO: Education Commission of the States.

Brown, Rexford. 1986. "A Personal Statement on Writing Assessment and Educational Policy." In *Writing Assessment: Issues and Strategies*, edited by Karen L. Greenberg, Harvey S. Wiener, and Richard A. Donovan, 44–52. New York: Longman.

Brown, Rexford, Ina Mullis, and Wendy Littlefair. 1976. *Expressive Writing: Selected Results from the Second National Assessment of Writing*. Report No. 05-W-02. Denver, CO: Education Commission of the States.

Bruce, George. 1969. *Secondary School Examinations: Facts and Commentary*. Oxford, UK: Pergamon Press.

Bunn, Geoff, A. D. Lovie, and G. D. Richards, eds. 2001. *Psychology in Britain: Historical Essays and Personal Reflections*. Leicester, UK: The British Psychological Society.

Burry, James, and Edys Quellmalz. 1983. *Assessing Students Writing Skills: The CSE Expository and Narrative Rating Scales*. Los Angeles: UCLA, Center for the Study of Evaluation. ERIC Document No. ED 238 942.

Burstein, Jill, Norbert Elliot, and Hillary Molloy. 2016. "Informing Automated Writing Evaluation Using the Lens of Genre: Two Studies." *CALICO Journal* 33 (1): 117–41.

Burstein, Jill, Norbert Elliot, Beata Beigman Klebanov, Nitin Madnani, Diane Napolitano, Maxwell Schwartz, Patrick Houghton, and Hilary Holloy. 2018. "Writing Mentor: Writing Progress Using Self-Regulated Writing Support." Paper presented at the Annual Meeting of the National Council on Measurement in Education, New York.

Burstein, Jill, Claudia Leacock, and Richard Swartz. 2001. *Automated Evaluation of Essays and Short Answers*. Princeton, NJ: Educational Testing Service.

Burt, Cyril. 1917. *The Distribution and Relations of Educational Abilities: Report by the Educational Officer Submitting Three Preliminary Memoranda*. London: London City Council.

Burt, Cyril. 1921. *Mental and Scholastic Tests: Report by the Education Officer Submitting Three Memoranda*. London: London County Council.

Caldwell, Keith. 1983. "Going Back: An Open Letter." *The Quarterly* 5 (1): 6–8.

California State Department of Education. 1979. *Technical Assistance Guide for Proficiency Assessment*. Sacramento, CA: California State Department of Education.

Campbell, Jay R., Kristen E. Voelkl, and Patricia L. Donahue. 1998. *NAEP 1996 Trends in Academic Progress. Achievement of U.S. Students in Science, 1969 to 1996; Mathematics, 1973 to 1996; Reading, 1971 to 1996; Writing, 1984 to 1996*. Revised. Washington, DC: US Government Printing Office.

Cannadine, David, Jenny Jeating, and Nicola Sheldon. 2011. *The Right Kind of History: Teaching the Past in Twentieth-Century England*. London: Palgrave Macmillan.

Caplan, Rebekah, and Catharine Keech. 1980. *Showing-Telling: A Training Program to Help Students Be Specific*. Collaborative Research Study, No. 2. Berkeley, CA: Bay Area Writing Project.

Carbado, Devon W., and Cheryl I. Harris. 2019. "Intersectionality at 30: Mapping the Margins of Anti-Essentialism, Intersectionality, and Dominance Theory." *Harvard Law Review* 132 (8): 2193–2239.

Carpenter, George R., Franklin T. Baker, and Fred N. Scott. 1903. "Philosophy of the Assignment." In *The Teaching of English in the Elementary and the Secondary School*, 319–26. London: Longmans, Green, and Company.

Cast, B. M. D. 1939. "The Efficiency of Different Methods of Marking English Compositions. Part I." *British Journal of Educational Psychology* 9 (3): 257–69.

Cast, B. M. D. 1940. "The Efficiency of Different Methods of Marking English Compositions. Part II." *British Journal of Educational Psychology* 10 (1): 49–60.

Chafe, William. 1980. "The Deployment of Consciousness in the Production of Narrative." In *The Pear Stories: Cognitive, Cultural and Linguistic Aspects of Narrative Production*, 9–50. Norwood, NJ: Ablex.

Charney, Davida. 1984. "The Validity of Using Holistic Scoring to Evaluate Writing: A Critical Overview." *Research in the Teaching of English* 18 (1): 65–83.

Cheng, Eileen Ka-May. 2012. *Historiography: An Introductory Guide*. London: Bloomsbury.

Cherry, Roger D., and Paul R. Meyer. 1993. "Reliability Issues in Holistic Assessment." In *Validating Holistic Scoring for Writing*, edited by Michael M. Williamson and Brian A. Huot, 109–41. Cresskill, NJ: Hampton.
Chomsky, Noam. 1957. *Syntactic Structures*. The Hague: Mouton.
Chomsky, Noam. 1965. *Aspects of the Theory of Syntax*. Cambridge, MA: MIT Press.
Citizens Advisory Commission. 1959. *Preliminary Progress Report of the Joint Interim Committee on the Public Education System*. Sacramento: Senate of the State of California.
Citizens Advisory Commission. 1961. *Final Report of the Joint Interim Committee on the Public Education System*. Sacramento: Senate of the State of California.
Cleary, T. Anne. 1968. "Test Bias: Prediction of Grades of Negro and White Students in Integrated Colleges." *Journal of Educational Measurement* 5 (2): 115–24.
Coffman, William. 1962. Proposal for a Study of the Feasibility of Reading a Twenty-Minute Essay as Part of the CEEB English Composition Test. Princeton: Educational Testing Service.
Coffman, William E. 1966. "On the Validity of Essay Tests of Achievement." *Journal of Educational Measurement* 3 (3): 151–56.
Cohen, Arthur M., M. Stephen Sheldon, and James P. Chadbourne. 1971. *Factors Accounting for the Variance in Junior College Students' Composition Writing*. Final Report. National Center for Education Research and Development. Dept. of Health, Education, and Welfare, Office of Education. Project O-I-051. Los Angeles: UCLA, School of Education.
Cole, Andrew. 2015. "The Function of Theory at the Present Time." *Publications of the Modern Language Association* 130 (3): 809–18.
Cole, Nancy. 1973. "Bias in Selection." *Journal of Educational Measurement* 10 (4): 237–55.
Collier, David, Jody LaPorte, and Jason Seawright. 2012. "Putting Typologies to Work: Concept Formation, Measurement, and Analytic Rigor." *Political Research Quarterly* 65 (1): 217–32.
Collingwood, R. G. 1947. *The Idea of History*. Oxford: Oxford University Press.
Commins, W. D. 1932. "Some Early Holistic Psychologists." *Journal of Philosophy* 29 (8): 208–17.
Commission on English. 1931. *Examining the Examination in English: A Report to the College Entrance Examination Board*. Cambridge, MA: Harvard University Press.
Committee of Examiners for the English Composition Test. 1962. "The Interlinear Section of the ECT." Memorandum to the Committee on Examinations of the College Entrance Examination Board, May 25. Princeton, NJ: Educational Testing Service.
Comprone, Joseph. 1975. "Cybernetics and Rhetoric: Freshman English in an Overdetermined World." *ADE Bulletin* 46: 22–31.
Congressional Globe. 1867. House of Representatives. Washington, DC: National Archives.
Congressional Record. 2001. May 9. Washington, DC: National Archives.
Conlan, Gertrude. 1976. *The Essay in Tests of Written Ability*. Internal report. Princeton, NJ: Educational Testing Service.
Conlan, Gertrude. 1978. *How the Essay in the CEEB English Test is Scored*. Internal Report. Princeton, NJ: Educational Testing Service.
Conlan, Gertrude. 1988. Draft of a Report by Fred Godshalk. Princeton, NJ: ETS Archives.
Conley, Valerie M., and Linda J. Zimbler. 1997. *1993 National Study of Postsecondary Faculty (NSOPF-93): Characteristics and Attitudes of Instructional Faculty and Staff in the Humanities*. Washington, DC: National Center for Education Statistics.
Conrad, Joseph. 1917. *The Shadow-Line: A Confession*. London: J. M. Dent & Sons.
Cooper, Charles R. 1977. "Holistic Evaluation of Writing." In *Evaluating Writing: Describing, Measuring, Judging*, edited by Charles R. Cooper and Lee Odell, 3–31. Urbana, IL: NCTE.
Cooper, Charles, and Beth Breneman. 1989. "California's New Writing Assessment." *The Quarterly* 11 (9): 9–14, 22.

Cooper, Charles, and Lee Odell. 1977. *Evaluating Writing: Describing, Measuring, Judging.* Urbana, IL: NCTE.

Council of Writing Program Administrators. 1999. "The WPA Outcomes Statement" *WPA: Writing Program Administration* 23 (1/2): 59–66.

Council of Writing Program Administrators, National Council of Teachers of English, and National Writing Project. 2011. *Framework for Success in Postsecondary Writing.*

Cousins, Norman. 1963. "Why Johnny Can't Write." *Saturday Review,* June 8, 20.

Coward, Ann F. 1950. "The Method of Reading the Foreign Service Examination in English Composition." ETS RB-50–57. Princeton, NJ: Educational Testing Service.

Coward, Ann F. 1952. "A Comparison of Two Methods of Grading English Compositions." *Journal of Educational Research* 46 (2): 81–93.

Crenshaw, Kimberle. 1991. "Mapping the Margins: Intersectionality, Identity Politics, and Violence against Women of Color." *Stanford Law Review* 43 (6): 1241–99.

Crew, Louie. 1977. "The New Alchemy." *College English* 38 (7): 707–11.

Cronbach, Lee J. 1960. *Essentials of Psychological Testing.* 2nd ed. New York: Harper and Row.

Cronbach, Lee J., and Paul E. Meehl. 1955. "Construct Validity in Psychological Tests." *Psychological Bulletin* 52 (4): 281–302.

Cronnell, Bruce. 1980. *The Scoring of Writing Samples: A Study.* Los Alamitos, CA: Southwest Regional Laboratory for Educational Research and Development.

Crowley, Sharon. 1985. "writing and Writing." In *Writing and Reading Differently: Deconstruction and the Teaching of Composition and Literature,* edited by D. Douglas Atkins and Michael J. Johnson, 93–100. Lawrence, KA: University Press of Kansas.

Crusius, Timothy W. 1989. *Discourse: A Critique and Synthesis of Major Theories.* New York: Modern Language Association.

Culham, Ruth 2003. *6 + 1 Traits of Writing.* New York: Scholastic Professional Books.

Cushman, Ellen. 2016. "Decolonizing Validity." *The Journal of Writing Assessment* 9 (1). Web.

Daiker, Donald, and Nedra Grogan. 1988. "Discrepancies in Holistic Scoring." *Notes from the National Testing Network* 8: 16.

Daniels, Harvey A. 1983. *Famous Last Words: The American Language Crisis Reconsidered.* Carbondale: Southern Illinois University Press.

Darwin, Francis, ed. 1887. *The Life and Letters of Charles Darwin, Including an Autobiographical Chapter.* Vol. 2. London: John Murray.

Davis, Barbara Gross, Michael Scriven, and Susan Thomas. 1981. *The Evaluation of Composition Instruction.* Pt. Reyes, CA: Edgepress.

Debeer, Dries, Rianne Janssen, and Paul de Boeck. 2017. "Model Skipped and Non-Reached Items Using IRTrees." *Journal of Educational Measurement* 54 (3): 333–63.

Dempster, J. J. B. 1954. *Selection for Secondary Education.* London: Methuen.

Diederich, Paul B. 1946a. "The Construction and Criticism of Comprehensive Examinations." Proposal for Ralph Tyler, dated May 22. Ralph Tyler papers, Box 5, Folder 13, University of Chicago Library Archives.

Diederich, Paul B. 1946b. "The Measurement of Skill in Writing." *School Review* 54 (10): 584–92.

Diederich, Paul B. 1946c. Untitled Memorandum to Ralph Tyler, dated May 12. Ralph Tyler papers, Box 5, Folder 13. University of Chicago Library Archives.

Diederich, Paul B. 1946d. Untitled Memorandum to Ralph Tyler, dated June 21. Ralph Tyler papers, Box 5, Folder 13. University of Chicago Library Archives.

Diederich, Paul B. 1949a. *Toward a Comprehensive Evaluation.* Internal ETS Report. Green File, Series 5, R 15. Princeton, NJ: Educational Testing Service.

Diederich, Paul B. 1949b. "Use of Essays to Measure Improvement." *College English* 10 (7): 395–99.

Diederich, Paul B. 1951. Memo for Mr. Dobbins: The CEEB General Composition Test. Princeton, NJ: Educational Testing Service.

Diederich, Paul B. 1954. "Notes on Grading Essays." Unpublished mimeographed document, dated February 23. Princeton, NJ: Educational Testing Service.

Diederich, Paul B. 1960. "The Rutgers Plan for Cutting Class Size in Two." *English Journal* 49 (4): 229–36, 266.

Diederich, Paul B. 1963. "Innovations in English Teaching." In *Needed Research in the Teaching of English*, edited by Erwin R. Steinberg, 72–79. Washington, DC: Office of Education.

Diederich, Paul B. 1965a. "Reading and Grading." In *Improving English Composition*, edited by Arno Jewett and Charles E. Bish, 81–91. Washington, DC: National Education Association.

Diederich, Paul B. 1965b. "The Use of External Tests in Public Schools in the United States." In *A Common Purpose: The Teaching of English in Great Britain, Canada, and the United States*, edited by James R. Squire, 146–152. Champaign, IL: NCTE.

Diederich, Paul B. 1966. "How to Measure Growth in Writing Ability." *English Journal* 55 (4): 435–49.

Diederich, Paul B. 1969a. "The Development of a National Assessment Program in English." *Research in the Teaching of Writing* 3 (1): 5–14.

Diederich, Paul B. 1969b. "Introduction." In *The Writing Problems of Remedial English Students in Community Colleges of the City University of New York*, by Richard M. Bossone, v. New York: CUNY Research and Evaluation Unit for Special Programs.

Diederich, Paul B. 1974. *Measuring Growth in English*. Urbana, IL: NCTE.

Diederich, Paul B., John W. French, and Sydell Carlton. 1961. *Factors in Judgments of Writing Ability*. Research Bulletin RB-61-15. Princeton, NJ: Educational Testing Service.

Diederich, Paul B., and Osmond E. Palmer. 1963. *Critical Thinking in Reading and Writing*. New York: Holt, Rinehart and Winston.

Dimock, Wai Chee. 2018. "Editor's Column: Historicism, Presentism, Futurism." *Publications of the Modern Language Association* 133 (2): 257–63.

Dorans, Neil J. 2011. "Holland's Advice for the Fourth Generation of Test Theory: Blood Tests Can Be Contests." In *Looking Back: Proceedings of a Conference in Honor of Paul W. Holland*, edited by Neil J. Dorans and Sandip Sinharay, 259–72. New York: Springer.

Douglas, Mary. 1986. *How Institutions Think*. Syracuse, NY: Syracuse University Press.

Dray, William. 1963. "The Historical Explanation of Actions Reconsidered." In *Philosophy and History: A Symposium*, edited by Sidney Hook, 108–10. New York: New York University Press.

Dressel, Paul L. 1954. "Evaluation as Instruction." In *Proceedings of the 1953 Invitational Conference on Testing Problems*, 23–34. Princeton, NJ: Educational Testing Service.

Dressel, Paul L. 1957. "Facts and Fancy in Assigning Grades." *Basic College Quarterly* 2: 6–12.

Dressel, Paul L., ed. 1958. *Evaluation in the Basic College at Michigan State University*. New York: Harper and Brothers.

Dressel, Paul L., ed. 1961. *Evaluation in Higher Education*. Boston, MA: Houghton Mifflin.

Dreyfus, Hubert. 1972. *What Computers Can't Do*. New York: Harper and Row.

Dryer, Dylan. 2013. "Scaling Writing Ability: A Corpus-Driven Inquiry." *Written Communication* 30 (1): 3–35.

Dudley, Martha. 1997. "The Rise and Fall of a Statewide Assessment System." *English Journal* 86 (1): 15–20.

Ebbitt, Wilma R., and Paul B. Diederich. 1950. "The Validity of an Examination in Writing." *College English* 11 (5): 285–86.

Edge, Donald. 1979. *Report of the New Jersey Basic Skills Council*. Trenton: New Jersey State Department of Higher Education. ERIC Document No. ED 185098.

Edgell, Beatrice. 1947. "The British Psychological Society." *British Journal of Psychology* 37 (3): 113–32.

Edgeworth, Francis Ysidro. 1888. "The Statistics of Examinations." *Journal of the Royal Statistical Society* 51 (3): 599–635.

Edgeworth, Francis Ysidro. 1890. "The Element of Chance in Competitive Examinations." *Journal of the Royal Statistical Society* 53 (4): 644–63.

Edwards Penfold, D. M. 1956. "Essay Marking Experiments: Shorter and Longer Essays." *British Journal of Educational Psychology* 26 (2): 128–36.

Elbow, Peter. 1973. *Writing without Teachers.* New York: Oxford University Press.

Eley, Earle G. 1953. "An Analysis of Writing Competence." PhD diss., University of Chicago.

Eley, Earle G. 1955. "The Test Satisfies an Educational Need." *College Board Review* 25: 9–13.

Eley, Earle G. 1956. "Testing the Language Arts." *The Modern Language Journal* 40 (6): 310–15.

Elliot, Norbert. 2005. *On a Scale: A Social History of Writing Assessment in America.* New York: Peter Lang.

Elliot, Norbert. 2014. *Henry Chauncey: An American Life.* New York: Peter Lang.

Elliot, Norbert. 2015. "Validation: The Pursuit." Review of *Standards for Educational and Psychological Testing. College Composition and Communication* 66 (4): 668–77.

Elliot, Norbert. 2016. "A Theory of Ethics for Writing Assessment." *The Journal of Writing Assessment* 9:1. Web.

Elliot, Norbert, Maximino Plata, Paul Zelhart. 1990. *A Program Assessment Handbook for the Holistic Assessment of Writing.* Lanham, MD: University Press of America.

Elliot, Norbert, et al. 2016. "ePortfolios: Foundational Measurement Issues." *The Journal of Writing Assessment* 9 (2).

Elliot, Norbert, Andre A. Rupp, and David M. Williamson. 2015. "Three Interpretative Frameworks: Assessment of English Language Arts-Writing in the Common Core State Standards Initiative." *The Journal of Writing Assessment* 8 (1).

Elman, Benjamin A. 2009. "Eight Legged Essay." In *Berkshire Encyclopedia of China,* vol. 5, edited by Linsun Cheng, 695–98. Great Barrington, MA: Berkshire.

Emig, Janet. 1971. *The Composing Process of Twelfth Graders.* Urbana, IL: NCTE.

Emmett, W. G. 1954. "Secondary Modern and Grammar Schools Performance Predicted by Tests Given in Primary School." *British Journal of Educational Psychology* 24 (2): 91–98.

Ericcson, Patricia Freitag, and Richard H. Haswell, ed. 2006. *Machine Scoring of Student Essays: Truth and Consequences.* Logan: Utah State University Press.

Eysenck, Hans Jürgen. 1939. "The Validity of Judgments as a Function of the Number of Judges." *Journal of Experimental Psychology* 25 (6): 650–54.

Faigley, Lester L. 1979. "Influence of Generative Rhetoric on the Syntactic Maturity and Writing Effectiveness of College Freshmen." *Research in the Teaching of English* 13 (3): 197–206.

Farrell, Edmund J. 1971. "Implications of National Assessment Writing Results." *English Journal* 60 (8): 1116–19.

Farrell, M. J., and N. Gilbert. 1960. "A Type of Bias in Marking Examination Scripts." *British Journal of Educational Psychology* 30 (1): 47–52.

Finder, Morris. 2004. *Educating America: How Ralph W. Tyler Taught America to Teach.* Westport, CT: Praeger.

Finlayson, Douglas Scott. 1951. "The Reliability of the Marking of Essays." *British Journal of Educational Psychology* 21 (2): 126–34.

Fisher, R. A. 1935. *The Design of Experiments.* Oxford: Oliver and Boyd.

Flower, Linda. 1994. *The Construction of Negotiated Meaning: A Social Cognitive Theory of Writing.* Carbondale: Southern Illinois University Press.

Frederick, Vicki. 1979. "Writing Assessment Research Report: A National Survey." Madison: Wisconsin Department of Public Instruction. ERIC Document No. ED 200 988.

Freedman, Sarah W. 1979. "How Characteristics of Student Essays Influence Teachers' Evaluations." *Journal of Educational Psychology* 71 (3): 328–38.

Friedrich, Gerhard. 1959. "Benefits to English Departments of the Advanced Placement Program." *College Composition and Communication* 10 (1): 11–14.

Fuess, Claude M. 1950. *The College Board: Its First Fifty Years.* New York: Columbia University Press.
Gaies, Stephen J. 1980. "College Freshman Writing Ability in 1963 and 1977: A Pilot Study Comparison." Washington, DC: National Institute of Education. ERIC Document No. ED 197 387.
Gallagher, Chris, ed. 2019. "Symposium: Standardization, Democratization, and Writing Programs." *College Composition and Communication* 70 (3): 476–507.
Galton, Francis. 1879. "Psychometric Experiments." *Brain* 2 (2):149–62.
Gannett, Cinthia, and John Brereton. Forthcoming. "Framing, Effacing, and Facing Histories of Rhetoric and Composition: Composition-Rhetoric in the Time of the Dartmouth Conference." In *Talking Back: Senior Scholars and Their Colleagues Deliberate the Past, Present, and Future of Writing Studies,* edited by Norbert Elliot and Alice Horning. Logan: Utah State University Press.
Gee, James Paul. 2012. *Social Linguistics and Literacy: Ideology in Discourses.* 4th ed. New York: Routledge.
Gerber, John C. 1948. "Testing and Evaluation in the Skills of Communication." *College English* 9 (7): 375–84.
Gipps, Caroline V., Stephen Steadman, Tessa Blackstone, and Barry Stierer. 1983. *Testing Children: Standardised Testing in Local Education Authorities and Schools.* London: Heinemann Educational Books.
Glenn, Cheryl. 2018. *Rhetorical Feminism and This Thing Called Hope.* Carbondale: Southern Illinois University Press.
Godshalk, Fred. 1961. Internal ETS memo to Henry Dyer, dated January 30. Princeton, NJ: Educational Testing Service.
Godshalk, Fred I. 1966. *Report of the Chief Reader: English Expression of Foreign Service Officer: Examination NSD2, December, 1965.* Princeton, NJ: Educational Testing Service.
Godshalk, Fred I. 1967. "Reply to the Critics." *Research in the Teaching of English* 1 (1): 84–88.
Godshalk, Fred. 1971. "A Survey of the Effect of the Essay upon ECT Scores." Internal ETS memorandum. Princeton, NJ: Educational Testing Service.
Godshalk, Fred. 1972. "Litmus Blue Books and Acid Tests, or Where are We Now and Why." Princeton, NJ: Educational Testing Service.
Godshalk, Fred I., Frances Swineford, and William E. Coffman. 1961. *A Study of the English Composition Tests of the College Entrance Examination Board as Predictors of an Essay Criterion.* ETS archives, Green File, Roll 13. Princeton, NJ: Educational Testing Service.
Godshalk, Fred I., Frances Swineford, and William E. Coffman. 1965. *Studies of the Question Types in the CEEB English Composition Test as Predictors of an Essay Criterion.* CEEB Research and Development Report RDR-64-5 No. 13. ETS SR-65-20. Princeton, NJ: Educational Testing Service.
Godshalk, Fred I., Frances Swineford, and William E. Coffman. 1966. *The Measurement of Writing Ability.* New York: College Entrance Examination Board.
Grabar, Terry, Leo Hines, and Irene Miranda. 1974. "Measuring Writing Progress: An Experiment." *College English* 35 (4): 484–85.
Graduate Management Admission Council. 2006. *GMAT® Analytic Rubric Study Report.* GMAC® Research Report 06–04.
Graham, Steve, Alisa Bollinger, Carol Booth Olson, Catherine D'Aoust, Charles MacArthur, Deborah McCutchen, and Natalie Olinghouse. 2012. *Teaching Elementary School Students to be Effective Writers: A Practice Guide.* NCEE 2012–4058. Washington, DC: National Center for Education Evaluation and Regional Assistance, Institute of Education Sciences, US Department of Education.
Graham, Steve, Julie Bruch, Linda D. Fitzgerald, Joshua Furgeson, Kathie Greene, James S. Kim, Julia Lyskawa, Carol Booth Olson, and Clair Smither Wulsin. 2016. *Teaching Secondary Students to Write Effectively.* NCEE 2017–4002. Washington, DC: National Center

for Education Evaluation and Regional Assistance, Institute of Education Sciences, US Department of Education.

Gray, James. 2000. *Teachers at the Center: A Memoir of the Early Years of the National Writing Project.* Berkeley, CA: National Writing Project. ERIC Document No. ED 230 576.

Gray, James, et al. 1982. *Properties of Writing Tasks: A Study of Alternative Procedures for Holistic Writing Assessment.* Berkeley, CA: Bay Area Writing Project.

Green, Jan, and Gale Goodrich. 1977. "Appendix C: The Working of a Controlled Essay Reading." In *Comparison and Contrast: The 1976 California State University and Colleges Freshman English Equivalency Examination,* edited by Edward M. White, 68–75. Los Angeles: Office of the Chancellor, the California State University and Colleges. ERIC Document No. ED 227 507.

Greenberg, Karen L., Harvey S. Wiener, and Richard A. Donovan. 1986. *Writing Assessment: Issues and Strategies.* New York: Longman.

Guba, Egon G., and Yvonna S. Lincoln. 1990. *Fourth Generation Evaluation.* Newbury Park, CA: SAGE.

Guite, Malcolm. 2010. *Faith, Hope and Poetry: Theology and the Poetic Imagination.* Abington, UK: Ashgate.

Guo, Hongwen, Paul D. Deane, Peter W. van Rijn, Mo Zhang, and Randy E. Bennett. 2018. "Modeling Basic Writing Processes from Keystroke Logs." *Journal of Educational Measurement* 55 (2): 194–216.

Guttman, L. 1954. "A New Approach to Factor Analysis: The Radex." In *Mathematical Thinking in the Social Sciences,* edited by Paul F. Lazarsfeld, 258–348. Glencoe, IL: Free Press.

Hach, Clarence W. 1960. "Needed: A Sequential Program in Composition." *English Journal* 57 (1): 69–78.

Hacker, Douglas J., Matt C. Keener, and John C. Kircher. 2017. "TRAKTEXT: Investigating Writing Processes Using Eye-Tracking Technology." *Methodological Innovations* 10 (2): 1–18.

Hake, Rosemary. 1978. "With No Apology: Teaching to the Test." *Journal of Basic Writing* 1 (4): 39–62.

Hake, Rosemary. 1986. "How Do We Judge What They Write." In *Writing Assessment: Issues and Strategies,* edited by Karen L. Greenberg, Harvey S. Wiener, and Ronald A. Donovan, 153–67. New York: Longman.

Hammond, J. W. 2018. "Toward a Social Justice Historiography for Writing Assessment." In *Writing Assessment, Social Justice, and the Advancement of Opportunity,* edited by Mya Poe, Asao B. Inoue, and Norbert Elliot, 41–70. Fort Collins, CO: WAC Clearinghouse and University Press of Colorado.

Hampel, Robert L. 2014. *Paul Diederich and the Progressive American High School.* Charlotte, NC: Information Age.

Hamp-Lyons, Liz. 1984. Review of *Testing ESL Composition: A Practical Approach,* by Holly L. Jacobs et al. *Language Testing* 1 (2): 241–44.

Hamp-Lyons, Liz. 1987. *"Testing Second Language Writing in Academic Settings."* PhD diss., University of Edinburgh.

Hamp-Lyons, Liz. 1991. "Reconstructing Academic Writing Proficiency." In *Assessing Second Language Writing in Academic Contexts,* edited by Liz Hamp-Lyons, 127–53. Norwood, NJ: Ablex.

Hamp-Lyons, Liz. 2012. "Linking Writing and Speaking in Assessing English as a Second Language Proficiency." In *Writing Assessment in the 21st Century: Essays in Honor of Edward M. White,* edited by Norbert Elliot and Les Perelman, 385–95. New York: Hampton.

Hamp-Lyons, Liz. 2016a. "Farewell to Holistic Scoring?" *Assessing Writing* 27: A1–A2.

Hamp-Lyons, Liz. 2016b. "Farewell to Holistic Scoring? Part Two: Why Build a House with Only One Brick?" *Assessing Writing* 29: A1–A5.

Hand, Harold. 1965. "National Assessment Viewed as the Camel's Nose." *Phi Delta Kappan* 47 (1): 8–17.
Hanna, Paul R. 1967. "A Response to the Reviewers." *Research in the Teaching of English* 1 (2): 214–23.
Hansard. 1944. *The Official Report of Debates in Parliament, House of Commons Debate, 19 January.* Vol. 396. Web.
Harms, Keith L. 2018. "Assessment's Hard Work: Early Twentieth Century American Imperialism and the Colonial Function of the Monolingual Writing Construct." In *Writing Assessment, Social Justice, and the Advancement of Opportunity,* edited by Mya Poe, Asao B. Inoue, and Norbert Elliot, 71–104. Fort Collins, Colorado: WAC Clearinghouse and University Press of Colorado.
Harned, Jon. 1986/1987. "Should English Teachers Oppose Minimal Competency Writing Tests?" *CEA Forum* 16 (4): 10–12.
Harris, David P. 1966. "The Testing of Student Writing Ability." In *Reflections on High School English,* edited by Gary Tate, 137–45. Tulsa, OK: University of Tulsa Press.
Hart, Gary K. 1978. "The California Pupil Proficiency Law as Viewed by Its Author." *Phi Delta Kappan* 59 (9): 592–95.
Hart, Ray, Michael Casserly, Renata Uzzell, Moses Palacios, Amanda Corcoran, and Liz Spurgeon. 2015. *Student Testing in America's Great City Schools: An Inventory and Preliminary Analysis.* Washington, DC: Council of the Great City Schools.
Hartog, Philip Joseph. 1918. *Examinations and their Relation to Culture and Efficiency.* London: Constable.
Hartog, Philip Joseph, Edmond Cecil Rhodes, and Cyril L. Burt. 1936. *The Marks of Examiners: Being a Comparison of Marks Allotted to Examination Scripts by Independent Examiners and Boards of Examiners, together with a Section on a Viva Voce Examination.* London: Macmillan.
Haswell, Richard H. 1988. "Contrasting Ways to Appraise Improvement in a Writing Course: Paired Comparison and Holistic." Paper presented at the Annual Meeting of the Conference on College Composition and Communication, St. Louis, MO. ERIC Document No. ED 294 215.
Haswell, Richard H. 1991. *Gaining Ground in College Writing: Tales of Development and Interpretation.* Dallas, TX: Southern Methodist University Press.
Haswell, Richard H. 1998. "Rubrics, Prototypes, and Exemplars: Categorization Theory and Systems of Writing Placement." *Assessing Writing* 5 (2): 231–69.
Haswell, Richard H. 2005. "NCTE/CCCC's Recent War on Scholarship." *Written Communication* 22 (2): 198–223.
Haswell, Richard H. 2006a. "Automatons and Automated Scoring: Drudges, Black Boxes, and *Dei Ex Machina.*" In *Machine Scoring of Student Essays: Truth and Consequences,* edited by Patricia Freitag Ericcson and Richard H. Haswell, 57–78. Logan: Utah State University Press.
Haswell, Richard H. 2006b. "On Writing Assessment and Writing Assessment." Review of *On a Scale: A Social History of Writing Assessment in America,* by Norbert Elliot. *Assessing Writing* 11: 140–44.
Haswell, Richard H., and Norbert Elliot. 2017. "Innovation and the California State University and Colleges English Equivalency Examination, 1973–1981: An Organizational Perspective." *The Journal of Writing Assessment* 10 (1). Web.
Haswell, Richard H., and Norbert Elliot. 2019. *Holistic Scoring of Written Discourse to 1985.* WPA-CompPile Research Bibliographies, no. 27. Web.
Haswell, Richard H., Susan Wyche-Smith, and Robin Magnuson. 1992. *Follow-up Study of the Washington State University Writing Placement Examination.* Internal report dated June 11. Pullman: Washington State University, Department of English.
Hayhoe, Mike. 1982. "A Historical Review of Essay Marking." In *New Directions in English Teaching,* edited by Anthony Adams, 99–109. Barcombe, UK: Falmer.

Hays, Frank Jr. 1962. "The Theme-a-Week Assumption: A Report of an Experiment." *English Journal* 51 (5): 320–22.

Head, J. J. 1966. "Multiple Marking of an Essay Item in Experimental 'O'-level Nuffield Biology Examinations." *Educational Review* 19 (1): 65–71.

Heenan, David K. 1961. "Evaluation in the Humanities." In *Evaluation in Higher Education*, edited by Paul L. Dressel, 157–91. Boston: Houghton Mifflin.

Heider, Grace M. 1977. "More about Hull and Koffka." *American Psychologist* 32 (5): 383–83.

Helmholtz, Hermann. (1847) 1971. "On the Conservation of Force: A Physical Memoir." *Selected Writings*, 3–55. Translated by John Tyndall. Middletown, CT: Wesleyan University Press.

Hendricks, Cecilia Hennel. 1940. "Exemption from Required Composition." *College English* 1 (7): 604–16.

Herbert, Auberon. 1889. *The Sacrifice of Education to Examinations: Letters from "All Sorts and Conditions of Men."* London: Williams and Norgate.

Heritage, Margaret, and Carolyne Wiley. 2018. "Reaping Benefits of Assessment for Learning: Achievement, Identity, and Equity." *ZDM: Mathematics Education* 50 (2): 729–41.

Hess, S. J. 2006. "Civilian Evacuation to Devon in the Second World War." PhD diss., University of Exeter.

Hickman, Mary Ann. 1972. "Study of the Relationships between Selected Antecedent Variables and the Language Skills Examination of the University System of Georgia." PhD diss., University of Georgia.

Hillegas, Milo Burdette. 1912. "A Scale for the Measurement of Quality in English Composition by Young People." *Teachers College Record* 13 (4): 1–55.

Hillocks, George Jr. 1986. *Research on Written Composition: New Directions in Teaching*. Urbana, IL: ERIC Clearinghouse on Reading and Communication Skills and National Conference on Research in English.

Holland, Bart K. 2002. *What Are the Changes? Voodoo Deaths, Office Gossip, and Other Adventures in Probability*. Baltimore: Johns Hopkins University Press.

Huddleston, Edith M. 1952. *Measurement of Writing Ability at the College-Entrance Level: Objective vs. Subjective Testing Techniques*. Princeton, NJ: Educational Testing Service.

Hudelson, Earl. 1923. "English Composition: Its Aims, Methods and Measurement." Yearbook of the National Society for Studies in Education, 22, Part 1. Bloomington, IL: Public Schools.

Hughes, David C., Brian Keeling, and Bryan F. Tuck. 1983. "The Effects of Instructions to Scorers Intended to Reduce Context Effects in Essay Scoring." *Educational and Psychological Measurement* 43 (4): 1047–50.

Hunt, Kellogg W. 1965. *Grammatical Structures Written at Three Grade Levels*. NCTE Research Report No. 3. Champaign, IL: NCTE.

Huot, Brian. 1990. "The Literature of Direct Writing Assessment: Major Concerns and Prevailing Trends." *Review of Educational Research* 60 (2): 237–63.

Huot, Brian. 1993. "The Influence of Holistic Scoring Procedures on Reading and Rating Student Essays." In *Validating Holistic Scoring for Writing Assessment: Theoretical and Empirical Foundations*, edited by Michael Williamson and Brian Huot, 206–36. Cresskill, NJ: Hampton Press.

Huot, Brian A. 2002. *(Re)Articulating Writing Assessment*. Logan: Utah State University Press.

Huot, Brian A., Peggy O'Neill, and Cindy Moore. 2010. "A Usable Past for Writing Assessment." *College English* 72 (5): 495–517.

Inglis, Sidney A. 2011. "A Political Firestorm Surrounds the Fisher Credential Reform (1950–1961)." In *A History of Policies and Forces Shaping California Teacher Credentialing*, edited by Helen Grant, 32–57. Sacramento: Commission on Teacher Credentialing, California Department of Education.

Inoue, Asao B. 2019. "How Do We Language So People Stop Killing Each Other, Or What Do We Do about White Language Supremacy?" Paper Presented at the Annual Meeting of the Conference on College Composition and Communication, Pittsburgh, PA.

Jackson, Brian, and Dennis Marsden. 1962. *Education and the Working Class: Some General Themes Raised by a Study of 88 Working-Class Children in a Northern Industrial City*. London: Harmondsworth.

Jacobs, Holly L., et al. 1981. *Testing ESL Composition: A Practical Approach*. Rowley, MA: Newbury House.

Jakobson, Roman. 1963. "Parts and Wholes in Language." In *Parts and Wholes: The Hayden Colloquium on Scientific Method and Concepts*, edited by Daniel Lerner, 157–62. New York: Free Press of Glencoe.

Jamison, Elizabeth B. 2015. "1890–1969—Early History of the Advanced Placement Program: An Argument for Reform of the AP Language and Composition Exam." PhD diss., Georgia State University.

Jewell, Ross M., John Cowley, and Gordon Rhum. 1966. *The Effectiveness of College-Level Instruction in Freshman Composition*. Interim Report, Project No. 2188. Washington, DC: US Department of Health, Education, and Welfare.

Jiles, Paulette. 1995. *North Spirit: Travels among the Cree and Ojibway Nations and Their Star Maps*. Toronto: Doubleday Canada.

Jin, Yan. 2014. "The Accidental Language Tester: An Interview with Liz Hamp-Lyons." *Language Assessment Quarterly* 11 (3): 338–51.

Kane, Michael T. 2013. "Validating the Interpretations and Uses of Test Scores." *Journal of Educational Measurement* 50 (1): 1–70.

Kant, Immanuel. 1783–2004. *Prolegomena to Any Future Metaphysics, with Selections from the Critique of Pure Reason*. Translated by Gary Hatfield. Cambridge: Cambridge University Press.

Katz, Irvin R., and Norbert Elliot. 2016. "Information Literacy in Digital Environments: Construct Mediation, Construct Modeling, and Validation Processes." In *Information Literacy: Research and Collaboration across Disciplines*, edited by Barbara J. D'Angelo et al., 93–111. Fort Collins: The WAC Clearinghouse and University Press of Colorado.

Keech, Catharine. 1978. "Michael's Criterion List for Evaluating Written Composition." Memorandum. In *Evaluation of the Bay Area Writing Project: Rubrics for Writing Assessment: A Technical Report*, Michael Scriven et al., Appendixes A5–A8. Berkeley, CA: Bay Area Writing Project.

Keech, Catharine. 1979a. "Rubrics for Writing Assessment." In *Evaluation of the Bay Area Writing Project: A Technical Report*, Michael Scriven et al., Appendix B. San Francisco: Evaluation Institute.

Keech, Catharine. 1979b. "Scoring Guides for General Impression Marking." In *Evaluation of the Bay Area Writing Project: A Technical Report*, Michael Scriven, Appendix B. San Francisco: Evaluation Institute

Keech, Catharine. 1979c. "Holistic Assessment and Proficiency Testing." *The Quarterly* 1 (3): 4–6.

Keech, Catharine. 1982. "Practices in Designing Writing Test Prompts: Analysis and Recommendations." In *Properties of Writing Tasks: A Study of Alternative Procedures for Holistic Writing Assessment*, edited by James Gray and Leo Ruth, 132–213. Berkeley, CA: Bay Area Writing Project.

Keech, Catharine, and Mary Ellen McNelly. 1982. "Comparison and Analysis of Rater Responses to Anchor Papers in the Writing Prompt Variation Study." In *Properties of Writing Tasks: A Study of Alternative Procedures for Holistic Writing Assessment*, edited by James Gray and Leo Ruth, 259–315. Berkeley, CA: Bay Area Writing Project.

Kelley, Truman Lee. 1927. *Interpretation of Educational Measurements*. Yonkers, NY: World Book.

REFERENCES

Kelly-Riley, Diane, Norbert Elliot, and Alex Rudniy. 2016. "An Empirical Framework for ePortfolio Assessment." *International Journal of ePortfolio* 6 (2), 95–116.

Kennedy, John F. 1963, June 11. A Report to the American People on Civil Rights. Radio and television address. New York: Columbia Broadcasting System.

Kennedy, Theodore. 1992. "Brief Biographical Sketches of Deceased and Retired Faculty, Department of American Thought & Language: Osmond Palmer, 1907–1974." Box 17, Folder 55. Michigan State University Archives.

Keppel, Francis. 1966. *The Necessary Revolution in American Education.* New York: Harper and Row.

Kessen, William. 1960. "Research Design in the Study of Developmental Problems." In *Handbook of Research Methods in Child Development*, edited by Paul Henry Mussen, 36–70. New York: Wiley

Kincaid, Gerald L. 1953. "Some Factors Affecting Variations in the Quality of Students' Writing." PhD diss., Michigan State University.

Kinneavy, James A. 1971. A *Theory of Discourse: The Aims of Discourse.* Englewood Cliffs, NJ: Prentice Hall.

Kitzhaber, Albert R. 1963. *Themes, Theories, and Therapy: Teaching of Writing in College.* New York: McGraw-Hill.

Klinkenborg, Verlyn. 1993. Introduction to *Turning toward Home: Reflections on the Family from Harper's Magazine*, edited by Katharine Whittemore and Ilena Silverman, 1–8. New York: Franklin Square.

Koffka, Kurt. 1922. "Perception: An Introduction to *Gestalt-Theorie*." *Psychological Bulletin* 19 (10): 531–85.

Köhler, Wolfgang. 1947. *Gestalt Psychology: An Introduction to New Concepts in Modern Psychology.* New York: New American Library.

Kridel, Craig, and Robert V. Bullough. 2007. *Stories of the Eight-Year Study: Reexamining Secondary Education in America.* Albany: State University of New York Press.

Kvernbekk, Tone. 2017. "Evidence-Based Educational Practice." In *Oxford Research Encyclopedia of Education*, edited by George W. Noblit, 1–21. Oxford: Oxford University Press.

Labov, William. 1972. *Language in the Inner City: Studies in the Black English Vernacular.* Philadelphia: University of Pennsylvania Press,

Lamb, H. 1953. "The English Essay in Secondary Selection Examinations: A Comparison of Two Systems of Marking." *British Journal of Educational Psychology* 23 (2): 131–33.

Lang, Albert R. 1930. *Modern Methods in Written Examinations.* NY: Houghton Miffllin.

Latour, Bruno. 1987. *Science in Action: How to Follow Scientists and Engineers through Society.* Cambridge, MA: Harvard University Press.

Law, Alexander I. 1977. *The Assessment of the Writing Performance of California High School Seniors.* Sacramento: Office of Program Evaluation and Research, California State Department of Education.

Lawley, Derek N. 1943. "On Problems Connected with Item Selection and Test Construction." *Proceedings of the Royal Statistical Society of Edinburgh* 61 (2): 273–87.

Lawton, Denis. 2005. *Education and Labor Party Ideologies: 1900–2001 and Beyond.* Abingdon, UK: Routledge Falmer.

Lazarín, Melissa. 2014. *Testing Overload in America's Schools.* Washington, DC: Center for American Progress.

Lederman, Marie Jean.1986. "Why Test?" In *Writing Assessment: Issues and Strategies*, edited by Karen L. Greenberg, Harvey S. Wiener, and Richard A. Donovan, 35–43. New York: Longman.

Linde, Charlotte. 1997. "Narrative: Experience, Memory, Folklore." *Journal of Narrative and Life Story* 7 (1–4): 281–89.

Lloyd-Jones, Richard. 1977. "Primary Trait Scoring." In *Evaluating Writing: Describing, Measuring, Judging*, edited by Charles R. Cooper and Lee Odell, 33–66. Urbana, IL: NCTE.

Lord, Frederick M. 1980. *Applications of Item Response Theory to Practical Testing Problems*. Mahwah, NJ: Lawrence Erlbaum.

Lubar, Steven. 1992. "'Do Not Fold, Spindle or Mutilate': A Cultural History of the Punch Card." *Journal of American Culture* 15 (4): 43–55.

Lucas, Catharine [Keech]. 1982. "Unexpected Directions of Change in Student Writing Performance." In *Properties of Writing Tasks: A Study of Alternative Procedures for Holistic Writing Assessment*, edited by James Gray and Leo Ruth, 386–471. Berkeley, CA: Bay Area Writing Project.

Lucas, Catharine [Keech]. 1984. "Apparent Regression in Student Writing Performance as a Function of Unrecognized Changes in Task Complexity." PhD diss., University of California, Berkeley.

Lucas, Catharine [Keech]. 1988. "Toward Ecological Evaluation." *The Quarterly*, 10 (1); 1–3, 12–17 and 10 (2): 4–10.

Lunsford, Karen J. 2017. Foreword to *Points of Departure: Rethinking Student Source Use and Writing Studies Research Methods*, edited by Tricia Serviss and Sandra Jamieson, xiii–xx. Logan: Utah State University Press.

Lutz, William D. 1980. "How to Read 55,000 Essays a Year, and Love It." Washington, DC: Government Printing Office. ERIC Document No. ED 185 563.

Lynd, Albert. 1953. *Quackery in the Public Schools*. New York: Little, Brown.

Mackenzie, Clayton G. 2006. "The Eleven-plus Examination in Developing Countries: A Case Study." *Educational Studies* 15 (3): 281–300.

Marcuse, Herbert. 1964. *One-Dimensional Man: Studies in the Ideology of Advanced Industrial Society*. Boston: Beacon.

Martin, W. Don. 1972. "The Sex Factor in Grading Composition." *Research in the Teaching of English* 6 (1): 36–47.

Maslow, Abraham H. 1943. "Dynamics of Personality Organization," *Psychological Review* 50 (5): 514–39.

Maslow, Abraham. 1962. *Toward a Psychology of Being*. New York: Van Nostrand.

Mather, Donald Raymond, Norman France, and G. T. Sare. 1965. *The Certificate of Secondary Education: A Handbook for Moderators*. London: Collins.

Maxwell, Scott E. 2000. "Sample Size and Multiple Regression Analysis." *Psychological Methods* 5 (4): 434–58.

McAdams, Dan P. 1993. *The Stories We Live By: Personal Myth and the Making of the Self*. New York: Morrow.

McColly, William. 1970. "Roundtable Review." *Research in the Teaching of English* 4 (1): 69–78.

McColly, William, and Robert Remstad. 1963. *Comparative Effectiveness of Composition Skills Learning Activities in the Secondary School*. Final Report, US Office of Education Cooperative Research Project 1528. Madison, WI: University of Wisconsin.

McCready, Michael A., and Virginia S. Melton. 1981. "Feasibility of Assessing Writing Using Multiple Assessment Techniques." Ruston: Louisiana Tech University. ERIC Document No. ED 220 871.

McLean, Kate C., and Monisha Pasupathi, eds. 2010. *Narrative Development in Adolescence: Creating the Storied Self*. New York: Springer.

McMahon, D. 1953. "Educational Selection and Allocation." In *Current Trends in British Psychology*, edited by C. A. Mace and Philip E. Vernon, 45–58. London: Methuen.

McNeil, William H. 2007. *Hutchins' University: A Memoir of the University of Chicago, 1929–1950*. Chicago, IL: University of Chicago Press.

Meadows, Michelle, and Lucy Billington. 2005. *A Review of the Literature on Marking Reliability*.

Mellon, John C. 1972. "Roundtable Review." *Research in the Teaching of English* 6 (1): 86–106.

Mellon, John C. 1975. *National Assessment and the Teaching of English: Results of the First National Assessment of Educational Progress in Writing, Reading, and Literature—Implications for Teaching and Measurement in the English Language Arts.* Urbana, IL: NCTE.

Messick, Samuel. 1989. "Validity." In *Educational Measurement*, 3rd ed., edited by Robert L. Linn, 13–103. New York: American Council on Education and Macmillan.

Meyerson, Rolf, and Elihu Katz. 1957. "Notes on a Natural History of Fads." *American Journal of Sociology* 62 (6): 594–601.

Mielenz, Mary Luella. 1939. "An Analysis of Background Factors and Their Possible Influence on Placement in Freshman English at the University of Nebraska–Lincoln." PhD diss., University of Nebraska.

Miller, Carolyn. 1984. "Genre as Social Action." *Quarterly Journal of Speech* 70:151–67.

Miller, David L. 2013. *Introduction to Collective Behavior and Collective Action.* 3rd ed. Long Grove, IL: Waveland.

"Minimum Essentials." 1921. *English Journal* 10 (9): 540–41.

Mislevy, Robert J. 2007. "Validity from the Perspective of Model-Based Reasoning." CRESST Report 752. Los Angeles: University of California, National Center for Research on Evaluation, Standards, and Student Testing.

Mislevy, Robert J. 2009. "Validity from the Perspective of Model-Based Reasoning." In *The Concept of Validity: Revisions, New Directions and Applications*, edited by Robert W. Lissitz, 83–108. Charlotte, NC: Information Age Publishing.

Mislevy, Robert J. 2017. *Sociocognitive Foundations of Educational Measurement.* New York: Routledge.

Mitchell, Richard. 1979. "The Three-Mile Island Syndrome." *Underground Grammarian* 3 (5).

Modu, Christopher C., and Eric Wimmers. 1981. "The Validity of the Advanced Placement English Language and Composition Examination." *College English* 43 (6): 609–20.

Molloy, Sean. 2018. "'Human Beings Engaging with Ideas': The 1960s SEEK Program as a Precursor Model of Ecological and Sociocultural Writing Pedagogy and Assessment." In *Writing Assessment, Social Justice, and the Advancement of Opportunity*, edited by Mya Poe, Asao B. Inoue, and Norbert Elliot, 71–104. Fort Collins, CO: WAC Clearinghouse and University Press of Colorado.

Morgan, Kerry L. 1985. *The Constitution and Federal Jurisdiction in American Education.* Lonang Institute.

Morris, William, Curt Greve, Elliot Knowles, and Brian Huot. 2015. "An Analysis of Writing Assessment Books Published before and after the Year 2000." *Teaching English in the Two-Year College* 43 (2): 118–40.

Morrison, R. J., and Philip E. Vernon. 1941. "A New Method of Marking English Compositions." *British Journal of Educational Psychology* 11 (2): 109–19.

Morton, Andrew. 1980. *Frames of Mind: Constraints on the Common-Sense Conception of the Mental.* Oxford: Clarendon.

Moslemi, Marlene H. 1975. "The Grading of Creative Writing Essays." *Research in the Teaching of English* 9 (2): 154–61.

Mullis, Ina V. S. 1976. "The Primary Trait System for Scoring Writing Tasks." Washington, DC: Office of Education. ERIC Document No. ED 124 942.

Myers, Albert E., Carolyn B. McConville, and William E. Coffman. 1966. "Simplex Structure in the Grading of Essay Tests." *Educational and Psychological Measurement* 26: 41–54.

Myers, Miles. 1980. *A Procedure for Writing Assessment and Holistic Scoring.* Urbana, IL: NCTE.

Nail, Pat, Rodney Fitch, John Halverson, Phil Grant, and N. Field Winn. 1960. *A Scale for Evaluation of High School Student Essays.* Champaign, IL: NCTE.

National Assessment of Educational Progress. 1975. *Writing Mechanics, 1969–1974: A Capsule Description of Changes in Writing Mechanics.* Writing Report No, 05-W-01. Washington, DC: US Government Printing Office. ERIC Document No. ED 113 736.

National Assessment of Educational Progress. 1978. *The Second National Assessment of Writing: New and Reassessed Exercises with Technical Information.* Washington, DC: National Center for Education Statistics.

National Assessment of Educational Progress. 1981. *The Third Assessment of Writing, 1978–79: Released Exercise Set.* Denver: Education Commission of the States.

National Assessment of Educational Progress. 2000. "Scoring of Twelfth-grade Persuasive Writing." *NAEPFacts* 5 (3): 1–6.

National Assessment Governing Board. 2011. *Writing Framework for the 2011 National Assessment of Educational Progress.* Washington, DC: National Assessment Governing Board.

National Union of Teachers. 1949. *Transfer from Primary to Secondary Schools.* London: Evans.

Neisser, Ulrich. 1967. *Cognitive Psychology.* New York: Appleton-Century-Crofts.

Nelson, Clarence H. 1961. "Evaluation in Natural Sciences." In *Evaluation in Higher Education,* edited by Paul L. Dressel, 113–56. Boston: Houghton Mifflin.

Nelson, Howard. 2013. *Testing More, Teaching Less: What America's Obsession with Student Testing Costs in Money and Lost Instructional Time.* Washington, DC: American Federation of Teachers.

Newkirk, Thomas. 1979. "How Competent Are the Writing Competency Tests?" Paper presented at the Alabama Symposium on English and American Literature, Alabama, October 18–20. ERIC Document No. ED 179 958.

Newkirk, Thomas. 2009. *Holding On to Good Ideas in a Time of Bad Ones: Six Literacy Principles Worth Fighting For.* Portsmouth, NH: Heinemann.

Newton, Paul. 2017. "There Is More to Educational Measurement than Measuring: The Importance of Embracing Purpose Pluralism." *Educational Measurement: Issues and Practice.* 26 (2): 5–15.

Nisbet, John Donald. 1955. "English Composition in Secondary School Selection." *British Journal of Educational Psychology* 25 (1): 51–54.

Nold, Ellen W., and Sarah W. Freedman. 1977. "An Analysis of Readers' Responses to Essays." *Research in the Teaching of English* 11 (2): 164–74.

Norris, Eleanor L. 1969. *Writing Objectives.* Committee on Assessing the Progress of Education. Denver: Education Commission of the States.

Noyes, Edward S. 1966. "Introduction." In *The Measurement of Writing Ability,* by Fred I. Godshalk, Frances Swineford, and William E. Coffman, iv–vi. New York: College Entrance Examination Board.

Noyes, Edward S., William Meritt Sale, and John M. Stalnaker. 1945. *Report on the First Six Tests in English Composition, with Sample Answers from the Tests of April and June.* New York: College Entrance Examination Board.

Nulton, Karen S., and Irvin Peckham. 2017. "Writing Program Assessment, Attitude, and Construct Representation: A Descriptive Study." In *Writing Assessment, Social Justice, and the Advancement of Opportunity,* edited by Mya Poe, Asao B. Inoue, and Norbert Elliot, 293–314. Fort Collins, CO: WAC Clearinghouse and University Press of Colorado. Web.

Nystrand, Martin. 1977. *Assessing Written Communicative Competence: A Textual Cognition Model.* Toronto: Ontario Institute for Studies in Education. ERIC Document No. ED 133 732.

Office of Qualifications and Examinations Regulation. 2014. *Review of Double Marking Research.* Coventry: Ofqual. Web.

O'Hare, Frank. 1973. *Sentence Combining: Improving Student Writing without Formal Grammar Instruction.* Champaign, IL: NCTE.

Olsen, Marjorie. 1956. *Summary of Main Findings on the Validity of the 1955 College Board General Composition Test.* Statistical Report 56-9. Princeton, NJ: Educational Testing Service.

Page, Ellis, and Dieter Paulus. 1968. *The Analysis of Essays by Computer.* Final report of Project No. 6–1318. Washington, DC: US Department of Health, Education and Welfare.

Palmer, Orville. 1962. "College Entrance English Examinations in America." *Use of English* 13 (4): 219–27.

Palmer, Osmond E. 1961. "Evaluation of Communication Skills." In *Evaluation in Higher Education*, edited by Paul L. Dressel, 192–226. Cambridge, MA: Riverside.

Palmer, Osmond E., and Clarence Nelson. 1958. "In Courses of Course." In *Evaluation in the Basic College at Michigan State University*, edited by Paul L. Dressel, 116–35. New York: Harper and Brothers.

Partnership for Assessment of Readiness for College and Careers. 2016. *Guide to English Language Arts/Literacy Released Items: Understanding Scoring.*

Peacocke, Christopher. 1979. *Holistic Explanation: Action, Space, Interpretation.* Oxford: Clarendon.

Peckham, Irvin. 1987. "Statewide Direct Writing Assessment." *English Journal* 76 (8): 30–33.

Pedley, R. R. 1949. "English in Exams 1: The General Certificate." *Use of English* 1 (1): 35–39.

Percival, E. 1966. "The Dimensions of Ability in English Composition." *Education Review* 18 (3): 205–12.

Perelman, Les. 2012. "Mass-Market Writing Assessments as Bullshit." In *Writing Assessment in the 21st Century: Essays in Honor of Edward M. White*, edited by Norbert Elliot and Les Perelman, 425–37. New York: Hampton.

Perelman, Les. 2013. "Critique of Mark D. Shermis & Ben Hamner, 'Contrasting State-of-the-Art Automated Scoring of Essays: Analysis.'" *The Journal of Writing Assessment* 6 (1). Web.

Perkins, Kyle. 1983. "On the Use of Composition Scoring Techniques, Objective Measures, and Objective Tests to Evaluate ESL Writing Ability." *TESOL Quarterly* 17 (4): 651–71.

Persky, Hilary. 2012. "Writing Assessment in the Context of the National Assessment of Educational Progress." In *Writing Assessment in the 21st Century: Essays in Honor of Edward M. White*, edited by Norbert Elliot and Les Perelman, 69–86. New York: Hampton.

Phelps, Louise Wetherbee. 1988. *Composition as a Human Science: Contributions to the Self-Understanding of a Discipline.* New York: Oxford University Press.

Piché, Gene, Donald L. Rubin, Lona J. Turner, and Michael L. Michlin. 1978. "Teachers' Subjective Evaluations of Standard and Black Nonstandard English Compositions: A Study of Written Language Attitudes." *Research in the Teaching of English* 12 (2): 107–18.

Pidgeon, Douglas A., and Alfred Yates. 1956. "Experimental Inquiries into the Use of Essay-Type English Papers." *British Journal of Educational Psychology* 26 (3): 37–47.

Pilkington, Gwendoline. 1967. "The Problem of Subjectivity in Marking in English Composition and the Effects of Using a Rapid Impressionistic Evaluation Procedure by Suitably Paired Markers." Master's thesis, McGill University, Montreal.

Poe, Mya, and John Cogan. 2016. "Civil Rights and Writing Assessment: Using the Disparate Impact Approach as a Fairness Methodology to Evaluate Social Impact." *The Journal of Writing Assessment* 9 (1).

Poe, Mya, Norbert Elliot, John Aloysius Cogan, and Tito G. Nurudeen. 2014. "The Legal and the Local: Using Disparate Impact Analysis to Understand the Consequences of Writing Assessment." *College Composition and Communication* 65 (4): 588–611.

Poe, Mya, Asao B. Inoue, and Norbert Elliot. 2018. *Writing Assessment, Social Justice, and the Advancement of Opportunity.* Perspectives on Writing. Fort Collins, CO: WAC Clearinghouse and University Press of Colorado.

Polkinghorne, Donald E. 1988. *Narrative Knowing and the Human Sciences.* Albany: SUNY Press.

Prather, James E., and G. Glynton Smith. 1975. *Factors Influencing Student Performances on a Language Skills Examination: The Regents' Test.* Atlanta: Office of Institutional Planning.

Purnell, Rosentene. 1982. "A Survey of the Testing of Writing Proficiency in College: A Progress Report." *College Composition and Communication* 34 (4): 409–10.

Putz, Joan M. 1969. "The Effectiveness of Non-Directive Teaching as a Method of Improving the Writing Ability of College Freshmen." PhD diss., New York University.

Putz, Joan M. 1970. "When the Teacher Stops Teaching—An Experiment with Freshman English." *College English* 32 (1): 50–57.

Quammen, David. 2017. *The Tangled Tree: A Radical New History of Life.* New York: Simon and Schuster.
Quellmalz, Edys. 1981a. "Designing Writing Assessments: Balancing Fairness, Utility, and Cost." In *Studies in Test Design: Annual Report*, edited by Edys Quellmalz, 230–48. Los Angeles: UCLA, Center for the Study of Evaluation. ERIC Document No. ED 212 650.
Quellmalz, Edys. 1981b. "Implications of Learning Research for Designing Competency-Based Assessment." In *Studies in Test Design: Annual Report*, edited by Edys Quellmalz, 39–63. Los Angeles: UCLA, Center for the Study of Evaluation. ERIC Document No. ED 212 650.
Quellmalz, Edys. 1981c. "Problems in Stabilizing the Judgment Process." In *Studies in Test Design: Annual Report*, edited by Edys Quellmalz, 129–52. Los Angeles: UCLA, Center for the Study of Evaluation. ERIC Document No. ED 212 650.
Rabinowitz, Paula. 2014. *American Pulp: How Paperbacks Brought Modernism to Main Street.* Princeton, NJ: Princeton University Press.
Rachels, James. 1986. *The Elements of Moral Philosophy.* Philadelphia: Temple University Press.
Reese, William J. 2005. *America's Public Schools: From the Common School to "No Child Left Behind."* Baltimore: Johns Hopkins University Press.
Resnick, Daniel P. 1968. *State Testing Programs: A Survey of Functions, Materials, and Services.* Princeton, NJ: Educational Testing Service.
Revelle, William, Joshua Wilt, and David M. Condon. 2011. "Individual Differences and Differential Psychology: A Brief History and Prospect." In *The Wiley-Blackwell Handbook of Individual Differences*, edited by Tomas Chamorro-Premuzic, Sophie von Stumm, and Adrian Furnham, 3–38. London: Wiley-Blackwell.
Richards, I. A. 1929. *Practical Criticism: A Study of Literary Judgment.* London: Kegan Paul.
Rohlinger, Deana A., and David A. Snow. 2006. "Social Psychological Perspectives on Crowds and Social Movements." In *Handbook of Social Psychology*, edited by John Delamater, 503–27. New York: Springer.
Rothschild, Eric. 1999. "Four Decades of the Advanced Placement Program." *History Teacher* 32 (2): 175–206.
Rubin, Edgar. 1915. *Synsoplevede figurer: Studier i psykologisk analyse.* [Visually perceived figures: Studies in psychological analysis]. Copenhagen: Gyldendalske Boghandel.
Ruth, Leo, and Catharine Keech. 1982. "Designing Prompts for Holistic Writing Assessments: Knowledge from Theory, Research, and Practice." In *Properties of Writing Tasks: A Study of Alternative Procedures for Holistic Writing Assessment*, edited by James Gray and Leo Ruth, 31–131. Berkeley, CA: Bay Area Writing Project.
Ruth, Leo, and Sandra Murphy. 1988. *Designing Writing Tasks for the Assessment of Writing.* Norwood, NJ: Ablex.
Sachse, Patricia P. 1984. "Writing Assessment in Texas: Practices and Problems." *Educational Measurement: Issues and Practice* 3 (1): 21–23.
Sartre, Jean-Paul. 1949. *Nausea.* Translated by Lloyd Alexander. New York: New Directions.
Saupe, Joe L. 1961. "Appendix A: Technical Considerations in Measurement." In *Evaluation in Higher Education*, edited by Paul L. Dressel, 433–56. Boston: Houghton Mifflin.
Savio, Mario. 1964. "Sit-in Address on the Steps of Sproul Hall." American Rhetoric: Top 100 Speeches. Web.
Schmidt, Jeff. 2000. *Disciplined Minds: A Critical Look at Salaried Professionals and the Soul-Battering System That Shapes Their Lives.* Lanham, MD: Rowman and Littlefield.
Schools Council. 1965. *English: A Programme for Research and Development in English Teaching.* Working Paper No. 3. London: Her Majesty's Stationery Office.
Scriven, Michael. 1959. "Logic of Criteria." *Journal of Philosophy* 56 (22): 857–68.
Scriven, Michael. 1966. *The Methodology of Evaluation.* Social Science Education Consortium, Publication No. 110. Lafayette, IN: Purdue University.

Scriven, Michael. 1974. "Evaluation Perspectives and Procedures." In *Evaluation in Education: Current Applications*, edited by W. James Popham, 1–93. Berkeley, CA: McCutchan.

Scriven, Michael. 1978. "General Categories for Assessment of Essay Work." Memorandum to the Evaluation Unit. In *Evaluation of the Bay Area Writing Project: Rubrics for Writing Assessment*, edited by Michael Scriven et al., Appendixes A1–A4. Berkeley, CA: Bay Area Writing Project.

Scriven, Michael, et al. 1978. *Evaluation of the Bay Area Writing Project: Rubrics for Writing Assessment: A Technical Report*. Berkeley, CA: Bay Area Writing Project.

Scriven, Michael. 2000/2005. *Logic and Methodology of Checklists*. Kalamazoo, MI: The Evaluation Center, Western Michigan University.

Shermis, Mark, and Ben Hammer. 2013. "Contrasting State-of-the-Art Automated Scoring of Essays." In *Handbook of Automated Essay Evaluation: Current Applications and New Directions*, edited by Mark Shermis and Jill Burstein, 313–46. New York: Routledge.

Sledd, James, and Wilma R. Ebbitt, eds. 1962. *Dictionaries and THAT Dictionary*. Chicago, IL: Scott, Foresman.

Sloan, Gary. 1979. "The Subversive Effects of an Oral Culture on Student Writing." *College Composition and Communication* 30 (2): 156–60.

Slotnick, Henry B. 1971. "Do Thirteen-Year-Olds Write as Well as Seventeen-Year-Olds?" *English Journal* 60 (8): 1109–15.

Slotnick, Henry B. 1972. "A Response." *Research in the Teaching of English* 6 (1): 112–21.

Smallwood, Mary Lovett. 1935. *An Historical Study of Examinations and Grading Systems in Early American Universities*. Harvard Studies in Education, Vol. 24. Cambridge, MA: Harvard University Press.

Smarter Balanced Assessment Consortium. 2014. *Smarter Balanced Scoring Guide: For Grades 3, 6 and 11, English/Language Arts, Performance Task Full-Write Baseline Sets*. https://portal.smarterbalanced.org/library/en/scoring-guide-for-ela-full-writes.pdf.

Smith, Clarence Ebblewhite, and Philip Joseph Hartog. 1941. *The Marking of English Essays: A Report on an Investigation Carried Out by a Sub-Committee of the International Examinations Enquiry Committee*. London: Macmillan.

Smith, Laura Spooner, Lynn Winters, Edys S. Quellmalz, and Eva L. Baker. 1980. *Characteristics of Student Writing Competence: An Investigation of Alternative Scoring Systems*. Center for the Study of Evaluation, Report No. 134. Los Angeles: University of California, Center for the Study of Evaluation.

Smith, Mary Ann. 1987. "Writing Projects and Writing Assessment." *The Quarterly* 9 (1): 6–7.

Smith, William L. 1992. "The Importance of Teacher Knowledge in College Composition Placement Testing." In *Reading Empirical Research Studies: The Rhetoric of Research*, edited by John R. Hayes, Richard E. Young, Michele L. Matchett, Maggie McCaffrey, Cynthia Cochran, and Thomas Hajduk, 289–313. Hillsdale, NJ: Erlbaum.

Smitherman, Geneva. 1992. "Black English, Diverging or Converging? The View from the National Assessment of Educational Progress." *Language and Education* 6 (1): 47–61.

Smitherman, Geneva, and Sandra Wright. 1984. "Black Students, Writers, Storks, and Familiar Places: What We Can Learn from the National Assessment of Educational Progress?" Paper presented at the Annual Meeting of the National Council of Teachers of English, Detroit, Michigan. ERIC Document No. ED 259 328.

Smuts, Jan Christiaan. 1926. *Holism and Evolution*. London: Macmillan.

Snyder, Thomas D. 1993. *120 Years of American Education: A Statistical Portrait*. Washington, DC: National Center for Education Statistics.

Snyder, Thomas D., Cristobal de Brey, and Sally A. Dillow. 2019. *Digest of Education Statistics 2017*. 53rd ed. NCES 2018–070. Washington, DC: National Center for Education Statistics, Institute of Education Sciences, US Department of Education.

Spearman, Charles. 1904. "General Intelligence: Objectively Determined and Measured." *American Journal of Psychology* 15 (2): 201–92.

Spencer, Ernest. 1979. *Folio Assessment of External Examinations? An Investigation into Alternative Means of Assessing SCE Ordinary Grade English.* Report to the Scottish Certificate of Education Examination Board from the Scottish Council for Research in Education. Dalkeith: Scottish Certificate of Education Examination Board. ERIC Document No. ED 194 555.
Spinuzzi, Clay. 2003. *Tracing Genres through Organizations.* Cambridge, MA: MIT Press.
Spinuzzi, Clay. 2015. *All Edge: Inside the New Workplace Networks.* Chicago, IL: University of Chicago Press.
Stalnaker, John N., and Ruth C. Stalnaker. 1934. "Reliable Reading of Essay Tests." *School Review* 42 (8): 599–605.
Stansfield, Charles W. 1986. "A History of the Test of Written English: The Developmental Year." *Language Testing* 3 (2): 224–34.
Starr, Kevin. 2009. *Golden Dreams: California in an Age of Abundance 1950–1963.* New York: Oxford University Press
Starring, Robert W. 1952. "A Study of Ratings of Comprehensive Examination Themes When Certain Elements Are Weakened." PhD diss., Michigan State University.
State of New Jersey Basic Skills Council. 1979. *Report of the New Jersey Basic Skills Council. 1979.* Princeton, NJ: Educational Testing Service. ERIC Document No. ED 185 098.
State of New Jersey Basic Skills Council. 1982. *Scoring the Essays for the New Jersey College Basic Skills Placement Test.* Princeton, NJ: Educational Testing Service.
Stedman, Lawrence C. 1998. "An Assessment of the Contemporary Debate over U.S. Achievement." In *Brookings Papers on Education Policy: 1998*, edited by Diane Ravitch, 53–121. Washington, DC: Brookings Institution.
Steinberg. Edwin R. 1963. *Needed Research in the Teaching of English.* Washington, DC: Office of Education.
Steinmann, Martin Jr. 1967. "A Conceptual Review." *Research in the Teaching of English* 1 (1): 79–84.
Stevens, Jane R. 2000. *University Committee on Preparatory Education Annual Report 1999–2000.* Oakland: University of California.
Stiggins, Richard. 1982. "A Comparison of Direct and Indirect Writing Assessment Methods." *Research in the Teaching of English* 16 (1): 101–14.
Sutherland, Gillian. 1977. "The Magic of Measurement: Mental Testing and English Education, 1900–1940." *Transactions of the Royal Historical Society* 27, 135–53.
Swineford, Frances. 1956a. *College Entrance Examination Board Advanced Placement Tests.* Princeton, NJ: Educational Testing Service.
Swineford, Frances. 1956b. *Test Analysis of College Entrance Examination Board—General Composition Tests.* Statistical Report 56–28. Princeton, NJ: Educational Testing Service.
Swineford, Frances. 1964. *Test Analysis: College Entrance Examination Board Advanced Placement Examination—English.* Statistical Report 64–49. Princeton, NJ: Educational Testing Service.
Swineford, Frances, and Fred I. Godshalk. 1961. "CEEB Research Proposal—Validity of the Interlinear." Unpublished internal College Board memorandum, October 6.
Tattersall, Kathleen. 2007. "A Brief History of Policies, Practices and Issues Relating to Comparability." In *Techniques for Monitoring the Comparability of Examination Standards*, edited by Paul Newton, Jo-Anne Baird, Harvey Goldstein, Helen Patrick, and Peter Tymms. London: Qualification and Curriculum Authority.
Taylor, David. 1984. "Much to Do about Writing." Review of *Teaching and Assessing Writing*, by Edward M. White. *College Teaching* 33 (3): 140–41.
Texas Education Agency. 1980. "Texas Assessment of Basic Skills: Focused Holistic Scoring of TABS Writing Samples: Exit Level." Austin: Texas Education Agency. ERIC Document No. ED 194 588.
Thompson, Thomas E. 1913. "Teaching and Testing the Teaching of Essentials." *Journal of Education* 78 (12): 102.

Thorndike, Edward L. 1920. "A Constant Error in Psychological Ratings." *Journal of Applied Psychology* 4 (1): 25–29.
Thorpe, Louis P., and Allen M. Schmuller. 1954. *Contemporary Theories of Learning, with Applications to Education and Psychology.* New York: Ronald.
Thurstone, Louis Leon. 1935. *The Vectors of Mind: Multiple Factor Analysis for the Isolation of Primary Traits.* Chicago: University of Chicago Press.
Titone, Renzo. 1973. "A Psycholinguistic Definition of the 'Glossodynamic Model' of Language Behavior and Language Learning." *Rassegna Italiana de linguistica applicata* 5 (1): 5–18.
Tolman, Edward Chace. 1932. *Purposive Behavior in Animal and Man.* New York: Century.
Trachsel, Mary. 1992. *Institutionalizing Literacy: The Historical Role of College Entrance Examinations in English.* Carbondale: Southern Illinois University Press.
Trimbur, John. 1994. "Taking the Social Turn: Teaching Writing Post-Process." *College Composition and Communication* 45 (1): 108–18.
Tripp, Janny Griswold. 1978. "The Positive Approach: Response-Evaluation of Children's Writing." *Language Arts* 55 (3): 358–61, 408.
Tyler, Ralph W. 1983. "Testing Writing Procedures Vary with Purposes." In *Literacy for Life: The Demand for Reading and Writing,* edited by Richard W. Bailey and Robin Melanie Fosheim, 197–206. New York: Modern Language Association.
United Nations Department of Economic and Social Affairs, Population Division. 2017. *International Migration Report 2017: Highlights.* New York: United Nations.
US Congress, Office of Technology Assessment. 1992. *Testing in American Schools: Asking the Right Questions.* OTA-SET-519. Washington, DC: Government Printing Office.
US Department of Education, Institute of Education Sciences. 2011. *Writing 2011: National Assessment of Educational Progress at Grades 8 and 11.* Washington, DC: Institute for Education Sciences.
US Department of Education, Institute of Education Sciences. 2017a. *Procedures Handbook.* Version 4.0. Washington, DC: What Works Clearinghouse.
US Department of Education, Institute of Education Sciences. 2017b. *Standards Handbook.* Version 4.0. Washington, DC: What Works Clearinghouse.
US National Assessment Governing Board 2017. *Writing Framework for the 2017 National Assessment of Educational Progress.* Washington, DC: National Assessment Governing Board.
Valentine, C. W., and W. G. Emmett. 1932. *The Reliability of Examinations.* London: University of London Press.
Valentine, John A. 1961. "The College Entrance Examination Board." *College Composition and Communication* 12 (2): 88–92.
Van Wagenen, M. J. 1921. "The Minnesota English Composition Scales: Their Derivation and Validity." *Educational Administration and Supervision* 7 (9): 481–99.
Vernon, Phillip. E., ed. 1957. *Secondary School Selection: A British Psychological Society Inquiry.* London: Methuen.
Vernon, Philip E. 1958. *Educational Testing and Test-Form Factors.* Princeton, NJ: Educational Testing Service.
Vernon, Philip E., and G. D. Millican. 1954. "A Further Study of the Reliability of English Essays." *British Journal of Statistical Psychology* 7 (2): 65–74.
Vespa, Jonathan, David M. Armstrong, and Lauren Medina. 2018. *Demographic Turning Points for the United States: Population Projections for 2020 to 2060.* P25–1144. Washington, DC: US Census Bureau.
von Ehrenfels, Christian. (1890) 1988. "On Gestalt Qualities." In *Foundations of Gestalt Psychology,* edited by Barry Smith, 82–117. Munich: Philosophia Verlag.
Vopat, James B. 1981. "Going APE: Reading the Advanced Placement Examination in English Literature and Composition." *College English* 43 (3): 284–92.
Wallis, Bertie Cotterell. 1927. *The Technique of Examining Children: A Quest for Capacity.* London: Macmillan.

Watts, Alan. 1966. *The Book: On the Taboo against Knowing Who You Are.* New York: Pantheon Books.
Watts, Alfred F., and Douglas A. Pidgeon. *Admission to Grammar Schools.* London: Newnes.
Weir, Cyril J., Ivana Vidakovic, and Evelina D. Galaczi. 2013. *Measured Constructs: A History of Cambridge English Language Examinations 1913–2012.* Cambridge: Cambridge University Press.
Weiss, Carol H. 1972. *Evaluation Research: Methods for Assessing Program Effectiveness.* New York: Prentice Hall.
Wells, Amy Stuart. 2019. "An Inconvenient Truth about the New Jim Crow of Education." Paper Presented at the Annual Meeting of the American Educational Research Association. Toronto, Canada.
Wertheimer, Max. (1912) 2012. "Experimental Studies on Seeing Motion." In *On Perceived Motion and Figural Organization,* edited by Lothar Spillman, 1–92. Cambridge, MA: MIT Press.
Whelton, Paul K., and Robert M. Carey. 2017. "Guideline for the Prevention, Detection, Evaluation, and Management of High Blood Pressure in Adults: A Report of the American College of Cardiology/American Heart Association Task Force on Clinical Practice Guidelines." *Journal of the American College of Cardiology* 71 (19): e127–e248.
White, Edward M. 1973. *Comparison and Contrast: The 1973 California State University and Colleges English Equivalency Examination.* Los Angeles: Office of the Chancellor, California State University and Colleges.
White, Edward M. 1984. "Holisticism." *College Composition and Communication* 35 (4): 400–409.
White, Edward M. 1985. *Teaching and Assessing Writing.* San Francisco: Jossey-Bass.
White, Edward M. 1993. "Holistic Scoring: Past Triumphs, Future Challenges." In *Validating Holistic Scoring for Writing Assessments: Theoretical and Empirical Foundations,* edited by Michael M. Williamson and Brian A. Huot, 79–108. Cresskill, NJ: Hampton.
White, Edward M. 2001. "The Opening of the Modern Era of Writing Assessment: A Narrative." *College English* 63 (3): 306–20.
White, Edward M. 2005. "The Scoring of Writing Portfolios: Phase 2." *College Composition and Communication* 56 (4): 581–600.
White, Edward M. 2010. "Six Writing Traits." WPA-L, Writing Program Association listserve. Web.
White, Edward M., and Leon L. Thomas. 1981. "Racial Minorities and Writing Skills Assessment in the California State University and Colleges." *College English* 43 (3): 276–83.
White, Edward M., Norbert Elliot, and Irvin Peckham. 2015. *Very Like a Whale: The Assessment of Writing Programs.* Logan: Utah State University Press.
White, Hayden. 1973. *Metahistory: The Historical Imagination in Nineteenth-Century Europe,* Baltimore: Johns Hopkins University Press.
White, Hayden. 1980. "The Value of Narrativity in the Representation of Reality." *Critical Inquiry* 7 (1): 5–27.
White, Timothy P. 2017. "Memorandum: Assessment of Academic Preparation and Placement in First-Year General Education Written Communication and Mathematics/Quantitative Reasoning Courses, Executive Order 1110." Web.
Whitehead, Alfred North. (1916) 1948. "Presidential Address: The Aims of Education: A Plea for Reform." *The Mathematical Gazette* 32 (300): 119.
Whithaus, Carl. 2010. Distributive Evaluation. WPA-CompPile Research Bibliographies, No. 3. Web.
Williamson, David M., Xiaoming Xi, and F. Jay Breyer. 2012. "A Framework for Evaluation and Use of Automated Scoring." *Educational Measurement: Issues and Practices* 31 (1): 2–13.
Williamson, Michael M. 1993. "An Introduction to Holistic Scoring: The Social, Historical, and Theoretical Context for Writing Assessment." In *Validating Holistic Scoring for Writing,* edited by Michael M. Williamson and Brian A. Huot, 1–43. Cresskill, NJ: Hampton.

Williamson, Michael M., and Brian A. Huot, eds. 1993. *Validating Holistic Scoring for Writing.* Cresskill, NJ: Hampton.
Willing, Matthew H. 1918. *Scale for Measuring Written Composition.* Bloomington, IL: Public School Publishing.
Willingham, Warren W., et al. 1997. "Test Performance." In *Gender and Fair Assessment,* edited by Warren W. Willingham and Nancy S. Cole, 55–126. Mahwah, NJ: Lawrence Erlbaum.
Wilson, Maja. 2006. *Rethinking Rubrics in Writing Assessment.* Portsmouth, NH: Heinemann.
Wise, Arthur. 1979. "Why Minimum Competency Testing Will Not Improve Education." *Educational Leadership* 36 (8): 546–49.
Wise, J. Hooper. 1953. "A Comprehensive Freshman English Course: Reading, Speaking, and Writing at the University of Florida." *College Composition and Communication* 4 (4): 131–35.
Wiseman, Stephen. 1949. "The Marking of English Composition in Grammar School Selection." *British Journal of Education Psychology* 19 (3): 200–209.
Wiseman, Stephen. 1956. "Symposium: The Use of Essays in Selection at 11+: III.—Reliability and Validity." *British Journal of Educational Psychology* 26 (3): 172–79.
Wiseman, Stephen, and Jack Wrigley. 1958. "Essay-Reliability: The Effect of Choice of Essay-Title." *Educational and Psychological Measurement* 18 (1): 129–38.
Witte, Stephen P., and Lester Faigley. 1983. *Evaluating College Writing Programs.* Urbana, IL: Conference on College Composition and Communication.
Witte, Stephen P., Mary Trachsel, and Keith Walters. 1986. "Literacy and the Direct Assessment of Writing: A Diachronic Perspective." In *Writing Assessment: Issues and Strategies,* edited by Karen L. Greenberg, Harvey S. Wiener, and Richard A. Donovan, 13–34. New York: Longman.
Wolcott, Willa, Patricia Dovell, and Dianne Buhr. 1988. "Discrepancies in Essay Scoring." Paper presented at the Annual Meeting of the American Educational Research Association, New Orleans, LA. ERIC Document No. ED 306 246.
Wolfe, Edward W., Carol M. Myford, George Engelhard Jr., and Johanna R. Manalo. 2007. *Monitoring Reader Performance and DRIFT in the AP® English Literature and Composition Examination Using Benchmark Essays.* Research Report 2007-2. New York: College Board.
Wood, Shane. 2018. "Intersections of Genre and Assessment: Systems, Uptakes, and Ideologies." PhD diss., University of Kansas.
Woodworth, Patrick, and Catharine Keech. 1980. *The Write Occasion.* Collaborative Research Study No. 1. Berkeley, CA: Bay Area Writing Project.
Wooldridge, Adrian. 1994. *Measuring the Mind: Education and Psychology in England 1850–1990.* Cambridge: Cambridge University Press.
Woese, Carl. 2005. "Evolving Biological Organizations." In *Microbial Phylogeny and Evolution: Concepts and Controversies,* edited by Jann Sapp, 99–118. New York: Oxford University Press.
Yancey, Kathleen Blake. 1999. "Looking Back as We Look Forward: Historicizing Writing Assessment." *College Composition and Communication* 50 (3): 483–503.
Zlatkin-Troitschanskaia, Olga, et al. 2019. "On the Complementarity of Holistic and Analytic Approaches to Performance Assessment Scoring" *British Journal of Educational Psychology.* ePUB ahead of print: 1–17.
Zuckerkandl, Victor. 1956. *Sound and Symbol: Music and the External World.* Translated by Willard R. Trask and Norbert Guterman. Princeton, NJ: Princeton University Press.
Zuckerkandl, Victor. 1973. *Man the Musician.* Translated by Willard R. Trask and Norbert Guterman. Princeton, NJ: Princeton University Press.
Zwick, Rebecca. 2017. *Who Gets In? Strategies for Fair and Effective College Admissions.* Cambridge, MA: Harvard University Press.

ABOUT THE AUTHORS

Richard Haswell retired from Texas A&M University, Corpus Christi, in 2005. At Washington State University he directed the composition program (1972–82) and the cross-campus writing-assessment program (1993–96). He is author of *Gaining Ground in College Writing* (1991), coauthor with Janis Haswell of *Authoring* (2010) and *Hospitality and Authoring* (2015), and coeditor of *Comp Tales* (2000), *Beyond Outcomes* (2001) and *Machine Scoring of Student Essays* (2006). With colleague Glenn Blalock, he created *CompPile*, an online bibliography of scholarship in composition and rhetoric.

Norbert Elliot is research professor at the University of South Florida and Professor Emeritus of English at the New Jersey Institute of Technology. He is coauthor of *Very Like a Whale: The Assessment of Writing Programs*, with Edward M. White and Irvin Peckham, and coeditor of *Writing Assessment, Social Justice, and the Advancement of Opportunity*, with Mya Poe and Asao B. Inoue, and *Talking Back: Senior Scholars Deliberate the Past, Present, and Future of Writing Studies*, with Alice Horning.

INDEX

ACT, 237, 244
adjusted rater scoring. *See* holistic scoring
Advanced Level Examinations (A-Level), 55, 56, 81, 82, 84, 96n6. *See also* General Certification of Education; General Certificate of Secondary Education; Ordinary Level Examinations
Advanced Placement Program, 25, 26, 47n6, 47n8, 99, 100, 109–111, 118n8, 120–121, 129, 147n1, 150n22, 160–163, 172–173, 209, 239, 259n5. *See also* College Board; holistic scoring; *An Informal History of the AP Readings, 1956–76*
Albrecht, Robert C., 116
Allison, Harold, 161
Alloway, Evans, 186n13, 189
Allport, Gordon W., 228, 230
American Psychological Association Committee on Test Standards, 245, 266
American Pulp: How Paperbacks Brought Modernism to Main Street (Rabinowitz), 40
Analysis of Background Factors and Their Possible Influence on Placement in Freshman English at the University of Nebraska-Lincoln, An (Mielenz), 223n4
analytic scoring, 18, 26, 52–53, 61, 62–63, 65, 66, 76, 80, 82, 171, 244, 250, 253, 255, 256. *See also* primary-trait scoring; schedule scoring; trait
Analytical Writing Placement Examination, 154. *See also* Entry Level Writing Requirement; Subject A Examination; University of California
anchors, 19, 44, 179, 196, 232, 233. *See also* exemplars; prototypes; range finders; sample essays
Anderson, C. C., 121–122, 147n3, 147–148n3, 151n23, 270. *See also* Sequential Tests of Educational Progress (STEP)
Anderson, Harold A., 117n3
Anglo American Seminar on the Teaching of English, 92. *See* Dartmouth Conference
Anrig, Gregory G., 225n20
Appiah, Kwamie Anthony, 277
Applebee, Arthur N., 216–219, 263, 276. *See also* NAEP; *Writing Trends Across the Decade, 1974–1984*

Ash, Mitchel G., 39, 41, 46. *See also* gestalt psychology
Asilomar Language Arts Conference, 159–160
Austen, Jane, 204
Assessing Writing, 28n3, 276
Assessment and Evaluation in Higher Education, 28n3
Assessment and Qualifications Alliance, 88
Assessment for Learning (AfL), 288
Assessment Reform Group, 286
authenticity, 173
Automated Writing Evaluation (AWE), 245–246, 254, 261n14, 261–262n15. *See also* computer scoring of essays; machine scoring

Backstrand, Jeffrey, 31–32
backwash, 54, 87, 89
Bain, Alexander, 264
Baker, Franklin T., 264
Ballard, Philip Boswood, 54–56, 65–67. See also *New Examiner*
Basic College, 27, 123–130, 136, 148n6. *See also* Michigan State University
Bay Area Writing Project, 27, 42, 47n8, 99, 112, 116, 147, 152, 167–184, 186n11, 188, 233, 257–258, 274. *See also* Keech, Catherine; Lavin, Albert ("Cap"); teacher consultant
Belanoff, Pat, 34, 254
Bennett, Randy Elliot, 288
Berg, Harry D., 125
Bernstein, Ruby S., 171, 172
Bennet, James, 9
Bettelheim, Bruno, 102
Blickhahn, Kate, 161–162, 165–166, 167, 170–171, 172, 173, 186n11, 186n12, 186n14, 186n18
Bloom, Benjamin, 105, 135, 150n18
Blos, Peter, 102
Board of Regents of the University System of Georgia, 25, 191, 200, 234n9, 290. *See also* Georgia Regents Testing Program
body of knowledge, 5, 27, 39, 47n6, 92, 184, 197, 201, 245

328   INDEX

Book, The: On the Taboo Against Knowing Who You Are (Watts), 164
Bossone, Richard, 81–82, 239–241, 246, 253, 262n16
Boston University, 210
Boucher, Chauncey S., 100, 117n5, 135. See also New Plan
Boyer, John W., 101, 106
Braddock, Richard, 93, 192
Brandeis University, 34
Breland, Hunter, 197–200, 258, 270, 278
Brereton, John C., 97n14
British Council, 248, 250
British Psychological Association, 266
Britton, James, 16, 26, 39, 58, 59, 60, 70, 71, 78, 79–80, 82–83, 89–90, 92, 93, 95n5, 144, 194, 204, 211, 236, 245, 247, 263, 264, 279
Brooks, Val, 79
Brown, Edmund Gerald ("Pat"), Sr., 154
Brown, Rexford, 27, 211, 220–221, 222, 224n13. See also NAEP
Bowker, Geoffrey C., 226, 227
Boyd, William, 49, 62–64, 68, 201, 241, 267, 289. See also Measuring Devices in Composition, Spelling and Arithmetic; Research Committee of the Educational Institute of Scotland
Brandt, Mark J., 279
Bunn, Geoff, 49
Burgess, Anthony, 220
Buros, Oscar, 102
Burstein, Jill, 261n15
Burt, Cyril L., 4, 23, 25, 26, 48n10, 51, 56, 61–67, 72n3, 74n12, 75, 76, 80, 94, 95n2, 99, 105, 143, 144, 150–151n23, 270, 271–272
Burnham, Philip E., 147n1
Butler, Richard. A., 55, 68 See also Education Act (1944)

Caldwell, Keith, 185n8
calibration, 152, 174, 178, 197, 216. See also rater training
California Assessment Program, 169–171. See also California Learning Assessment System
California Association of Teachers of English, 160
California Community Colleges (public university system), 153, 262n16
California High School Proficiency Examination, 171, 173
California Learning Assessment System, 183–184. See also California Assessment Program

California Pupil Proficiency Law, 170
California State University (public university system), 15, 25, 47n8, 98, 116, 146, 150n22, 153, 172–173, 191, 198, 213, 259n5. See also English Equivalency Examination; White, Edward M.
California Teachers Association, 185n7
California Writing Evaluation Scale, 160
Cambridge English Language Assessment, 248
Camp, Roberta, 173, 174
Canada, 16
Carnegie Foundation for the Advancement of Teaching, 64, 175, 191
Carlton, Sydell T., 16, 79, 81–82, 91, 98, 107, 108, 111, 112, 122, 123, 128, 149n11, 151n23, 194, 197, 244, 261n12, 267, 272, 279. See also Factors in Judgments of Writing Ability
Carpenter, George R., 264
Carpenter, William, 116
Cast, B. M. D., 66–67, 76–77, 80, 82, 94, 95n1, 146, 151n23, 246, 272–273, 289
Category of Evidence (CoE) framework, 28, 260n12, 264–290
Cattell, Raymond, 228
Center for American Progress, 28n2, 184n2
Center for the Study of Evaluation, 190, 223n3. See also National Center for Research on Evaluation, Standards, and Student Testing; University of California, Los Angeles
Certificate of Secondary Education, 55, 81, 82, 83, 84, 92, 97n15
Chafe, Wallace, 264
Charney, Davida, 150n20, 197, 254
Chauncey, Henry, 98
checklists, 176–177, 178, 242. See also rubrics; scoring guide
Cheng, Eileen Ka-May, 12
Cherry, Roger, 197
Chomsky, Noam, 36, 37, 230
Christensen, Frances, 192, 195
Citizens Advisory Commission, 156–157, 158. See also Joint Interim Committee on the Public Education System
City University of New York, 82, 239
Civil Rights Act (1964), 200, 270
Civil Rights Address (1963), 200. See Kennedy, John F.
Claggett, Mary Francis, 170, 172
classical test theory, 58, 59, 73n11
Clear English (Finlayson), 95n3
Cleary, T. Anne, 198
Coffman, William E., 13–14, 27, 89–90, 93, 94, 95n4, 102, 118n9, 119, 120, 137–

147, 151n23, 151n25, 192, 211, 224n7. *See also* NAEP
Cogan, John Aloysius, Jr., 200
Cognitive Psychology (Neisser), 35–37
Cole, Andrew, 281
Cole, Nancy S., 198
Colman, Ronald, 40
collective judgment. *See* holistic scoring
College Board (College Entrance Examination Board), 3, 13, 14, 47n8, 51, 74n13, 89, 90, 94, 96n13, 98, 99, 109, 110, 111, 115, 117n4, 118n9, 119, 120, 126, 137, 139–140, 141, 142, 143, 144, 145, 146, 152, 169, 188, 197, 239. *See also* Advanced Placement Program; Test of Standard Written English
College Level Examination Program (CLEP), 146, 171
College of Staten Island, 262n16
Collier, David, 271
Collingwood, R. G.(Robin George), 11
Columbia University, 64, 101, 120, 131, 147n1
Combs, William, 223n5
Condon, David M., 228
Cooper, Charles, 182–183, 185n9, 201. See also *Evaluating Writing: Describing, Measuring, Judging*
Committee on Assessing the Progress of Education, 207, 209
Composing Processes of Twelfth Graders, The (Emig), 23
Comprehensive Examination in English, 100–109, 117n2, 132, 135. *See also* Comprehensive Examinations; Diederich, Paul B.; New Plan
Comprehensive Examinations, 101–102, 149n14. *See also* Hutchins, Robert Manyard
Comprone, Joseph, 9
computer scoring of essays, 256. *See also* Automated Writing Evaluation
Concord High School (California), 160
Conlan, Gertrude, 25, 144, 145, 150n21, 224n9
Conrad, Joseph, 256. See *Shadow-Line, The*
Consistency Index Number (CIN), 118n10
connoisseurship scoring. *See* holistic scoring
consensus scoring. *See* holistic scoring
construct inferences, 229
construct representation, 23, 52, 61, 122, 188, 199, 207, 227, 270, 281. *See also* validity
consulted scoring. *See* holistic scoring

content scheme scoring. *See* holistic scoring
Cooper, Charles, 182, 185n9
Cooperative Research Program, 190
Cornell University, 46
Cousins, Norman, 170
Coward, Ann F., 50, 51, 93, 138, 139, 140, 144, 150n19, 151n23
Cowley, John, 111, 112, 238
Crew, Louie, 149n14, 200, 290
Criper, Clive, 249
Criterion® Online Writing Evaluation Service, 246
Cronbach, Lee J., 125, 169
Crowley, Sharon, 224n10
Crusius, Timothy W., 281
Cubberly High School, 118n11

Daiker, Donald A., 223n5
Danforth Foundation, 207
Daniels, Harvey A., 158–159
Department of Health, Education, and Welfare, 191, 206
Dartmouth College, 92–93, 208
Dartmouth Conference, 16, 92–93, 97n14, 126, 161. *See also* Anglo American Seminar on the Teaching of English
Darwin, Charles, 226, 230, 236, 242, 253. See also *On The Origin of Species*
Davies, Alan, 248, 249
Davis, Barbara Gross, 202–203, 274
decision inferences, 229
DeFunis v. Odegaard, 198
Design for Assessment (DFA), 280–281
Designing Writing Tasks for the Assessment of Writing (Ruth and Murphy), 182, 187n19
Deukmejian, George, 183, 185n4
Devon County, 13, 25, 26, 51, 67–71, 77, 80, 93, 94, 97n15, 105–106, 150n19, 182, 279. *See also* Robertson, R. K.
Diederich, Paul B., 14, 16, 24, 25, 26, 27, 47n5, 74n13, 77, 79, 81, 82, 90, 91, 94, 98–118, 122–123, 128, 129, 130–137, 148n4, 149n9, 149n10, 149n11, 149n14, 151n23, 151n25, 160, 161, 166, 173, 175–176, 178, 182, 183, 194, 197, 201, 207–208, 215, 223n3, 225n15, 238–239, 244, 258, 261n12, 267, 272, 279, 289. *See also* Comprehensive Examination in English; Comprehensive Examinations; ETS; *Factors in Judgments of Writing Ability*; NAEP; New Plan; Palmer, Osmond E.
differential accuracy, 20, 261n13. *See also* DRIFT; reliability

differential prediction, 198, 200, 267, 270, 278
differential scale category use, 20, 261n13. *See also* DRIFT; reliability
differential severity, 20, 261n13. *See also* DRIFT; reliability
differential validity, 270, 278
Dimock, Wai Chee, 266
discrepancy, 65, 270, 271. *See also* reliability
Dixon, John, 92
Donahoe Higher Education Act, 154, 155
Dorans, Neil, 73n11
double marking, in UK, 21–22, 79. *See also* Ofqual
Douglas, Mary, 230, 243, 260n9
Dressel, Paul D., 124, 135, 148n6, 148–149n8, 149n16, 201. *See also* *Evaluation in Higher Education*
Dreyfus, Hubers, 164. *See also* *What Computers Can't Do*
DRIFT (Differential Reader Functioning over Time), 20, 261n13. *See also* differential accuracy; differential scale category use; differential severity; reliability
Duke University, 168, 200
Dyer, Henry, 150n21

East Texas State University, 17
Ebbit, Wilma R., 117n4, 137, 150n18
ecological evaluation, 178, 223n1, 277, 280. *See also* Keech, Catherine
Edinburgh ELTS Validation Project, 81, 219, 248–251
Education Act (1944), 49, 55, 57, 72n6, 75, 84. *See also* Butler, Richard A.
Education Act (1976), 84
Educational Assessment, 28n3
Educational Institute of Scotland, 62, 267
Educational Testing Service. *See* ETS
Educational Wastelands, 158
Education Commission of the States, 207, 208, 211, 220, 225n20
Edgeworth, Francis, 52, 58, 59, 63, 64, 65, 68, 73n10, 76, 77, 82, 256
Education Commission of the States, 27, 207, 208, 211, 220, 225n20
effect size, 245
Effectiveness of Non-directive Teaching as a Method of Improving the Writing Ability of College Freshmen, The (Putz), 192
Eight-Legged Essay, 5
Eight-Year Study, 102, 135. *See also* Tyler, Ralph
Einstein, Albert, 41
Eisenhower, Dwight D., 206

Elbow, Peter, 35–37, 40, 116, 254
11-Plus Examinations, 13, 25, 54, 55, 57, 62, 64, 67–71, 72n5, 72n6, 73n7, 75, 79, 80, 81, 84, 85, 91, 96n8, 96n9, 105, 150n19
Eley, Earl G., 48n10, 117n6, 135–136, 150n17, 259n5. *See also* General Composition Test
Elliott, T. J., 28n1
Elliot, Norbert, 3, 17, 48n10, 118n8, 150n21, 225n20, 261–262n15, 278. *See also* *Writing Assessment, Social Justice, and the Advancement of Opportunity*
Encina High School, 115
Emig, Janet, 23
emplotment, 10–13, 14, 28n5, 147, 206, 219–220, 230. *See also* White, Hayden
English Composition Test (ECT), 25, 27, 50, 89–90, 99, 111, 119–123, 137–147, 151n24, 152, 160, 186n13, 193, 211, 224n9, 239, 259n5
English Equivalency Examination, 25, 32, 47n8, 98, 116, 117n7, 146, 150n22, 173, 179, 213, 259n5, 267, 273. *See also* California State University; English Placement Test
English Language Testing System Validation Project, 4, 81, 248–251. *See also* International English Language Testing System
English Placement Test, 15, 198–199. *See also* California State University; English Equivalency Examination
Entry Level Writing Requirement, 154. *See also* Analytical Writing Placement Examination; Subject A Examination; University of California
ESL Composition Profile, 203–204. *See also* Jacobs, Holly L.
EQ (English Quotient) testing, 78, 91
e-rater® scoring engine, 246, 261n14
error (statistical), 58–59, 65, 68, 73n10, 73n11
Essay on Criticism, An (Pope) 263
Essay on Man, An (Pope), 264
ETS (Educational Testing Service), 3, 13–14, 15, 16, 17, 25, 26, 27, 29n7, 32–33, 50–51, 90, 93–94, 97n15, 98–99, 107, 109, 110, 112, 117n4, 117n7, 118n9, 119, 120, 128, 135, 136, 137–147, 147n2, 147–148n3, 148n8, 150n21, 151n24, 151n25, 154, 160, 161, 162, 171, 173, 174, 183, 186n13, 186n15, 186n16, 189, 197, 207–222, 223n3, 224n9, 225n20, 237, 244, 246, 259n5, 261n14. *See also* Coffman, William E.;

Diederich, Paul B.; Godshalk, Fred I.; NAEP; Swineford, Frances
Evaluating College Writing Programs (Witte and Faigley), 204
Evaluating Writing: Describing, Measuring, Judging (Cooper and Odell), 201–201.
Evaluation of Composition Instruction (Davis, Scriven, Thomas), 190–191, 202–203, 222n3, 275
Evaluation Research: Methods for Assessing Program Effectiveness (Weiss), 177
Evaluation Review, 28n3
Evaluation in Higher Education (Dressel), 124, 126. *See also* writing in the disciplines
Evaluation Institute, 190, 202. *See also* University of San Francisco
evidence-based practice, 265–266
exemplars, 19. *See also* anchors; prototypes; range finders; sample essays
extrapolation inferences, 229

factor analysis, 16, 73–74n11, 90, 107, 122, 148n4, 194, 196, 197, 228, 224, 260–261n12, 270, 272, 279
Factors in Judgments of Writing Ability (Diederich, French, and Carlton), 122, 128
Faribanks, Douglas, 40
Faigley, Leser, 204, 257. *See also Evaluating College Writing Programs*
fairness: bias, 59, 73n7, 107–108, 201, 257, 282, 287–288; consequence, 12, 24, 84, 199, 227, 231, 238, 239, 245, 253, 254, 256, 257, 258, 261n13, 268–269, 273–274, 275, 278, 280, 282, 286, 287–288; consistency, 23, 45, 70, 77, 82, 111, 117n3, 118n10, 125, 133, 268, 269, 270, 284, 287–288; fair decision, 23; group comparisons, 197–201; information use, 286; inferred fairness, 45, 267, 270; reliability as evidence of fairness, 20, 23; typology, 271, 274. *See also* English Equivalency Examination; NAEP; reliability; social justice; validity
Finlayson, Douglas S., 77–79, 82, 91, 94, 95n3, 122, 150–151n23, 270–271
Finn, Patrick J., 201
First Six Tests in English Composition, The (Noyes, Sale, and Stalker), 120
Fisher, Ronald, 245
Florida State University, 191, 223n5
Foreign Service Examination in English Composition, 33, 111, 138–139, 186n13
formal holistic scoring. *See* holistic scoring
Flower, Linda, 41
Ford Foundation, 191, 207

FORTRAN, 14
Fowles, Mary, 154
Frames of Mind: Constraints on the Common-Sense Concepion of the Mental (Morton), 39
Framework for Success in Postsecondary Writing (CWPA, NCTE, NWP), 245
France, Norman, 83, 235, 96n6
Freedman, Sarah, 194–196, 224n6, 267, 279
French, John W., 26, 79, 81–82, 91, 102, 111, 112, 122–123, 128, 148n4, 149n11, 150–151n23, 194, 197, 244, 260–261n12, 267, 272, 279. *See also Factors in Judgments of Writing Ability*
Freud, Sigmund, 230
Frey, James, 116
Friedrich, Gerhard, 114, 116, 150n22, 160, 259n5
Frye, Northrop, 28n5

Gadda, George, 154, 184n1
Galaczi, Evelina D., 21
Galton, Francis, 59, 85, 236, 266
Gannett, Cinthia, 97n14
Garfield, James A., 206, 207, 220
Gauss, Carl Frederick, 260n10
Gaussian distribution, 139, 199, 260n10
GED (General Educational Development tests), 101
gender inferences, 229
General Certificate of Education, 55, 79, 99. *See also* Advanced Level Examinations; Ordinary Level Examinations
General Certificate of Secondary Education, 81, 84, 88
general impression marking. *See* holistic scoring
generalization inferences, 45, 178, 228, 246, 260–261n12
genre: constitutive, 23–24, 276; discourse community, 257; essay, 29n9, 180; research, 281–286; writing assessment, 5–6, 12, 28, 163, 245, 260–261n12, 280, 289
General Certificate Examination, 54. *See also* Advanced Level Examinations; Ordinary Level Examinations
General Composition Test, 117n4, 135
general impression marking. *See* holistic scoring
Georgia Regents Testing Program, 25. *See also* Board of Regents of the University System of Georgia
gestalt psychology: aesthetics, 35–37, 47; cognition, 35–37; departure from

332   INDEX

mechanistic views, 37; Great Britain, 49; history and theory, 33–42, 46–47; language, 36–37; music, 36–37; perception theory, 33–35, 38, 39–42, 50, 114, 144, 166, 251; psychology of motion, 37. *See also* Ash, Mitchel G.; holistic scoring; Koffka, Kurt; Köhler, Wolfgang; Neisser, Ulrich; Wertheimer, Max; Zuckerkandl, Viktor

Gestalt Psychology: An Introduction to New Concepts in Modern Psychology (Köhler) 40–42, 46

Ginsberg, Allan, 152, 164. *See Howl*

Godshalk, Fred I., 13–14, 25, 27, 32–33, 89–90, 93, 94, 95n4, 102, 111, 112, 118n9, 119–151, 186n13, 189, 192, 193, 211, 238, 258

Gorrell, Robert. 211. *See also* NAEP

grading, 19, 24, 52, 65, 68, 72n3, 99, 102, 108, 123, 127, 128, 133, 134, 136, 151n25, 155, 160, 176, 193, 202, 241

Graduate Management Admission Council, 255

Gray, James, 39–40, 98, 99, 161, 167, 168, 169, 172, 175, 181, 186–187n18, 187n19, 190, 245, 258, 264, 265

Greve, Curt, 14

Grinnell, Josiah B., 221, 222

Guttman, Louis, 90

Hach, Clarence W., 147n1

halo effect, 127, 128, 146, 148n7, 177, 194, 196, 224n7, 241, 242

Hammond, J. W., 14, 12, 299

Hamp-Lyons, Liz, 14, 24, 27, 71n1, 81, 88, 203–204, 247–251, 254, 262n17. *See also* English Language Testing System; *Testing Second Language Writing in Academic Settings*

Hand, Harold, 207. *See also* NAEP

Hanna, Paul, 9

Hannaford, Reginald, 116

Harcourt Brace and World, 222

Harms, Keith L., 4

Hartog, Phillip Joseph, 4, 19, 23, 25, 26, 51, 58, 61–67, 74n12, 77, 80, 96–97n13, 99, 104, 105, 143, 144, 150–151n23, 259n5, 270, 271

Harvard University, 36, 96n13, 102, 148n4, 177, 191, 194, 203, 225n16

Harvard University Commission on English, 96n13

Haswell, Richard 3, 17, 184n2, 223–224n5, 258n12, 279

Hayes, John R., 42

Hayhoe, Mike, 96n11

Head, J. J., 79

Heenan, David K., 125

Helmholtz, Hermann, 46

Herbert, Auberon, 54

Heritage, Margaret, 288

Hillegas, Milo B. (Burdette), 52, 63, 102, 129. *See also* sample matching

Hillocks, George, Jr., 196, 235

history: as annals, 11; as global journey, 12; as social exploration, 12; as story, 11–12; as trajectory 12, 28–29n6

Hitler, Adolf, 46

Holder, Carol, 15

Holism and Evolution (Smuts), 8

holism: cognition, 260n9; in composition and rhetoric, education, learning theory, literature, linguistics, psychoanalysis, psychology, 18; holism, 223n1, 389; holistic scoring, 63, 90, 135, 165, 251; organicism, 8–9; phi phenomenon, 38–39. *See also* Elbow, Peter; gestalt psychology; Neisser, Ulrich; Zuckerkandl, Viktor

holistic scoring: adjusted rater scoring, 21, 25, 26, 32, 47n8, 275; collective judgment, 19; conformism, 134; connoisseurship scoring, 24, 52, 57, 63, 76, 87, 154; consensus scoring, 19; consulted scoring, 19, 103, 120, 132, 236; content scheme scoring, 19, 81, 86, 87, 117n5; definition, 4, 21; end of, 251–258; formal, 4, 10, 19–20, 21, 22, 24, 26, 49, 53, 63, 65, 96–97n13, 107; general impression marking, 13, 51, 66, 70, 144; gestalt qualities, 26, 33–47, 48n9, 48n10, 49–50, 61, 62, 70–71, 114, 123, 135, 166, 188, 197, 207, 230, 231, 242, 251; Great Britain, 49–97; informal, 19; marking scheme, 18, 23, 65–66, 82, 88; multiple marking, 19, 22, 59, 60, 62, 63, 66, 70, 75, 79, 80, 84, 86, 92, 93; office adjusted rater scoring, 19, 22, 80; open ranking, 19, 22, 66, 80, 141, 144, 152; pooled rater scoring, 13, 14, 19, 20, 22, 24–25, 26, 32, 50, 51, 53–61, 62, 66, 67, 71, 73n7, 73n10, 76, 77, 78, 79, 80, 82, 85, 86, 87, 88, 89, 91, 93, 94, 94n3, 105, 108, 113, 120, 122, 123, 137, 138, 139, 141, 142, 144, 146, 147–148n3, 150n19, 151n25, 193, 211, 236, 238, 253, 269, 271, 272; practitioner guides, 269(table); pragmatic reasons for success, 30–31; profile, 22, 24, 26, 27, 81, 203, 220, 227, 232, 247–251, 253, 254, 256; racial prejudice, 234; rapid impression reading, 24,

51, 70, 77, 80, 82, 89, 92, 93, 150n19, 160; research studies, 268–269(table); rubrics, 7, 14, 16, 19, 21, 22, 24, 25, 27, 44, 50, 60, 72n3, 80, 81, 82, 87, 94, 95n2, 109, 114, 115, 116, 141, 145, 152, 161, 166, 173, 174, 175, 176, 177, 179, 186n17, 190, 209, 211, 212, 215, 216, 218, 219, 221, 225n17, 227, 229, 233, 237–247, 251, 253, 254, 255, 256, 259n5, 260–261n6, 260n8, 275; sample matching, 19, 52, 63, 83, 129, 160, 185n10, 193; splitters, 16, 27, 36, 227, 231–236; student peer review, 201; total effect, 173; United States, 98–225; wholistic, 30, 138, 150–151n23. *See also* fairness; gestalt psychology; grading; reliability; social justice; validity
holisticism, 275. *See also* White, Edward M.
Hooker, Joseph Dalton, 226
Houghton Mifflin Tests of Academic Progress, 155
House Un-American Activities Committee, 158
Hove, Mary Rion, 116
Howl (Ginsburg), 152, 164
Hughes-Hart Education Reform and Finance Act, 185n4
Hunt, Kellogg, 201, 208
Huot, Brian, 4, 48n10, 271, 276
Hutchins, Robert Manyard, 100–101, 104, 106, 149n15. *See also* Comprehensive Examination in English; Comprehensive Examinations; New Plan

individual differences, 89, 133, 135, 204, 228, 231, 236, 251, 254, 255, 258
Informal History of AP Readings, An (Advanced Placement Program of the College Board), 109, 113
Indiana University, 191, 193
informal holistic scoring. *See* holistic scoring
Inoue, Asao B., 278. See also *Writing Assessment, Social Justice, and the Advancement of Opportunity*
Institute of Education Sciences, 265. *See also Procedures Handbook*; *Standards Handbook*; US Department of Education
interlinear exercise, 89, 120, 126, 139, 141, 142, 143, 144
International Conference on Examinations, 64, 105
International English Language Testing System (IELTS), 248. *See also* English Language Testing System Validation Project

interpretation and use argument, 228–231, 234
interval scale, 21, 200, 224n11
Irmscher, William, 211. *See also* NAEP
Ironson, Gail H., 198
IQ (Intelligence Quotient) testing, 78, 85, 91, 96n8, 184n2, 271, 274
item testing, 52, 56, 96n8, 101

Jackson, Brian, 83
Jacobs, Holly L., 81, 203–204. *See also* ESL Composition Profile
Jakobson, Roman, 9
Jamison, Elizabeth, 118n8
jangle fallacy, 18, 19, 20
Jefferson School District (Colorado), 241
Jewell, Ross M., 111, 112, 238
Jiles, Paulette, 7, 16
Jin, Yan, 247–248
Johnson, Wendell, 116
Joint Interim Committee on the Public Education System, 156. *See also* Citizens Advisory Commission
Journal of Educational Measurement, 30, 143
Journal of Writing Analytics, The, 28n3
Journal of Writing Assessment, The, 28n3, 276

Kane, Michael T., 228–231. *See also* interpretation and use argument
Kant, Immanuel, 37, 281
Keech, Catherine (Catherine Keech Lucas), 27, 112, 113, 114, 115, 150n17, 163, 165, 167, 172, 173, 174, 175–179, 180, 181, 185–186n11, 186–187n18, 191, 194, 197, 205, 223n1, 233–235, 244, 253, 254, 265, 273. *See also* Bay Area Writing Project; ecological evaluation; *The Write Occasion*
Keller-Cohen, Deborah, 248
Kelley, Truman Lee, 18
Kennedy, John F., 185n5, 220. *See also* Civil Rights Address (1963)
Kennedy, Theodore R., 127
Keppel, Francis, 206–207. *See also* NAEP
Kerr, Clark, 165
Kerrie, Marjorie, 115
Kinneavy, James, 264
Kitzhaber, Albert, 208, 209, 244
Klaus, Carl H., 211, 222
Klinkenborg, Verlyn, 12
Knowles, Elliot, 4
Koffka, Kurt, 38–39, 41, 42, 46–47, 49. *See also* gestalt psychology
Köhler, Wolfgang, 36, 38, 39–42, 46–47, 49. *See also* gestalt psychology; *Gestalt*

Psychology: An Introduction to New Concepts in Modern Psychology
Kvernbekk, Tone, 265, 279–280

Labov, William, 264
Lamb, H., 77
Langer, Judith A., 216–219, 263, 264, 275. See also NAEP; *Writing Trends Across the Decade, 1974–1984*
language arts curricular model, 97n14, 126–127, 164, 183. See also Palmer, Osmond
Lanham, Richard A., 154
LaPorte, Jody, 271
Latour, Bruno, 257
Law of Large Numbers, 58, 144
Lavin, Albert ("Cap"), 27, 116, 159–163, 165, 167, 168, 172, 173, 179, 185–186n11, 186n12, 186n13, 186n14, 205, 225n15. See also Bay Area Writing Project; Dartmouth Conference; NAEP; Sir Frances Drake High School
Lawley, Derek N., 73–74n11
Lederman, Marie Jean, 116
Lee, Robert E., 206
Levering Act, 157. See also University of California
Lévi-Strauss, Claude, 230
Linde, Charlotte, 15
Linnaeus, Carl, 229–230. See *Systema Naturae*
Lloyd-Jones, Richard, 93, 201, 211, 213, 225n17, 275. See also NAEP
Lorge-Thorndike Intelligence Tests, 155
Lowell High School (California), 167
Lucas, Catherine Keech. See Keech, Catherine
Lubar, Steven, 165
Lunsford, Karen J., 279
Lynd, Albert, 158. See *Quackery in the Public Schools*

machine scoring, 108, 154, 155, 156, 165, 222. See also Automated Writing Evaluation
Marcuse, Herbert, 164. See *One-Dimensional Man: Studies in the Ideology of Advanced Industrial Society*
Marks of Examiners, The (Hartog, Rhodes, Burt), 4, 26, 64–66, 150–151n23
Marsden, Dennis, 83
Martin, Nancy C., 26, 39, 58, 78, 82–83, 89, 90, 236, 263–264, 279
Maslow, Abraham, 236. See also *Toward a Psychology of Being*
Mather, Donald Raymond, 83, 95–96n6

matrix sampling, 169, 183, 207
matrix theory, 148n4
McCarthy, Joseph, 157
McColly, William, 193
McConvlle, Carolyn B., 90, 224n7
McGill University, 235
McNelly, Mary Ellen, 233–235, 253
Measurement of Writing Ability, The (Godshalk, Coffman, Swineford), 27, 89–90, 94, 95n4, 107, 118n9, 119–120, 137–147, 151n24
Measurement Research Center, 222. See also University of Iowa
Measuring Devices in Composition, Spelling and Arithmetic (Boyd), 49, 62–64
Measuring the Mind: Education and Psychology in England, 1860–1990 (Wooldridge), 48
Mellon, John C., 191, 210–211, 225n16. See also NAEP
Mental and Scholastic Tests (Burt), 72n3
meritocracy, 55, 60, 73n7, 87
Messick, Samuel J., 225n20
Michigan State University, 16, 99, 120, 121, 123–130, 148n6. See also Basic College
Michlin, Michael L., 200–201
Middendorf, John H., 120, 147n1
Middlebury College, 220
Midsummer Night's Dream, A (Shakespeare), 263
Mielenz, Mary Luella. See *Analysis of Background Factors and Their Possible Influence on Placement in Freshman English at the University of Nebraska-Lincoln, An*
Milic, Louis, 211. See also NAEP
Miller, Carolyn R., 257
minority student groups, 197–201, 224n9, 233
Mislevy, Robert J., 47n6
Mitchell, Robert, 224n10
Modu, Christopher C., 116, 259n5
Molloy, Hillary, 261–262n15
Molloy, Sean, 4
Moore, Cindy, 4
Moray House Tests, 57, 73n7, 91
Morenberg, Max, 223n5
Morgan Hill High School (California), 185n8
Morris, William, 14
Morton, Andrew, 281
Moslemi, Marlene, 328
Mullins, Ina V. S., 211, 216–219, 225n17, 263, 264, 275. See also NAEP; *Writing Trends Across the Decade, 1974–1984*
multiple marking. See holistic scoring; *Multiple Marking of English Compositions: An Account of an Experiment*

Multiple Marking of English Compositions: An Account of an Experiment (Britton, Martin, Rosen), 26, 39, 58, 89, 263
multiple regression, 194–195
Muirden, Marjorie, 120, 147n1
Muss i den (German folk song), 38
Murphy, Sandra, 180, 187n19, 265
Myers, Albert E., 90, 224n7
Myers, Miles, 19, 42–46, 47n8, 48n9, 87, 116, 147–148n3, 159–161, 167, 171, 172, 173, 175, 185n9, 185–186n11, 186n12, 186n13, 186n17, 187–188n18, 187n19, 202–203, 204, 232–233, 255, 259n2, 274. See also *A Procedure for Writing Assessment and Holistic Scoring*; prototypes

NAEP (National Assessment of Educational Progress), 27, 31, 47n2, 135, 147, 161, 169, 188–189, 201, 206–222, 224n12, 224n13, 224n14, 225n15, 225n16, 225n18, 225n20, 241, 255, 257, 259n3, 275. See also Applebee, Arthur N.; Brown, Rexford; Coffman, William; Diederich, Paul B.; Gorrell, Robert; Hand, Harold; Hunt, Kellogg; Irmscher, William; Keppel, Francis; Kitzhaber, Albert; Klaus, Carl H.; Langer, Judith A.; Lavin, Albert ("Cap"); Lloyd-Jones, Richard; Mellon, John C.; Milic, Louis; Mullis, Ina V.S.; Page, Ellis; Persky, Hillary; Sebold, Donald; Slotnick, Henry
Nail, Pat, 185n10. See also *Scale for Evaluation of High School Student Essays*
Nardin, James T., 116
National Association of State and City School Superintendents, 206
National Center for Education Statistics, 31, 214
National Center for Research on Evaluation, Standards, and Student Testing, 223n3. See also Center for the Study of Evaluation
National Council of Teachers of English, 42, 45, 147n1, 166, 245
National Defense Education Act, 156, 185n3, 185n4
National Endowment for the Humanities, 32, 175, 191
National Evaluation Systems, 237
National Institute of Education, 15, 180, 191, 265
National Science Foundation, 32
National Writing Project, 113, 114, 115, 116, 168, 169, 176, 192, 235, 245

Neisser, Ulrich, 35–37. See also gestalt psychology
Nelson, Clarence H., 125
New Criticism, 260n9
New Examiner, The, 56, 67. See also Ballard, Philip Boswood
Newkirk, Thomas, 186n15
New Jersey Basic Skills Assessment Program, 237
New Jersey Basic Skills Placement Test, 32
New Orleans, 15, 260n8
New Plan (Chicago College Plan), 100–101, 104, 106, 117n5, 135, 150n18. See also Boucher, Chauncey S.; Hutchins, Robert Manyard
Newton, Paul, 71n1, 96n7, 278, 285
New York University, 192
Nisbet, John Donald, 94, 146
No Child Left Behind Act, 215
Nold, Ellen, 194–196, 224n6
Notes from the National Testing Network in Writing, 28n3
Noyes, Edward S., 120, 142–143. See also *The First Six Tests in English Composition*
Nulton, Karen, 260n11

Oakland High School (California), 42, 160
Odell, Lee, 201–202, 223n5. See also *Evaluating Writing: Describing, Measuring, Judging*
office adjusted rater scoring, See holistic scoring
Ofqual (Office of Qualifications and Examinations Regulation), 20, 96n7. See also double marking
O'Hare, Frank, 223n5
Olsen, Marjorie, 224n7
On a Scale: A Social History of Writing Assessment in America (Elliot), 3, 4
One-Dimensional Man: Studies in the Ideology of Advanced Industrial Society (Marcuse), 164
O'Neill, Peggy, 4
On the Origin of Species (Darwin), 226
Open ranking. See holistic scoring
Oregon State University at Ashland, 168
Ordinary Level Examinations (O-level), 79, 82, 84, 87, 89, 256. See also Advanced Level Examinations; General Certificate of Education
organicism, 8–9
Oxford University, 33, 202

Pace College, 168
Page, Ellis B., 14, 211. See also NAEP

336 INDEX

Palmer, Osmond E., 27, 99, 119–151. *See also* Comprehensive Examination in English; Diederich, Paul B.; language arts curricular model
PARE: Practical Assessment, Research & Evaluation, 28n3
Parsons, Talcott, 230
Partnership for Assessment of Readiness for College and Careers, 256
Parts and Wholes (Jacobson), 9
Paulus, Dieter, 14
Peacocke, Christopher, 242, 260n9
Pearl Harbor, 13, 74n13, 108
Peckham, Irvin, 171, 172, 173, 260n11
Pedley, R. R., 54
Penfold, D. M. Edwards, 79, 94, 95n1, 146
Percival, E., 91–92
Perelman, Les, 260n11, 261–262n15
Perkins, Kyle, 82
Persky, Hillary, 47n1, 219. *See also* NAEP
perspectivism, 59–60
Phelps, Louise Wetherbee, 14–15, 203
phi phenomenon, 38–39. *See also* gestalt psychology; Wertheimer, Max
Piaget, Jean, 230
Piché, Gene, 200–201
Pidgeon, Douglas A., 75, 81
Pilkington, Gwendolyn, 235–236
Pilliner, Albert, 73–74n11
Planck, Max, 51
Planning, Development and Evaluation Association, 237
Poe, Mya, 200, 278. See also *Writing Assessment, Social Justice, and the Advancement of Opportunity*
Polkinghorne, Donald D., 11
Pollitt, Alastair, 71n1, 73n7, 73–74n1, 87, 96n10
Polanyi, Michael, 221
Pomona, 31
pooled rater scoring. *See* holistic scoring
Pope, Alexander, 263–264. See also *An Essay on Criticism*; *An Essay on Man*
Portland State College, 120, 147n1
Portola Junior High School, 262n16
Powers, Gary, 157
Practical Criticism (Richards), 60
primary-trait scoring, 18, 19, 22, 27, 146, 188, 201, 209, 211–220, 221, 222, 250, 254, 275. *See also* analytic scoring; scaled criteria; trait
Procedure for Writing Assessment and Holistic Scoring, A (Myers), 42, 45, 186–187n18, 202
Procedures Handbook (US Department of Education), 256. *See also* Institute of Education Sciences; *Standards Handbook*; Department of Education, US
profile scoring. *See* holistic scoring
Progressive Education Association, 102
prompt, 45, 105, 118n9, 141, 162–163, 178, 181, 183, 186n12, 190, 194, 218, 223n1
Properties of Writing Tasks: A Study of Alternative Procedures for Holistic Writing Assessment (Gray, Ruth), 39–40, 181, 186–187n18, 190, 223n1, 240–241, 250n18, 301n1, 352
prototypes, 19, 43–44, 111. *See also* anchors; exemplars; Myers, Miles; range finders; Rosch, Eleanor; sample essays
Princeton, 14, 32, 94, 97n15, 98, 110, 145, 174
Purves, Alan C., 116
Putz, Joan M., 192
Psychology in Britain: Historical Essays and Personal Reflections (Bunn), 49

Quackery in the Public Schools (Lynd), 158
Qualifications and Curriculum Authority, 87–88
Quellmalz, Edys, 190, 245

Rabinowitz, Paula, 40
Rachels, James, 253
RAD (replicable, agreeable, and data-supported) research, 279–280. *See also* Haswell, Richard
random variation, 23
range finders, 19. *See also* anchors; exemplars; prototypes
rapid impression reading. *See* holistic scoring
rater training, 21, 25, 32, 50, 80, 133, 152, 197, 237, 238, 254, 260n9. *See also* calibration
Raths, Louis E., 102
Rauner Special Collections Library (Dartmouth College), 16
Reese, William J., 158
Reid, Stephen, 116
Regional Educational Laboratory Northwest, 190, 237
Regional Educational Laboratory Southwest, 239
reliability: differential accuracy, 20; differential scale category use, 20; differential severity, 20; evidence of fairness, 70, 217; evidence of validity, 20, 23; inter-rater agreement, 7, 20, 51, 95n5, 117n4, 122, 232, 235, 238, 239, 261n13; inter-rater reliability, 7, 20, 21, 26, 27, 29n8,

45, 51, 70, 76, 78, 80, 82, 86n4, 90, 107, 112, 117n3, 117n4, 125, 134, 138, 142, 150–151n23, 188, 194, 232, 235, 245, 261n13, 267, 270, 271, 275; intrarater reliability, 20, 80, 86, 113, 267, 270; prerequisite to validity, 23; single rater, 65, 138, 142, 209, 250; test reliability, 20, 86, 267; typology, 271–272; writer reliability, 20, 66, 86, 102, 103, 132, 181, 267. *See also* discrepancy; double marking; DRIFT; English Equivalency Examination; fairness; NAEP; splitters; validity

Remstad, Robert, 193

replication studies, 93, 144, 150–151n23, 279–280. *See also* Brandt, Mark J.; Haswell, Richard

Republic, The (Plato), 102

Research Committee of the Educational Institute of Scotland, 366. *See also* Boyd, William

Research in Written Communication (Braddock, Lloyd-Jones, Schoer), 267

Revelle, William, 228.

Rhodes, Edmond Cecil, 4, 23, 25, 26, 51, 58, 61–67, 68, 74n12, 75, 76, 86, 90, 94, 99, 105, 143, 144, 150–151n23, 270, 271

Rhum, Gordon, 111, 112, 238

Richards, I. A. (Ivor Armstrong), 60, 102, 260n9. See also *Practical Criticism*

Rider College, 116

Robertson, R. K., 13–14, 25, 67–71, 74n13, 75, 77, 78, 79, 94, 97n15, 105, 106, 144, 150n19

Rogers, Andrew, 206, 207, 221, 222

Roquentin, Antoine (protagonist in *Nausea*), 28n4

Rosch, Eleanor, 42–43, 47n7, 230. *See also* prototypes

Rosen, Harold, 26, 39, 58, 78, 82–83, 89, 90, 236, 263–264, 279

Rosner, Benjamin, 107

Rubin, Donald L., 200–201

Rubin, Edgar, 34

Rutgers, The State University of New Jersey, 168

rubrics. *See* checklists; holistic scoring; scoring guide

Ruth, Leo, 180–181, 186–187n18, 187n19, 258

Sacrifice of Education to Examinations, The (Herbert), 54

Sale, William Meritt, 120. *See also First Six Tests in English Composition, The*

sample essays, 19, 132, 141, 209

sample matching, 19, 52, 63, 83, 129, 160, 185n10, 193. *See also* Hillegas, Milo B.; holistic scoring; Palmer, Osmond E.

sampling plan design, 45, 148n4, 170, 189, 198, 227, 249, 260–261n12, 279, 285, 289

San Francisco Bay Area, 15, 155

Sare, G. T., 83, 95n6

Saretzky, Gary, 150n21

Saupe, Joe L., 125

Savio, Mario, 164–165, 184

scaled criteria, 18, 22, 241. *See also* primary-trait scoring

Scale for Evaluation of High School Student Essays, A (Nail), 185n10

Schoer, Lowell, 93–94

Scholes, Robert E., 116

Scotland qualifying examination, 62

schedule scoring, 18, 53, 69, 91, 95n6, 241. *See also* holistic scoring: marking scheme

Schmuller, Allen, 9

score use, 45, 71, 199, 233, 250, 278

scoring grid, 18, 241. *See also* holistic scoring: marking scheme

scoring guide, 19, 21, 22, 24, 25, 50, 60, 72n3, 81, 87, 103, 109, 113, 114, 116, 145, 152, 162, 171, 172, 173, 174, 175, 178, 179, 186n12, 186n17, 213, 214, 216, 219, 224n7, 227, 239, 241, 242, 244, 247, 253, 259n5, 261n13. *See also* checklist; holistic scoring

Scriven, Michael, 27, 99, 110, 175–179, 186–187n18, 190, 202–203, 204, 205, 242, 243, 244, 245, 257, 274. *See also Evaluation of Composition Instruction*

Seawright, Jason, 271

Sebold, Donald, 211. *See also* NAEP

Secondary School Selection (Vernon), 84, 94, 119, 143, 274

Seder, Alan, 173

Sequential Tests of Educational Progress (STEP), 121–122, 129, 147n2, 160, 147–148n3. *See also* Anderson, C. C.

Shadow-Line, The (Conrad), 256

Shakespeare, William, 263–264. See also *Midsummer Night's Dream, A*

Sheldon, Nicola, 95–96n6

Shermis, Mark, 261–262n15

Sir Frances Drake High School (California), 27, 167. *See also* Lavin, Albert ("Cap")

Skinner, B. F. (Burrhus Frederick), 46

Sledd, James, 150n18

Slotnick, Henry B., 94, 211, 212

Smarter Balanced Assessment Consortium, 256
Smith, Clarence Ebblewhite, 76, 77
Smith, Mary Ann, 167, 172, 182, 186n14, 186n16
Smith, Ruth F., 259n5
Smitherman, Geneva, 201
Smuts, Jan, 8, 221, 223n1
Snyder, Thomas D., 237
Slotnick, Henry, 211. *See also* NAEP
social contagion, 26, 31–33, 42, 43, 44, 47n8, 254
social justice, 4, 12, 86, 88, 130, 266–267, 289. *See also* fairness; *Writing Assessment, Social Justice, and the Advancement of Opportunity* (Poe, Inoue, and Elliot),
Sound and Symbol: Man the Musician (Zuckerkandl), 37
Sound and Symbol: Music and the External World (Zuckerkandl), 35, 37
Spearman, Charles E., 61, 148n4, 228, 244
Spencer, Herbert, 49
Spinuzzi, Clay, 257
splitters. 16, 27, 36, 227, 231–237, 251, 256. *See* holistic scoring; reliability
Spitz, Mark, 147
Sputnik, 157, 166
Stalnaker, John M, 117n2, 120. See also *First Six Tests in English Composition, The*
Stalnaker, Ruth, 117n2
Stanford Reading Tests, 155
Stanford University, 194, 196
Standards for Educational and Psychological Testing, 291
Standards Handbook (US Department of Education), 265. *See also* Institute of Education Sciences; *Procedures Handbook*; US Department of Education
Star, Susan Leigh, 226, 227
Statler, Charles R., 192
Steinmann, Martin, Jr., 119–120
St. John's College (Maryland), 37
State University of New York at Stony Brook, 34
Studies in Educational Evaluation, 28n3
Subject A Examination, 24, 108, 153–154, 169, 184n1. *See also* Analytical Writing Placement Examination; Entry Level Writing Requirement; Gadda, George; University of California
Sutherland, Gillian, 59
Swales, John, 248
Swarthmore College, 36
Swineford, Frances, 13–14, 27, 32, 89, 93–94, 95n4, 102, 109, 112, 119, 120, 121, 123, 126, 128, 137–147, 150–151n23, 151n25, 192, 224n7
Systema Naturae (Linnaeus), 229–230

Taba, Hilda, 102
Tanner, Bernard R., 116, 118n11, 171, 172
Taylor, David, 204
teacher consultant, 168. *See also* Bay Area Writing Project
Teaching and Assessing Writing (White), 204–205
Teaching ESL Composition: Principles and Techniques (Hughey, Wormuth, Hartfield, Jacobs), 203
Technical Assistance Guide for Proficiency Assessment, 171
Technical Recommendations for Psychological Tests and Diagnostic Techniques: Preliminary Proposal, 291
Testing ESL Composition: A Practical Approach (Jacobs, Zinkgarf, Wormuth, Hartfield, Hugley), 203–204
Testing Second Language Writing in Academic Settings (Hamp-Lyons), 248
Test of English as a Foreign Language (TOEFL®), 248
Test of Standard Written English, 197–199
Texas A&M College Station, 203
Texas A&M Commerce, 17
Thatcher, Margaret, 88, 96n10
think-aloud protocols, 41, 181
Thomas, Leon L., 198–201, 258, 270
Thomas, Susan, 202, 274
Thompson, Thomas E., 164
Thomson, Godfrey, 73n7, 73–73n11, 78
Thorndike, Edward L., 196–197
Thorpe, Louis, 9
Thurstone, L. L. (Louis Lee), 148n4, 228. *See also Vectors of Mind*
Toward a Psychology of Being (Maslow), 236
trait, 10, 18, 22, 24, 27, 43, 44, 71, 91–92, 103, 109, 116, 125, 126, 127, 136, 148n7, 194, 196, 197, 203, 209, 210, 212, 214, 218, 219, 223n5, 242, 243–244, 247, 250, 251, 252, 253, 254, 255, 260n7, 271, 272. *See also* holistic scoring; *Vectors of Mind*
Trachsel, Mary, 92
Traxler, Arthur A., 117n3
Tripp, Janny Griswold, 224n10
true score, 59
Turner, Lorna J, 200–201
Tyler, Ralph, 47n5, 101–102, 103, 106, 107, 131, 133, 135, 136, 207, 225n20. *See also* Eight-Year Study; NAEP
typology, 271, 281, 286

United Nations Department of Economic and Social Affairs, 277
University College London, 66, 95n1
University of Alberta, 121
University of Cambridge, 82
University of California (public university system), 153, 157, 164, 257. *See also* Analytical Writing Placement Examination; California State University; Entry Level Writing Requirement; Levering Act; Subject A Examination
University of California, Berkeley, 42, 153, 164, 165, 167, 169, 173, 175, 185–186n11, 187n19, 202, 234, 262n16
University of California, Los Angeles, 154, 190, 223n3. *See also* Center for the Study of Evaluation; National Center for Research on Evaluation, Standards, and Student Testing
University of California, Riverside, 262n16
University of California, San Diego, 153, 182
University of Chicago, 16, 25, 26, 27, 47n5, 74n13, 94, 98, 99–109, 117n1, 117n2, 117n3, 124, 127, 130–137, 148n4, 149n12, 149n13, 150n18, 182, 191
University of Colorado Boulder, 168
University of Connecticut, 14
University of East Anglia, 96n11
University of Edinburgh, 4, 73n7, 73–74n11, 95n3, 248, 249, 271
University of Exeter, 248
University of Glasgow, 62, 76
University of Illinois, 191, 207
University of Iowa, 148n5, 192, 211, 220, 222
University of London, 61, 64
University of Michigan, 248
University of Minnesota, 200
University of Nebraska, 191, 223n4
University of North Carolina at Chapel Hill, 154
University of Pittsburgh, 254
University of Prague, 37
University of San Francisco, 190, 202. *See also* Evaluation Institute
University of Southern California, 14
University System of Georgia (public university system), 191, 200, 290
US Census Bureau, 267
US Department of Education, 206, 214, 265. *See also* Institute of Education Sciences; NAEP; *Procedures Handbook*; *Standards Handbook*

Valentine, Charles W., 52
Validating Holistic Scoring for Writing Assessment (Williamson and Huot), 276
validity: conceptually-related evidence, 23, 45, 67, 125, 201; concurrent, 23, 125, 201, 267, 270; construct, 23, 45, 52, 59, 61, 67, 70, 78, 89, 91, 107, 122, 125, 170, 188, 198, 199, 201–202, 207, 216, 218, 219, 227, 229, 244, 249, 250, 256, 267, 269, 270, 271, 272, 273, 275, 278, 281; content, 23, 267, 270; criterion measures, 70, 89, 108, 120, 146, 192; inferred validity, 45; predictive, 23, 70, 78, 125, 201, 267, 270; reliability as prerequisite to validity, 23; reliability as validity, 20, 23; typology, 273. *See also* English Equivalency Examination; fairness; NAEP; reliability
Valley, John R., 110
Vectors of Mind: Multiple-Factor Analysis for the Isolation of Primary Traits, 148n4. *See also* Thurstone, L. L.
Vernon, Philip, E., 76, 77, 82, 84, 85, 86, 94, 97n15, 119, 143, 144, 146, 151n25, 201, 274. *See also Secondary School Selection*
Vidakovic, Ivana, 21
Vienna University, 37
von Ehrenfels, Christian, 37–38
von Helmholtz, Hermann, 46
Vopat, James, 114
Voss, Ralph F., 116

Wallis, Bertie Cottrell, 53
Walters, Keith, 92
Warren, Thomas B., 116
Washington High School (California), 159–160
Washington State University, 17, 254
Watts, Alan, 164. See *The Book*
Watts, Alfred F., 75
Weir, Cyril, 21
Weimar Republic, 39
Weiss, Carol H., 177, 203, 257. *See Evaluation Research: Methods for Assessing Program Effectiveness*
Wellesley College, 37
Wertheimer, Max, 38–39, 41, 42, 46–47, 47n7, 49, 230
West Yorkshire, 83
Westminster Choir College, 110
What Computers Can't Do (Dreyfus), 164
White, Edward M., 47n3, 116, 117–118n7, 154, 198–201, 204–205, 213, 236, 257n10, 258, 259n5, 267, 270, 275–276, 278. *See also* English Equivalency

Examination; *Teaching and Assessing Writing*
White, Hayden, 11, 14, 28n5, 28–29n6, 138, 147, 206, 219, 230
Whitehead, Alfred North, 96n12
Williamson, Michael M., 276
Wilson, Peter Barton, 183
Wilt, Joshua, 228
Wimmers, Eric, 259n5
Winterowd, Ross, 213
Wise, Arthur, 235
Wiseman, Stephen, 48n10, 59, 61, 67–71, 75, 76, 77, 78, 79, 80, 82, 93, 94, 95n3, 96n7, 97n15, 105, 106, 120, 142, 143, 144, 146, 150n19, 150–151n23, 182, 194, 236, 247, 272
Witte, Stephen, 92, 204, 257. *See also Evaluating College Writing Programs*
wholistic. *See* holistic scoring
Woese, Carl, 231
Woodworth, Patrick, 180, 181, 223n1, 273. *See also* Bay Area Writing Project; *Write Occasion, The*
Wooldridge, Adrian, 49, 75, 83, 85, 96n8, 266

WPA-CompPile Research Bibliography No. 27 (Haswell and Elliot), 5, 28, 291
WPA Outcomes Statement (CWPA), 245
Wrigley, James, 194
Writing Assessment, Social Justice, and the Advancement of Opportunity (Poe, Inoue, and Elliot), 266–267. *See also* fairness; social justice
Write Occasion, The (Woodworth and Keech), 180
writing in the disciplines, 126. *See also Evaluation in Higher Education*
Writing Trends Across the Decade, 1974–1984 (Applebee, Langer, Mullins), 216–219, 263
Wylie, Caroline, 288

Yale University, 72n2, 90, 142
Yancey, Kathleen Blake, 12
Yates, Alfred, 101

Zuckerkandl, Viktor, 35, 37–38, 41. *See also Sound and Symbol: Man the Musician; Sound and Symbol: Music and the External World;* gestalt psychology

www.ingramcontent.com/pod-product-compliance
Lightning Source LLC
Chambersburg PA
CBHW030441090526
44586CB00044B/468